Social and Cultural Foundations of Counseling and Human Services

Multiple Influences on Self-Concept Development

John J. Schmidt

East Carolina University

Boston New York San Francisco
Mexico City Montreal Toronto London Madrid Munich Paris
Hong Kong Singapore Tokyo Cape Town Sydney

Executive Editor: *Virginia Lanigan*
Series Editorial Assistant: *Scott Blaszak*
Marketing Manager: *Kris Ellis-Levy*
Production Editor: *Janet Domingo*
Editorial Production Service: *Walsh & Associates, Inc.*
Composition Buyer: *Linda Cox*
Manufacturing Buyer: *Andrew Turso*
Electronic Composition: *Omegatype Typography, Inc.*
Cover Administrator: *Kristina Mose-Libon*

For related titles and support materials, visit our online catalog at www.ablongman.com.

Copyright © 2006 Pearson Education, Inc.

All rights reserved. No part of the material protected by this copyright notice may be reproduced or utilized in any form or by any means, electronic or mechanical, including photocopying, recording, or by any information storage and retrieval system, without written permission from the copyright owner.

To obtain permission(s) to use material from this work, please submit a written request to Allyn and Bacon, Permissions Department, 75 Arlington Street, Boston, MA 02116 or fax your request to 617-848-7320.

Between the time website information is gathered and then published, it is not unusual for some sites to have closed. Also, the transcription of URLs can result in typographical errors. The publisher would appreciate notification where these errors occur so that they may be corrected in subsequent editions.

Library of Congress Cataloging-in-Publication Data
Schmidt, John J., 1946–
Social and cultural foundations of counseling and human services : multiple influences on self-concept development / John J. Schmidt.—1st ed.
p. cm
Includes bibliographical references and index.
ISBN 0-205-40333-6
1. Counseling—Textbooks. I. Title.
BF637.C6S3265 2006
361'.06—dc22

2005045922

Printed in the United States of America
10 9 8 7 6 5 4 3 2 1 09 08 07 06 05

To Pat and Dawn,
with deepest admiration, affection, and appreciation

Contents

Preface

Diversity is the manifestation of social and cultural phenomena among and within populations, and in recent years, it has become a significant topic of study, discussion, and policy-making in countless educational, political, business, and mental health arenas. For several decades, the counseling profession and related human service professions have focused on diversity issues, and most importantly, have attempted to establish a knowledge base and skill development for preparing counselors and human service providers to serve diverse clientele appropriately and effectively. This text provides an overview of social and cultural foundations and issues related to this knowledge base and skill development for professional counselors and human service workers within a broad arena of helpers.

Social and Cultural Foundations of Counseling and Human Services: Multiple Influences on Self-Concept Development adds to the professional literature that addresses the social and cultural knowledge base and standards required of professional counselor education and other human service preparation programs. In general, accreditation bodies such as the Council for Accreditation of Counseling and Related Education Programs (CACREP) and the Council for Standards in Human Service Education (CSHSE) of the National Organization for Human Service Education (NOHSE), as well as certification bodies such as the National Board of Certified Counselors (NBCC), have established these standards of preparation and practice. This text provides a broad foundation of knowledge about social and cultural concepts for students preparing for careers in counseling, human services, and other helping professions. By acquiring this foundation, counselors and other professional helpers are in a stronger position to understand the social/cultural context of helping relationships as filtered through the individual perceptions of their clients.

Many texts about multicultural counseling are available. Some are classic works and several are excellent sources of how clients from specific cultures might respond to traditional approaches. Not all, however, address the fundamental social and cultural foundations upon which counselors and other helpers develop the knowledge and skill to work effectively with diverse populations. A basic premise of this current text is that such foundational knowledge includes learning about self-concept development within a cultural and sociological context and about the impact that both individual differences and collectivistic philosophies have on cultural identity. In addition, this text presents issues and factors related to counseling diverse populations, such as culture, ethnicity, nationality, age, gender, sexual orientation, mental and physical ability, socioeconomic status, family functioning, religion and spirituality, and other unique characteristics of individuals, family structure, ethnic groups, and communities.

A distinctive feature of this text is its social psychology perspective of diversity, complemented by an understanding of self-concept theory and its interaction with other theories of identity development. As such, this text addresses the "individualistic" versus "collective" debate with a balanced view that attempts to understand the value of both perspectives. The stance taken suggests that one view is not more important than the other is, but rather each contributes in different ways to human development and the concerns that diverse people bring to professional counseling and other helping relationships.

Social and Cultural Foundations of Counseling and Human Services considers aspects of a client's social and cultural heritage within the context of perceptual psychology and the person's emerging self-concept. Accordingly, this text encourages the use of approaches that consider not only the client's perception of problems and life decisions, but also the social and cultural influences that help clients create respective self-views and worldviews. As such, it is essential for counselors and other human service providers to understand that the process of helping diverse clients depends on knowledge about the social and cultural influences on human development and awareness of clients' unique perceptions about these life experiences. Similarly, successful professionals are aware of the social and cultural influences on everyone's development and the ways those experiences affect their own self-concept development and, subsequently, the choices they make in their helping relationships.

Social and cultural experiences and their limitless nuances greatly influence counseling and other helping relationships established with diverse clients. Equally important, the unique perceptions and understanding that individual clients accord to these experiences assign them personal meaning. To help clients from diverse backgrounds, professional helpers learn the multitude of ways that clients' perceptions merge or conflict with a plethora of social/cultural experiences, and how helpers' and clients' views interact in this process.

Social and Cultural Foundations of Counseling and Human Services consists of twelve chapters, beginning with a definition of society and culture and a brief explanation of the significant role that cultural diversity plays in establishing effective counseling relationships. This introductory chapter also explains various differences in time orientation, language, unearned privilege, and nature orientation as some diversity aspects that might influence the helping relationship. Chapter 2 presents a theoretical discussion of *self*-development, including the structure of *self*-concept, ways the *self* changes, the stability of *self*-views, and the relationship between *self*-view and worldview. In addition, the second chapter reviews social psychology theories of learning and highlights some social phenomena, such as violence and substance abuse, and their relationship to self-development.

Chapter 3 introduces several existing theories related to social development and identity as well as cultural identity formation. Chapter 4 continues this discussion by presenting several models of racial and cultural identity found in the literature.

Chapters 5 through 9 include race, ethnicity, sex, gender, sexual orientation, physical attractiveness, ability, aging, family structure and function, spirituality and religion, and socioeconomic class. Chapter 10 incorporates the lessons learned from earlier chapters into an appreciation of how multicultural knowledge and awareness relate to skill development and selection of counseling approaches when working with diverse clients. This learning includes an appreciation of cultural bias in counseling, an overview of multicultural approaches and culturally effective skills, knowledge of issues related to assessment, diagnosis, and treatment in counseling, information about group procedures with culturally diverse clients, and the role of advocacy and activism that counselors and other professional helpers might assume in encouraging clients and society to move toward greater social justice.

The last two chapters of this text present ethical and legal issues relative to counseling diverse clients, multicultural competencies presented in professional literature, research concerns, and future trends and issues related counseling diverse clients. All the chapters in the text end with a section titled "Counseling Inferences," to help students explore the content of each chapter in the context of counseling and other human service relationships.

Throughout the text, narratives and exercises give practical meaning to the theoretical presentation. Experiential activities, dispersed throughout the book, encourage individual students and classes to gain further understanding of the concepts presented. In addition, websites and references at the end of the text direct students to additional information about these concepts.

This text is the product of several years of teaching a graduate course in social/cultural issues in counseling, as well as teaching other theoretical and practical courses to help prepare students for the counseling and human service professions. During those years, my students and I used many excellent books as primary and secondary sources, and they are cited throughout this text. At the same time, my research and writing efforts have focused on self-concept theory and its relationship to helping processes. Those experiences combined with my interest in sociology that began in undergraduate school led to the desire to write this book.

I have learned much during the process of researching and writing this text and want to thank several people whose efforts and contributions helped in its development and publication. I sincerely appreciate Virginia Lanigan, the Allyn and Bacon editor who directed this project, and am grateful to reviewers of the initial proposal and earlier drafts of the book: Y. Barry Chung, Georgia State University; Bruce J. Diamond, William Paterson University; and Margaret Olson, University of Wisconsin, Oshkosh. I also thank Julia Powell, graduate assistant at East Carolina University, who helped with the websites in the Appendix; other graduate assistants Jenna Clemente and Jessica Smith, who helped with additional research; Dr. Pat Partin of Gardner Webb University for sharing pertinent websites; Dr. Keith Waters and Gene Hayworth of Colorado University for their suggestions; and Dr. José Villalba of The University of North Carolina at Greensboro for his review and helpful comments. Special thanks are extended to former students Fran Hutchison, Aletha Hudson, Thomas Dean, and Patrick Hinson for their insightful contributions. Finally, my affection and appreciation to my partner in life, Pat, whose patience during the lengthy process of researching and writing this book meant so much to its successful completion.

J. J. S.

1

Society, Culture, Counseling, and Human Services

As relatively young professions, the fields of counseling and human services continue to emerge and develop as important members of the expanding helping and health care professions. Marking its beginning at the turn of the twentieth century (Gladding, 2000; Vacc & Loesch, 2000), the counseling profession of the twenty-first century consists of many specialty areas including school and educational counseling, mental health services, community counseling, family counseling, career development and placement, geriatric counseling, spiritual counseling, and a host of others. Similarly, the human services profession developed in response to human needs and challenges emerging from the late twentieth century to the present day (National Organization for Human Service Education, 2004a).

Established in 1975, the National Organization for Human Service Education (NOHSE) brings together professionals and paraprofessionals from a wide array of settings that include community mental health centers, group homes and halfway houses, family, youth, and geriatric agencies, correctional facilities, and many others that parallel those of the counseling profession. In fact, the term *counselor* is found among many of the human service job titles. A sample listing of occupational titles used by human service workers includes residential counselor, eligibility counselor, drug abuse counselor, crisis intervention counselor, and halfway house counselor (National Organization for Human Service Education, 2004b).

Regardless of the setting in which they deliver services, counselors in all these specialties have a common knowledge base of counseling theory, helping skills, and professional practice. This knowledge base has developed over the profession's lifetime due to the effort of several associations including the American Counseling Association (ACA) and its divisions, the Council for Accreditation of Counseling and Related Education Programs (CACREP), and the National Board for Certified Counselors (NBCC), which combined have set standards for counselor preparation and professional practice (Gladding, 2000; Vacc & Loesch, 2000). At the same time, the National Organization for Human Service Education (NOHSE, 2004a) promotes preparation standards, professional competencies, and ethical standards of practice for human services.

This text focuses on one area of professional preparation and practice: social and cultural foundations. Specifically, it considers the influence of these foundations on effective and ethical counseling and human service relationships.

The influence of social and cultural foundations in counseling and human services has received wide attention in recent decades. In part, this attention is a consequence of the increasing diversity of clients in schools, mental health centers, family clinics, hospitals, and other health care arenas. In addition, the focus on social and cultural factors has been a response to what some theorists and practitioners view as a narrowly developed theoretical basis for the practice of counseling and other forms of helping with diverse populations (Pedersen, 2000). As part of this response, CACREP includes "Social and Cultural Diversity" among its core areas of preparation for professional counselors. In addition, the NBCC requires applicants to document study in social and cultural foundations. Similarly, the Ethical Standards of Human Service Professionals developed by the Council for Standards in Human Service Education, a body of NOHSE, pay particular attention to human diversity issues and services rendered within the context of social communities (NOHSE, 2004a).

The CACREP standards specifically state that preparation in counseling will

> provide an understanding of the cultural context of relationships, issues and trends in a multicultural and diverse society related to such factors as culture, ethnicity, nationality, age, gender, sexual orientation, mental and physical characteristics, education, family values, religious and spiritual values, socioeconomic status and unique characteristics of individuals, couples, families, ethnic groups and communities. (Council for Accreditation of Counseling and Related Educational Programs, 2001)

The National Board of Certified Counselors is an organization that awards national certification to eligible professionally prepared counselors. Eligibility is determined, in part, by the academic preparation of applicants. According to the NBCC, counselors who are eligible for certification "hold an advanced degree with a major study in counseling" with "graduate-level counseling coursework at a regionally accredited institution of higher education, with at least one course" in each of eight areas of study designated by the NBCC (National Board of Certified Counselors, 2004, p. 4). Among the eight areas of study is Social and Cultural Foundations, which consists of coursework that provides "an understanding of issues and trends in a multicultural and diverse society" (p. 4).

In its ethical standards, the National Organization for Human Service Education (NOHSE, 2004a) includes several statements pertaining to diverse clientele. In particular, human service professionals

- Advocate for the rights of all members of society, particularly those who are members of minorities and groups at which discriminatory practices have historically been directed. *(Statement 16)*
- Provide services without discrimination or preference based on age, ethnicity, culture, race, disability, gender, religion, sexual orientation, or socioeconomic status. *(Statement 17)*
- Are knowledgeable about the cultures and communities within which they practice. They are aware of multiculturalism in society and its impact on the community as

well as individuals with the community. They respect individuals and groups and their cultures and beliefs. *(Statement 18)*
- Are aware of their own cultural backgrounds, beliefs, and values, recognizing the potential for impact on their relationships with others *(Statement 19).*
- Are aware of sociopolitical issues that differentially affect clients from diverse backgrounds. *(Statement 20)*
- Seek the training, experience, education, and supervision necessary to ensure their effectiveness in working with culturally diverse client populations. *(Statement 21)*

Furthermore, NOHSE standards for human service educators include that

- Human service educators develop and demonstrate culturally sensitive knowledge, awareness, and teaching methodology. *(Statement 44)* (NOHSE 2004a)

The goal of this text is to provide basic information about the social and cultural foundations that guide counselors and human service professionals and, more importantly, assist clients in making decisions about personal and professional goals, career choices, educational plans, personal relationships, and other behaviors to bring more beneficial meaning to their lives. For this reason, this text gives particular attention to social and cultural influences in the context of self-concept development. We begin in this chapter by exploring the meaning of society and culture and their relationship to counseling and human services.

Society

The Random House Unabridged Dictionary (Flexner, 1993) cites its first definition of society as "an organized group of persons associated together for religious, benevolent, cultural, scientific, political, patriotic, or other purposes" and follows with "a body of individuals living as members of a community" (p. 1811). This dictionary definition of society concludes with "a highly structured system of human organization for large-scale community living that normally furnishes protection, continuity, security, and a national identity for its members" (p. 1811). Each of the above definitions confirms the foundational influence that society plays in the development of human beings.

At first appearance, societies seem simple in design and structure, but as they develop, they become complex, consisting of divisions and substructures that are more diverse and numerous as a society grows. A key to the development of a social structure and a vital factor for counselors and human service professionals to remember is the interaction between an evolving society and the emerging individual. Through the ages, history has taught that great societies emerge, change, and disintegrate because of the rise or fall of individual leaders, or sometimes due to a single act by one person or small group of people. In many of these instances, we identify unique perceptions and actions that began with one individual and ultimately changed the course of events for a particular society. Certainly, on the negative side, we can cite many world leaders who, because of their twisted perceptions and warped personalities, caused grief and sorrow for societies and people. In a more positive vein, we find numerous accounts of politicians, scientists, educators,

Exercise 1.1

Think of a historic world figure or some notable personality that you have admired for her or his accomplishments. As you recall the life of this person, list personal factors that distinguished this individual from others of his or her time and place. Share these factors and discuss them with a classmate. Among the factors that you listed, which tend to be socially/culturally influenced? Which, if any, tend to be characteristics that were individually created or developed by the person?

---

activists, and ordinary citizens who lessened the daily suffering of people by their positive decisions and caring actions. Exercise 1.1 asks you to choose and reflect on the life of one historic leader.

Society is the main structure, the overarching influence if you will, of human development and interaction. As such, society is the framework that guides the development of social norms, educational goals and policies, political systems, culture, religious doctrine, family structure, and countless qualities, attributes, and traits embraced by its members. The influence of society is highlighted in sociology as "a central concept . . . because it is on the level of societies that the most important elements of social life are created and organized" (Johnson, 1995, p. 268). Although counselors and other professionals are most concerned about current issues of society and their influence on the lives of clients, a basic understanding of the evolution of society gives us a historical context from which to understand the present.

The development of human society is a complex phenomenon, particularly when discussions focus on where modern humans first emerged (Bogucki, 1999). Nevertheless, there seems to be agreement that the earliest societies were groups, or "bands," of people that formed flexible organizations into which members came and went. It also seems that these early groups survived and developed because of their ability to form social relationships, establish friendships, share basic resources, build settlements for protection and shelter, and accumulate materials for the common good of the group. These early groups formed the first societies, what some sociologists refer to as a social structure (Barber, 1992). These social structures allow scientists a mechanism for grouping various people. Identify your own society in Exercise 1.2.

For centuries, scientists have attempted to classify and categorize human beings. Zoologists have based their classification on anatomical morphology—the study of the form

Exercise 1.2

My Society

Review the definition of society, and consider the main society to which you belong. Write the name of this society. Now consider other subsocieties to which you belong and write down those names. (Subsocieties would be organizations and groups to which you belong because of family, cultural, or ethnic influence.) When finished making your list of societies, meet with a classmate and compare/discuss your list of major and subsocieties.

---

and structure of the human organism—and have declared modern humans as *Homo sapiens sapiens*. For most of the twentieth century, an established practice among anthropologists was to divide humans into subgroups based on geography or race (Campbell, 1975). During this period, biologists also grouped human populations by similar genes or gene combinations, referred to as "gene pools," that were thought to typify a particular race. Recent genetic studies, however, have demonstrated that no genetic distinction exists within the human population to tell groups apart (Jones, 1993). Therefore, classifications that attempt to group humans by race or some other biological trait are unreliable. Modern genetic findings indicate that variation between individuals that come from the same group or classification might be far greater than any dissimilarity found between individuals from different geographic areas, nations, or countries (Jones, 1993). Despite the conflicts and inconsistencies regarding biological theories of human classification, the start of human society has its basis in biology and evolutionary theory (Megarry, 1995).

A useful video series from the Public Broadcasting Service (PBS, http://www.pbs.org/race/000) is *Race—The Power of an Illusion,* which asks the basic question, What is this thing called race? The series explores assumptions about race, including the largely held belief that people across the globe can be divided biologically along racial lines, and debunks these popular conceptions.

Another equally important sociological structure is culture. While social structure might consist of formal and informal association, communication, gender, economy, kinship, and other factors basic to a society, cultural aspects, such as literature, music, religion, law, philosophy, and values, give each society an identity. More important, it is cultural aspects that more directly influence the identity of individuals and the groups with which they associate.

Culture

Culture is sometimes thought of as "the quality in a person or society that arises from a concern for what is regarded as excellent in arts, letters, manners, scholarly pursuits, etc." (Flexner, 1993, p. 488). In addition, culture is relevant to common behaviors and beliefs demonstrated and embraced by various social, ethnic, and other societal groups. Perhaps more important to counselors and other helping professionals is the anthropological definition that culture is "the sum total of ways of living built up by a group of human beings and transmitted from one generation to another" (Flexner, 1993, p. 488).

The concept of culture in the helping professions finds broad definition and interpretation. For example, Harper (2003) defined culture "as the sum of intergenerationally transmitted and cross-culturally acquired lifestyle ways, behavior patterns, and products of a people that include their language, music, arts and artifacts, beliefs, interpersonal styles, values, habits, history, eating preferences, customs, and social rules (p. 1). Similarly, Baruth and Manning (1999) wrote that culture consists of "institutions, languages, values, religions, genders, sexual orientations, thinking, artistic expressions, and social and interpersonal relationships" (p. 7). In an earlier yet expanded definition for counselors, Sodowsky, Lai, and Plake (1991) noted that culture is "shared values; custom, habits, and rituals; systems of labeling, explanation, and evaluation; social rules of behavior; perceptions regarding human nature, natural phenomena, interpersonal relationships, time, and activity; symbols, art and artifacts; and historical developments" (p. 194).

Today's literature continues to expand the definition of culture making it a more inclusive concept. When we speak of culture in the sense of its influence on human development, we usually include a range of traits, characteristics, behaviors, beliefs, and other attributes that people incorporate into their own self-concept development and worldview. The counseling literature includes several terms related to culture that are important in understanding clients' development and perceptions. Among common terms are *enculturation, acculturation, assimilation, encapsulation, collectivism, individualism, interculture, intraculture, subculture,* and *worldview.* Each of these concepts is also important in understanding and empathizing with clients, so this text briefly introduces and defines them in the following sections.

Enculturation

Aponte and Johnson (2000a) reported that enculturation is the process of a person becoming a member of a cultural group. It combines both formal and informal relationships to convey knowledge, history, language, awareness, and other aspects of a particular culture to the individual. These learning processes are initiated, influenced, and encouraged through many channels including parents, family, peer groups, and institutions of society that embrace the culture.

The strength with which people become enculturated, that is, identify with a particular culture or group, influences how amenable they might be to other culturally related processes (Aponte & Johnson, 2000a). For example, a Native American child who grows up on a reservation embracing the heritage and legacy of the tribe's culture might have some difficulty moving into mainstream society where the history of oppression is relived daily through this individual's unique perceptions. Aponte and Johnson (2000a) noted that if a person is successful through the enculturation process "then an individual will have the competencies needed to function effectively in his or her cultural group of origin" (p. 20). Implicit in this point is that a person who is unsuccessful in the enculturation process would not identify sufficiently with his or her cultural group to function effectively in it. The question left unanswered in this process is, What determines, or who decides, which cultural aspects are accepted or rejected as the person develops? As counselors and human service professionals strive to become culturally competent, they consider this question when starting each new helping relationship.

Acculturation

Acculturation is the process of assuming new ways and behaviors of a culture that is different from one's culture of origin, while retaining some of the beliefs and attributes of one's native culture. It is a dynamic process that occurs when different cultural groups interact, exchange aspects of their cultures, and adapt to these exchanges. Most often in research and professional literature, acculturation refers to adaptation of the beliefs, traits, and behaviors of a dominant culture by persons of a minority group who have significant contact with the dominant group. At the same time, acculturation processes can happen at global or local levels of interaction, are multidimensional, multifaceted, and multidirec-

Exercise 1.3

My Culture and Counseling

Think about three dominant cultural aspects that have influenced your development as a person and write them down. Now, write down three cultural aspects that have influenced your decision to become a counselor or other professional helper. Share your lists with a classmate and discuss.

---

tional, and can include two or many cultures. Identify cultural aspects that influenced your personal development in Exercise 1.3.

Roysircar (2003) noted that acculturation has received wide attention from researchers in recent decades and that population projections for the United States through the next fifty years and across various ethnic groups should encourage further investigation of this process. Furthermore, she emphasized that the research thus far has found that "due to each group's unique culture and sociopolitical history with the dominant group, certain issues are more salient for one ethnic group than for others" (Roysircar, 2003, pp. 165–166). Nevertheless, despite these differences it appears that, at least among immigrants to the United States, "researchers have increasingly come to recognize that all ethnic minority individuals can, at some level, relate to issues of acculturation and retention of ethnic identity in White American society" (p. 166). Nearly thirty survey instruments developed during the past twenty years to measure perceptions about acculturation and ethnic identity highlight this finding (Roysircar, 2003).

Acculturation not only occurs when immigrants come to a new country. It also happens when people migrate within a society that consists of multiple cultures. We observe and experience this frequently in the United States, where it is commonplace for people to relocate to various parts of the country for career, educational, family, or health reasons. Frequently, people talk about their relocation in terms of "culture shock" experienced in the first few months or years of living in a new region. College students who attend school in unfamiliar parts of the country often express feelings of being out of place and sometimes have difficulty adjusting to their chosen college or university because of cultural differences. People who adjust to these moves successfully experience an acculturation process through which they adapt to certain traditions, beliefs, and behaviors while retaining aspects of their former or original culture that are important to them. Perhaps you can relate to this process to some degree because of an experience in your life. Read my account of "Moving South" in Narrative 1.1 and see if you have had a similar experience with acculturation in your development.

NARRATIVE 1.1 • *Moving South*

My wife and I grew up on Long Island, N.Y., as post–World War II "baby boomers." I left in the mid-1960s to attend college in Vermont. After graduation, we married and returned to Vermont, where I began graduate school and accepted a teaching position in social studies at a rural secondary school. After finishing my master's degree, I became a school counselor in a junior high school. Two years later, we moved to North Carolina, where I took an elementary counseling position and soon after began doctoral study in counseling.

(Continued)

NARRATIVE 1.1 • *Moving South* *(Continued)*

Our move to this beautiful part of the country introduced many new cultural experiences. We learned early about the important role religion plays in southern community life. When meeting people for the first time, we were often asked, "What church will you join?" We perceived this as an unusual question, one that we could not recall ever being asked by New Englanders or New Yorkers.

Of course, we spoke differently than the southern people we met, and that often became a source of humor for our new acquaintances and us. In the elementary school for example, it took a while to get used to the common greeting, "Hey!" and my female colleagues often chuckled when I addressed them as "You guys." I will always remember the puzzled look on one student who asked, "Are you a Yankee?" when I responded, "No, I am a Dodger fan."

This was the early 1970s and many southern communities had begun to desegregate their schools. Having grown up in a community where students of all races and backgrounds attended the same public schools, I was puzzled by some of my White colleagues' comments and behaviors toward Black students, colleagues, and parents. What I did not realize was that they too were learning to adjust to cultural changes perhaps more significant than mine were. At the same time, the Black students and community were adjusting to new opportunities and challenges brought about through school desegregation. As I reflect on these experiences, I now see that acculturation also occurs among members within a society because of social and political changes. People who are successful in adapting to the changes move forward in productive ways with their lives. Those who are not successful tend to falter. In my experience of moving to North Carolina and working in the public schools of that place and time, I recall teachers and students of different racial and social backgrounds who accepted the changes, embraced the opportunity to expand their cultural views, and as a result, became better teachers and stronger students.

One aspect of acculturation that is of particular importance to counselors and other professional helpers is the related stress of incorporating new cultural aspects into one's life while holding to an ethnic identity. Berry (1980), Roysircar (2003), and others have noted that acculturative stress occurs when individuals do not have sufficient support and resources to make the necessary adjustments to adapt to a new culture. Therefore, stress might result from culture shock fueled by great differences in beliefs and patterns, lack of resources such as financial support to become educated or trained, perceived discrimination or hatefulness, feelings of rejection, fear for one's safety, sense of isolation, lack of encouragement and support from family, guilt about leaving one's homeland or family, homesickness, or other factors. Sometimes, acculturative stress is disabling enough to require intervention or treatment, which a counselor or other professional helper might provide. This text considers stress as a social/cultural issue in a later chapter.

Assimilation

Learning theorists define assimilation as the cognitive process by which people bring new information in the form of mental structures into their understanding of the world around them. For example, a young child forms mental structures of dogs, cats, horses, and cows and is able to understand them as animals. When the child views an unfamiliar creature, say a platypus, for the first time, existing mental structures allow him or her to assimilate this new knowledge (the platypus) as "most likely another animal."

From a sociological perspective, assimilation is the process by which a person (or group) is accepted, absorbed, and integrated into a new culture (Helms & Cook, 1999). As such, assimilation is likely to interact and intertwine with acculturation that was defined earlier. Similar to acculturation, assimilative processes might contribute to stressful experiences particularly as related to an individual's ethnic identity. Writing about Asian Americans, Maki and Kitano (2002) noted that assimilation "refers to the processes of acculturation and becoming 'Americanized' " (p. 113). They presented a two-by-two model that illustrates the interaction between assimilation processes and the person's level of ethnic identity. Their model will be presented in Chapter 4 of this text.

Ivey (2000) noted that cultural assimilation, as used in the United States, highlights the impact of the environment, especially when considering the expectation the U.S. has had for immigrants to embrace the American standard. "The impact of culture is so strong that those who come to our country have little choice but to assimilate . . . the power of an environment to shape and direct behavior in the largest sense should be evident" (p. 212).

Encapsulation

When people are unaware, unreceptive, and intolerant of the views of other cultures, to the point where they live as if there is only one culture and one worldview, they become encapsulated in their own culture. To encapsulate something means to put it into capsule form or a nutshell, an efficient way of behaving or summarizing life events. The danger inherent in encapsultation is that in the process of summarizing, we may exclude other perspectives. In the field of perceptual psychology, the phrase "phenomenal absolutism" describes the process or stance where a person maintains a righteous posture, believing that he or she is most always correct and that people who disagree are wrong or untrustworthy (Schmidt, 1994). When people become encapsulated in their own worldview, it is similar to this posture of *phenomenal absolutism.*

Professional counselors and human service workers avoid becoming encapsulated in their cultural views. To do otherwise would jeopardize their helping relationships, because cultural competency is required in every instance. Before the professions began emphasizing and researching cultural aspects and diversity in helping relationships, counselors and other helpers learned to apply theories and techniques uniformly without regard for, or sensitivity to, cultural differences. Today, as noted earlier, the professions require an understanding, awareness, and acceptance of the cultural differences that exist in all helping relationships (CACREP, 2001; NBCC, 2004; NOHSE, 2004a).

Exercise 1.4

Encapsulation

Reflect on some strong values you hold. Write down these values. As you reflect on them, consider their influence on your decisions as a counselor or other professional helper. How will these beliefs allow you to interact with clients who do not hold the same view? What will you do if these beliefs prevent you from helping a client?

Collectivism

In recent years, one aspect of cultural difference that authorities have highlighted is the collectivistic philosophy of some groups in contrast to the individualistic emphasis of others, particularly Western and White cultures (Helms & Cook, 1999; Parham & Brown, 2003; Pedersen, 2002; Robinson, 2005). *Collectivism* describes the belief that the group is more important than individuals are because everyone is part of a group, tribe, family, or other type of unit. Furthermore, each individual owes a debt to the group to which he or she belongs because survival and development would be less likely without the culture and support of that network. In summary, collectivistic influence is particularly important in societies and cultures that value interdependence more than independence.

Counseling and other helping professions historically have embraced theories of practice that focus on the goals and aspirations of the individual and egocentric concepts such as self-development, self-confidence, and independence. In contrast, collectivistic perspectives tend to embrace values that are socially centered, such as community goals, group responsibility, social interest, social welfare, and dependence on group authority. For this reason, some experts in the field of multicultural counseling have questioned the limitations of Western psychological theories when applied to diverse client populations (Pedersen, 2002; Robinson, 2005).

In certain instances, proponents of psychological and counseling theories, many of which have been popular among counselors and human service professions for decades, have attempted to show how "individualistic" approaches retain some sensitivity to cultural diversity. As one example, Sweeney (1998) reviewed the tenets of Adlerian counseling, also known as Individual Psychology, within the context of multicultural counseling. He noted that researchers and theorists who examined different approaches "reaffirm the Adlerian contention that the values that move persons toward social interest are also those that promote the individual and the community. . . . By being congruent with the philosophy, values, and practices of Adlerian theory, however, counseling practitioners increase the probability of being appropriate in their interventions with culturally diverse groups" (Sweeney, 1998, pp. 33–34). Furthermore, Sweeney (1998) listed personal characteristics of Alfred Adler and the promise his theory might hold as an approach to use with clients across cultures. These characteristics include his advocacy for women's rights (with his wife), a holistic view of human development, sensitivity to what is considered normal and abnormal in mental health, the role of spirituality and religion in life, group responsibility and the importance of family and community, tolerance of sexual preference and orientation, conflict in gender roles, and the influence of oppression and discrimination on lifestyle development of individuals (Sweeney, 1998, pp. 31–37).

Other authorities have also attempted to adapt existing theories for appropriate use with diverse clients. In explaining his theory of developmental counseling and therapy (DCT), Ivey (1993) noted, "Traditional Western therapy too often seeks to change individuals and families in isolation. . . . full awareness that an entire community network of extended family and professional helpers may be required to bring about significant and lasting change" (p. 232). He also illustrated that professional helpers need to understand the core condition of empathy in a broader context across helping relationships with many different clients. Rather than understanding counseling and other helping relationships as simply interactions between two participants, the therapist and client, Ivey (2000) wrote,

"It could be said that *four* participants may be found in the interview: the therapist, with his or her cultural and historical background, and the client, with his or her cultural and historical background" (p. 317).

As important as collectivism is in counseling across cultural groups, counselors and other helpers (who, themselves, are also culturally diverse) most often work with *individual* people to help them make appropriate life decisions. While these decisions are made within a holistic context considering the cultural and historical background of both the client and the therapist, it remains the ultimate responsibility of the client, that individual person, to make decisions. Therefore, successful counselors and human service professionals balance their understanding and appreciation of collectivism with an acceptance for the unique perceptions of individuals from all different cultural backgrounds.

Individualism

An individualistic culture is, as the name implies, one that emphasizes and prefers individual development often to the extent that it disregards group welfare. Helms and Cook (1999) defined an individualistic culture as one "based on gratification of the individual's personal needs and desires. Consequently, in such cultures, a person's behavior is more likely to be motivated by the quest for personal fulfillment and self-interests rather than group survival" (p. 21). When taken to this extreme, counselors and other helping professionals who focus on individual clients without regard to cultural perspectives have the potential to do more harm than good.

Within multicultural counseling, authorities give significant attention to the individualistic philosophy of Western culture and, subsequently, the psychological and counseling theories generated over the past hundred years. Essentially, this focus describes the differences between individualistic and collectivistic philosophies and the cultural biases inherent in an individualistic stance. Attention given to individualism has focused particularly on American and Western European cultures. As one example, Robinson (2005) stated, "In individualism, the person is regarded as discrete from other beings and is considered the essential cornerstone of society," and furthermore, "because Western society is philosophically oriented to individualism, individuals are the primary referent point and are separate from others" (p. 7).

Pedersen (2000) noted that when counseling theories focus on individual development while ignoring the contribution and influence of families, groups, cultures, and societies to which clients belong, they make assumptions that demonstrate bias against more collective perspectives. By neglecting collective worldviews and overemphasizing self-development, Western theories of counseling and professional helping demonstrate that a "lack of sensitivity to the discomfort engendered in an ethnic client by such a focus can lead to ineffective treatment and early termination" (Aponte & Johnson, 2000a, p. 32).

Terminology used to describe goals and outcomes of counseling and therapy might confirm this apparent overemphasis on individualism. Frequently, we read and hear about clinical or educational objectives to help clients focus on their self-development, gain self-confidence, discover their true self, reach self-fulfillment, or become more self-reliant. While these goals may seem appropriate on the surface, such focus might bother clients whose cultures emphasize humility and deference to group welfare over self-interest. At the same time, the language and terminology used in Western practice unnecessarily dichotomizes individual development and collective perspectives. For example, mental health practitioners often use terms contrary to "self" definitions that indicate supposed deficient traits and characteristics. These include descriptions such as immature, enmeshed, needy, and dependent, which therapists, counselors, teachers, and others use to label clients and students who remain attached to and inseparable from their family or other supportive group (Helms & Cook, 1999).

The lesson here is not to discount the individual in the counseling process, but to find balance between what the client wants to achieve or change in life and the cultural influences from family, tribe, community, or other unit to which the client feels allegiance. Many collective cultures embrace aspects of self-development within the context of the group. For example, African perspectives assume that self-knowledge is an essential ingredient to achieve mental health (Parham & Brown, 2003). Similarly, individualistic societies, such as the United States, place emphasis on community, family, and other group structures as making significant contribution to healthy human development. Therefore, it is not an *either-or* proposition for the helping professions. The point is that professional counselors and human service providers understand collectivistic and individualistic philosophies, have command of the approaches they use, and know their relationship to divergent views. Most important, culturally competent professionals learn about their clients' backgrounds and the collective influences that contribute to and guide their worldviews.

Chapters 2 and 3 of this text consider the emerging self in the counseling process and attempt to relate self-perceptions to collective influences. In this way, this text appreciates and encourages a balanced perspective between these two important concepts. Counselors and human service providers who work with diverse populations want to be knowledgeable about how their clients operate according to collective and individual viewpoints.

Interculture and Intraculture

Meaning "between or across cultures," *intercultural* experiences help people expand their perspective of self and others and subsequently their worldview. When individuals perceive cross-cultural experiences in a positive fashion, they increase their intercultural sensitivity. By becoming sensitive to other cultural views, people move away from an encapsulated framework that limits their development as fully functioning, mentally healthy participants in a broader, more inclusive society. In contrast, when fear and ignorance of other cultures guide perspectives, or when limited exposure to intercultural experiences has not been positive, people are less inclined to be sensitive to differing views and cultural patterns.

Intraculture refers to those factors within a culture that affect development and influence behavior. In counseling, intracultural factors might include a client's economic status, social class, educational background, degree of acculturation, family background and functioning, and rural or urban identification.

Pedersen (1996) emphasized that the significance of within-culture differences may be more important than apparent between-culture differences. By attaining a full picture of between- and within-group differences, counselors and other helpers are less inclined to place all clients from particular cultures into single or stereotypical categories. For example, because a particular client happens to be an Asian American does not automatically mean that the client shares the common intracultural attributes and characteristics associated with that culture. By listening and giving full attention to the client's concerns and perspectives, a counselor or other helper is in better position to assess the cultural, intercultural, intracultural, and individual differences expressed by each client and avoid stereotypical responses.

Subculture

In every society and culture, subgroups form, and members of those particular societies and cultures distinguish themselves by identifying with and belonging to certain subgroups, subsystems, or subcultures. These communities consist of members who join because of an ethnic, religious, economic, educational, social, or other attraction. To illustrate the important role that subgroups play in U.S. society and individual development, consider for a moment high school students and the countless opportunities they have to join groups. To begin, each student takes a schedule of classes, oftentimes assigned based on academic ability and past achievement. Students might follow this schedule with the same classmates for an entire school year. They might also join organizations such as the drama club, forensic society, newspaper staff, band, and others. Some win positions on athletic teams such as football, lacrosse, swimming, baseball, softball, track, and basketball. All these formal opportunities to join subgroups are supplemented by the informal peer groups that students establish. Consequently, school counselors must consider not only the dominant culture in a student's life, but also the numerous subcultures in and out of school that influence a student's perceptions and development (Pedersen & Carey, 2003).

When recognizing the subcultures with which clients identify, professional helpers again use caution not to overcategorize or overclassify because of assumptions commonly made about those groups. A prison counselor working with an inmate who identifies with a particular gang is careful not to assume that the inmate embraces all the tenets and beliefs espoused by that subculture. Instead, the counselor seeks to understand which views and values the prisoner follows, and helps to assess whether the prisoner believes that those views are beneficial in reaching long-term goals.

All the subcultures and subgroups to which people belong stimulate the perspectives they have incorporated from their dominant culture. This complex process gives each individual a multifaceted view of themselves and the world in which they live. All these factors come together to be processed by each person in a unique manner and incorporated into a private worldview.

Exercise 1.5

Subcultures and Values

Make a list of the subcultures and subgroups to which you belong. Write down as many as you want. Next to each group or organization, write down the most important value that encouraged you to join that group. In a third column, write down any value or belief held by the group or organization that you do not hold to be true. Share your lists with another classmate or person. What have you learned from this exercise? How will this learning help you as a counselor or human service provider?

Worldview

People's experiences combine with family, societal, cultural, educational, spiritual, and other encounters to help them construct a worldview. All these influences notwithstanding, establishing a worldview by an individual person is a private process by which he or she forms a belief system. Regardless of how society and culture are dominant influences in a person's development, people's psychic makeup allows them to process information and construct a *unique* worldview. The creation of a unique worldview presents challenges for the person as she or he interacts with other perspectives. In counseling, for example, the client's worldview interacts with his or her primary cultural worldview as well as with the counselor's worldview. In addition, if a dominant cultural worldview differs from the client's cultural worldview, the interaction of those perspectives might also influence the helping process, particularly if the counselor's views reflect the dominant cultural perspective.

Use of the term *worldview* sometimes identifies an essential aspect of ethnic groups and cultures. As one example, Aponte and Johnson (2000a) stated, "Worldview constitutes part of the cultural characteristics of ethnic groups as well as the dominant culture" (p. 31). Therefore, counselors and other helpers typically use the term *worldview* in attempting to understand both the client's perspective of society, culture, family, and other life influences and the minority and dominant cultural worldviews that coexist in society.

In some respects, the construction of an individual's worldview is analogous to other constructs found in counseling theory. For example, as we will explore in Chapter 2, self-concept theory maintains that the self is "our own private mental image of ourselves, a collection of beliefs about the kind of person we are" (Hamachek, 1992, p. 26). In constructing a self-concept (an unconscious process), people incorporate many of the characteristics and beliefs that comprise a worldview. As an illustration, Alfred Adler's theory of lifestyle development poses "a combination of beliefs about self, others, and the world on which his or her expectations are based" (Sweeney, 1998, p. 267). Although most counseling theories have emerged from European culture and were largely developed by White, male theorists, many nevertheless consist of constructs that parallel the concept of a worldview. Therefore, it is important that professional helpers understand the theoretical approaches they choose and determine the appropriateness of various theories when working with clients of divergent worldviews.

Diversity and Counseling

In U.S. society, many people relate diversity to multiculturalism, minority groups, affirmative action, political correctness, and other terms or concepts that evoke emotional responses. In part, these responses are a reflection of the conflict inherent between opposing views on a wide continuum of perspectives about divergent groups and cultures. On one end of this continuum, views value social sameness, uniformity, and similarity because they contribute to feelings of security, safety, and comfort. Diversity, multiculturalism, integration, and related concepts threaten this perspective. At the other end of the spectrum is the view that embraces and celebrates cultural, ethnic, spiritual, and other differences in the belief that variety adds richness to life, contributes to acceptance and compassion, elevates learning, and enhances the human spirit. Segregation, egocentricity, strict individualism, superiority, and similar ideas are contrary to this worldview.

Although diversity is related to the concept of multiculturalism, it is not a belief or value. Rather, the term *diversity* helps to describe society according to certain identifiers. In the spectrum of perceptions about diversity, the view that desires sameness and conformity might conclude that diversity weakens society, while an opposing view maintains that acceptance of differences leads to a peaceful, long-lasting social order. Robinson (2005) noted, "Diversity across age, ethnicity, gender, race, religion, sexual orientation, and socioeconomic class attests to the strengths of a heterogeneous culture" (p. 2).

With diversity comes a need to understand different conceptualizations of shared experiences. For illustrative purposes, we consider concepts about which awareness and understanding might prove beneficial when working with diverse clientele. These concepts are time, language, privilege, and orientation to nature.

Orientation to Time

Cultures conceptualize time in various ways. As one popular expression exclaims, "Time flies!" A Western or American perception, this expression perpetuates a *monochronic* belief that time is a finite concept that is best focused on individual tasks, scheduled carefully, and monitored rigidly. In contrast, other world cultures conceptualize time as *polychronic,* meaning that people prefer doing several tasks at a time, view time as flexible, and change plans often and easily (Hall, 1983).

As an example of polychronic culture, Spanish people tend to act as though time is in limitless abundance. Consequently, they might appear more at ease about time schedules and work deadlines. In contrast, European Americans often strictly organize their time and maintain a full schedule of activity to make life more fulfilling. If "time flies" in America, it might crawl in Spain. It is not that Spanish people or members of other polychronic cultures are not task minded and proud of the work they accomplish; they simply go about completing their work with different views about time and schedules.

Polychronic cultures focus on time spent developing working relationships. This perspective views personal relationships as essential to the performance of scheduled tasks. The two concepts—tasks and personal relationships—are inseparable. Consequently, polychronic cultures distribute time among the most important tasks, including personal relationships. Sometimes, if relationships become more important than the scheduled task, the task may take longer to accomplish, and that is acceptable.

A monochronic lifestyle values punctuality. For many Americans, being on time is extremely important. As a diverse society, not all Americans are consistent in their punctuality, but generally, the public remains conscious of time. For example, customary manners expect that people will keep appointments on time and even arrive before the time indicated. Some events, such as social gatherings and parties, might have flexibility, but a phone call or other form of notification is expected when people are going to be late or unable to keep an engagement. Other cultures do not necessarily demonstrate such rigidity. For people from more polychronic cultures, behaving in a timely manner is a matter of how a particular situation feels to a person rather than a need to "be on schedule" or "finish the task on time." In this sense, time is not simply an objective fact related to a given situation. Instead, time is only one of countless elements that comprise the whole experience.

Robinson (2005) observed that Americans also value the future, as demonstrated by the propensity to look ahead and make plans. In contrast, other cultures value the past and present more than the future. Counselors and human service providers who know how their perspective of past, present, and future influences their self-concept development are in better position to understand their clients' views of past events, present time, and future promises. Exercise 1.6 asks you to explore some of these time-related elements.

Culturally effective professionals consider varying perspectives about time and elements related to time such as past, present, and future. By understanding monochronic or polychronic views, counselors and other helpers place themselves in better position to learn

Exercise 1.6

Instructions: Draw three circles to represent the past, present, and future. You may draw circles of any size, realizing that the size of a circle represents its importance to you. The larger a circle, the more important that particular concept of time is to you. You may also place the circles any distance from one another or may have them interacting in some fashion with each other. The sample below gives an illustration and explanation.

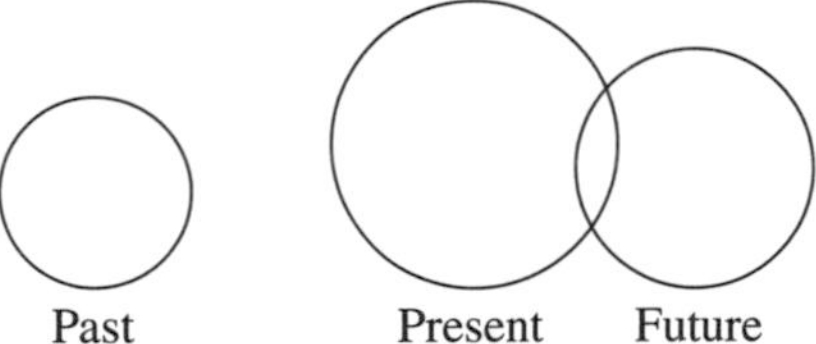

In the sample above, the person apparently sees the past as separate from the present and future. The past is also the smallest circle, and therefore least important, while the present is the largest, or most important, of these time concepts.

After drawing your circles to represent past, present, and future, share with a classmate and answer the questions below.

1. What element of time is most important to you? How does this view influence your relationships, and how might it affect your practice as a counselor?
2. What relationships did you illustrate among the three circles? How do these views about past, present, and future manifest themselves in your behavior?
3. What role do you think development plays in these perceptions? For example, at a younger age would you have drawn a different illustration? How about at an older age? What might these differences mean in counseling clients from diverse cultures at various developmental levels?

Exercise 1.7

Understanding Monochronic and Polychronic Perspectives

Instructions: Review the statements in each column and make a judgment about them. After considering all the statements, determine how close you are to being monochronic or polychronic in your attitudes about time and tasks.

Monochronic

- Prefer to handle one task at a time
- Time is measurable and inflexible
- Work time and personal time are separate concepts
- Works tasks are focused and well organized
- When late for an appointment, I apologize
- When people are late, I get annoyed, angry, frustrated, impatient (etc.)

Polychronic

- Like multi-tasking (doing several things at once)
- Time is unpredictable and flexible
- Work time and personal matters often blend or overlap
- Work schedules are flexible and change readily
- When I am late, most people will understand
- When people are late, I think something has held them up and hope they are alright

---

about and appreciate the time references of their clients. Exercise 1.7 asks you to explore different perspectives of time and task orientation. By using this exercise, you might have better understanding of your own perspective on time and work schedules, and at the same time develop greater appreciation for alternative views.

Language

Language is an essential element in every relationship, but it is especially important when counseling clients from divergent backgrounds, particularly refugees and immigrants who often have no knowledge of the dominant language. In the United States, lack of proficiency in English presents numerous barriers preventing access to social services, educational programs, and employment opportunities. At the same time, weak command of English by U.S. native citizens also creates obstacles and might become fuel for existing racist or classist attitudes.

Linear research models have considered the *use* of language in acculturation studies to measure increased usage of the dominant language in comparison to a decreased use of people's language of origin (Roysircar, 2003). When such relationships are noted, the result is typically perceived as increased acculturation. Padilla (1980) noted that *preference* for, in addition to *use* of, a language plays an important role in acculturation. Combined, preference for a particular language and use of that language establish the social playing field for members of society.

When a society limits itself to one acceptable language, it sends a clear message of isolation and exclusion to people who do not have command of that language. By demonstrating acceptance of other languages (such as bilingual application forms), a society

Exercise 1.8

What Did You Say?

Instructions: Think of a place where you did not understand the language spoken. Perhaps you were visiting another country, or maybe you were eating in a fine European, Asian, Indian, or other restaurant that did not use English translations on its menus. Maybe you were in a college lecture where the professor used English, yet you could not understand much of the vocabulary in the lesson! (Sometimes, our own native tongue can seem foreign to us.) After you recall the experience, answer the questions below.

1. What feelings about this experience come to mind?
2. What did you try to do about the situation?
3. Was anyone helpful? Hurtful?
4. Thinking back to that time and place, what could have made it a better experience?

---

extends itself to diverse groups, allowing them to retain preference for their native language while learning to use the dominant language.

Knowing how it feels not to speak the language of an adopted country is a first step in understanding diversity and the difficulties immigrants and refugees face. Likewise, when counselors and other helpers reflect upon their personal beliefs about languages that are different from their native tongue, they move closer to appreciating diverse cultures and understanding the frustrations that some clients might experience in adapting to a new society. Exercise 1.8 asks you to revisit an experience when language was a serious barrier.

Advocacy is another important element when working with clients who do not have command of the dominant language. What professionals do to seek assistance through interpreters, supportive networks, referrals to services that speak a client's language, and translation material is indicative of their understanding and empathy as well as advocacy beyond the helping relationship.

Unearned Privilege

When people hold membership in a dominant group, they automatically have privilege bestowed upon them by association. In contrast, people in minority, oppressed groups often retain labels such as "disadvantaged" or "underprivileged." Both of these conclusions are unearned. The privilege held by dominant group members is due mostly to social position, while they relegate less fortunate members to lower status by virtue of race, religion, culture, or other factors.

Privilege knows no culture, race, social class, or other status variable. We find privilege expressed within groups and between groups. As such, among members of the poorest segment of a society, some have more privilege than others do. Likewise, in wealthier levels of society there is also a hierarchy of privilege—the richest among the rich. Sometimes, people earn privilege due to effort and productivity, or due to qualities of acceptance and sensitivity. Other times, people receive privilege because of unearned qualities such as

Exercise 1.9

Privilege: Those Who Have It and What They Say

Instructions: Read each of the statements and decide how each fits into your perceptual world. Determine how each statement might contain misguided perceptions related to privilege, both earned and unearned.

"If he only would apply himself, he could succeed."
"That group needs to help itself, like we do."
"They cannot continue to blame past history for their present failings."
"It's always racial. When are they going to get over it?"
"I worked my way up to this position, and I expect others to do the same."
"All this complaining helps no one."
"Without her sex appeal, she would not have been as successful."
"Women [or men] don't realize how good they have it."
"It seems like the more the government does for them, they more they want."
"There's no free lunch."

---

attractiveness, height, skin tone, racial identity, gender, employment, perceived social class, or other status.

People with privilege often take it for granted. In addition, they mistakenly assume other members of society have equal privilege and, consequently, equal opportunity. Such misguided notions "may lead to expectations that blind us to the experiences of others" (Smith, Richards, & MacGranley, 2004, p. 7). When such assumptions persist, they become part of the fabric of society and everyday life, and they counteract hopes of moving society toward democratic ideals of fairness, equity, and liberty. One way to check your assumptions regarding privilege is to examine common thoughts expressed in frequently heard statements. Exercise 1.9 lists some common expressions related to assumptions about the concept of privilege.

White unearned privilege became the norm in the United States as an outcome of intentional and unintentional segregation of the Black and White races, continued oppression of Native Americans, abuse of Chinese laborers, and internment of thousands of Japanese families during World War II. Only through policies that have demanded racial inclusion and promoted social justice has the United States started in recent decades to eradicate White privilege (Arredondo & Rice, 2004). More than a decade ago, McIntosh (1989) published a list of provocative notions related to White unearned privilege. In the article, she listed 25 privileges associated with skin color that she doubted her African American associates could equally rely on. Much of what she listed then still applies today.

Privilege pervades all aspects of society. It is not just blatant racism, sexism, or other forms of prejudice demonstrated in specific incidents. Privilege is generalized and affects residency, educational attendance, choice of religious worship, social participation, consumer treatment, and countless other functions of a society. Narrative 1.2 gives an example of common gender bias and unearned male privilege.

NARRATIVE 1.2 • *Gender and Privilege*

An exercise I use when teaching the social and cultural foundations class to counselor education students is to ask them to recall a time when they felt slighted, excluded, rejected, or otherwise discriminated because of something over which they had no control. In past years, I have noticed how many female students have recalled incidents in the marketplace involving gender discrimination. Often, these recollections of women being mistreated were interactions with car dealers or auto service stations about buying an automobile or having it repaired. In subsequent class discussions, other female students would universally recall and comment about similar experiences. In one such discussion, a woman recalled that she could not get satisfaction from a car dealer on a repair she thought should be covered under warranty. Later that same day, her husband went down to the dealership, and the service department repaired the car under warranty without hassle.

Culturally adept counselors and other helping professionals understand the function of privilege, and they particularly understand how their racial identity, social class, or other status might influence counseling relationships. By taking time in the counseling relationship to learn about clients' perceptions and feelings regarding privileges they have or do not have, counselors might learn more about their clients' worldviews.

Orientation to Nature

Related to spiritual aspects of self-view and worldview is a person's orientation to nature and its relationship to humankind. According to formative work by Kluckhohn and Strodtbeck (1961), one theory of the nature orientation includes three different perspectives that suggest people either (a) obey and submit to nature as an all-influencing force, (b) achieve harmony with nature, or (c) attain mastery over nature. By understanding perceptions people have regarding their environment and natural surroundings, counselors and other helpers gain some awareness about how clients might view internal and external controls in their lives.

Using Kluckhohn and Strodtbeck's theory (1961), professional helpers might conclude that people who view nature as all-powerful relinquish responsibility to an external force over which they feel there is no control. Clients who operate from this assumption might believe that when nature takes its course, nothing people can do will protect them from inevitable fate. Consequently, natural hazards such as hurricanes, monsoons, and avalanches are unavoidable and the destruction they cause is inescapable. Likewise, supernatural events such as divine intervention and miracles are beyond the power of humankind. Therefore, such clients live with the belief that nature determines fate.

The perspective of living in harmony with nature includes a holistic view of life. As we will learn in a later chapter, Native American philosophy often incorporates a harmonious view of human–nature relationships. Clients who tend to have a harmonious relationship with nature recognize the interaction and connectedness among humans, nature, and the supernatural rather than viewing them as three separate entities. The notion of living in harmony conveys a responsibility to care for nature, respect its power, and achieve peaceful coexistence to benefit all humankind.

Mastery of nature includes the belief that natural forces are to be harnessed and controlled for the betterment of humankind. Exploring, conquering, changing, and otherwise mastering the environment is the ultimate goal to benefit society. Robinson (2005) posited that this nature orientation describes American culture, and pointed to the example of how land was taken from Native Americans by the White man's government.

Several other theories of the human–nature orientation exist in scientific and philosophic literature (Thompson, Ellis, & Wildavsky, 1990; Worster, 1994). Various theories speculate many possibilities about the status of nature and its relationship to humans. Some views include (a) that nature is random and unpredictable, (b) that nature is stable and resilient, yet vulnerable to major disturbance or catastrophic change, (c) that nature is stable and capable of repairing itself no matter how much destruction humans or natural events cause, and (d) that nature is vulnerable and its balance can be undermined by the smallest of interferences (Thompson et al., 1990). At the same time, other theories of nature emphasize faith in a Creator and caution that interference by humans should be minimized out of respect for all that is nature and that which nature offers. These varying perspectives present models for counselors and other professional helpers to understand how clients view themselves in relation to natural and supernatural phenomena. More specifically, they provide ideas around which professionals can assess how clients view spirituality, religious beliefs, natural phenomena, and their connectedness with the environment. Through such assessment, counselors and clients are better able to understand beliefs about fate, responsibility, internal and external control, free will, and other factors that influence self-development and worldview.

This text explores various factors, including inherent biases, related to the practice of counseling and human services, and considers models or approaches that address these issues while building cultural sensitivity. In addition, this text presents foundational theories related to self-concept development that might influence the selection of approaches to use when counseling or providing other human services. The process of selecting appropriate approaches to counseling and other forms of helping, applying credible assessment procedures, and using culturally sensitive skills and interventions requires thoughtful consideration of various implications for the counselor (or human service worker), the client, and the helping relationship. For this reason, each chapter throughout this text will conclude with a section titled "Counseling Inferences."

Exercise 1.10

Diversity Experience

This exercise is a private reflection about an experience you may have had with a person who seemed culturally different from you. Use it to explore your developing worldview.

Instructions: Think of an interaction or observation you have had concerning a person who appeared culturally different from you. Reflect on your thoughts and reaction to what the person said or did. Recall your feelings and responses. Did you say anything? How do you feel about your reaction today? If the same situation occurred again, how might you react?

Counseling Inferences

This chapter has introduced concepts and terms related to social and cultural foundations of professional counseling and human services. As counselors and other helpers learn about these concepts and incorporate the language of diversity into their professional practice, they become aware of the impact and meaning this knowledge might have on their effectiveness with different clients.

Increasing diversity among and within groups in the United States has implications for counselors and other professional helpers who work in a variety of settings. The literature and research seem to indicate that helping a broad spectrum of clients requires self-awareness, communication skills compatible with clients' language and nonverbal cues, understanding and appreciation of clients' cultural values, attitudes, and behaviors, and resource information that will be helpful to different clients (Pedersen, Draguns, Lonner, & Trimble, 2002; Robinson, 2005). The first step in achieving this level of competency is for professional helpers to become aware of how their culture and background will influence choices made in relationships formed with clients who are different from them. Knowledge of cultural, ethnic, spiritual, and other diverse identities is another area counselors and human service providers need in working with a wide range of clients. Equally important is their appreciation of the strengths that a client's culture contributes to healthy development and a full life.

Competent professionals also understand that the resistance within their own profession to accepting multiculturalism is a major force in the development of approaches to counseling. Sue (1998) compiled a number of bases for this resistance. For example, many people see a connection between multiculturalism and concepts such as affirmative action, civil rights, and reverse discrimination, which provoke negative responses. In addition, some counselors favor a more universal perspective believing that all traditional practices in counseling and therapy will work equally well across client groups regardless of cultural differences. A lack of measurable competencies for cross-cultural approaches and adequate standards of professional practice also have contributed to this resistance, as has the dearth of research findings to validate such approaches and standards. Scarcity of empirical research, however, has long been a challenge of the counseling and human service professions regardless of the approaches used in therapy and other helping relationships.

A final point for professional counselors and human service providers to consider in working across populations is that no person is defined entirely by his or her cultural background. Human beings are born into this world with the capacity to perceive events and draw conclusions about those experiences. It is those conclusions that help define a person's worldview. At the same time, it is the helper's role and responsibility to understand the unique worldview of a person within the context of the society and cultures that influence his or her development. In the next chapter, we will explore the emerging self of the person and learn how self-concept development interacts with society and culture.

2

The Emerging Self and Social Learning

If society and culture comprise the foundation, lumber, mortar, and brick that form a person's worldview, then self-concept, or self-view, is the blueprint. In theory, a person's self-concept consists of countless perceptions incorporated into a unique understanding of oneself and the surrounding world. This incorporation of perceptions is an unconscious process of constructing a self-identity and developing a personality (Hamachek, 1992; Purkey, 1970, 2000; Purkey & Schmidt, 1996). As such, this process is common to human development across societies and cultures, and results in a unique and personal understanding that guides each person in daily decisions and lifelong endeavors.

This chapter explores self-concept theory and the influence of society and culture in human development. The hypothesis suggested is that, while society and culture play a prominent role in a person's development, it is the emerging self-concept, interacting with particular social and cultural influences, that filters experiences, information, traditions, and knowledge, and structures them into a distinctive view of *self* and the world. Self-concept theory explains the structure and stability of this construct. Social learning theory, presented later in this chapter, explains the behavioral and cognitive processes involved in its construction.

Self-Concept Theory

A person's perceptions and subsequent construction of a self-concept are processes and products influenced by family, society, and culture. Robinson (2005) highlighted these influences by noting several identity constructs, among them gender, race, social class, and education, that interact with and affect self-perceptions. To appreciate the interaction between self-concept and perceptions of self, family, society, and culture, we begin by understanding the process of self-development.

Numerous educators, philosophers, and theorists have contributed to self-concept theory and there are differences in concepts, constructs, and terms created in all these efforts (Allport, 1937, 1955; Combs, 1962; Cooley, 1902; Dewey, 1930; Goldstein, 1939; James, 1890; Jourard, 1964, 1968; Kelly, 1955; Maslow, 1968; Mead, 1934; Purkey, 1970, 2000; Rogers, 1951, 1986). Nevertheless, common beliefs exist across these views about how the self emerges. For example, we can articulate beliefs about self-concept's structure, how people create it, and its consistency over time (Purkey & Schmidt, 1996). This understanding is important in comprehending how individuals from divergent backgrounds process perceptions to arrive at their own unique *self*-views and worldviews.

The Structure of Self-Concept

In theory, the self-concept consists of an orderly structure that provides harmony and concurrence among the limitless perceptions a person accumulates to form a self-view and ultimately a unique worldview. In an early book, Purkey (1970) offered a drawing to illustrate this theoretical structure. His drawing depicted the self-concept as a large spiral consisting of a core (center) and infinite boundary. On this larger spiral, smaller spirals existed displaying similar structure and a harmony with the larger self-concept. Later work expanded this illustration to show more clearly how these smaller units of "sub-selves" not only have many of the qualities of the larger structure, but also exist in a dynamic relationship with each other and the larger, global self-concept (Purkey & Schmidt, 1996).

Figure 2.1 provides an illustration of the self-concept spiral with its core and related sub-selves. Note that the essential structure of the smaller units (sub-selves) is the same as the spiral of the larger, global self-concept.

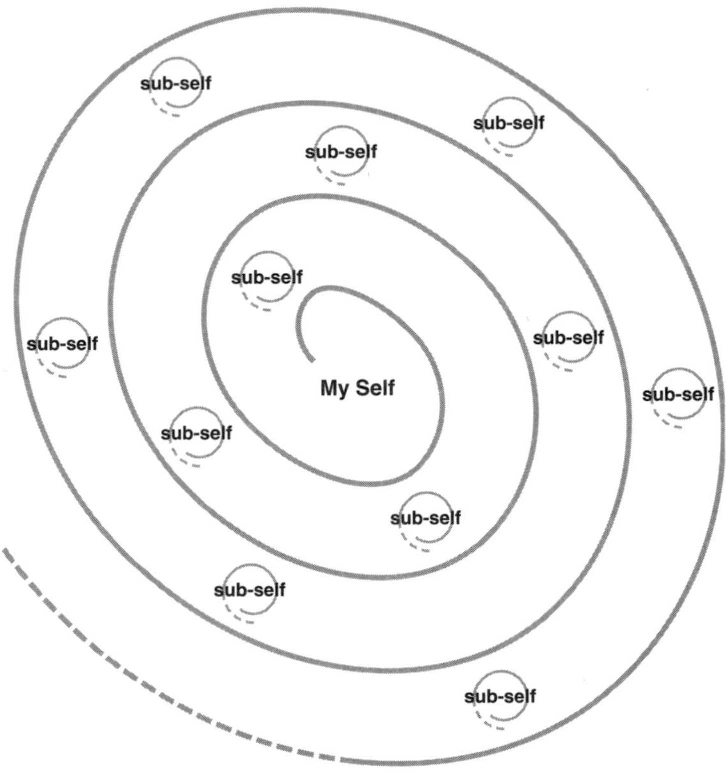

FIGURE 2.1 ***Structure of the Self-Concept***

Theoretically, the sub-selves within the self-concept are the countless perceptions that people hold about themselves and the world around them. As such, these sub-selves incorporate not only perceptions about objects and events, but also about beliefs, values, and attitudes that surround those things and happenings. For example, a professional counselor might have a sub-self that says, "I am a counselor." This sub-self gives the counselor a professional identity with which to function in the world of work as a mental health practitioner. At the same time, this counselor might hold the belief that "counseling is not a well-understood profession." Such a sub-self gives additional meaning to the perception "I am a counselor," and presents the counselor with a professional challenge. How the counselor uses these sub-selves in defining her or his professional role depends on many other sub-selves within the counselor's global self-concept. If the counselor has a sub-self of confidence and passion about the chosen profession, he or she might become active in state and national associations to elevate the counseling profession and educate the public about it as an important branch of mental health services. On the other hand, if the counselor lacks confidence and professional passion, but instead holds negative beliefs about the profession, then apathy, withdrawal, or resignation might become the chosen responses.

At the center of the larger, global self-concept is "My Self." This core of the self-concept is the part that remains a constant sum of all the sub-selves (Purkey, 1970). As such, individual perceptions and beliefs might change during a lifetime, but the core (My Self) always is the collective view offered by the combined sub-selves. In addition, the sub-selves closest to the core are, according to this model, most valued and important to the person. Over time and with life experiences, the positions of these perceptions and beliefs might change, thus assigning them different values as the person develops. In this way, the self-concept is a dynamic structure that, while not usually changing readily, can adjust slowly and deliberately (Purkey & Schmidt, 1996).

Self-Structure and Cultural Influence

Labeling the sub-selves of a self-concept structure (Figure 2.1) enables us to understand the influence of society and culture on the development of a person's global self-view. Figure 2.2 embellishes the original diagram to show how particular sub-selves, defined by social and cultural factors, play an essential role in a person's self-concept. In this second illustration, certain aspects of a person's life have more importance than others do (as indicated by their relative distance from My Self). According to the diagram, the three most important perceptions in this person's self-concept are closeness to family, the meaning of racial identity, and the value of culture in life. Other perceptions, such as spirituality and gender, are also highly valued by this person. Relatively speaking, perceptions about self-worth, wealth, and prosperity might have less influence on this person's day-to-day decisions because of their illustrated distance from the core. Nevertheless, they are perceptions that help define the individual to some degree, and as mentioned earlier, might change their relative position depending on immediate situations or on the conclusions the person draws over time about particular life experiences.

Under certain circumstances, perceptions (sub-selves) within the self-concept alter their position, depending on the situation at hand and the decisions an individual needs to make. For example, using Figure 2.2 we can illustrate how family, culture, spirituality, and

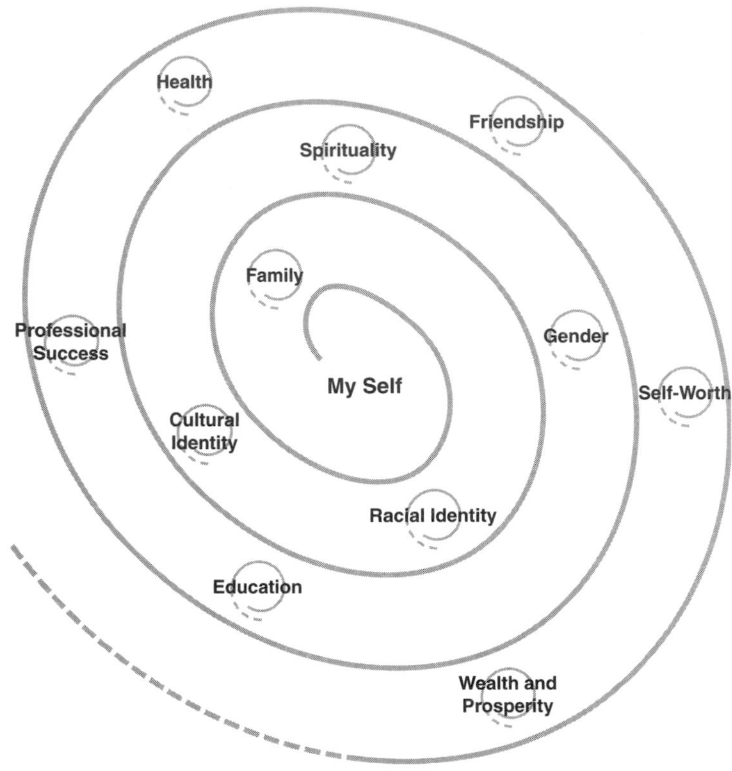

FIGURE 2.2 ***Influence of Society and Culture on the Self-Concept***

gender might vie for favored position depending on the situation. Suppose the person is a preadolescent, Islamic female in a family that has immigrated to the United States from the Middle East. Family ties are strong, and respect for parental authority and religious beliefs have guided her early development. As this young woman passes through adolescence and adapts to different American customs and values, the gender role she embraced earlier in life might be tested—not only for her, but also for her family and religious beliefs. As she makes decisions about these competing values, the relative positions of particular subselves—family, culture, spirituality, and gender—might change over time. If such adjustment occurs, corresponding changes in behavior and attitudes about being an Islamic female living in American society could occur. Altered dress, emerging relationships with male and female friends, and attitudes about careers are examples of changes that we might observe.

Conflicts and challenges between old perceptions and new experiences occur daily in everyone's life. Most often, these are minor and people readily make adjustments. Occasionally, conflicts occur due to major life changes, traumatic or tragic experiences, or other life-altering encounters. When new experiences do not fit a person's self-view or worldview,

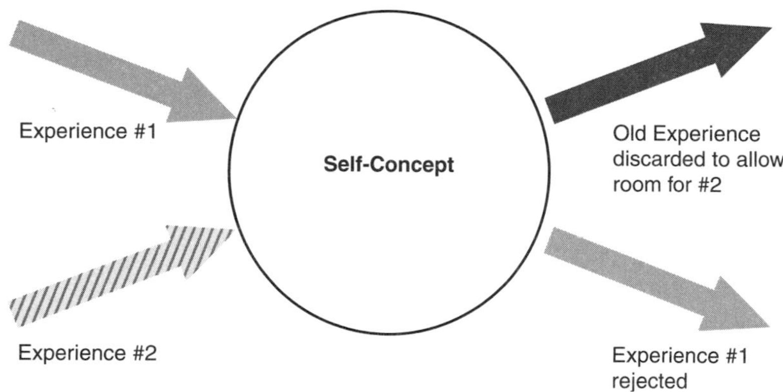

FIGURE 2.3 ***Adjusting and Accommodating for New Experiences***

the individual either accommodates the new experience by adjusting or discarding existing perceptions or rejects the new experience by excluding it from the present self-concept structure. Figure 2.3 illustrates this phenomenon. The example shows two experiences (#1 and #2). In the illustration, the individual accepts Experience #2, and makes room for it in the self-concept (belief system) by discarding an older, perhaps competing perception. In contrast, the person considers and rejects Experience #1. Apparently, this event and the perceptions involved did not fit with existing perceptions. The processes involved in accepting new beliefs or rejecting incompatible perceptions are not necessarily conscious operations. They might happen without full awareness of the person. Exercise 2.1 gives you an opportunity to explore the phenomena illustrated by Figure 2.3 more personally.

By understanding self-concept development through a conceptual model or structure, we comprehend that free people typically have control in creating a unique self-view, and a compatible worldview. Society and culture are tremendously strong influences, but in the final analysis, an individual experiences these conditions, considers their value (consciously and unconsciously), and determines (consciously or unconsciously) whether to include them is his or her life's view. Through this process, people attempt to balance individual desires and goals with collective values of the society or group to which she or he belongs and identifies. Achieving such balance may relate to specific events and circumstances that influence alterations in the self-concept.

Exercise 2.1

Think of a time in your life when you had an experience or an event occur that you seriously considered, but ultimately rejected. What perceptions allowed you to consider this opportunity? What other strongly held views guided you not to accept it into your worldview? If you had the same experience today, would the outcome be different? If so, how? Share your thoughts with classmates or colleagues, and ask them to share a similar experience.

Altering the Self-Concept

Self-views are dynamic and fluid within the structure of the self-concept (Purkey, 1970; Purkey & Schmidt, 1996). We saw this earlier in the example of the Islamic young woman who immigrated with her family to the United States. Her beliefs about family, culture, gender roles, and other self-views possibly shifted in importance and influence as she adapted to experiences in her newly adopted country. If such a shift occurs, it would not mean necessarily that she dismissed past beliefs, but rather that she reorganized them within the structure of her personal belief system. In similar ways, other people adjust their self-structures to fit a direction they want to go in life. As such, "the self-concept serves as a road map for living" (Purkey & Schmidt, 1996, p. 35).

The link between self-concept and behavior is not a causal one, although this is a common misperception (Purkey, 1970; Purkey & Schmidt, 1996). For example, we might hear a school counselor mistakenly conclude that a student is doing poorly in school *because* "he has low self-esteem." Although the conclusion that the student has low self-esteem might be correct, there are many other factors, including self-responsibility, to consider in determining why the student is performing poorly in school.

The self-concept serves as a guidance system, perhaps a compass, which helps people choose goals in life. Furthermore, people select behaviors that maintain, protect, and enrich their self-view (Combs & Gonzalez, 1994). By returning to the example of the poorly performing student, we might ascertain that he chooses, perhaps unintentionally, to do poorly in school because to try harder would threaten his perception that he is "not very smart." He might wonder, "If I try harder and succeed, will I be able to maintain that level of performance?" On the other hand, he might think, "I know I'm not smart, so why bother trying?" Sometimes, people maintain self-views of inadequacy when such perceptions are an integral and valued part of their self-belief system. Exercise 2.2 offers an opportunity to explore some of your personal views and explore why you maintain them.

If people strive to maintain the self-concept, yet at the same time want to alter aspects of its organization, the challenge for counselors and other helpers is to understand how self-views change. Brown (1998) noted that most research suggests that the self-concept is relatively stable, and pointed out differences between self-concept *activation* and self-concept *change.* Returning to the spiral diagrams in Figures 2.1 and 2.2, we might assume that *activation* is the constant movement of different beliefs or views in the hierarchy of one's self-belief system depending on the situation at hand. Such activation allows for flexibility in daily functioning. Substantive *change,* however, is less frequently observed. As Brown (1998) explained, "The evidence here is clear and straightforward: Numerous factors (e.g., the social context) influence the salience or accessibility of our various self-views" (p. 121). Furthermore, he claimed, "the most reasonable conclusion is

Exercise 2.2

Think of a behavior or belief that you hold about yourself that is unflattering, demeaning, or otherwise unhelpful to you. Write the belief down in your own words. Now think about it. What is it about this belief that encourages you to hold on to it? What would you have to do, or what would have to happen, to alter this belief?

that although people's ideas about themselves *can* be changed, they typically do not" (p. 122).

In the next sections, we explore five possible ways that self-views might change. Some are external events, while others are internal and initiated by the individual, but they are not exhaustive examples. Furthermore, some of these events are sudden and sometimes tragic happenings, while others might last a lifetime. Each type of event has social or cultural aspects that directly or indirectly influence the impact on individuals and groups of people.

Ecstatic Events

Sometimes, people have life-altering experiences that are ecstatic and joyous events. These might happen suddenly, such as being spiritually reborn due to an emotional event, or could take place over time, such as becoming deeply in love with a partner, acquaintance, or friend. Whatever the occasion, these experiences could have great effect on people's views of themselves, others, and life. The birth of a child, an unexpected marriage proposal, the survival of a near-death experience, an inspiring commencement address, and a life-saving encounter are a few examples of ecstatic events that might have a powerful influence on a person's development. Exercise 2.3 gives you an opportunity to reflect on a joyous experience in your life.

Joyous and ecstatic events can be powerful influences. They are also pleasant to recall and remember with others. Another way that self-concept might change is through tragic or traumatic events, which are equally powerful but less enjoyable and comfortable to remember.

Traumatic Events

Tragedy and trauma often have an immediate and devastating effect on people's lives. These experiences not only influence how individuals view themselves, but also how they view others, groups, institutions, and life in general. Most people can recall events when they, or someone they knew, experienced sudden trauma such as a car accident, senseless crime, medical surgery, natural disaster, disease, or other unforgettable happening that caused harm, loss, or death. In most tragic and traumatic experiences, social and cultural influences have an impact on how people deal with the events. For example, religious views about death and the hereafter might help a person accept the tragic and untimely death of a loved one. On the other hand, some social values might hinder self-development, or worse, contribute to human misery suffered through traumatic events. An example is domestic

Exercise 2.3

Think of an event in your life that you would describe as ecstatic or joyous. Recall the event in as much detail as possible and recount it to a friend or classmate. As you reflect on this event, what impact do you think it had on your self-views at that time in your life? If there were significant changes in how you viewed yourself or others, have you sustained these perceptions?

violence, particularly as perpetrated on women. Sadly, stereotypical views, maintained by particular social and cultural beliefs, frequently perpetuate debilitating gender roles and permit the physical, sexual, and emotional abuse of spouses and children in families.

War is a special case of trauma comprised of significant social and cultural aspects and ingredients. As such, war is often the consequence of social and cultural views held by one group and in conflict with the views of another group. Hatred toward different groups of people has borne countless skirmishes, battles, and wars between families, villages, regions, nations, and countries since the dawn of humankind, but we do not have to rely solely on major world conflicts to understand the impact of violent action on self-development. Tormented individuals bullied by predators often live with emotional and psychological scars that inhibit their development and relationships with others. A lifetime of being harassed, humiliated, and degraded takes its toll and influences self-perception. Later in this chapter, we will revisit violent behavior as a social phenomenon related to self-development.

Intervention

As a particular form of human service, counseling encourages people to examine their perceptions and beliefs. Such examination might ultimately enable people to alter behaviors that eventually will help them reorganize their beliefs, let go of long-held counterproductive values, or incorporate new, healthier perceptions into their self-views. For example, through cognitive behavior modification, Meichenbaum (1977) encouraged counselors and therapists to teach specific problem-solving and coping skills to their clients. Through this process, clients learn how to use their internal dialogue, also known as *self-talk,* to listen and talk with themselves in mediating and changing thoughts and behaviors. Meichenbaum (1977) referred to this process as cognitive restructuring, a way to help clients examine perceptions and beliefs while taking responsibility for altering destructive thought patterns and related behaviors. Other forms of cognitive therapy and counseling approaches founded on self-concept theory also advocate interventions that encourage self-examination of thoughts, beliefs, and perceptions (Ellis, 1996; Purkey, 2000; Purkey & Schmidt, 1996).

Countless interventions through counseling and other professional approaches have potential impact on people's self-perceptions. Medical intervention, such as surgery or medication, frequently has an effect on patients' self-views. From a social/cultural perspective, other interventions might include alternative healing methods, which are sometimes performed by laypeople rather than professionals, creative expression through art, dance, and music, and holistic approaches to wellness including emotional, social, vocational, educational, physical, and spiritual aspects of healthy living.

When considering interventions to help clients examine self-views, professional helpers practice from a broad understanding of social-cultural influence and make every attempt to select from a range of approaches that clients might find appropriate and useful. By doing so, counselors and other professionals maintain a respectful posture that recognizes the autonomy of the client within the helping relationship, while at the same time creating a flexible and open approach (Schmidt, 2002).

Self-Determination

Another way that people adjust views is through self-action and self-determination. Most people move through life with minimal counseling or other formal help because they have developed high levels of self-reliance, determination, and perseverance, and these traits are complemented by family ties and community support. They are able to ascertain what views are inhibiting their development, plan strategies to alter these views, and adopt new behaviors to bring about desired change in their lives. Sometimes, people seek out guidance and suggestions from professional helpers, or from family, friends, or another supportive network. Ultimately, however, they choose strategies and determine a direction for change to take place. When successful, such people are able to make significant shifts in their views and behaviors that bring about noticeable differences in their self-concept and lifestyle.

People make countless choices everyday that are illustrations of how self-determination can alter self-concept. Some examples include quitting smoking, eating healthier, ending a destructive relationship, moving away from family, joining or leaving a church, mosque, or temple, proposing marriage or asking for a divorce, coming out to family and friends, going back to school, and changing career direction. When people rid themselves of unhealthy habits, seek more education, leave oppressive relationships, identify their sexual orientation, establish helpful and caring relationships to enrich their lives, or recognize the career they have chosen is unfulfilling, they take the initial step to determine what interventions will enable them to move forward in a responsible manner.

When family, friends, teachers, and others encourage people to establish goals, make plans, and choose strategies for achieving these goals, their confidence becomes stronger and nurtures self-determination. For counselors and other helping professionals, understanding how self-determination emerges and the subsequent social or cultural implications for the client, family, and community is important. Self-concept can change through individual self-determination, but fostering such behavior without understanding its impact on a client's relationships with family members, friends, and community might not be helpful. Counselors and other helping professionals foster self-determination with clients within the context of particular social and cultural influences each client must consider. For example, clients with a cultural heritage that embraces collective views more that individualistic achievement balance their self-determination with what is best for themselves, family, and community as a whole.

Determination, as with other qualities of the *self,* is vulnerable to countless experiences. It can be strengthened or weakened by repeated events that influence people's belief system. Therefore, a fifth way that self-concept might change is through repetition of similar events and experiences.

Repeated Life Events

In addition to ecstatic events, trauma, intervention, and self-determination, another way that self-concept might change is by repeated positive or negative events in a person's life (Purkey & Novak, 1996; Purkey & Schmidt, 1996). Classroom teachers and school counselors see the effects of this phenomenon every day with students they teach and counsel.

Young students who have learned from their parents, grandparents, and extended family members that they are valued, respected, and capable often succeed in school. In contrast, students who constantly hear how awful, dumb, uncoordinated, and irresponsible they are might conclude that they are worthless and incapable. Understandably, they might rebel against the rigors of academic lessons and high standards expected in school.

When people hear continuously that they have potential and are loved by others, these remarks have a powerful cumulative effect. At the same time, if people observe genuine kind and nurturing behaviors that validate the comments they hear, the positive effect could be magnified. In such instances, we might be more certain that individuals will be successful and productive in their lives. Still, a caveat is important to note here. According to self-concept theory, as mentioned earlier, through unconscious processes, people ultimately determine which perceptions fit and which to reject from the self-views that construct their belief system (Purkey & Schmidt, 1996). For this reason, we occasionally see people who have grown up in seemingly ideal environments, yet nevertheless choose destructive and counterproductive behaviors. Such cases of deviant behavior are often confusing to counselors and other professional helpers. They struggle to understand why people who seem to have *everything going for them* make such inappropriate decisions or choose such destructive behaviors. Later in this chapter, we will consider deviancy in more detail. For now, suffice to say that these cases show that other factors, such as biological traits and psychological conditions, work in tandem with phenomenological processes to influence people's choices. Understanding these combined influences gives increased credence to holistic approaches used in counseling and human service—approaches that consider self-perceptions, environmental influences, biological makeup, cultural heritage, social pressures, and other aspects related to human development.

As mentioned, repeated negative events might have a devastating effect on people's development. This could be particularly true in the early stages of development, as children begin creating belief systems about themselves and the world around them. However, in later years such negative repeated experiences could also take their toll. As an illustration, think of a young man who has excelled in sports during childhood and adolescent years. His relationships with coaches have been mostly positive, helping him develop a strong belief in his athletic abilities. Then, in college, a new coach relies on constant aversive language and physical exercise to motivate players. The young man begins to doubt his athletic ability, eventually becoming so discouraged that he quits the team. Some other players might take the coach's negative style and fight back by motivating themselves and saying, in essence, "I'll show him!" They reject the coach's taunts and comments and succeed in spite of his approach. The young man in question, however, may not have experienced such abuse before, and ultimately accepts defeat by concluding that he does not have the mental and emotional stamina to compete successfully under such stressful conditions.

Repeated experiences are important factors that relate to social and cultural influences in a person's development of a belief system. Cultural traditions practiced within families and communities and passed on to youth become part of a child's existence and worldview. Similarly, spiritual beliefs emerge through repeated practice of religious ceremonies or other sacred experiences. Counselors and other professional helpers who practice with social and cultural sensitivity are interested in all the experiences that influence people's development, and pay particular attention to their clients' perceptions about these significant events.

Factors that influence change in self-concept include more than the examples presented here. Joyful events, trauma, intervention, self-determination, and repeated experiences offer a sampling of sources for self-concept development and change. Although all these events have significant influence on people's lives and belief systems, the self-concept is a relatively stable and consistent part of a person's personality (Hamacheck, 1992; Purkey, 1970, 2000; Purkey & Schmidt, 1996).

Stability of the Self-Concept

In theory, self-concept is a stable structure that perpetuates consistent behavior (Brown, 1998). Without consistency, we might see widespread chaos and unpredictability in people's behavior. Change, as we have noted, does take place, and people do alter views, but the fundamental beliefs that guide who they are in life demonstrate a reliability that manifests itself in the consistent behaviors people choose. As such, we might expect all the significant "sub-selves" of the self-concept (in Figure 2.1, those closest to the core) to show a degree of stability and dependability in how people view themselves and their surrounding world. Earlier, this chapter discussed how people experience events and either accept or reject them as an illustration of "fitting" or "not fitting" their current belief system. When people accept contrary beliefs or incompatible perceptions, they invite *cognitive dissonance,* which can lead to behaviors that are inconsistent with the person's usual pattern. A common phrase used to illustrate these instances is "I'm just not myself today!" However, inviting such dissonance is not necessarily a negative event. Often, contrary circumstances encourage people to make changes, alter views, and take positive steps toward self-development.

Counselors and human service providers understand the stability of the self-concept because they appreciate the consistency that comes from an *internal* frame of reference. They understand that what might appear to be conflicting perceptions within a client's belief system are assessed by the counselor and others from an external point of view. If such apparent conflicting sub-selves exist without inner turmoil for the client, then consistency prevails. However, the conflict that exists from external perspectives often causes problems for the person and community. An example is a man who has been unable to hold a job—an external view. From his perspective, he is much better and more talented than what these jobs offer, so by constantly quitting them, he maintains a consistent perspective about himself and the unworthiness of these occupations. Others, especially his spouse and family, draw different conclusions, and wonder if he will ever accept responsibility by keeping a job. Therein lies the conflict.

Understanding the difference between an external assessment and an internal point of view is particularly important when helping people who are from different cultural and social backgrounds, or who have belief systems contrary to the helper. Counselors and other providers who learn about their clients' traditions and values might have less difficulty comprehending social and cultural perspectives different from theirs. In practice, such professionals may have the potential to be successful with a range of clients. In addition, counselors and human service workers who understand the stability of self-concept and the importance of its consistency also appreciate the time it might take for a person to make changes and bring about transformations in life.

Related Developmental Theories

Over the years, various authorities have created numerous developmental theories to explain psychosocial, cognitive, and other aspects of human growth and maturation (Chickering, 1969; Erikson, 1968; Kohlberg, 1976; Piaget, 1952). In many respects, these developmental theories incorporate factors related to the emerging self-concept and identity development. For example, Erikson's (1968) ideas about stages of identity development and Piaget's (1952) work on cognitive development both consider the role of environment and a person's interpretation of and reaction to external events in the process of growing and maturing from childhood to adulthood.

Likewise, Chickering's (1969) pioneering study with undergraduate college students is an example of adult development models. Chickering and Reisser (1993) used contemporary research findings to revise this original theory and proposed seven vectors of development, each contributing to a person's identity development. In his original work, Chickering (1969) selected the term *vector* to describe the various stages of development (students' tasks) because of the degree and purpose attributed to each of the vectors. The seven vectors (tasks) in the revised model included (1) Developing Competence, (2) Managing Emotions, (3) Moving through Autonomy toward Interdependence, (4) Developing Mature Interpersonal Relationships, (5) Establishing Identity, (6) Developing Purpose, and (7) Developing Integrity. Regarding the task of establishing an identity, Chickering and Reisser (1993) included several aspects such as body image and appearance, gender role and sexual orientation, clarity of self-concept and lifestyle, an understanding of social and cultural heritage, secure sense of self, self-acceptance, and personal stability and integration (Evans, 2003). Researchers have studied the applicability of this theory across various population groups (e.g., women, Asian Americans, African Americans, those of alternative sexual orientation) and have noted gender and cultural differences in prioritizing the various vectors (Evans, Forney, & Guido-DiBrito, 1998).

Other theories of adult development have proposed stages of life, particular life events, and the timing of life events as different perspectives on the maturation process. Some of these models lend understanding to self-development from a social and cultural perspective. For example, Schlossberg, Waters, and Goodman (1995) suggested a life events' model that views significant happenings as part of a process over a period of time in which people accomplish certain tasks. Evans (2003) noted that life events' models consider the manner in which individuals accomplish these important tasks and related the process to many factors including personality traits as well as support networks and resources. Furthermore, she observed that the "focus on variability, interconnectedness, and environmental influence" suggests that life events' models are "well-suited for explaining women's development across the life span" (Evans, 2003, p. 185).

Many other theories related to self-evolution (Kegan, 1994), moral development (Gilligan, 1982; Kohlberg, 1976), spiritual development (Parks, 2000), and career development (Super, 1990) exist, and contribute to the knowledge base and understanding of self-concept. A final supposition presented here is that all aspects related to a person's self-view tie distinctively to that person's worldview. In a sense, self-view is the core belief system that creates, promulgates, and affirms the belief system that comprises a worldview, which was defined in Chapter 1. Figure 2.4 illustrates one depiction of this relationship.

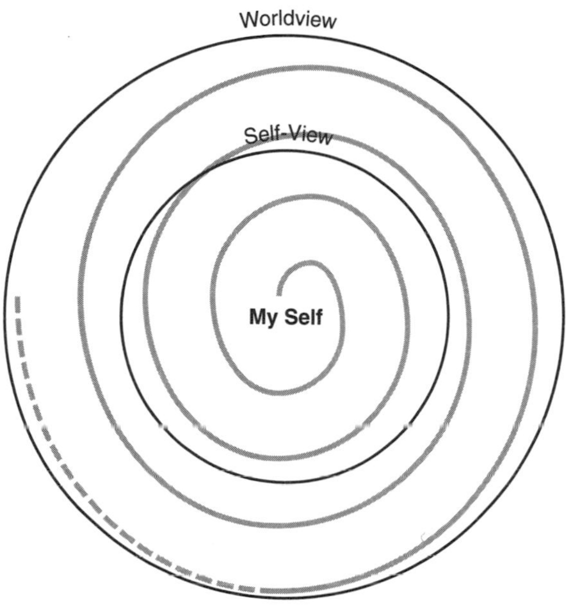

FIGURE 2.4 ***Relationship of Self-View and Worldview***

Strongly held values, beliefs, customs, and language of cultural and ethnic groups to which an individual belongs are influential in the formation and organization of a worldview.

The ideas presented thus far in this chapter explain the organization, function, and stability of self-concept as depicted through various theories. An understanding of how human perception constructs this internal belief system is useful to professional helpers in expressing empathy regarding their clients' point of view. Counselors and other human service providers might also find self-concept theory and related developmental theories helpful in constructing and appreciating how their clients view the world in which they live. At the same time, they might gain appreciation for the learning processes that comprise the creation of a *self-* and worldview. The next part of this chapter connects self-development and worldview with social learning theory.

Self-View, Worldview, and Social Learning

If, as theorists propose, people construct self-concepts, they do so within a particular environment, which itself is also created, nurtured, ignored, or harmed by various social and cultural forces. Human development, including an emerging self-concept, is either enhanced and supported or neglected and depreciated by the societies and groups in which, and with whom, people live. In concert with a person's unique perceptual power, these assorted social and cultural elements contribute to the development of a self-view and corresponding worldview that fill a continuum of human thought and beliefs about oneself, other people, and life in general. For counselors and other professional helpers, an understanding of the dynamic relationship between a person's view of *self* and the cultural context in which she or he was born and nurtured is imperative.

The following sections explore two schools of thought related to social learning theory. The first is Vygotsky's (1962, 1935/1978) social cognition learning model and a second is the social learning theory of Albert Bandura (1971, 1986; Bandura & Walters, 1963), also known as social cognitive theory. Of particular interest for premises put forth in this text is the relationship Bandura (1997) and others (Maddux & Gosselin, 2003) have highlighted between social learning and self-efficacy.

Social Cognition Learning Model

Born in 1896 in Byelorussia of the former Soviet Union, psychologist Len Semyonovitch Vygotsky was a contemporary of notable stimulus-response psychologists including Ivan Pavlov and John B. Watson, and of the Gestalt theorists of that period. In contrast with other speculation of the time, Vygotsky (1935/1978, 1962) attempted to develop a theory of cognitive development with particular relevance to an ever-changing society, the impact of culture on human development, and practical implications for education and learning.

Three basic premises set the foundation for his theory. First is the significant role a person's culture plays in the process of human development. Everything that people experience from birth through death in the process of developing a personal identity filters through limitless cultural and social contexts. Beginning with the birth setting, trauma, and celebration into which they are born, continuing with family experiences and interactions, and moving through childhood, adolescence, and adult learning, people experience a plethora of cultural events and influences that have a tremendous impact on who they become.

A second important theme in Vygotsky's theory is the central role of language in human development. Through language, adults teach children. Consequently, language is a fundamental feature of culture. As children learn about culture through the transmission of language (e.g., words, concepts, beliefs), they adapt this knowledge to internalize language in developing their thought processes. In this way, children acquire an internal language by which they learn to direct their thoughts and behaviors. The common term for this internal language or dialogue today is *self-talk* (Purkey, 2000). A key notion in this theme is that language not only helps people with their cognitive development, it also helps shape society and culture. As people develop the ability to think and solve problems, they create fresh cultural features or adjust old ones to fit new patterns and trends. In this way, culture has significant influence on the emerging person, who in turn has the potential to have an impact on the culture.

The third premise of social cognitive learning theory is the *zone of proximal development* (Vygotsky, 1935/1978). This idea focuses on what children are capable of doing on their own in comparison to what they are able to do with help from others. As such, this concept defines human functions that are in the process of developing as well as those that are mature. We might expect that children surrounded by social institutions, cultural traditions, nurturing parents, competent teachers, and inviting friends would benefit intellectually. In theory, the more expansive a child's *zone of proximal development,* the more potential exists for maximum learning. This concept has implications for assessing children in educational settings and for counseling. Counselors, for example, want to ascertain what their clients currently know and understand, as well as the potential for learning more information and understanding more complex matters. These three principles of Vygotsky's social cognitive learning theory have relevance for understanding self-development.

Vygotsky's work (1935/1978, 1962) was cut short by his death in 1934 due to tuberculosis. However, his ideas have had an influence on educational theory and self-concept theory (Purkey, 2000), and may have importance in counseling a broad spectrum of clients, particularly children. Because so much of what children learn is influenced by society and culture, counselors who work with children from diverse backgrounds avoid assessing them in isolation. Parental influence, family experiences, and other important social and cultural considerations are taken into account.

Social Learning Theory

In behavioral theory, operant conditioning maintains that learning occurs through a reinforcement paradigm (Kazdin, 2001). That is, all human learning is an outcome of direct reinforcement schedules. Albert Bandura's lifetime work has contested this conclusion (1997, 1998). Early in his career as a clinical psychology professor at Stanford University, in the 1960s, Albert Bandura began studying the relationship between modeling behaviors of parents and social aggression by adolescent boys. Over time, his research showed that learning often takes place through observation without any identifiable or direct reinforcement. Furthermore, social learning research found that learning through modeling does not necessarily result in behavior change (Kazdin, 2001). Sometimes, learning through modeling simply is integrated into a person's pattern of cognitive functioning (i.e., into the construction of self-concept).

During the past decades of social learning research, theorists have placed increased emphasis on the role cognition plays in the understanding and interpretation of human learning and behavior. This makes particular sense when considering cultural learning and the integration of cultural traditions and beliefs into a person's self-concept. For example, as a young child learns religious rituals and beliefs by observing ceremonies in a mosque, synagogue, or church, we may not see overt behavioral change. Gradually, as the child matures, he or she may incorporate new behaviors based on the earlier observational learning, particularly if family and society encourage and reinforce such behaviors. However, the child may never demonstrate much of the observed learning by specific behavior changes. Rather, the child might simply incorporate these observations into a global belief system that serves as a guide to spiritual and religious functioning.

Reinforcement and Social Learning. Reinforcement of modeling occurs in several ways. For one, a learner might be reinforced by the model. For example, a young child who has observed parents and older siblings eating with utensils might suddenly pick up a spoon and begin using it. Subsequent praise and encouragement by the parents will likely result in continued use of the spoon and eventual adaptation of other utensils at future meals.

Another example of reinforced modeling is when a third person intervenes. As an illustration, say a basketball player has been observing how a teammate uses a certain technique for shooting foul shots. The player watches and attempts to incorporate this technique into her style of shooting, and while practicing it, is encouraged by the coach, who notes that the new way of shooting will improve her foul-shot percentage. Of course, the ultimate reinforcement for adapting this shooting technique will be increased foul shots scored during the game.

Vicarious reinforcement is another way that people learn through modeling. Sometimes, models win accolades, achieve goals, make money, or perform tasks. Research shows that under certain conditions, observers will adapt behaviors of the model if they perceive those behaviors are valued by people who are important to them. Some of Bandura's earliest research studied vicarious learning by having children watch films of an inflated plastic doll (the now famous Bobo doll) being hit by a model. Children who observed the model receiving praise began to hit the doll also, without receiving praise themselves (Bandura, 1973).

Imitated behaviors result in self-gratification, fun, or other form of pleasure that reinforces their use. First, the behaviors are observed. Next, the observer concludes that the behaviors might be worth trying, and finally, the individual makes the attempt. If the person feels the expected enjoyment or pleasure assumed from the observations, then the behaviors are reinforced. On the other hand, if those expected feelings are not realized, it is likely the person would not integrate the observed learning into his or her behavioral repertoire.

Social Learning and Cognition. One factor related to learning that is receiving increased consideration among contemporary learning theorists is the influence of expectation on cognitive functioning. In particular, an individual's expectation of reward or punishment regarding a particular behavior is influential in determining whether the person ultimately uses the observed behavior. Closely tied to this notion of expected reinforcement is the person's degree or level of attention during the learning process. With expected reinforcement, therefore, attention might be more likely and learning will result (Bandura, 1997, 1998). Putting this in the context of self-development and cultural identity, we might conclude that when a person finds a particular cultural experience meaningful, she or he will attend to the details of the event more so than will someone who does not find it satisfying or worthwhile.

Social Learning and Self-Efficacy

Much of Bandura's work in the 1990s focused on development of self-efficacy and its link to social learning theory (1998). Efficacy relates to perceived value, worthiness, and effectiveness. As such, *self*-efficacy is the sum of perceived beliefs that people hold about their ability to behave in productive ways to have a beneficial influence on their life. A person's beliefs about self-efficacy, therefore, are important and integral pieces of his or her larger, more global self-concept (Maddux & Gosselin, 2003).

Bandura (1998) highlighted several sources for developing self-efficacy. The first is through mastery learning. As people learn to master certain tasks in life, and repeated successes reinforce this learning, they tend to develop a stronger sense of capability. Such success should include experience in overcoming obstacles. Achievement without challenge may not lead to an efficacy built on fortitude and perseverance, and without those qualities, feelings of self-worth might be short-lived. At the same time, failures, particularly repeated and harsh failures that occur before a strong sense of efficacy develops, tend to demoralize people and weaken their chances to gain self-fulfillment.

Social learning, as we have seen, is another source of self-efficacy, and one that is particularly tied to groups, societies, and cultures. Observing how other people perform, particularly people in groups with which we identify, provides powerful information about our self-efficacy. Behaviors, attitudes, and customs observed in families, peer groups, and through other social encounters are sources of self-efficacy beliefs. When the groups with whom we associate are successful in their endeavors, we integrate our observations of that success into an assessment of ourselves. On the other hand, when our primary groups are unsuccessful or perceived as less valuable by larger segments of society, this might have a negative effect on our feeling of self-worth.

Having our social or cultural group perceived as less valuable by the larger society might have a countereffect if our group is persuasive in convincing us of its *true* value. Persuasiveness is another source of self efficacy and one that can counteract beliefs of inferiority whether professed by individuals or groups. Bandura (1998) cautioned that persuasion alone without corresponding success might lead to unrealistic expectation that will quickly deteriorate into disappointment with the onset of a first setback or failure.

As noted above, self-efficacy relates to self-identity. Understanding self-views, and having a structure or model, such as the self-concept spiral or social learning theory, to increase this understanding is valuable in comprehending a clients' development, appreciating the social and cultural influences on developmental processes, and ultimately understanding the behavioral choices people make in their daily lives.

Because counseling and human services often have a remedial focus in helping people address fears, inhibitions, and behaviors that thwart personal development, negative issues such as deviance, violence, and substance abuse are often central to difficult cases. In contrast, helping professionals also provide access to and acceptance of educational opportunity, including new technology, which complements interventions to help people redirect their lives. The next sections offer a sample of human behaviors and developmental opportunities to help connect self-concept theory with social learning. The sample includes both positive and negative behaviors, presented here to explore how they might relate to self-development. In that regard, while reading each of the following sections, you might consider how the self-view and worldview of people who use these selected behaviors or socially learned traits might be structured (returning to Figure 2.1 might assist you in this analysis). The first topic is deviant behavior.

Deviant Behavior

Sociologists, criminologists, psychologists, and other behavioral scientists have studied deviancy since humankind began observing differences among members of social groups (Kelly & Clarke, 2003). Numerous theories of criminal deviance have been proposed, investigated, analyzed, and criticized over the years (Downes & Rock, 2003). For our purposes here, we consider deviance in a broad sense, not necessarily confined to criminal behavior.

By considering a broad definition of deviance, we acknowledge that not only has deviant behavior existed since the formation of early societies, but it also remains a consistent phenomenon in the study of social structure and individual development. As Curra (2000) observed, "Social deviance is a persistent and common feature of societies, communities, and groups" (p. 1). At the same time, deviance is a social construct uniquely defined by particular groups according to their "ideal culture—shared understandings about exemplary ways of acting, thinking, and feeling" (Curra, 2000, p. 16). Consequently, deviance is socially and culturally defined, and therefore manifests itself in various forms not necessarily evaluated consistently across social groups. Deviancy also includes aspects of motivation, opportunity, continuity, positive reinforcement, and adverse consequences (Kaplan & Johnson, 2001). What motivational conditions, opportunities, reinforcements, or punishment does society have in place that help to define deviant behavior? How these aspects operate in a given society or particular cultural group helps define deviancy and its relativity to proper and improper ways of behaving.

Earlier conceptions that deviancy results from biological characteristics remain unsupported by research findings (Gibbs, 2003). A new emerging view rejects the notion that physical, biological, or other intrinsic features relate to deviant behavior. Instead, deviancy is identified and defined only by the reaction of society to particular acts. Because certain behaviors are considered deviant by one society and not another, this theory maintains that biological or other characteristics alone cannot define deviance. "Purely biological variables may explain why some persons commit certain acts, but they do not explain why the acts are crimes" (Gibbs, 2003, p. 18). Accordingly, we can assume that deviant behavior is socially defined and learned.

Depending on the particular social group and motivations and opportunities that exist, some behaviors defined as deviant by external observers in retrospect might be perceived as noble and even heroic by internal group members. Helms and Cook (1999) reminded us that the early American colonies and the United States of America were established largely due to rebellious opportunities accepted by deviants and misfits from Europe. For example, the Sons of Liberty who staged the Boston Tea Party in 1773 were defying England's tax policies and their deviant behavior was the precursor to further confrontation that eventually led to a successful rebellion, proudly referred to today as the American Revolution.

Some authorities have proposed the concept of *positive deviance* (Heckert, 2003). Although there is debate about the existence of positive deviance, its definition includes behavior that society recognizes as superior in nature and that typically deviates from the expected norm. Heckert (2003) offered numerous examples of positive deviance across categories that include innovative and creative people, extremely physically attractive people, Nobel Prize winners, geniuses, and others. Exercise 2.4 offers a list of exceptional historical and contemporary figures. Review the names you know, and decide whether you consider them examples of positive deviants.

Deviance is both socially constructed and situational (or contextual) by definition (Goode, 2002). Social construction, as noted earlier in this text, consists of rules and behavioral norms established both formally and informally and intended for members of a particular society or group. An example of deviant behavior from a social perspective might be the act of arson. Burning down an inhabited building or intentionally torching a forest are crimes and likely to result in punishment by imprisonment.

Exercise 2.4

Positive Deviancy?

Instructions: Review the list below and identify names about which you have some knowledge. Based on that knowledge, decide whether you could appropriately label the person as a positive deviant. Form a rationale for each decision and share with a classmate.

Person	*Positive Deviant?*
Mother Theresa	______________
Dr. Martin Luther King, Jr.	______________
Michelangelo	______________
Galileo	______________
Jesus Christ	______________
Jefferson Davis	______________
Rosa Parks	______________
Albert Einstein	______________
Thomas Edison	______________
Mahatma Gandhi	______________
The Dalai Lama	______________

Socially constructed norms might change over time, and consequently, behavior once thought of as deviant could be redefined or reconsidered. For example, in the United States during the 1940s and 1950s, marital divorce had different social meaning than it does today. Although divorce is still not a positive event in anyone's life, it no longer has the social stigma attached to it in earlier years.

Situational deviance occurs when a person or people within a group break a rule or violate a norm that relates to a specific circumstance or context. As an illustration, the U.S. Episcopal Church installed an openly gay bishop in 2004. This historic event caused much consternation and fragmentation among church members because it deviated from what some believed to be church doctrine. However, the larger society did not condemn or punish this act, so its deviancy is contextual or situational in nature. Although we might define the act of naming a gay bishop as situational deviance, the act of being homosexual might be defined as a socially constructed deviance because the larger society continues to reject such sexual orientation (Goode, 2002). Within particular communities or cultural groups, however, members view homosexuality as an acceptable orientation, and this is another example of situational rather than social judgment.

Deviant behavior is important to understand from both social and situational perspectives when working with clients from diverse cultures. People who deviate from the normal practices of groups with which they identify, whether with negative or positive deviation, face rejection, punishment, criticism, or other stressors that affect their *self*-development. Understanding how society, cultural groups, families, and individual clients perceive and evaluate the deviant behavior in question is an important starting point to establishing helpful relationships. Key to this understanding is being able to differentiate between deviant behavior that is destructive to social order, human welfare, or the individual's *self*-development and deviant behavior that simply violates cultural norms and customs. This may be an oversimplification of the issue, but perhaps it is the difference between criminal (or destructive) deviance and cultural (or individual) deviance. Consider the examples of deviant behavior in Exercise 2.5 and decide whether each is a destructive deviance or cultural/individual deviance.

Understanding situational deviance could be important when working with clients who violate existing social codes of a dominant culture or reject customs and traditions of their family and culture. Many young people who immigrate with their families to the United States assimilate into Western or American ways of behaving, dressing, and dating, thus causing conflict within their families. Helping young clients understand their actions within the context of social and situational deviance might be an initial step to learning negotiation and compromise skills that enable parents and other family members to view new behaviors in positive ways. Similarly, clients from diverse backgrounds who struggle to adjust in a new society might want to learn how to navigate through new cultural experiences without drawing negative attention to customs and traditions they continue to embrace.

Exercise 2.5

Understanding Deviance

Instructions: Review the list of behaviors and decide whether each is criminal (destructive) or cultural (individual) in nature. Leave blank any you cannot label. Share your responses with the class.

Behavior	***Criminal, Destructive, Cultural, or Individual***
Dressing in sexually provocative ways	________________
Robbing a bank	________________
Protesting at a political rally	________________
Stealing food from a grocery	________________
Wearing culturally authentic clothes	________________
Using profanity in public	________________
Worshiping in public places	________________
Preaching on a street corner	________________
Looking down when talking to someone	________________
Changing religious affiliation	________________
Having extramarital affairs	________________
Marrying more than one spouse	________________
Children sleeping in same bed with parents	________________
Driving over the speed limit	________________
Hitting a child for discipline/punishment	________________
Hitting a spouse for discipline/punishment	________________
Not worshiping at a mosque, synagogue, or church	________________
Boycotting a popular product	________________
Running away from home	________________
Achieving the highest academic goals	________________
Dropping out of school	________________
Being sexual active as a single adult	________________
Being sexually active as an adolescent	________________

Equally important in addressing various forms of deviant behavior are strategies and services that help society, families, and other groups understand and empathize with people from diverse backgrounds or people who chose unconventional behaviors and customs to express themselves. Counselors and other professional helpers not only work with individuals, they also have responsibility to educate the larger group, be it society, family, peer group, or other social group, about behaviors that some might perceive as deviant or simply different. School counselors, for example, are keenly aware of the need to help students understand the behavior, dress, and customs of their classmates who come from diverse backgrounds. Integrating guidance lessons into daily instruction, arranging cultural celebrations, and inviting speakers from various cultures into the school are a few ways that schools inform their communities while teaching tolerance and acceptance of behaviors that appear to deviate from the norm.

Violence and Abuse

Violence and abuse are two factors related to deviancy that social scientists and psychologists have studied for years. Despite volumes of research, full understanding of violent behavior and how people become violent eludes us. As Stewart and Strathern (2002) surmised, violence is "an enduring phenomenon that is part of our lives and cannot be ignored, yet has proved difficult to understand and analyse" (p. 1).

An understanding of the relationship between violent behavior, personal development, and social status variables such as gender and class is important for designing effecting strategies that help clients, communities, and organizations address this issue. At the same time, counselors and other professional helpers want to understand the effects of violence on victims, families, communities, and the larger society.

In addition to commonly known forms of violence condemned by most societies, such as murder and rape, there are also culturally specific forms of violence, which in contrast are often encouraged within certain social groups. These culturally accepted forms of violence include bullfighting, animal sacrifice, cattle raids, public executions, male socialization rituals, hazes, and many types of sport, among other forms of condoned violent behavior. Also, warfare is a specific type of organized violence that, as noted earlier, has been used by social structures such as kingdoms, empires, countries, tribes, and governments throughout history for political, territorial, or social gain. Organized violence perpetuated by social structures, such as states and countries, also takes the form of widespread aggression against ethnic groups (Stewart & Strathern, 2002).

Violence and Homicide

Statistics indicate that "the United States is the most violent industrialized country in the world" (Hoffman & Summers, 2001, p. xiv). In the United States, African Americans tend to be more at risk of violent behaviors than White Americans and Black men are seven to ten times more likely to be murdered than White males (Aponte & D[illegible], 2000). Similarly, Black women have a 1 in 194 probability of being murdered, while White females have a 1 in 369 chance (Aponte & Bracco, 2000). In cultural and sociopolitical contexts, violence is perpetuated against women throughout the globe in various forms including genital mutilation and rape. Traditional practices in some cultures and societies raise conflicts for American and other Western cultures and legal processes.

Violence among African American teens is at a rate of 61 percent, as opposed to 36 percent for White youth (Hoffman & Summers, 2001). Among Black youths between the ages of 15 and 19 in 2001, the homicide rate per 100,000 was 58.2, compared with 7.9 for White males. Likewise, among Black females the rate was 6.4, compared to 2.0 for White females (Child Trends Data Bank, 2003). In general, older teens and young adults have the highest rates across age groups as both victims and offenders of homicide. Since 1993, homicide rates in the United States have declined, but they remain higher than rates reported in the 1980s (Bureau of Justice Statistics, 2002).

In a majority of Black homicides, the murderer is a family member, friend, or associate of the victim. Consequently, most often the murders of African Americans in the United States reflect the phenomenon of Black-on-Black violence "in the context of familiar interpersonal relationships" (Aponte & Bracco, 2000, p. 140).

Homicide is the seventh leading cause of death among Hispanics and the second leading cause of death for Hispanic youth (Violence Policy Center, 2003). Rates among Hispanic youth reported from 1999 through 2001 were higher than non-Hispanic populations (Child Trends Data Bank, 2003). In 2001, the rate of Hispanic homicides among males between the ages of 15 and 19 was three times greater than among non-Hispanic males. Alcohol and substance abuse are often variables in these killings (Aponte & Bracco, 2000).

Suicide

Suicide, a special form of violence, is also significant in the United States, although the rates have been relatively stable for most groups in recent years. The rate of suicide among males ages 15 to 19 in 2001 was almost 13 per 100,000, and under 3 per 100,000 for females (Child Trends Data Bank, 2003). Suicide is a leading cause of death among Native American youth, for whom alcohol abuse is a related factor (Aponte & Bracco, 2000; Harper & McFadden, 2003). The 2001 suicide rate for Native American males in the 15-to-19 age group was 27.7 per 100,000 versus a rate of 14.0 for White males (Child Trends Data Bank, 2003). Rates for male and female African Americans were lower than Whites in 2001, although Porter (2000b) suggested that suicide rates among Black adolescents might be underestimated. Study of suicidal thinking among gays and lesbians indicates about a third of respondents reveal actual attempts (McBee & Rogers, 1997). In these instances, a majority of subjects cited sexual orientation as their reason for attempting suicide.

Age is another correlate of suicide found within some populations. For example, Alston, Rankin, and Harris (1995) wondered about the rising rates among elderly African American males, which increased about 42 percent in the 1980s. Likewise, Baruth and Manning (1999) reported "an alarmingly high rate of drug use and suicide among older Asian Americans . . . especially in older men without family or ideological ties to the larger community" (p. 184). In 2000, suicide rates for White males, in contrast to females and Black males, climbed sharply after the age of 70 (National Institute of Mental Health, 2003).

Physical and Sexual Abuse

Child and spousal abuse are two areas of violent behavior of major concern in the United States. The law requires that suspected physical, sexual, or emotional abuse and the neglect of children be reported to appropriate authorities. Specifically, the Child Abuse Prevention and Treatment Act of 1974 and related statutes require that helping professionals report suspicions of such situations. As the date of passage for the child abuse act indicates, serious attention to this matter is relatively recent—during the past three decades. In part, this is because cultural attitudes about raising children and the rights of children under the law have evolved over time. Not all cultures share these views. Within the United States, a wide range of opinion exists regarding child-rearing practices, discipline and punishment, and children's legal rights. Variance across cultural groups, religious beliefs, and family traditions contribute to differing views. Professionals who work with families and children from diverse cultures are aware of legal requirements and ethical responsibilities and at the same time balance their knowledge with sensitivity toward subtle and obvious cultural and family differences.

Estimates are that over 3 million reports of child abuse and neglect are made each year in the United States (Child Abuse Data, 2003). Fatalities cross ethnic groups, and depending on the type of statistical analysis performed, African American and Hispanic children may be somewhat more likely to suffer a fatality than White children. Furthermore, younger children have a greater likelihood of dying than older abused children do.

Spousal abuse or battering comes under the rubric of domestic violence. As has child abuse, domestic violence has received increased attention in the United States in recent years. Johnson (2000) reported that between 2 and 4 million women are abused each year—about one incident every 18 seconds. Regarding spousal abuse and battering, the largest percent of cases involved men abusing female partners in either married or live-in relationships. According to Crespi and Howe (2000), about a third of all married couples have physical altercations. Gladding (2002) noted from a number of sources that each year over 1.5 million wives are battered by their husbands, and about 13 percent of murders in the United States are husbands killing their wives. As with other forms of violence, alcohol abuse is closely associated with spousal abuse.

Sexual abuse is another form of domestic violence. Forced sexual intimacy, even in marital relationships, is abusive and considered rape in the United States. Additional forms of sexual coercion and abuse include intimidation and threats to force sexual consent and obligatory exposure to sexual media and activities that the victim would otherwise not want to see or perform (Volpe, 1996).

As do views about child punishment, cultural attitudes about marital relationships interact with the issue of domestic violence. These attitudes become part of social learning processes that distinguish people's views about domestic violence. For example, adults from nonabusive relationships frequently express confusion and frustration with women who remain in abusive marriages or other partnerships. Such confusion and frustration, however, are not necessarily translated into community action. Theories have proposed several factors that influence a woman's decision to stay in an abusive relationship, including psychological stress and fear for safety, emotional dependence, economic need, and cultural beliefs such as gender-role differentiation.

The link between violent behavior and self-concept development remains uncertain. Scientists have long considered the possible link between violent behavior and biological characteristics, but no specific gene, brain functioning, or other physical trait has emerged as a clear link thus far.

Substance Abuse

According to the office of Substance Abuse and Mental Health Services Administration (SAMHSA) of the U.S. Department of Health and Human Services, an estimated 19.5 million Americans in 2002 used illicit drugs, and 120 million 12 years of age and older indicated they drank alcoholic beverages (SAMHSA, 2003). The rate of illicit drug usage among youth 12 to 17 years of age was over 11 percent and increased to more than 20 percent for young adults ages 18 to 25. Of people who drank alcoholic beverages, nearly 7 percent in the 2002 sample were heavy drinkers (SAMHSA, 2003) and over 22 percent participated in binge drinking. These data do not include people who misuse or overuse prescribed medications, which is another form of substance abuse in U.S. society.

Substance abuse is a correlative factor with certain deviant and violent behaviors. At the same time, research of substance and alcohol abuse indicates, "the stress of coping with poverty, unemployment, discrimination, and inadequate housing could contribute to substance abuse" among various people and across cultural groups (Thurman, Plested, Edwards, Chen, & Swaim, 2000, p. 217). The etiology of the problem varies from case to case, and is, therefore, difficult to ascertain in terms of psychological, social learning, genetic, or other biological factors, or a combination of these contributors as essential determiners of substance abuse behavior.

Although research indicates that substance abuse crosses all cultural and ethnic groups, it is impossible to generalize about the problem due to variances within groups (Thurman et al., 2000). According to U.S. data, the rate of substance dependency or abuse in 2002 was highest among Native Americans including Alaskan Natives—over 14 percent (SAMHSA, 2003). The same data show people of biracial or multiple racial backgrounds with the next highest rate (13 percent), Hispanics at over 10 percent, Whites and African Americans with about the same rate (9.5% and 9.3% respectively), and Asians with the lowest rate of dependency or abuse (over 4%).

Education

In the United States, the more educated a person becomes, the more likely she or he will have opportunity to reap the economic rewards of career success and higher income. In addition, combined educational achievement and career satisfaction can help people acculturate into mainstream society. Consequently, personal attitudes and beliefs about education interact with social policies to create educational pathways and achieve educational goals that benefit both the individual and society.

Various cultural groups and nationalities have strong beliefs about the importance of education in *self*-development and in bringing honor to the family. At the same time, education offers avenues to free people from oppressive and discriminatory practices of the past against their race, gender, culture, religion, or other social variable. Before the U.S. civil rights movement of the 1960s, educational opportunity and correlated career success were not equally available to all people. School segregation policies deprived African American children of equal advantage due to inferior facilities and outdated resources found in Black schools. Progress made because of school desegregation is evident by the percentage of African Americans completing college and the economic gains made over the past few decades.

Despite the progress made, however, many challenges in the educational arena continue. Some of these challenges come from policies that place certain groups at a disadvantage. Across less educated cultural groups, we find traces of unfair practices and unequal treatment in schools. The relatively high percentage of minority students placed in exceptional children's classes is an example of well-intended programs being implemented in ways that place students disproportionately in remedial, lower-level classes. At the same time, other challenges come from within cultural groups. For example, the attitudes of some African American students say that to excel in school is to be like White students, thereby criticizing and ostracizing their peers who achieve academically (Polk, 2000).

As each person interacts with educational programs and policies, the perceptions formed from experiences with family background and history, by encouragement or discouragement received in early school experiences, and by beliefs about education learned from associating with relatives, peers, and the community, all contribute to *self*-concept development as a student. Educational views become established through unique personal perceptions interacting with family beliefs in concert with numerous societal factors.

Technology and Self-Development

An added dimension to educational opportunity is the increasing use of computers and other technology at home and in the workplace. This exploding phenomenon of "high tech" culture introduces another variable to consider in understanding a person's self-concept development within the larger society. Use of new technology presents several social challenges and opportunities for counselors and other helping professionals to consider (Bloom & Walz, 2000).

Lee (2000) cautioned the counseling profession about relying too heavily on new technology to provide mental health and educational services. Noting that the United States is the most industrialized country with the widest economic gap between wealthiest and poorest groups, Lee commented that "basing the opportunity for quality mental health and educational services on access to the new network technologies is potentially to consign many to marginalization and disenfranchisement" (p. 85). This condition is analogous the medieval times when scribes were about the only people who could read or write and therefore held great social and political power. If the cost of obtaining access to new technology and, subsequently, communication, resources, education, and other services prohibits a large segment of society from participating, then the educational and economic gaps that exist now will widen in the future. Such a result would leave disenfranchised groups and individuals more powerless to make positive gains.

Recent news reports have indicated that the "digital divide"—the increasing social divisions across cultural groups as result of inability to access the Internet—has not been as dramatic as once predicted (Stone, 2003). An increasing number of schools, for example, provide access across student populations. Some experts predict that as new technology continues to decline in cost and economic growth enhances the position of all social groups, Internet usage will greatly expand. Generational differences and normal daily routines may contribute more to decreased Internet usage than other social factors. Still, a digital divide of some degree will exist as long as economic disparities continue. Efforts to ensure equal access might include government sponsored community centers and other initiatives that will eliminate the digital divide across cultural and socioeconomic groups (Lee, 2000; Stone, 2003).

Another factor that new technology has introduced into the human development formula is risk of increased personal isolation. Although new technology has had tremendous impact on information processing and communication, it carries a corresponding risk of people spending more time alone, as noted by the number of children and adults who work or play on the computer a large portion of time and more often than in more social activities. Exercise 2.6 permits you to self-assess the time you spend alone using new technology.

The use of a wide array of technology, from television viewing to Internet chat rooms, also has an effect on public attendance at social events and live performances. Yin (2003) reported that according to findings in the 2002 Survey of Public Participation in the Arts, "Americans are increasingly less likely to go out for a dose of the arts, and more likely to stay home and enjoy performances in front of their home entertainment centers" (p. 1). As such, we might deduce that social interaction might decrease as the use of new technology increases.

New technology might also contribute to changes in social interaction at the workplace. As computers and robots perform more tasks, people may spend less time in cooperative work experiences. If so, the decrease in social contact might increase workers' sense of personal isolation. As a university professor who has entered the realm of teaching online courses, I sometimes worry about the lack of student contact and decrease in "real time" student interaction that result from Internet classes. I am not convinced that discus-

Exercise 2.7

Alone with My Technology

Instructions: Keep a log for the next two weeks. On your log, record the time you spend alone or with one other person doing the activities listed. Total the time, and compare results with classmates.

Activity	*Total Time*
Listening to music	_____
Watching television	_____
Doing school/job-related work on computer	_____
Surfing the Internet	_____
Talking on the phone	_____
Playing on the computer	_____
Watching videos or DVDs	_____
Total Combined Time:	_____

sion boards, virtual classrooms, and other high-tech processes fully take the place of face-to-face contact in optimal learning environments, especially in the helping professions. Yet, I understand the power of this new technology to deliver convenient information and instruction to a broader audience.

Access to the Internet and other new technologies also presents challenges to families across cultural groups. Less interaction between spouses and with children is unhealthy for family functioning (Gladding, 2002). Increased individual time working or playing on the computer by husbands, wives, and children likely adds to the challenges of marital relationships and responsible child rearing. In addition, children from diverse families who access the Internet are exposed to cultural attractions that might violate or otherwise threaten traditional values and customs that parents wish to uphold. On one hand, parents want children to use new technology for educational and other advantages, but on the other hand, they want to ensure that accessed information does not interfere with parental guidance and family functioning. Using technology to enhance family functioning and nurture self-development will be a challenge in the future.

Counseling Inferences

This chapter presented the structure of self-concept, certain qualities about this theory, and its relationship to social and cultural influences in human development. It considered a few ways that self-concept changes during a person's lifetime, and related these events to social and cultural factors that frequently play mitigating roles in the process of growth and development.

For counselors and other helpers, there are a few fundamental teachings about self-concept that are essential. First and foremost is that the self-concept is just that, a *concept,* a theory. It is not something clients show us. We cannot see, touch, measure (in a literal sense), hear, or smell it. Clients do not carry their self-concepts in a tote bag to have counselors or others examine them. Therefore, we are careful not to be overly precise with, or dependent on, the clinical conclusions drawn based on self-concept speculation. As a theory, self-concept is most helpful in allowing counselors and clients to construct assumptions about influential beliefs and values, explore self-talk that might be inhibiting development, and gain general understanding of how clients view themselves and the world around them. From this exploration, clients then choose aspects of their self-views they want to change in making life decisions.

Another inference from the teachings about self-concept is that, although they can change, self-views, particularly as related to personality, remain relatively stable over a lifetime. Counselors and clients can focus on changing behaviors that might ultimately bring about different self-views. New behaviors might be selected and incorporated expeditiously, but any adjustment to self-concept will usually take time.

Counselors and human service providers also understand the powerful influence they have in establishing an effective helping relationship with clients. How they use that power while respecting the social and cultural background and experiences of each client is the hallmark of ethical and professional practice. Perhaps most importantly, successful professionals take time to learn about and understand their own self-views. Helping people examine and explore their perceptions about themselves and the world is best facilitated by counselors and other professionals who willingly engage in their own self-reflection for the purpose of identifying behaviors, views, and values that might inhibit their performance and helpfulness.

This chapter also introduced different theories of social learning and related them to self-development. For counselors and other professional helpers, the theoretical development and research performed by scholars in the arenas of social learning theory and self-development have provided knowledge of possible processes by which people construct self-views. The inferences of this knowledge for professional helpers touch on four areas of awareness and understanding: (a) awareness of learning processes, (b) understanding of client social learning, (c) awareness of the helper's own learning, and (d) awareness of the client's subsequent self-identity and worldview. As noted, counselors and human service providers who attain high levels of self-awareness and understanding of clients' identity are in position to perform adequate assessment of clients' situations and concerns, and subsequently to choose culturally appropriate therapeutic approaches (Robinson, 2005). In later chapters, this text examines the competencies of professional helpers in doing assessment and choosing appropriate strategies and interventions.

A significant aspect of self-development is the interaction of the person with society. Final sections of this chapter presented several social aspects that might have an impact on people's individual development as well as how they function in families and society. Brief treatments about deviancy, violence and abuse, substance abuse, education, and new technology were presented. How counselors and other helping professionals assist clients in handling any or all of these factors is dependent, first, on the knowledge they have about facts and issues related to various social conditions, trends, and behaviors. Second, and equally important, is the professional's use of appropriate skill and interventions when working with clients who exhibit deviant behavior, are prone to violence, abuse drugs and alcohol, fail to attain educationally, or misuse new technology.

Few professionals are equipped or prepared to handle any or all issues that clients might bring to helping relationships. For this reason, training in specialized areas is important, as is appreciation of one's limitations as a helping professional. Expertise is needed for many of the social factors covered in this chapter. In particular, certain deviant, violent, and abusive behaviors demand knowledge and practice beyond the usual preparation required to help with normal developmental issues. Knowing your limitations, seeking additional knowledge and skill, or referring clients to more appropriate sources for assistance are essential ingredients in being an intentionally effective counselor or human service worker (Schmidt, 2002).

Helping clients work through various social factors that impede *self*-development or damage personal relationships must also take into account cultural beliefs and differences. The focus of this text is on social and cultural foundations that relate to and affect helping relationships. When working with clients who exhibit behaviors or face challenges related to any of the variables presented in this chapter, successful counselors and human service providers learn about family and cultural background to help clients work through issues within an appropriate context. Ignoring ethnic or cultural factors places the *helper* at risk of encapsulation, which inhibits empathic understanding and limits the likelihood of successful helping relationships.

The next chapter continues the discussion of self-concept development and social learning by examining additional theories related to identity. These include models of social identity, racial identity, and cultural identity.

3

Social, Cultural, and Racial Identity

If people construct self-concepts and identities as theorists propose, they do so within a particular environment, which itself is also created, nurtured, ignored, or harmed by various social and cultural forces. Human development, including an emerging self-concept, is either enhanced and supported, or neglected and depreciated, by the societies and groups in which, and with whom, people live. These assorted social and cultural elements in concert with a person's unique perceptual power contribute to the development of a self-view and worldview that fill a continuum of human thought and beliefs about oneself, other people, and life in general. For counselors and other professional helpers who apply the principles of self-concept theory and related social learning theories of human development presented in Chapter 2, an understanding of the dynamic relationship between a person's view of self and the social-cultural context in which she or he was born and nurtured is imperative.

The next two chapters explore several theories related to social, cultural, and racial identity. To begin, this chapter provides a broad overview of social identity, cultural identity, and racial identity theories, which provide the foundations for cultural and racial identity models proposed by theorists over the years. First, it explores social identity theory developed by Tajfel and Turner (1979, 1986). Second, this chapter considers cultural identity theory as reported in the multicultural counseling literature (Ibrahim, 1999; Ivey, D'Andrea, Ivey, & Simek-Morgan, 2002), and reviews some of the criticisms of these models as well as research challenges. Lastly, it examines racial identity as a social construction. In addition to these theoretical presentations, this chapter explains in greater depth the concepts of collectivism and individualism introduced in the first chapter, and explores the construct of self-consciousness in relationship to identity.

Social Identity Theory

Social identity theory links self-concept and social learning theory. Hogg (2003) defined social identity as "that aspect of the self-concept that derives from group membership and is associated with cognitive, motivational, and social processes that are associated with group and intergroup behaviors" (p. 474). The theory of social identity, introduced by Tajfel and Turner (1979, 1986), involves the three primary concepts of categorization, identification, and comparison. Connected to these concepts is the notion that all people have a basic need to achieve positive self-esteem as part of their identity, which consists of personal and social descriptions. Examples of personal identity descriptors might include "I prefer small groups to large crowds," " I am diabetic," and "I am outgoing." Social identifiers might be "I am of Asian heritage," "I am a member of the tennis club," and "I am a social activist." Exercises 3.1 and 3.2 ask you to explore some social identity descriptors. Try them out, and discuss your descriptors with others, such as family members, friends, or classmates.

As you process Exercise 3.2, consider the social and cultural factors that have had an impact on the social groups with which you identify and those with which you do not identify. Regarding the groups to which you belong but do not have a strong identity, how much of this decision comes from your *self*-view? How much of it is the result of social and cultural influence? What elements are most significant in maintaining your identity with particular groups? Answering these questions is not a simple process because all these factors highlight the complexity of social identity. Understanding the three primary concepts of social identity theory might be helpful in learning about your *self.* It will also help you learn about the development of clients with whom you might work as a professional helper in the future. The first concept of social identity theory is *categorization.*

Categorization

Social identity theory suggests that people categorize themselves, others, and groups using concepts and language to make sense of their social environment. The outcome of this process reveals countless social categories such as middle class, African American, European, White, Muslim, agnostic, faculty, family, athlete, peer, attorney, and student. By establishing social categories, people assign themselves and others to different groups, thereby lending an understanding to their social environment. At the same time, this

Exercise 3.1

Personal Descriptors

Instructions: List ten things about yourself that follow the stem "I am . . . " It might be best to list them quickly as they come to mind without much thought or reflection about each.

1. I am ____________________
2. I am ____________________
3. I am ____________________
4. I am ____________________
5. I am ____________________
6. I am ____________________
7. I am ____________________
8. I am ____________________
9. I am ____________________
10. I am ____________________

Exercise 3.2

Social Descriptors

Part I

Instructions: List five groups to which you belong and with which you strongly identify. Write down a belief or attribute for each group that helps you identify with it.

Social Group	*Belief or Attribute*
1. ____________	____________
2. ____________	____________
3. ____________	____________
4. ____________	____________
5. ____________	____________

Part II

Instructions: List groups to which you belong, *but* with which you *do not* strongly identify. Write down a belief or descriptor about each group that prevents you from having *strong* identification.

Social Group	*Belief or Descriptor*
1. ____________	____________
2. ____________	____________
3. ____________	____________
4. ____________	____________
5. ____________	____________

Part III

Instructions: List groups that you have knowledge of, but to which you *do not belong*. Write down a belief or descriptor that prevents you from belonging to the group.

Social Group	*Belief or Descriptor*
1. ____________	____________
2. ____________	____________
3. ____________	____________
4. ____________	____________
5. ____________	____________

---

process helps people select appropriate behavior as preferred by the groups to which they belong. For example, if college students belong to a fraternity or sorority, they embrace certain traditions and customs as part of their affiliation with those societies. Following such traditions and customs becomes the "norm" for members of the students' fraternity or sorority. Of course, members of other fraternities and sororities (i.e., other groups) might have quite different customs, which could put their behaviors at odds with the other societies. Therefore, defining normal behavior (i.e., behaviors that follow the norms of a particular group) is a complex process because it is *group specific*.

Return to Exercise 3.2 to see if you find a connection between the social groups with which you identify and the descriptors used as evidence of your relationship with those groups. Reexamine Parts II and III of Exercise 3.2. Of the groups to which you belong but do not strongly identify, and the groups to which you do not belong, how many of the beliefs and descriptors would you say potentially or actually violate your standards of normal conduct? Because categorization helps people determine to which groups they belong, it also leads them to personal and social *identification,* the next important concept of social identity theory.

Identification

Tajfel and Turner (1979, 1986) noted that identification is a twofold process. This is probably apparent from the previous discussion of personal and social identity. Both aspects of this process relate to the development of self-concept. People are individuals who identify with social groups (in-group identification). Consequently, at times they think and define themselves with the personal pronouns "I" and "me." Similarly, they distinguish other individuals as "you" and "he or she." In this way, language helps to distinguish between a person's unique individuality and that of other people. At other times, however, the pluralistic pronouns of "we" and "us" give a collective identity to a person's *self.* People govern the decision whether to respond from their unique individual identity or from their social identity according to the situations in which they find themselves. In addition, social and cultural factors regarding individualism and collectivism play an influential role. We will return to this idea later in this chapter.

According to social identity theory, this *in-group* identification is as significant to the development of self-concept as are personal descriptors and identifiers. Likewise, the categorization of *out-groups* is equally important in establishing a person's social identity. Norms and customs of groups with which people do not identify (out-groups) often do not fit within the purview of their self-concept. This is not to imply that social identity is a stagnant or unchangeable dimension. Similar to the way self-concept might adjust over time, social identity could change as people rethink their affiliation with certain groups. This happens in different ways. On one hand, they might continue to belong to groups with which they no longer have strong identity. On the other hand, they might leave membership in groups because particular views have changed. Now other groups make more sense to their social identity.

Related to this process of social group identity is the third theme of social identity theory. In order to select groups with which to identify and decide whether to remain in those groups, people need a process. Social identity theory calls the process *social comparison.*

Social Comparison

Based on Festinger's (1954) earlier work, *social comparison* is the cognitive process of noticing and realizing that differences and similarities exist between oneself and other people. These differences and similarities cross all aspects of the human condition from physical appearance to philosophical beliefs. Theoretically, this process is rooted in the belief that human beings have the propensity to evaluate their *self.* The starting point for such self-assessment is social comparison.

The process of social comparison begins at birth as people enter an environment of family, relatives, friends, and community. Within this environment, people interact with others who provide information about which to make judgments. Among the people that they trust and to whom they are closest, each gathers opinions about others and themselves, and filters these ideas through a perceptual framework. In this process, people observe and listen to evaluative comments that allow them to establish standards for self-assessment. As people examine these standards and measure themselves accordingly, they continue to create a meaningful self-concept.

As an example of social comparison and its impact on self-development, think of a child who is borne to a family where differences and similarities among all people are viewed in the most positive ways. This is a family where members accept and celebrate cultural differences, and where they highlight commonalities among people by openly expressing positive opinions and behaving in the most respectful manner. In contrast, think of another child in a family of members defined by fear of people who look and act differently than they do. How might the standards of measurement differ between these two children as they process social comparisons toward their self-assessment? For an analysis closer to home, complete Exercise 3.3 and glance at your self-assessment.

You will notice in Exercise 3.3 that all the descriptors are subjective. Not all comparisons are, but the tendency is to use subjective social comparisons when objective data are not readily available. When people think or talk about objective features, such as height and weight, measurements are usually available to make comparisons. When they put these descriptors into relative or subjective context, however, social comparisons become more likely. For example, "I wish I was not so tall" and "I need to gain weight" are two statements probably based on social comparisons.

Exercise 3.3

Self-Assessment

Instructions: In the left column, write down your thoughts about each of the descriptors. In right column on the corresponding space, write down the source of this information (from whom did you learn it?).

Descriptor	***Source***
My Appearance ________________	__________
My Academic Ability ___________	__________
My Athletic Ability ____________	__________
My Political Views ____________	__________
My Tolerance __________________	__________
My Emotional Stability _________	__________
My Patience ___________________	__________
My Confidence ________________	__________

Social comparison has implications for group assessment as well. Similar to the way social comparison helps individuals attain a degree of self-worth, groups also use this process to assess their status. Tajfel and Turner (1979, 1986) posited that groups tend to compare themselves to other groups as a means of seeing themselves (the group members) in a positive light. Two possible outcomes occur through this process of group assessment. One outcome might be that the group learns about its distinctive qualities, which in the eyes of the group members places them in a relatively higher position than other similar groups. A second possibility might be that the comparison reveals some negative qualities of the group, in which case group members may tend to de-emphasize these traits to minimize their effect on the group's favorable standing. From a social/cultural perspective, groups frequently make these comparisons and judgments.

Wood (1989) contributed another dimension of social comparison by introducing the ideas of *upward* and *downward* comparisons. Each of these concepts relates to the process of self-assessment, particularly as related to the notion of self-improvement and self-enhancement. When people think in terms of self-improvement, they might look at individuals whom they view as better or more superior to them for comparison. The phrase "I want to get as good grades as she does" might be an *upward comparison* and possible precursor to a student changing study habits to perform better in school. Sometimes, people use *downward comparisons* to lift their self-assessment. For example, "I'm glad my family's house is on higher ground and not flooded" compares one's providence with others who are less fortunate during a disastrous flood. To summarize, people tend to use upward comparisons for *self*-motivation to achieve goals, attain knowledge and skill, and otherwise improve their lives. People use downward comparisons to feel better about their *self,* appreciate their relative position in society, and generate an overall positive self-assessment.

The three concepts of categorization, identification, and social comparison add dimensions to help understand self-concept development. All of these dimensions require individuals to observe, draw conclusions, learn, and integrate this learning into their repertoire of behaviors, attitudes, and beliefs. As noted in Chapter 2, these principles form the basis of self-concept and social learning theory. Similarly, the assumptions put forth by these principles relate to cultural identity theory.

Cultural Identity Theory

Cultural identity theory consists of several perspectives about how self-concept development incorporates learning about culture, race, and related issues through a sequence of progressive stages (Ivey, D'Andrea, Ivey, & Simek-Morgan, 2002). Specific theories developed over the past 30 years and more include several racial identity models such as Cross's (1971, 1991, 1995; Cross, Smith, & Payne, 2002) Negro-to-Black conversion experience (also known as Nigresence), Poston (1990) and Root's (1990, 1992, 1998) biracial identity models, and Helms's (1984, 1994, 1995, 2003) White racial identity model.

Other models of racial and cultural identity development include Ponterotto's racial consciousness development model for White counselor trainees (1988), Casas and Pytluk's (1995) work on Hispanic (Latino and Latina) development, and an optimal development model presented by Myers and her associates (Myers, Speight, Highlen, Cox, Reynolds,

Adams, & Hanley, 1991). The optimal development model proposed by Myers and colleagues (1991) criticizes past models of psychosocial development for neglecting the individual in the process of developing a self-identity. This criticism focuses on the emphasis that past models placed on external validation instead of valuing internal self-worth and spiritual development of the person.

Counselors and human service professionals want to be knowledgeable about different identity models because clients who bring a multitude of issues might be at various stages depending on which issues are the primary focus of the helping relationship. Chapter 4 will highlight some of the more notable identity models. For the purpose of this chapter, we consider some critiques of identity models and explore related research issues.

Critique of Identity Models

Several authorities have noted the limitations of identity models and raised concern about their lack of logical development and research to validate their conceptualization and usefulness (Myers et al., 1991). In addition, Root (1990, 1996, 2002) questioned the value of monoracial and monoethnic models in understanding identity, and the omission of other important variables such as family environment and unique personal characteristics.

Although the models have been positively received for the most part, criticism and concern about their development and efficacy revolve around several issues. These issues include that (a) some models were developed as reaction to contemporary events; (b) they are based on Euro-American worldviews; (c) they omit individuals with multiple oppressions; and (d) they neglect the power and role of the person in filtering perceptions and creating a unique view of self and worldview (Myers et al., 1991).

Criticism regarding the development of identity models in reaction to contemporary events addresses a number of theories. For example, Cross's (1971) early Nigrescence model might have been a reaction to the civil rights movement of the times rather than a depiction of universal elements that Black people process while adjusting to a dominant White culture. Similarly, feminist and sexual identity models within a temporal context might be reactions or responses to particular social movements regarding women's role in society and gay rights. Myers and colleagues (1991) noted that a weakness in such responses is that the resulting models ultimately might reflect more of the social conditions in a particular period or era than they depict common processes empirically verified across designated groups.

Myers and colleagues (1991) noted that some identity models are criticized for being "based upon a Eurocentric worldview, which may not be applicable to the group in question" (p. 55). At the same time, these authors commented that common characteristics among different models suggest a universal model might be more appropriate.

Poston (1990) and Speight, Myers, Cox, and Highlen (1991) noted that most identity models overlook individuals with multiple oppressions, such as ethnic groups from lower socioeconomic classes and biracial individuals. Myers and colleagues (1991) suggested that such oversight might result in an oversimplification of how people deal with multiple challenges (e.g., ethnicity, sexual orientation, gender roles) within an oppressive society.

Root (1990, 1996, 2002) moved away from stage models of identity and "emphasized the multiple variables that may give rise to different processes resulting in different resolutions of identity, such as family environment, place of birth, temperament, and so forth" (p. 175). For example, in her quintessential volume of research and reviews about the development of multiracial individuals, Root (1996) noted the complexity of identity formation, which cannot be explained by a single, simple paradigm. Her research of multiracial subjects suggested the development of identity models that focus on specific processes for resolving identity dilemmas (Root, 1990, 2002). As noted in the next chapter, her research has continued to emphasize the importance of multiple processes that explain variations in identity and subsequent de-emphasis on single models of racial identity formation (Root, 1999).

All of the criticism mentioned thus far relates to the last concern, and perhaps the most significant for this text—neglect of the individual in the process. As Myers and colleagues (1991) indicated, all the models seem to de-emphasize the role of the person and the power of self-perception and self-creativity in constructing a unique view of oneself and the surrounding world. In most cultural identity models, the person becomes merely a player in the process, reacting to environmental conditions and cultural traditions. Although environmental and cultural effects are significant, this text takes the position that within the realm of awareness, individuals decide (albeit through unconscious processes) the relativity and usefulness of environmental and cultural influences.

Cultural Identity Research

Over the past several decades much research on racial and cultural identity has been generated (Howard-Hamilton & Frazier, 2005; Robinson, 2005). Specific theoretical models, however, have not been validated or disputed, yet certain descriptors used to define particular stages of development have been found to correlate with other psychosocial characteristics. For example, some research notes that among Black women higher levels of "womanist" attitudes correlated with higher levels of internalization (Parks, Carter, & Gushue, 1996). For White female participants, however, the study found no relationships between racial and "womanist" identities. According to Robinson (2005), womanist identity characteristics are female attitudes and behavioral patterns used by theorists to develop identity measurement instruments such as the *Racist Identity Attitudes Scale* (Helms & Parham, 1984) and the *Womanist Identity Attitude Scale* (Ossana, Helms, & Leonard, 1992).

In another study of womanist identity, Poindexter-Cameron and Robinson (1997) found a negative correlation between the preencounter stage of development (Cross's model) and self-esteem. At the same time, they noted a positive correlation between internalization and self-esteem. This study included Black women from both historically Black and predominantly White universities. The researchers concluded that measures of self-esteem produced higher scores for Black women at predominantly White institutions than for women on historically Black campuses. From their findings, these researchers suggested that proposed identity models might be consistent with self-esteem theory that suggests higher stages of identity development are related to higher levels of mental health (Robinson, 2005).

Closely related to formation of cultural identity is the development of *self* and the corresponding constructs self-view and worldview discussed in Chapter 2. As seen from the earlier exploration of social learning and cultural identity theories, both of these concepts involve processes such as cognitive and emotional development, modeling, and reinforcement. Williams (2003) noted that counseling research has focused mostly on variations of worldviews across different racial, ethnic, and national groups. He encouraged further research to examine the relationship between worldview and "and various psychological processes" (p. 370).

In a selective review of research, Carter (1991) concluded that many factors and variables interact to establish a cultural identity and the expression of cultural values. At the same time, the expression of cultural values is a complex process; one in which it is difficult to distinguish clearly between different ethnic and racial groups, yet indicates greater variation within similar groups than between diverse groups. Carter (1991) called for research to examine how many of the factors related to self-concept development (e.g., family, social learning, gender, social class) might better help counselors and other helpers understand the development and articulation of cultural identity.

The call for more research was also echoed by Harper and McFadden (2003) who noted that although self-reporting instruments have improved, other methods are required to verify constructs and processes proposed in multicultural literature. They suggested more direct observation of counseling relationships "to better understand the content and process of what happens between individuals of two or more different cultures" (p. 391). Harper and McFadden (2003) also encouraged an expansion of research methods and statistical analyses to include nonparametric statistics when studying small populations, multiple regression analysis, factor analysis, qualitative and quantitative analyses of nontraditional cross-cultural variables, historical study of various helping processes found in diverse cultures, and case study designs.

Although research has related certain attitudes and traits to descriptors used by stage theorists in denoting levels of development, more research will help to verify how the process of cultural identity interacts with self-concept development. Williams (2003) reviewed the meta-analyses of 170 studies on multicultural constructs by Oyserman, Coon, and Kemmelmeier (2002) and noted, "these studies provided empirical support for the theorized links that exist between worldview and the psychological variables of self-concept, well-being, attribution style, and relationality" (p. 370). Of particular importance to self-concept development and its significance in helping relationships was analyses that examined the constructs of individualism and collectivism, which Williams (2003) observed, "make up a portion of a culture's core set of values and serve as organizing principles for both interpersonal and intrapersonal relationships" (p. 370). The remaining sections of this chapter revisit the concepts of collectivism and individualism and introduce additional ones to elaborate on the relationship between self-concept development and racial/cultural identity.

Race, Ethnicity, and Identity

Laypeople and professionals often mistakenly use the terms race, ethnicity, and culture interchangeably. This can be confusing to students who are learning to become professional helpers working with broad clientele. As Dobbins and Skillings (1991) noted, "the problem resides in the concept of race and its often blurred connotations with culture and the social processes that structure our society" (p. 39). In recent years, multicultural authorities have attempted to clarify these terms, establishing their differences to bring better understanding to multicultural perspectives (Aponte & Johnson, 2000a; Comstock, 2005; Helms & Cook, 1999; Robinson, 2005; Scupin, 2003a).

This section presents an overview of race and ethnicity and the relationship these concepts have with self-identity. Current thinking, discussion, and debate regarding these concepts are considered to lend broader understanding of the relationship among the terms race, ethnicity (or ethnic group), and culture. We begin with a discussion of racial identity.

Racial Identity

Perhaps no other term in the multicultural literature stirs more emotion and debate than *race.* Robinson (2005) suggested, "it is an extremely volatile and divisive force" that "accounts for huge variations in income, occupational distribution, educational levels, quality of and access to health care, and longevity" (p. 9). For one word to acquire such reputation and significance, we might think that its meaning is understood by everyone, but that is not the case. Exactly what is this trait called race?

Historically, race meant a biological identification based on physical traits such as skin color, facial features, and hair texture. This biological categorization is evident by how the U.S. Bureau of the Census classified groups into five races during the middle to late nineteenth century: White, Colored (Black), Colored (mulatto), Chinese, and Indian (Root, 1992). Since then, scientists and others have debated this method of classification, and as mentioned in Chapter 1, research has failed to identify reliable genetic or other biological distinctions among these so-called races. Consequently, research has neither defined nor identified biological or physiological traits that enable researchers or laypeople to distinguish races consistently. Actually, research of biological traits has found greater within-group variation among particular group members than between supposed different groups when examining the same traits (e.g., skin tone, blood type) (Allen & Adams, 1992; Zuckerman, 1990).

Despite the lack of scientific verification of racial identity, most people have common knowledge of what they mean by "race." Furthermore, from an early age most people can identify with which racial group they belong (Helms & Cook, 1999). So, if there are no scientifically sound biological bases for racial identity, what is the foundation for this labeling process? It is the process of social construction.

Race as Social Construction

The lack of scientific evidence to distinguish racial groups has led many scholars to view race as a social construction (Helms & Cook, 1999; Robinson 2005; Spickard, 1992). Since humankind began forming groups, societies have created social constructs to perpetuate and maintain particular norms, customs, and traditions. For example, the ancient caste system in India consisted of a complex arrangement of separate social divisions. Although no longer sanctioned by the Indian government, this hierarchical system, with origins in Hindu tradition, continues to influence social, economical, and political processes in modern India. In similar ways, the U.S. media, government, and other institutions use the classifications of *lower, middle,* and *upper class* to distinguish economic or educational levels across groups.

Race is another category constructed by society to place people into groups that supposedly designate similar phenotypes and physical appearances. Today, despite the lack of scientific evidence to support these biological differences, U.S. society persists in using racial categories. This is true in formal functions of institutions and government and for everyday interactions among people in societies, such as the United States, that rely on racial classification. The 2000 U.S. census changed (U.S. Bureau of the Census, 2000a, 2000b, 2003), with respondents self-identifying from several racial categories including "White," "Black or African American," "American Indian and Alaska Native," "Asian," "Native Hawaiian and other Pacific Islander," or "some other race." In addition, respondents could select "two or more races" (2.4% did so), and they could select whether they were of "Hispanic or Latino" origin (12.5% indicated they were Hispanic or Latino). Over 280 million respondents to the 2000 census selected a racial identity of either a single race (97.6%) or a combination of races (2.4%).

Race as a social construct maintains societal expectations in similar fashion to other class explanations. According to Helms and Cook (1999), "race is a social construction intended to maintain certain societal norms—in the case of race, the norm of between-group disparity" (p. 16). Of course, these supposed between-group disparities are socially perceived rather than scientifically confirmed. People see different skin color, facial features, hair color and texture, and other physical differences, and with the help of socially constructed categories (e.g., White, Black, Asian, etc.), use their perception to place people with particular appearances into corresponding categories. Notwithstanding a lack of scientific support, this process of classification is fraught with all the common weaknesses known to human perception.

Despite the lack of scientific evidence to support the continued use of race to classify people, the scientific community continues to use it as a nominal category. Psychology, sociology, counseling, and other fields of research and practice persist in using racial categories to study behavior and other attributes. This practice has spurred some authorities to declare that *race,* as a biological construct, is no longer a valid or reliable way to categorize people (Aponte & Johnson, 2000a). Others, however, maintain that as a social construction, racial identification continues to be a principal method of formally and informally including or excluding people in social and political processes (Helms & Talleyrand, 1997). Thus, physical appearances tend to influence people's judgment and subsequent classification of others whether or not formally institutionalized categories exist.

In an editorial piece, Jackson and Vontress (2003) encouraged counselors to place more emphasis on culture than on racial or ethnic groups to which clients might identify. Their concern was that the mistaken idea that culture and race were the same had caused the counseling profession to neglect an adequate definition of culture and its impact on helping relationships. In their opinion, this failure to define and understand culture led to countless groups identifying themselves as culturally distinct to the point where so much cultural diversity now exists that no cultural differences are at all present. Regarding the distinction between race and culture, Jackson and Vontress (2003) commented, "A client's race or heritage may have little or nothing to do with culture or the presenting problem. Counselors who respond stereotypically to their clients run the risk of being anti-therapeutic" (p. 10).

Helms and Cook (1999) noted that the use of perceived racial grouping is so powerful that "the person's 'racial' demographic identity typically obliterates his or her membership in other demographic categories or social affiliations" (p. 16). As such, a Black person born in Europe who migrates to the United States might be classified as racially Black, and would suffer the discrimination and face the historic obstacles that people of color have endured in the United States. In the process, this person's European heritage and ethnicity would be diminished, if not lost entirely. In contrast, Helms and Cook (1999) continued that a White person of similar European background who migrates to the United States would be classified racially, and consequently, would benefit from the customs and privileges normally granted White people. This observation is noteworthy because such racial classification and identity frequently allow or deny access to societal resources. They can also be a source of conflict and confusion for members within a racial group who do not always conform or fit the group's expectations. An African American student in counseling, who grew up in a large family in a rural Southern town, illustrated this phenomenon. In class, the student commented:

> My family was always very close, but my father's death drew us even closer. We were labeled as "different" by many people in our neighborhood because my parents stressed education over farm work. This was unusual for a Black family of sharecroppers during the 1950s and '60s. We were called "stuck up," "wanna-be's," and "Oreos" by many people in the community. Today I am still troubled by people of my own race who say I am 'acting White' because I value education.

If racial classification and identity are so predominant, particularly in U.S. society, it follows that they would have a significant impact on self-concept development and identity. This student's story indicates a struggle with racial identity in conjunction with cultural influences and conflicts. As such, it is one example of how the *self* emerges as a product of many influences including culture.

Self as a Cultural Product

Throughout this chapter, we have explored different theories and assumptions to better understand how the *self* develops within a social, cultural, and racial context. Previously, Chapter 2 presented self-concept development as largely an individual process. Now, we have learned that to complete our understanding of self-concept theory, we must consider the social environment in which a person develops. This is not a new concept. Psychologists, sociologists, and others have studied, researched, debated, and discussed this notion for decades.

What is of particular importance about a discussion regarding self-concept development and environmental influence for professional counseling and other helping disciplines is how the constructs of individualism, collectivism, independence, and interdependence are conceptualized and applied in practice. Chapter 1 introduced two of these constructs, individualism and collectivism, and now we explore them in detail. In particular, this section highlights the complexity of these concepts and notes the significance of how professional counselors and other helpers choose to define these constructs and apply them in daily practice. With this goal in mind, let us revisit the constructs of individualism and collectivism and add the dimensions of independence and interdependence.

Individualism and Collectivism

Oyserman and colleagues (2002) presented the concepts of *individualism* and *collectivism* as two forms of worldviews that distinguish themselves according to the issues that are most important to each. Accordingly, they defined *individualism* as a worldview that assigns central importance to the person while giving less significance to social/cultural influences. In contrast, they defined *collectivism* as a worldview that assumes group cohesiveness is paramount and individuals feel compelled to work toward that goal. As such, according to a collective worldview, personal attributes, personal goals, and personal uniqueness are less significant aspects of the larger social and cultural group.

Common definitions of individualism and collectivism place these two constructs apparently on opposite ends of a worldview continuum (Landrine, 1992; Williams, 2003). Figure 3.1 illustrates this notion. According to this perspective, a person and culture would fall somewhere on the continuum, illustrating some level of individualistic or collectivistic value. Many definitions found in current professional literature about counseling and diversity favor this bipolar perspective, noting conflicting perspectives between individualistic and collectivistic societies. For example, in their comments on the "American Dream," Helms and Cook (1999) noted that it "included a heavy emphasis on individualism, religious freedom (for Christian Protestants), and materialism. Each successive generation was encouraged to buy a share of this dream by abandoning its traditional cultural mores in order to be assimilated into the larger White and more politically powerful group" (p. 39).

Draguns (2002) highlighted the work of Chang (1988) and Hofstede (1991) and subsequent research by Triandis (1995) and others that confirmed attitudes related to individualism and collectivism across different nationalities. Chang (1988) described the "individualistic self" as viewing the individual as apart from other people. This perspective is prevalent in Western Europe and North American cultures. Contrastingly, "sociocentric milieus" such as in Asian cultures hold views of the *self* that "bind a person to

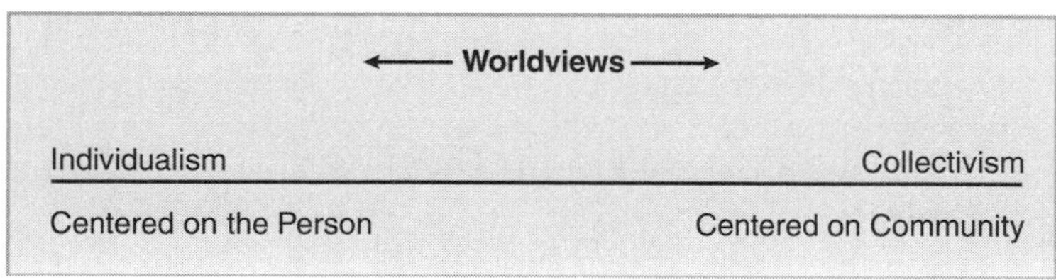

FIGURE 3.1 ***Individualism–Collectivism Continuum***

others, especially his or her family, neighbors, and friends" (Draguns, 2002, p. 34). Similarly, Hofstede (1991) noted that individualistic societies include attitudes that express casual ties among people and expectations that individuals are responsible for themselves and their immediate family. On the other hand, Hofstede (1991), painted collective societies as ones where "people from birth onward are integrated into strong, cohesive ingroups, which throughout the people's lifetime continue to protect them in exchange for unquestioning loyalty" (p. 51).

Draguns (2002) continued that the years following Hofstede's (1991) findings saw research and further speculation about these individualistic and collectivistic aspects of society. The two perspectives also identified emerging advantages and disadvantages of each. For example, the creativity, responsibility, and personal development associated with individualism might contrast with feelings of isolationism, loneliness, and alienation. Likewise, the collective advantages of group support, social bonding, and security might be counterbalanced by personal stagnation due to social duty and allegiance. Perhaps Triandis's (1995) observation about the importance of finding balance between the notion of individualism and collectivism is significant for understanding and helping people with their self-development. "We need societies that would do well both in the citizen-authorities and the person-to-person fronts, that provide both freedom and security, that have something for their most competent members but also for the majority of their members" (Triandis, 1995, pp. 186–187).

Another possibility raised among debaters is that rather than a bipolar relationship on a continuum of worldviews, individualism and collectivism might have properties that allow persons and cultures to include aspects of both. With this perspective, attributes of both constructs become significant to the person and to the culture. Figure 3.2 attempts to illustrate such an inclusive relationship. In Figure 3.2, a particular person's worldview includes aspects of both collectivism and individualism. As such, collectivistic and individualistic attitudes are influenced and provoked by a person's perceptions and subsequent conclusions about various situations. The overlapping portion of the collectivistic and individualistic views in the diagram indicates the possibility of both perspectives working in harmony in making life decisions.

Williams's (2003) review of the meta-analyses by Oyserman and colleagues (2002) concludes, "multicultural models, which categorize variations in worldview based on racial, ethnic, or national group membership, might be unwarranted" (p. 373). One noteworthy finding, for example, was that among 46 studies of national groups, European American subjects were found to be higher in collectivism than were Korean and Japanese subjects. At the same time, mixed findings were noted among 35 studies of European Americans and subjects from other groups in the United States. For example, (a) European Americans were found to be significantly higher in individualism only when compared with Asian Americans, (b) African Americans were found to be higher in individualism than European Americans, (c) no difference in individualism was found between European Americans and Latin Americans, (d) European Americans were found to be lower in collectivism than Latino Americans and Asian Americans, and (e) no difference in collectivism was noted between European Americans and African Americans. Overall, findings from Oyserman and colleagues' (2002) meta-analyses seem to indicate that while the constructs of collectivism and individualism are useful in understanding some differences

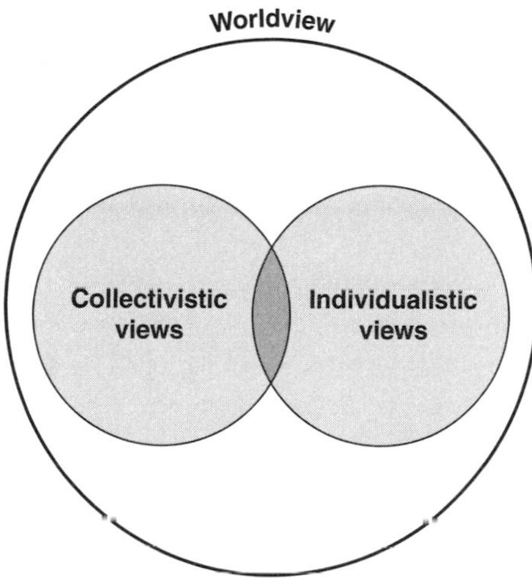

FIGURE 3.2 ***An Inclusive Relationship for Collectivism and Individualism***

among societies, they may be more relevant in understanding how persons perceive collective and individual values within their particular self-concept development. Related to these perspectives are the notions of independence and interdependence.

Independence and Interdependence

Independence is the quality of being free from subjection, external control, or support, or exempt from the influence of other people or groups. Interdependence is the expression of mutual reliance, trust, and confidence in other people to create a culture of dependency on each other. Multicultural literature and research have often associated these two concepts with individualism and collectivism. Some authorities, for example, view independence as an essential theme of individualism, whereas interdependence is central to collectivism. A fundamental problem with these positions is that they create stereotypic views of people and cultural groups. That is, if a female client tends to exhibit individualistic attitudes, we may mistakenly conclude that she must be an independent person. Similarly, if a male client demonstrates collective beliefs, we might incorrectly assume that he strongly relies on others, such as family and friends, when making life decisions. Likewise, when considering cultural groups, we might assign unfound significance to independent attitudes for societies that tend to have higher individualistic qualities or to interdependent beliefs for groups that have higher collectivistic views.

When considering self-concept or cultural influence, dichotomous views of independence and interdependence ignore the complexity of human development. At the same time, they neglect differing views within diverse cultures about these concepts. Raeff (1997) noted that independence and interdependence are important aspects of human development and behavior in all cultures, and to appreciate how they influence and affect people differently, "it is necessary to discern how independence and interdependence are understood and enacted around the world" (p. 252). Across cultures, we see a blending of views related to independence and interdependence that give diverse groups another dimension of identity. For example, the notion of *American individualism* is tempered, and in some sense balanced, by various collective attributes including regional and community identity, labor unions, religious affiliations, political allegiance, and family to name a few. In similar fashion, African American culture balances its view of harmony—importance of the relatedness of self to one's surroundings—with creativity and uniqueness in self-expression of one's personality (Helms & Cook, 1999). In using concepts such as independent, interdependent, individualistic, and collective, therefore, we must understand how various cultures adapt these notions and enact them in daily life.

Counseling Inferences

In this chapter, we have learned about different constructs related to social, cultural, and racial identity and connected these ideas to self-concept development. Self-awareness, including an understanding of ones social, cultural, and racial identity, is the foundation of competent practice in counseling and other human services. This is true for working with all clients, but it is especially noteworthy when attempting to help clients who are culturally different from the helping professional. Understanding of one's own self-concept development—how you came to be who you are today—is crucial in being able to reach out in genuine ways to help others. When professionals know which critical life events and learning experiences have helped them construct their self-view, they are in a better position to understand how other people, including clients, have come to establish their self-concepts. Such understanding allows helpers to demonstrate genuine empathy for clients' problems, concerns, and life struggles. Connected to this understanding of self-concept development is knowledge about and appreciation for one's own identity.

Through exploration of cultural influences, counselors and human service providers have greater understanding of family structure and dynamics, spiritual beliefs, and other influences that have had an impact on their development. They also know and understand the biases, prejudices, and attitudes regarding culturally different people. When counselors, for example, attain such knowledge and understanding, we might speculate that they are more able to put aside these views and genuinely try to help clients from varied backgrounds. As noted later in this text, however, much speculation exists about helping relationships between diverse counselors and clients, but little empirical research has verified many of the assumptions and assertions purported in the counseling literature. As Ponterotto, Costa, and Werner-Lin (2002) noted, "with regard to cross-cultural counseling process and outcome, more questions remain unanswered than have been answered" (p. 411).

Understanding of a client's cultural identity and worldview is a next step in establishing an appropriate helping relationship. Here, knowledge of current research and culture-specific literature will be of value to counselors and other human service providers. For example, learning about Asian culture and research about assisting Asian clients might offer background information from which to enter helping relationships with clients of Asian heritage. This will be of particular importance when the professional helper is of

African American, Latino, European, or another culture. One caveat in using such background information is to be certain not to assume that *every* client of a particular heritage has the traits, customs, beliefs, or attitudes commonly found among people of that culture. For this reason, it is especially important for helping professionals to assess clients' perspectives and ask clients how their ethnicity, race, gender, or other cultural factors have contributed to their identity.

Supposition about how effective counselors and other professionals incorporate knowledge of racial and ethnic identity into helping relationships begins with self-understanding and knowledge of one's cultural heritage, the influence of race and past racial encounters, and an understanding and appreciation of one's ethnic development. For example, counselors who know where they are ethnically and racially and comprehend the biases and prejudices that continue to influence their behavior are in a stronger position to make ethical decisions about which clients they are most capable of helping. Likewise, helpers who have worked through their guilt, shame, anger, or resentment about past racial encounters are in better emotional condition to reach out to diverse populations without overcompensating for past transgressions or being too assertive with clients whose racial appearance opens old wounds.

When working with clients from diverse racial and ethnic backgrounds, another important consideration is to determine whether racial or ethnic identity factors have played or are playing a role in the concerns currently presented. For example, a client who appears to be multiracial does not necessarily have racial identity issues that relate to the presenting reason for services. The client's immediate concerns may have little or nothing to do with biracial identity. By using culturally appropriate attending skills early in the helping relationship, counselors and other professionals assess the influence of racial and ethnic identity on current issues that clients present. Helms and Cook (1999) suggested that three possibilities emerge from this early assessment. First, counselors and other human service professionals might conclude that "yes, either implicitly or explicitly the client's problem involves race, racism, or racial identity" (p. 96). The second possibility is that racial or ethnic factors might be relevant but their influence is not evident, and the third conclusion is that racial/ethnic identity issues or experiences are not relevant to the presenting concern. The first two conclusions might lead professional helpers to rely on racial and ethnic models to achieve better understanding of past events and current perceptions that have been and continue to be influential in the client's development. In the next chapter, we will consider some prominent racial and ethnic identity models found in the professional literature.

4

Cultural, Racial, and Ethnic Identity Models

The preceding chapter presented an overview of social, cultural, and racial identity theories, and connected them to self-concept development. This chapter continues the discussion of cultural and racial identity while considering notable race and ethnicity models. In addition, it gives further thought to the relationship of these concepts with overall self-identity.

As models, stage theories of racial and cultural identity might be helpful in assessing where clients are as they enter and proceed through counseling or other helping relationships. Equally important is the understanding theoretical models might offer about your own cultural identity. Throughout this chapter, you will have opportunities to explore your cultural identity.

Space in a single chapter cannot do justice to a multitude of theoretical models developed over the years. Furthermore, not all conceptual models of understanding human differences are stage oriented. For example, Arredondo (1992) demonstrated a three-dimensional approach to counseling with diverse clientele. Her model identifies the first group of dimensions (A Dimensions) as personal characteristics with which, or into which, people are born, including language, culture, sex, sexual orientation identity, age, social class, and physical status. The second set (B Dimensions) includes traits and characteristics that, while not always visible, influence a person's behavior and achievement. These factors include regional residency, educational and career background, economic status, leisure activities, religion, marital status, and citizenship, among others. The final group of traits (C Dimensions) identify encounters and events that have influenced a person's development. These include major events such as leaving a homeland because of religious oppression or political upheaval and changing lifestyles due to health epidemics, economic disasters, or constant terrorism (Robinson, 2005). Arredondo's A-B-C approach (1992) encourages a holistic perspective that considers many internal and external factors, each of which might have meaning for various stages of human development.

Another reason the following sections are not all-inclusive is that new theoretical models are emerging. For example, Relational-Cultural Theory (RCT) (Jordan & Hartling, 2002) is a relatively new school of thought that proposes alternative perspectives and emphasizes the complexity of developmental patterns across the life span (Comstock & Qin, 2005). In particular, the model focuses on creating and nurturing interpersonal connections rather than aspects of individual development. Readers are encouraged to review original sources cited throughout this chapter to gain a fuller appreciation of the various models and approaches presented. Table 4.1 provides a list of various stage models of cultural identity.

Racial Identity Models

This section examines a few racial identity models that have gained prominence in the multicultural literature and research. It begins with Cross's (1991) Nigrescence theory and more recent references to "activity approaches" to understanding Black identity (Cross, Smith, & Payne, 2002). Each of the following summaries provides a sample perspective and is not intended as inclusive of all racial models or all perspectives about a particular racial identity.

Black Identity

Cross (1971, 1991) differentiated between personal identity and group identity, what he referred to as "reference group orientation" (RGO). He related personal identity to self-esteem and interpersonal relationships, while he associated RGO with racial identity and esteem (Helms, 2003; Robinson, 2005). According to his five-stage model, African Americans create a self-identity through a developmental process within which they replace negative self-images with positive beliefs about themselves.

In the first stage of this model, *preencounter,* the Black person in America begins creating a self-image and worldview by looking through the lens of a dominant White culture. Here, the person uses identifiers unrelated to race and more reflective of the dominant culture. Such descriptors might include career, school, and church connections rather than identifiers linked with the Black experience. Consequently, Cross (1991) hypothesized that at this first stage of development, African Americans tend to behave in accordance with a White-centered cultural perspective.

The second stage, *encounter,* occurs when a Black person has a traumatic or other life-altering experience that challenges views established during the earlier stage. This stage is twofold. First, the person must encounter a challenging experience, and next, she or he must internalize the experience personally. This second phase of internalization is essential to move through the encounter stage. Without personal internalization of the event, the person will not fully process the encounter stage.

Cross's (1991) third stage consists of *immersion and emersion.* By internalizing the belief-altering experience in the *encounter* stage, the person now focuses more on being Black, even to the exclusion of other races, especially members of the dominant White culture. Now the person feels a strong connection and common bond with Black people. In some instances, this stage might be accompanied by anger and hostility towards the dominant culture.

Internalization is the fourth stage of this model, and at this level, the person shows evidence of maturation and resolution of the negative feelings espoused in the previous stage. Still, a greater value is assigned to one's Blackness, and assertive, confident behaviors replace the dissension and conflict sparked in the earlier stage characterized by *immersion and emersion.*

TABLE 4.1 *Stages of Various Cultural Identity Models**

Cultural Identity Development Theory (Ivey et al., 2012)	*Cross's Nigrescence Model (Cross, 1971, 1991, 1995)*	*Racial/Cultural Identity Development Model (Sue & Sue, 1999)*	*White Racial Development Model (Helms, 1984, 1995)*	*Identity Development Theory for White Counselors (Ponterotto, 1988; Ponterotto & Pedersen, 1993)*	*Biracial Development Model (Poston, 1990)*	*Root's Resolution Model of Identity Development (1990, 1996, 2002)* Five Resolutions:
Stage 1: Naïveté	Stage 1: Preencounter	Stage 1: Conformity	Status 1: Contact	Stage 1: Preexposure	Stage 1: Personal Identity	(a) accept the default monoracial and monoethnic identity through a hypodescent process,
Stage 2: Encounter	Stage 2: Encounter	Stage 2: Dissonance	Status 2: Disintegration	Stage 2: Exposure	Stage 2: Choice of Group Categorization	(b) identify with multiple groups,
Stage 3: Naming	Stage 3: Immersion and Emersion	Stage 3: Resistance and Immersion	Status 3: Reintegration	Stage 3: Zealotry or Defensiveness	Stage 3: Enmeshment/Denial	(c) actively resolve a single racial or ethnic identity,
Stage 4: Reflection on Self as Cultural Being	Stage 4: Internalization	Stage 4: Introspection	Status 4: Pseudoindependence	Stage 4: Integration	Stage 4: Appreciation	(d) identify as new ethnic or racial group,
Stage 5: Multiperspective Internalization	Stage 5: Internalization and Commitment	Stage 5: Integrative Awareness	Status 5: Immersion-Emersion		Stage 5: Integration	(e) adopt a symbolic race of ethnicity (Root, 2002, p. 175).
			Status 6: Autonomy			

* This table offers only a sampling of the many cultural identity models presented in the literature.

Full understanding and appreciation of the destructive force of "racism" marks the entry into the fifth stage of development—*internalization* and *commitment.* In contrast to the brief life periods reflected in earlier stages, this stage is characterized by long-term involvement and commitment to fighting racism and other forms of oppression for all people in society and across the world.

In later work, Cross and colleagues focused on the continuous everyday activities that influence the development of a Black identity (Cross et al., 2002). Although the original stage model (Cross, 1971) is useful in understanding some of the basic traits and processes that Black people might live through in developing a racial identity, "conceptualizing identity as operations, functions, negotiations, enactments, or activities" (Cross et al., 2002, p. 93) helps to appreciate the complexity of this process. Using "activity theory," which he developed from Vygotsky's (1935/1978) work on social learning (see Chapter 2), Cross and his associates (Cross et al., 2002; Cross & Strauss, 1998) suggested a "constellation of five Black identity operations: buffering, code switching, bridging, bonding, and individualism" (Cross et al., 2002, p. 94). These identity functions are learned, and they involve Black and non-Black people in a range of situations from negative and possibly harmful to positive and nurturing. According to Cross and colleagues (2002), with the exception of the fifth operation, *individualism,* "the Black identity functions are *race and Black culture sensitive,*" and their purpose is to help the person affirm and establish "a sense of collective identity and attachment to the Black experience" (p. 96).

Buffering is an operation characterized by protecting the person against the racist behaviors of other people or racist environments created by institutions. In a sense, buffering behavior lessens the hurt and suffering often associated with racism and in some instances avoids feelings of degradation and humiliation altogether.

Cross and colleagues (2002) noted that racist situations are often complex in that a Black person must distinguish between those racially discriminatory behaviors, policies, and processes, and other aspects within a given situation that are "race-neutral" and of possible benefit to the person (p. 97). Buffering allows the Black person to diminish the negative effects of racist experiences while considering and benefiting from the neutral elements within those same situations. For example, a Black employee might use buffering to negotiate around the unintentional racist behaviors of a boss because the job is very important to the person's immediate financial goals and long-term career plans.

Individuals and groups use buffering behaviors. Cross and colleagues (2002) explained, "when Black people join together to protest racism, that is a form of collective or group buffering" (p. 97). When group buffering evolves into formal group functioning (e.g., NAACP or the Legal Defense Fund), it establishes an institution advocating for the Black community.

Code switching is a function that enables Black people to move back and forth from their community to the dominant, non-Black society. In an increasingly multicultural society where most Blacks continue to live and interact in predominantly Black communities, schools, and churches, they often need to switch from their normal way of behaving in order to conform with situations governed by people who are not Black. Cross and colleagues (2002) noted that this "code switching" might require a Black person to master non-Black routines, expressions, and other competencies to become gainfully employed, achieve educationally, and receive customary services. Code switching does not necessarily involve situations that are difficult, discomforting, or otherwise challenging from a racial perspective. Sometimes, code-switching behavior might appear similar to buffering. However, "buffering always involves a *racist threat,* whereas a code-switching situation is typically non-threatening" (Cross et al., 2002, p. 97).

Bridging occurs when Black people form strong relationships, even intimate ones, with non-Blacks. In these instances, they are able to bridge differences in establishing deep friendships and loving unions. Bridging does not ignore racial and cultural differences. Rather, it celebrates them as each person in the relationship "relishes, examines, and assumes it is a privilege to share the other's culture and lived experiences" (Cross et al., 2002, p. 98). Considering the racial history and challenges to overcome in these relationships, it is evident that bridging, as defined here, is a difficult and perhaps laborious process. Yet, the rewards of personal growth and understanding for Blacks and non-Blacks who achieve such valued friendships and intimate relationships are indeed unique and special.

Bonding forms strong ties with being Black. Beyond learning to use different operations to survive, function, and flourish in a predominantly White society, persons establish a Black identity to emphasize their cultural uniqueness and richness. Bonding among Black people exists at all social levels and in countless forms, from grand events to solitary experiences of reflection and contemplation. Cross and colleagues (2002) explained that Black people from all social levels who attain a positive identity "like and accept themselves, like other Black people, like the lived experience of Blackness" and sense a "fundamental attachment to Blackness" (p. 98).

Individualism is an operation by which people establish a self-identity that extends beyond their Black experience. Although the first four functions in this theory of Black identity—buffering, code switching, bridging, and bonding—have significance and lend meaning to the notion of collective identity, researchers have found that the last element, individualism, plays an important role in establishing personal identity (Cross et al., 2002). In early studies of these operations, Black participants tended to rely on "acting as an individual" in their responses more than in using any of the other functions. Different focus groups noted varied reasons for this result, such as "their sense of individuality was part of their group identity to the extent that their collective sense of self was always in the background," or "they tended to see themselves in less racial and Black cultural terms, and more as Americans and individuals" (p. 99). Cross and colleagues (2002) noted several social and political trends (e.g., increased Black membership in the national Republican Party) that might be indicative of the function of individualism and its relationship to Black identity.

White Identity

Rowe, Bennett, and Atkinson (1994), Helms (1995), Ponterotto (1988), and others have proposed stages of White racial development. Rowe and colleagues (1994) presented a White racial consciousness model consisting of two major statuses and seven attitudinal categories. The two primary statuses are *unachieved* and *achieved* status. Accordingly, either White people achieve a level of consciousness that enables them to have a psychologically healthy identity, or they do not. In this model, the achievement of White consciousness is the awareness of being White and an understanding of what that means to people of color.

The attitudinal categories of the Rowe and colleagues (1994) model begin with *avoidant,* which is the lack of any thought about one's Whiteness and a disregard for racial issues in general. *Dependent* is the second attitude and it is indicative of people who rely on White perceptions, beliefs, and values learned through experience, often from family members and close associates. Omitted from this category are any internalized attitudes or consideration of alternative perspectives.

The third attitudinal category is *dissonant,* which reflects confusion and uncertainty about being White and about common racial issues in society. In this category, White people face dissonance because they either lack information and knowledge or they have experienced discomfort over new experiences that conflict with their long-held attitudes and beliefs.

A fourth category is *dominative.* It includes people who hold views that Whites are superior to people of other races and cultures, and therefore, White people are entitled to certain privileges over others. This category of people takes one of two forms: active or passive. Active membership in this category is depicted by overt behaviors aimed at discrimination and degradation of people of color. Passive expression of dominative racial attitudes might include an avoidance of contact with people of other races except in situations where the White person holds a position of authority or supervision.

Rowe and colleagues (1994) proposed a *conflictive* category that includes people who are generally opposed to racist views, yet do not favor or support changes in policies and programs that would diminish or eliminate such practices in society. For example, they voice objection to commonly held stereotypic and racist views, but vote against government initiatives that might help society reduce inequities. Thus, they are in conflict in terms of value and attitudinal development.

A sixth category of this White racial development model is *reactive.* In this category, people understand the benefits Whites have garnered at the price of discriminatory practices and attitudes toward people of color. They are sensitive about societal inequities and might tend to overlook the implications of individual choice and responsibility in assessing the impact of institutional racism on minority groups. People in this category might also fall on a continuum of passive to active behaviors. They might be active in combating the effects of racism by joining community initiatives with members of different racial groups, or they might demonstrate more passive stances by being accepting of diverse populations, behaving appropriately in the company of non-Whites, and being able to defend their accepting behaviors to other Whites.

The last attitudinal category of this model is *integrative,* where people do more than tolerate cultural diversity; they value and celebrate it. At the same time, people in this category have come to understand and accept their "Whiteness" as part of their being and development. Although people in this category also span a full range of passive and active behavioral patterns regarding their attitudes about cultural diversity, racism, and social justice, they routinely express themselves and join initiatives to bring about appropriate social change.

An underlying premise of Helms's (1995) model is that White people "are privileged relative to other groups" and subsequently "learn to perceive themselves (and their group) as being entitled to similar privileges" (Helms & Cook, 1999, p. 89). In a two-phase, seven-stage model of White racial-identity ego statuses, Helms proposed an evolutionary process that begins with a "primitive status" and ends with "advanced status" (Helms & Cook, 1999, pp. 92–93). The two primary phases of this model are (a) abandonment of racist attitudes and (b) development of a healthy and positive racial identity (Block & Carter, 1996). The attitudinal statuses cross these two phases.

Contact is the initial status or stage of this White racial identity model, and is distinguished by simplistic thinking and complete oblivion regarding the privileges and benefits derived from being White. When considering racial situations or conflicts, people at this stage commonly express denial, avoidance, and ignorance, particularly when responsibility by the White group is indicative of the problem.

The second stage of White identity development is *disintegration,* which a person enters when provoked by some racial conflict or dilemma. In this stage, the person becomes aware that White people have different status and are valued differently than people of color. The moral dilemmas that arise from these encounters place the person in a quandary of deciding between a just society and risking the wrath of the White society. People who remain at this stage suffer from confusion, stress, and anxiety about these challenging conflicts. Movement to the next stage, *reintegration,* allows people to avoid or absolve themselves from responsibility for racist attitudes and events in White society. According to Helms and Cook (1999), "The general theme of this status and correlated schema is idealization of one's own socioracial group, denigration and intolerance toward other groups, and protection and enhancement of the White group and thereby the maintenance of the racism status quo" (p. 92).

Movement to the fourth status, *pseudoindependence,* shows an intellectualization by the person to identify with positive nonracist attributes of Whites while rejecting racist attitudes. However, nothing substantially changes about the individual's awareness of racism or understanding of the responsibility Whites have in perpetuating a racist society. Instead, "White norms continue to be used to interpret cultural or racial differences" (Robinson, 2005, p. 136) and the person attempts, sometimes unwittingly, to resolve racial conflict by helping Blacks and other people of color to assimilate into White culture.

A continuing search for accurate information about racism and its meaning to the person's development leads to the *immersion* status. Characterized by a mission to reexamine and redefine "Whiteness," this stage also consists of behaviors aimed at debunking myths and replacing stereotypic beliefs and behaviors. *Immersion* becomes an active stage of reeducation and resolve that leads to an *emersion* status where the person experiences "a sense of discovery, security, sanity, and group solidarity and pride that accompanies being with other White people who are embarked on the mission of rediscovering Whiteness" (Helms & Cooks, 1999, p. 90). In this status, the person joins with other people in fighting racism, not by assisting people of color to assimilate, but by working within the White culture to educate and bring about change in beliefs, behaviors, and attitudes.

Autonomy is the last stage of Helms's model (1995). During this continuous status of racial development, people express realistic responses to racial situations, no longer inhibited by past emotions, arbitrary definitions, or stereotypic attitudes and behaviors. Now the individual is secure in experiencing and reacting to all types of racial dilemmas with an understanding of her or his racial essence and acceptance of its collective identity. At the same time, this autonomy allows flexible responses to express one's views about various racial situations and issues.

Asian Identity

Asian Americans (including Pacific Islanders) are a rapidly growing group in the United States, increasing from more than 3 million in 1980 to over 10.6 million in the 2000 U.S. census (U.S. Bureau of the Census, 2003). For the most part, this tremendous growth can be attributed to immigration patterns (Maki & Kitano, 2002). As with other minority groups in the United States, the Asian American experience, including subsequent identity development, is a complex phenomenon that is "characterized by continuity, change, diversity, and marginality" (Maki & Kitano, 2002, p. 110). Furthermore, consensus is lacking about the number of different groups that make up Asian American heritage. According to Sandhu (1997), upwards of more than forty different ethnic groups can be placed within Asian and Pacific Islander populations.

In noting multiracial and multiethnic issues confronted by Asian Americans, Spickard (2000) mentioned two opposing views about identity formation. According to one view, "to make satisfactory places for themselves in American society, minorities must either retain the ethnic culture of their youth, family, and community, or eschew their ethnicity and adopt the culture, values, and viewpoints of the dominant Anglo-American group" (p. 256). He further noted an opposing view presented in the nineteenth century by W. E. B. DuBois, who wrote of African Americans being "possessed by a double consciousness, two identities in a dialectical conversation" (p. 256). Accordingly, "An increasing number of people who are of mixed ancestry are choosing to embrace multiple identities," and research suggests "that the choice of a biracial identity is, for most mixed people, a healthier one than being forced to make an artificial choice" (Spickard, 2000, p. 265). Family support in this process is essential.

A two-by-two model (see Figure 4.1) presented by Maki and Kitano (2002) describes how Asian Americans or other ethnic groups with either low or high ethnic identity might interact with high or low assimilation into American society. Their model produces four possible types from this interaction:

- Type A indicates a person who realizes high assimilation into the new culture with low ethnic identity.
- Type B describes a person with high assimilation and high ethnic identity, what Maki and Kitano (2002) referred to as "bicultural adaptation" (p. 113).
- Type C reveals an individual with high ethnic identity and low assimilation. This is often a new person, an immigrant to the country, or "old timers who have little contact with the dominant society" (p. 114).
- Type D illustrates people with low ethnic identity and low assimilation. These individuals are rejected by the dominant culture and alienated by their own group. People who fit into this category most likely are the ones served by substance and alcohol abuse clinics, the criminal justice system, homeless shelters, and other services for the most delinquent and needy members of society.

Maki and Kitano (2002) noted that their model does not consider fully the different perspectives of ethnic groups that comprise Asian Americans. That is, as Asian cultures establish Americanized versions of their ethnic identities, they add an important dimension to this model. This is also true for other ethnic groups that have come to the United States. As an example, Maki and Kitano (2002) noted, "a Japanese American who is a Type A (high in acculturation, low in traditional Japanese culture) could strongly identify as Japanese American" (p. 114). Active involvement in the Japanese community for this person might provide appropriate balance between assimilation and ethnic identity.

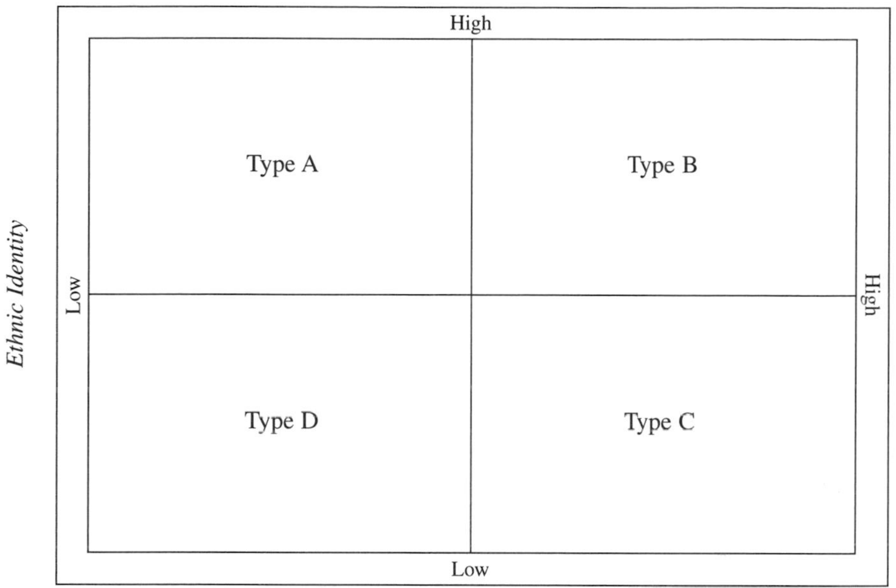

FIGURE 4.1 ***Interaction of Assimilation and Ethnic Identity***

Source: Adapted from Maki & Kitano (2002).

The previous sections have reviewed racial identity models with respect to people who view themselves as being from one particular race. As noted earlier in this text, not all authorities in counseling and related helping professions view racial identity as a useful aspect of establishing beneficial helping relationships with clients (Aponte & Johnson, 2000a; Jackson & Vontress, 2003). At the same time, other authorities have noted that an increasing portion of the world population has begun identifying with more than one racial classification. This has encouraged discussion and development of biracial identity models.

Biracial Identity

As seen from the 2000 U.S. census data, a segment of society views itself as biracial or as coming from a multitude of races rather than as monoracial (U.S. Bureau of the Census, 2000b). Nearly 7 million respondents in the 2000 census (2.4% of the U.S. population) indicated their makeup as of two or more races. In recent decades, "three important demographic trends have changed the face of America and its race relations: first, *the percentage of people of color has increased;* second, *the percentage of people of color who are not black has increased;* and third, *the number of people who consider themselves multiracial has increased"* (Ramirez, 1996, p. 51). In addition, concurrent social changes find that the term "minority" is no longer synonymous with Black people. Consequently, the increasing number of multiracial groups is eliminating the assumption of monoracial identity.

An increase in multiracial people makes stereotypical appearance factors less authoritative in identifying the backgrounds of individuals. As such, existing racial categories are becoming less useful for identification purposes. Exercise 4.1 gives you an opportunity to examine how people might classify different persons using their perception and using racial categories.

Root (1996) defined biracial as "a person whose parents are of two different *socially* designated racial groups, for example, black mother, white father." She also noted, "a less commonly used, but perfectly accurate meaning, biracial can also refer to someone who has parents of the same socially designated race, when one or both parents are biracial or there is racial mixing in the family history that is important to the individual" (p. xiv). These meanings blend both social construction and individual definitions.

Until recent decades, researchers and theorists have ignored this increasing population. Furthermore, Poston (1990) criticized the monoracial developmental models, noting several problems when applying them to biracial clients. In response, he proposed a five-stage developmental model of biracial identity.

The first stage of Poston's (1990) model is *personal identity* and it includes young people who are beginning to learn about their *self* independently from an awareness of race and ethnicity. As children become older, an increasing sense of race and identity with ethnic group members complements their self-development.

In the second stage of development, the person may begin to feel pressure to belong to a single ethnic group. During this period, the biracial individual chooses between a multicultural way of life or one parent's racial and ethnic background. Many factors influence this decision, including the valued status of each parent's background, attitudes of the

Exercise 4.1

Perception and Racial Classification

Instructions: Listed below are the names of prominent celebrities and sports figures. Using racial categories of your own choosing, assign a category to each name and write it in the right-hand column. If you do not know the name, skip it and go on to the next. When finished, compare your responses with classmates.

Prominent Figure	***Racial Classification***
Emeril Lagasse	________________
Tiger Woods	________________
Andre Agassi	________________
Vijay Singh	________________
Ricky Martin	________________
Paula Abdul	________________
Celine Dion	________________
Jennifer Lopez	________________
Selma Hayek	________________
Se Ri Pak	________________
Halle Berry	________________

dominant culture, physical characteristics, personality traits of the individual, peer group influence, and understanding of multiple cultures and languages.

Poston's third stage is *enmeshment/denial* during which the individual processes feelings of guilt about having to choose between two parents and confusion about selecting a racial identity that does not fully define his or her background. In this stage, anger about having to make the decision might impede development. In addition, shame about the biracial union of parents might embarrass the young person when establishing meaningful peer relationships. The *enmeshment/denial* stage is critical in the developmental process for biracial persons. Accordingly, successful resolution of this stage is imperative for healthy self-development and in learning to accept, celebrate, and appreciate the cultural background of both parents.

Appreciation is the fourth stage of this model. Now the person begins to see the richness of a biracial background and begins to expand her or his identity to a broader population. Still, some of the factors that mitigated the decision to identify with a particular group (see stage 2 above) influence the choice to identify with one group.

Integration is the final stage of this biracial developmental model, and it is characterized by increased self-esteem and perceived value in all racial distinctiveness that has contributed to the individual's identity. In addition, biracial people at this stage sense a oneness or wholeness about their self-development—they are an integrated self-entity.

From Poston's (1990) model, we can identify several issues of biracial identity that distinguish it from monoracial identity. Most obvious is the number of choices and factors that influence a biracial person's identity decision. Parents of different races, siblings of different races, peers that identify with different races, and countless other factors have an effect on this identity process. In addition to the difficulty incumbent in these choices, a biracial person also risks alienating people whose support is most crucial to her or his development. For example, if a biracial person chooses to identify strongly with the race of one parent, how might that choice affect relationships with the other parent? The feelings associated with these choices (e.g., guilt, remorse, betrayal, etc.) further complicate the identity process.

As noted in Chapter 3, Root (1990, 2002) also criticized monoracial and monocultural models of identity. Thornton (1996) supported this premise and suggested three prominent research themes that had attempted to understand multiracial people: "The first was an approach to multiracials as problems. The second theme was what we called the equivalent approach, which described mixed and mainstream identities as comparable. Last the variant approach envisioned mixed racial identity as a new phenomenon, presumably different than any before" (p. 108). All these themes focused on either differences or similarities, which, Thornton (1996) held, misses "an understanding of mundane, normal, and indeed, unique aspects of their lives, such as the dynamics of family life and peer pressure, as well as how members of this group feel about topics other than race" (p. 114). He continued that research should highlight this uniqueness by focusing on different sets of factors than previous studies have done.

Specifically, Thornton suggested that ethnic identity, social content, and developmental analysis across the life span might provide new direction for research themes of multiracial people. He placed combined emphasis on individual perception and social/cultural influences. For example, he noted, "Identity means to join with some people and depart from others, both within and without the group. Although society may try to impose identity in an absolute way, individuals often differ in how they define group boundaries and how strongly they identity with their own and other groups" (1996, p. 115). At the same time, Thornton (1996) noted, "we must address cultural and structural forces that determine how multiracials view themselves and are viewed by others" (p. 119).

Root (1990, 2002) suggested five aspects of identity formation based on social and cultural contexts and a person's flexibility to change, rather than predetermined stages. Through one or more of these five processes, she hypothesized, multiracial individuals resolve their identity development. The five resolutions include:

> **a.** Accept the default monoracial and monoethnic identity through a hypodescent process.
> **b.** Identify with multiple groups.
> **c.** Actively resolve a single racial or ethnic identity.
> **d.** Identify as new ethnic or racial group.
> **e.** Adopt a symbolic race of ethnicity. (Root, 2002, p. 175)

In an ecological framework for understanding racial identity development, Root (1999) chose a sociological and interactionist approach to examine the greatest number of influences on identity development and suggested, "the main lenses of influence are gender, class, regional history of race relations, and community" (p. 175). In addition, she noted that other lenses such as sexual orientation, family, and generations, among others, also influence the process.

Research of self-concept development and multiracial people identified adjustment difficulties in early studies, but later analyses of these reports found sampling and methodological problems that weakened the findings. In a more promising study, Field (1996) found biracial adolescents' self-concepts to be as positive as comparison groups of African American and Caucasian adolescents. She concluded, "The overall finding that biracial adolescents had positive self-concepts is extremely important in light of the historical pathologizing of biracial children in the popular media" (p. 222).

Racial and Cultural Identity Model (R/CID)

Sue and Sue (1999) developed one of the most noted and inclusive models of racial and cultural identity. Their model consists of five stages, and although Sue and Sue (1999) presented it as a racial and cultural identity development model (R/CID) to understand the experiences all people have as they establish a clearer identity, we review it here to make comparisons with other models presented earlier. Readers are encouraged to review other stage models of racial development that parallel the R/CID model. For example, Helms (Helms & Cook, 1999) presented a six-stage model of ego-statuses that contains many similarities (and some differences) to the R/CID model.

The first stage of the R/CID model is *conformity.* In this stage, the person views the dominant race and culture as superior and tends to deemphasize one's native culture (high assimilation–low ethnic identity). Stereotypic views espoused by the dominant race are accepted. For example, an Asian American's development that includes low self-esteem and denial regarding traditional cultural values and physical characteristics might at the same time demonstrate acceptance of White, Euro-American culture at the expense of Asian traditions, beliefs, and values.

As experiences begin to conflict with some of these "conforming" values, *dissonance* becomes more prevalent. This second stage sees a transformation from high assimilation–low ethnic identity to rethinking of one's racial and cultural identity. Confusion, disorientation, and uncertainty about one's racial group are elements observed early in this stage of development. Now the Asian American observes external contradictions and attempts to resolve conflicts towards self-development, one's racial group, and the White majority (Robinson, 2005).

Resistance and immersion mark the next stage of Sue and Sue's model (1999). During this stage of development, group members identify more strongly with beliefs and values held by their racial group, while they reject many views held by society's dominant race. For example, Asian Americans might express regret for having ignored or diminished their Asian heritage in previous years, and now want to rediscover the cultural influence and meaning it has had in their life. At the same time, they might feel angry towards the dominant group for fostering ignorance and devaluing their Asian culture.

In this stage, a member of the dominant racial group might also begin resisting and challenging values and beliefs that have perpetuated myths about minority groups and encouraged society's oppressive attitudes, customs, and policies. For example, White people who process the resistant and immersion stage might question their own racist views. For the first time in their life, they begin to become aware and understand the meaning and impact of racism on individuals and society as a whole. In an attempt to compensate for past beliefs and behaviors, White people who experience resistance and immersion might express guilt and negative feelings about their "Whiteness." In some instances, they might overly immerse themselves in other groups in the process of rejecting and detaching from the White culture.

The fourth stage of the R/CID model is the *introspective* stage in which people begin to assess their direction and purpose, particularly in the context of racial development and understanding. Expressions of independence now find balance with group identity. This stage might reflect an increasing ability to self-explore and self-analyze one's identity development. At the same time, people gain an appreciation for the complexity of racial identity and racial relationships. For oppressed people, this stage marks a search for meaningful personal goals and movement beyond an emotional reaction to racism. Successful development through this stage brings people to the final stage of *integrative awareness.*

In the final stage of the R/CID model of racial development, people are able to self-affirm and achieve a sense of independence and self-worth beyond racial identity. Pride in one's ethnicity remains strong, but more important is active commitment to fight oppression in any form by any group against another. In this process of becoming secure with oneself, people gain an understanding that all racial groups have aspects that are beneficial as well as some that are not. They also recognize the power of the individual within any group to capitalize on the benefits and diminish the negative attributes of that group. The autonomy that characterizes this last stage of development allows the individual to maintain a collective identity while responding as an independent person to racial situations. As such, a White person in this stage might respond to the oppression and degradation of other racial groups out of compassion and genuine commitment to equality rather than from a posture of guilt, shame, anger, or other rationalized emotion.

Optimal Theory Model

From their research, Myers and colleagues (1991) proposed an identity theory, which they called Optimal Theory Applied to Identity Development (OTAID). Relying on Erikson's (1968) assumptions about the emergence of self-identity and Jung's (1953) emphasis on spiritual awareness, Myers and colleagues (1991) defined identity development "as a continuous process of interaction between individuals and the sociocultural environment that they encounter" (p. 58). The authors presented their theory as neither linear nor categorical, but rather an "expanding spiral" of developing self-knowledge and an awareness "of belonging to the cycle of life" (p. 58). Furthermore, the OTAID model views identity development from the foundation of a worldview, constructed and altered by the person through "observation, examination, reflection, discussion, and conclusions" (p. 58). All these processes combine to create a more global one of self-learning, which ultimately results in greater self-awareness and awareness of others. Table 4.2 illustrates the seven phases of the OTAID model (including Phase 0) with brief descriptions of each.

Ivey's Cultural Identity Model

Ivey and colleagues (2002) presented a summary of a five-stage model of cultural identity development theory that illustrates movement from a lack of awareness of self to a higher level of awareness and action to fight against all forms of oppression and other aspects of society that demean, degrade, and discriminate against individuals or groups of people. The first stage in this summary is *Naïveté,* which manifests in lack of "awareness of self as a cultural being" (Ivey et al., 2002, p. 321). Different models of racial and cultural identity propose that at this lowest level of learning and functioning, people are unaware of differences in skin color and do not understand the significance of skin color as a status variable in certain societies. For example, many White Americans are unaware of "White unearned privilege" in their society. Simply being White gains them access to institutions, programs, services, and privileges that are routinely denied people of color in American society, and they do not comprehend this reality. This early stage of development might also reflect denial by people of having been oppressed and discriminated against in their life.

The second stage of this summary model by Ivey and colleagues (2002) is *Encounter.* This is a period of development when a person realizes that something about herself or himself or about other people is different, and they experience some form of discrimination or somehow witness it in society. The next stage is *Naming,* where the acts of discrimination observed in the earlier stage now have an identity of their own. Ivey and colleagues (2002) noted that in this stage of transformation, members of the majority group who are sympathetic and supportive of the oppressed minority would be challenged to maintain a positive identity for themselves. At the same time, members of the oppressed group might feel great anger and hostility and withdraw from contact with their oppressors (often the majority group), immersing themselves in the traditions and customs of their cultural group.

TABLE 4.2 *Phases of Optimal Theory Applied to Identity Development*

Phases	*Description*
Phase 0: Absence of Conscious Awareness	Generally associated with infancy, people have a lack of awareness of self or surroundings.
Phase 1: Individuation	An egocentric phase where: **1.** Individuals rarely identify or value particular parts of their *self.* **2.** Family values influence personal identity. **3.** Individuals may be unaware of how others devalue them. **4.** Societal reinforcement of certain views might preclude movement to higher phases.
Phase 2: Dissonance	Individual begins to explore aspects of identity that may be devalued by others. Conflict emerges and feelings of anger, confusion, isolation, guilt, and insecurity may be associated with a devalued sense of self. Some people in this phase might incorporate societal values and views into their identity, while others might reject such attitudes to remove or distance themselves from negative self-identities.
Phase 3: Immersion	People identify with the devalued group. They learn about and appreciate the devalued aspects, and feel joy and pride with a sense of belonging. Negative feelings toward a dominant group might persist, and some people might withdraw from, ignore, or reject the norms, customs, and values of the dominant culture.
Phase 4: Internalization	Individuals achieve a positive feeling about self. They translate feelings of self-worth into acceptance of others who are nonthreatening to their sense of self, resulting in an increased sense of security.
Phase 5: Integration	An increased sense of security with oneself helps individuals move toward a greater sense of community and genuine acceptance of others. The person has clearer understanding of oppression and how all people have the potential to oppress others and, depending on their self-views, all people can feel oppressed by others.
Phase 6: Transformation	Redefinition of the self allows individuals to experience an altered worldview that now understands the interrelatedness and interdependence of all things. Greater spiritual awareness occurs rather than reliance on external explanations.

Source: Adapted from Speight et al. (1991), pp. 59–60.

Reflection of Self as a Cultural Being is the fourth stage in this summary of cultural identity models. In this phase of development, the person becomes more aware of heritage, ethnicity, sexual orientation, physical challenges, or other traits that help to define her or his culture. According to Ivey and colleagues (2002), this stage includes an understanding that "the majority society is less relevant" and the individual's "developmental task is the establishment of a definite cultural consciousness" (p. 321).

The fifth and final stage of this summary is *Multiperspective Internalization.* Here, the person has achieved the ability to view life and world issues through many lenses.

People at this stage of development are comfortable with self, proud of their heritage and culture, and celebrate the similarities and differences they find across cultures and groups within society. They accept the beneficial aspects of the dominant culture in which they live, and still actively protest and combat all elements of degradation and discrimination that exist, such as racism, sexism, homophobia, and other forms of oppression.

As a summary of many models of cultural identity, the above stages should be processed by counselors and other professional helpers with caution. Ivey and his colleagues (2002) noted that clients might often express more than one form of cultural issue.

The developmental perspectives presented throughout this section are samples of models created to describe stages or statuses that people experience while moving toward an identity of *self*. Combined, they are indicative of the complexity of cultural and racial identity. Of course, this complexity begins with the debate of whether or not racial identity is a salient process in the larger scope of personal identity. This debate seems to have led counselors and other helping professionals to distinguish between racial identity as associated with biological/physical traits and racial identity as an outcome of social construction. Assuming that scientific discovery continues to debunk a biological distinction among human "races," we will be able to operate from a more confident position that racial identity is an important socially based element of self-identification. As such, racial identity develops through an individual's perceptual framework—experiencing, observing, learning, assessing, and drawing conclusions about countless factors that influence a person's decision about the *self* within the context of socially constructed meanings about race and racial groups. Exercise 4.2 offers an opportunity for you to explore your cultural and/or racial identity using one or more of the models presented in this chapter.

Closely related to the processes that comprise racial and cultural identity is the development of an ethnic identity. Ethnic identity, sometimes mistakenly considered synonymous with racial identity, is the topic explored in the next section of this chapter.

Ethnic Identity

Derivation of the word ethnicity comes from the Greek word *ethnos*. The ancient Greeks used the word *ethnos* when referring to non-Greeks and others who shared physical and

Exercise 4.2

My Cultural/Racial Identity

1. Using one or more of the stage models above, determine what stage you are at in your personal development. What traits or characteristics have you identified about yourself that led to this conclusion?
2. Retrace earlier stages of your life. What views did you hold during early phases of development, and how did you come to alter these views and move to subsequent stage or stages?
3. As a future counselor, what biases and prejudices do you still have to address and confront to elevate your level of professional practice and multicultural competency?

cultural traits. In time, European languages adopted forms of the word to denote racial associations (Scupin, 2003b).

In recent years, social scientists have used the terms *ethnicity* and *ethnic group* as indicators of people's cultural identity and heritage, apart from racial characteristics. At the same time, ethnicity does not imply an absolute sameness of identification among all members of a group. Researchers have noted that subgroups within an ethnic group often have disparate perceptions. An example applied across cultural groups would be differences found between male and female samples within the same ethnic group.

On occasion, the two terms—racial identity and ethnicity—combine to convey a thought about human development that implies a link or close association between them. Nevertheless, while these terms are closely related and share common influences, racial identity and ethnic identity formation are distinctive processes. We have seen that racial identity is greatly influenced by the value and meaning a society assigns to specific physical characteristics. In contrast, an individual's ethnic identity develops through countless personal, family, and social experiences.

As with racial identity, ethnic identity is a complex process. Some people are willing to give their lives fighting for ethnic beliefs including recognition and inclusion of their ethnic group. Other people seem oblivious and unconcerned about ethnic identity. Furthermore, society tends to classify people into ethnic groups, often without people knowing or agreeing with the identification (Scupin, 2003b). All of these aspects and dynamics are important to studying and understanding ethnicity and models of ethnic identification.

Ethnic Models

Scupin (2003b) summarized two major anthropological models of ethnic identity. The first, *primordialist,* comes from the work of Geertz (1973). *Primordial* refers to essential and fundamental connections that the group values and assigns historic meaning. In the primordialist model, several observations help us understand ethnic attachment and the dynamics that hold people to their identified groups. These observations include the following:

- **a.** People base their ethnic attachments on deeply rooted family and social connections and bonds such as religious traditions.
- **b.** Ethnic attachment persists because it is a fundamental aspect of personal identity.
- **c.** Strong emotional sentiments involving visible symbols such as dress, language, and food mark a person's ethnic attachment and identity.
- **d.** Ethnic identity conveys strong personal meaning for the individual.
- **e.** Individuals differ in how much attention they pay to primordial attachments.

An example of using the primordialist model to understand ethnic attachment might come from observing the Amish people and communities in the United States (Scupin, 2003b). Some of the visible ethnic attachments we might find are the similar dress of the Amish people, their use of a German dialect for language, a traditional way of life, and lack of modern conveniences and new technology in their day-to-day functions.

Another ethnic model is the *circumstantialist* perspective, which comes from a subjective definition of ethnic identity. This model offers a more complex process of groups revising boundaries and markers according to the circumstances the groups encounter. The circumstantialist model notes that ethnic markers often change when it is advantageous to the group (Scupin, 2003b). As such, ethnic groups are not always locked to particular markers as posited in the primordial model. Rather, they adapt to economic, political, and social circumstances in order to maintain an ethnic identity. For example, many European groups came to the United States in the late nineteenth and early twentieth centuries. To adjust to the social climate of this adopted country, while retaining some of their cultural heritage, these people often embraced identities that merged the old and new. For example, Irish immigrants became Irish Americans.

Today, social scientists tend to draw from both models in attempting to understand the complex process of ethnic identity. Essential markers are important in the study of ethnicity, but it is also reasonable to measure circumstantial influences over time that have an impact on group development.

Ethnicity and Self-Concept Development

Several social conditions and types of personal experiences are evidence of the influences that affect ethnic identity. Migration, adoption, interracial marriage, religious conversion, and change in financial status are a few conditions that might influence a person's ethnic choice. When people migrate from one place to another, they often acculturate to their new surroundings and subsequently adjust ethnic views. In the United States, we see this phenomenon played out daily as families, particularly children, from Asia, Europe, South America, and other parts of the world settle in the States and ultimately make decisions about who they are and to what ethnic group they belong (Roysircar, 2003). Similarly, adopted children of ethnically different parents will likely make adjustments in ethnic perceptions as they develop and mature. Such experiences illustrate the dynamics of ethnic identity. Indeed, it is a fluid and complex process rather than an unwavering stagnant one. Instead of portraying the *self* as a rigid and unchanging entity, ethnicity allows us to confirm the vibrant nature of self-concept. In today's evolving global society, it is common to find people whose ethnic identity is continually adjusting and changing. Exercise 4.3 asks you to explore your own ethnic development.

When professional counselors and other helpers do not distinguish between racial and ethnic identity, mistaken assumptions might lead them to believe that because clients associate with a particular socially constructed race, they must therefore identify with specific ethnic groups. This assumption might be erroneous because, as noted above, numerous social conditions, personal experiences, and individual choices might lead clients to choose an ethnic identification quite different from the identity socially assigned to their supposed racial group. Inherent in gaining a clearer understanding of racial and ethnic identity is recognition that the terms used are imprecise at best. Indeed, we struggle to find a language that accurately depicts who we are.

Ethnic identity is the process of associating, connecting, and linking with a particular cultural group. The ethnicity of a group is the mixture and fusion of countless traits, beliefs, behaviors, languages, and traditions that distinguish it from other groups. This does not mean that all members of a particular ethnic group embrace the same beliefs, display the same characteristics, or behave in identical ways. Every ethnic group consists of individuals, who form subgroups within the larger culture, and these subgroups sometimes dif-

Exercise 4.3

Developing Ethnicity

Instructions: In Column A, identify the ethnic group(s) to which you identified during particular periods of your life. In Column B, name significant events and experiences that influenced movement or changes in your ethnic identity. Share your exercise with a classmate and discuss.

Column A—*Ethnic Groups*	**Column B—*Significant Events That Influence Change***
Early Childhood	
____________________	____________________
____________________	____________________
Childhood	
____________________	____________________
____________________	____________________
Adolescence	
____________________	____________________
____________________	____________________
Young Adulthood	
____________________	____________________
____________________	____________________
Adulthood	
____________________	____________________
____________________	____________________

fer in the emphasis and importance they assign to various aspects of the group. Helms and Cook (1999) noted that loyalty and identification with a particular ethnic group by people who have immigrated to the United States relate to three factors:

a. Family's history of migration
b. Family and individual's experiences of being separated from their ethnic group of origin and subsequent assimilation by other groups
c. The visibility, density, and connectedness of their group of origin in the locality where they live

Understanding how all three factors impact a person's decision to identify with a particular ethnic group or to make adjustments in one's ethnic identity is essential in coming to know and help that person. In the journey for an ethnic identity, everyone's story is different, much the same way that each person's self-concept is unique and special. More important, the journey for an ethnic identity often includes stressful encounters, alienation, persecution, and other situations that affect the developing *self.* Counselors and other professional helpers who appreciate these challenges are in better position to help clients from diverse ethnic backgrounds.

In the previous sections, we have considered several racial and ethnic identity models that may assist counselors and other professional helpers in working with diverse populations. Although informative, these models focus on specific social constructions of race and cultural influences related to ethnicity. Such attention on singular identity factors omits some of the other identity features that contribute to self-concept development. These aspects might include gender, spirituality, religion, geographic region, social class, and other factors that in combination lend themselves to the notion of multiple identities.

Multiple Identities

McEwen (2003) reported, "Multiple oppressions and multiple identities are beginning to be addressed in the psychological literature" (p. 223), and Weber (1998) suggested that examination of the relationships among various identity factors is overdue. Examination of multiple identities and their combined impact on self-concept development seems like a logical progression for professional helpers to make. This is the case made by Robinson (2005) in her text about *converging* social statuses with other identity factors. For example, to consider ethnic identity issues without examining gender differences disregards the unique contributions of feminine and masculine perspectives in the complex process of self-development. Similarly, viewing socioeconomic status in a vacuum ignores race, sex, and physical ability as oppressive issues and possible identity correlates worthy of study.

Reynolds and Pope (1991) proposed a Multidimensional Identity Model (MIM) with which they constructed two identity dimensions, each consisting of two choices. One dimension involves a person's choice of whether to identify with a single aspect or multiple aspects of self-concept development. The other dimension indicates whether the person is passive or active in this selection process (McEwen, 2003). Table 4.3 depicts these two dimensions and the corresponding choices.

According to McEwen (2003), the MIM model does not reveal "how and under what conditions an individual's pattern may change over time" (p. 224). However, a basic premise of the model parallels the fundamental ideas put forth is this text by suggesting that self-concept development "involves an interaction between what happens within a person and what takes place in his or her environment" (McEwen, 2003, p. 224). As such,

TABLE 4.3 *Multidimensional Identity Model (MIM)*

	Single Factor	*Multiple Factors*
Passive	One aspect of self-identity (passive acceptance)	
Active	One aspect of self-identity (purposeful identification)	Multiple factors of self identified in a segmented manner
Active		Combined factors of self identified in an interactive manner.

MIM suggests active and passive stances that *react to or accept* external events in a complex process of self-concept development.

Another multiple identity model, presented by Jones and McEwen (2000), addresses multiple social identities within various *contexts* that surround the individual's personal attributes, characteristics, and identity factors, which form the *core,* the center, of the person's identity. According to McEwen (2003), the contextual variables, such as culture, social class, gender, and spirituality, rotate around the core in such a way as to illustrate their "relative salience to the individual and the degree of connectedness to the core at any one point in time" (p. 225). At the same time, these multiple rotations intersect with one another at various times, and these intersections indicate that a person's "social identities must be understood collectively rather than singularly" (McEwen, 2003, p. 225). Figure 4.2 illustrates an adaptation of Jones and McEwen's multiple dimensions of identity.

In Figure 4.2, the *core* resembles "My Self" in the self-concept spiral illustrated earlier in Chapter 2 (Figures 2.1 and 2.2), and the multiple dimensions of *context* are similar to the "sub-selves" in those two diagrams. Another similarity between these two theoretical

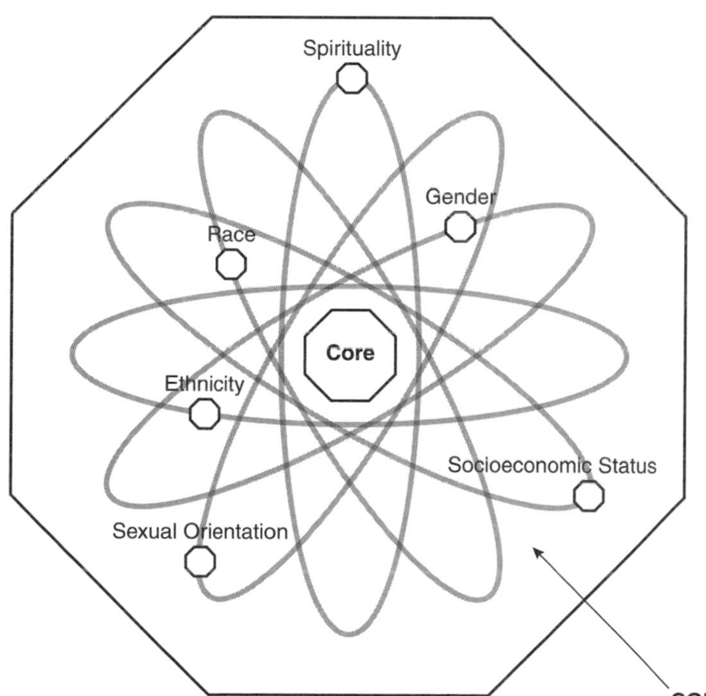

FIGURE 4.1 ***Multiple Dimensions of Identity***
Source: Adapted from Jones & McEwen (2000).

models is that the distance between the *core* (i.e., "My Self") and the multiple dimensions of *context* (i.e., "sub-selves") is indicative of the relative value particular dimensions have to the individual at any given period or point in time (McEwen, 2003; Purkey & Schmidt, 1996). In addition, both models advocate an understanding of self-concept development and identity development as a complex dynamic process that incorporates unique perspectives of individuals within the broad context of multiple social constructions and other essential contexts. This process, as noted in Chapter 2, is adaptable and flexible, yet the overall product (i.e., the emerging self-concept) is relatively stable over a lifetime.

In this chapter, we have explored several identity models that consider racial, cultural, ethnic, and multiple identities. Such models can help counselors and human service professionals to gain greater comprehension of how these factors might influence self-development of diverse populations. Equally if not more important to the process of counseling is an understanding of how different clients perceive and integrate these multiple concepts into their self-development. This integration of perceptions establishes a level of self-consciousness that every client uses in creating and maintaining a personal identity.

Self-Consciousness and Identity

We use the term *self-consciousness* here not in the common sense of being overly anxious about attention received from others, but rather being conscious of ones *self* regarding thoughts, beliefs, and attitudes. *Self*-consciousness gives the person an identity, a stance if you will, from which to behave. As noted in the second chapter, the behaviors people choose are typically consistent with the beliefs and perceptions that form their self-concept.

The process of developing self-consciousness (also referred to as self-awareness) begins early in life as children learn that they are physically separate beings. Later in the developmental process, children attain clearer definition of their *self* by learning to categorize themselves and other objects (color, size, gender, etc.). As seen throughout this chapter, social and cultural influences including language, traditions, and application of individualistic, collectivistic, independent, and interdependent views play a significant role in this process. Ultimately, however, the person's integration of all these influences into a self-view establishes a self-identity. Self-concept theory suggests that the basic foundation for this identification process is set about the age of five (Hamachek, 1992), and as children grow, progress through school, learn about customs, and experience life within society, they begin to internalize these observations and this learning into an increasingly complex view of themselves and their surroundings.

Helms and Cook (1999) presented a table of descriptions to illustrate how people might express views of themselves across individualistic and collectivistic perspectives. They cautioned that although the table suggests two mutually exclusive cultural forms, "in fact, it is possible for a person to be collectivistic or individualistic with respect to some of the dimensions and the opposite with respect to the others" (Helms & Cook, 1999, p. 104). Their descriptions suggest that counselors and other professional helpers can assess self-consciousness by listening to how clients describe their thoughts, emotions, and behaviors. For example, clients with individualistic leanings might tend to use descriptions beginning with "I" statements, such as "I am outgoing." In contrast, clients with collec-

Exercise 4.4

Exploring Self-Consciousness

1. Where do you see yourself on a continuum of individualistic and collectivistic views?
2. Are you interdependent or independent?
3. How strong are your family ties?
4. What have been the most significant influences in making major life decisions (e.g., educational plans, career choices, marriage, etc.)?
5. What beliefs do you hold about expressing emotions, negative or positive?
6. What are the most important aspects that define who you are?

---

tivistic attitudes might refer more to group orientations, as in "My family thinks I am the most outgoing."

These examples illustrate how social and cultural aspects interact with a person's unique processing and filtering of life experiences to form an identity. The better that people understand this process and the influences they have integrated into their development, the higher their level of self-consciousness. Exercise 4.4 offers you an opportunity to explore your level of self-consciousness.

Counseling Inferences

As noted earlier, when using proposed models in the helping process, counselors and other professionals avoid labeling or categorizing clients simply because they appear to belong to a particular racial or ethnic group. More appropriate interventions using these models ask clients if they can relate to the language and significance of particular stages of development and what meaning these factors might have for their present concerns or problems. The key is to learn from clients rather than to use one's own perceptions in forming misguided or mistaken conclusions. This danger was illustrated in an ethnobiography written by a former graduate student. Narrative 3.1 summarizes his story.

NARRATIVE 3.1 • *The Story of Timothy*

Born in a southeastern state in 1972, the oldest of three children, Timothy reported, "I have red hair, brown eyes, and happen to be Caucasian. The general belief is that I am from Irish decent, but to my parents' knowledge our family name is Dutch-German." The family was "lower-middle class" and lived mostly in apartments and duplexes while Timothy, his brother, and sister were growing up.

In primary school, Timothy became "best friends" with a Black boy, and although they went to different elementary schools for a few years, the two "reunited in junior high school and started hanging out again." This friend taught Timothy "a lot about defending myself and speaking up for the things I believed in most. I adopted many of his beliefs." Timothy played

(Continued)

NARRATIVE 3.1 • *The Story of Timothy (Continued)*

on the basketball team in school and gained respect for his athletic abilities on the court. "The only downfall to this newfound glory was the negative attention received from my White friends. They did not approve of my association with Black kids, and referred to me as 'White Knight' and 'Wigger.' "

Growing up in a multicultural neighborhood with Black, Asian, Latino, Greek and Euro-American ancestries living together, Timothy felt "Blessed to experience so much diversity. It was always entertaining when I stayed the night at my friends' houses due to the differences in our cultures." He credits his parents for instilling positive values. "The values, manners, and respect that my parents have instilled in me have carried on throughout adulthood. In 1992, I accepted Christ into my life and have tried to live my life according to His word ever since. I am proud to be a Christian and consider it to be a great success in my life."

Timothy's experiences with diversity and his embracement of values and beliefs that cross cultural boundaries have posed personal challenges. "I am a constant outcast because of the things I am attracted to in life. No matter the crowd I am in, I seem to be different." He explained, "My favorite music is hip-hop, a predominantly Black music and culture. Music plays a huge part in my life because it makes me feel better when I'm down, happier when I am unhappy, and safe when I feel exposed. Most people tend to judge me simply by the music and culture I live by." As a White, educated adult, Timothy reported that this "is frustrating, but I feel a certain comfort in being different, so it balances out. I guess I have strived to be different my entire life and it appears to bother other people."

A final suggestion in using racial and ethnic identity models is to become knowledgeable of cultural behaviors and nuances that might influence the helping skills you choose. Learn about behavioral differences and cultural sensitivities common among the people with whom you will work. Search out resources to learn about Native Americans, Asian Americans, Latinos/as, and people of other heritage, and use them judiciously. Learn from clients what is important. For example, what behaviors offer them comfort or present uncomfortable situations? Use their perspectives in creating healthy and helpful relationships. The remaining chapters of this text continue to explore different aspects of cultural identity and self-concept development that will help in this process. To begin, Chapter 5 examines, sex, gender, and sexual orientation identity as contributing factors.

5

Sex, Gender, and Sexual Orientation Identity

Sex and gender are other influential factors in self-concept development—ones also affected by values and statuses assigned by society and cultural groups. In some situations and under certain circumstances, sex or gender may be a dominant factor influencing people to make particular decisions that establish their personal identity. In addition, unwarranted fears and oppressive acts cross social and cultural groups and unfairly discriminate against people because of their gender, sexuality, and sexual orientation identity (Robinson, 2005). Sexism, when acted out by a single person, embraced by certain groups, or promulgated through socially accepted customs, has an impact on both individual development and the collective beliefs of society. Therefore, sex, gender, sexuality, and sexual orientation identity are significant social and cultural variables for professional helpers to consider and understand in providing effective assistance with all clients.

This chapter explores the meaning of sex, gender, and sexual orientation identity as they relate to and influence self-concept development. According to Hamachek (1992), a first step in the process of self-identity is to establish a *gender identity,* "which is a boy's and girl's awareness and acceptance of his or her basic biological nature as a male or female" (p. 236). Biological sex, therefore, is the precursor to gender identity and ultimately sexual orientation identity. The title of this chapter includes all three factors in a seemingly sequential process, realizing that they do not illustrate stages of development, nor do they convey distinct terms unrelated to one another. Sex, gender, and sexuality are closely related concepts that interact with biological traits, social constructs, and cultural beliefs in a complex process of influences to a person's identity. To comprehend this influence, we begin with a brief exploration of biological sex.

Sex

The human body is a marvelous and complex organism that under normal circumstances produces offspring as one of two possible sexes, female or male. What distinguishes these two sexes biologically is a single pair of chromosomes in each human cell. In the usual case, human cells have 46 chromosomes arranged in 23 pairs. The first 22 pairs of chromosomes are *autosomes* and they consist of identical genetic material in males and females. The 23rd pair of chromosomes, called *sex chromosomes,* is different for females and males (Wachtel, 1994).

The resulting sex of a newborn is a biological outcome that begins during the second month of gestation. Genetic material in the sex chromosome activates production of proteins thereby causing a successive chain of hormonal activity, ultimately leading to the development of either an XY (normal male) or XX (normal female) sex chromosome. On rare occasions, aberrant development results. For example, sometimes only 45 chromosomes (XO, female) exist, known as Turner's syndrome, or an additional 47th chromosome (XXY, male) is found, called Klinefelter's syndrome. Turner's syndrome is a rare chromosomal disorder of females that typically results in shortness of height and minimal sexual development, and occasionally other physical abnormalities. Klinefelter's syndrome affects males and results in minimal testicle growth with low sperm count, which generally leaves subjects infertile. Behavioral indicators of Klinefelter's syndrome include delayed speech, motor function, and maturational development. Examination of normal and aberrant chromosome counts concludes that the absence or presence of the Y chromosome triggers hormonal and protein activity that determines the sex of a human being (Ridley, 1999; Wachtel, 1994).

Research on biological sex has found some differences between females and males. A few years ago, such a statement would have been an affront to women and their strides toward equality for both sexes. Today, through scientific discovery and particularly genetic research, we know that at first glance, the male-determining Y chromosome, consisting of only 25 genes, seems deficient in comparison to the female-determining X chromosome with over 1,000 genes. However, a part of the Y chromosome has one powerful gene, called *Sry,* which triggers hormones that play a dominant role in male development (Therman & Susman, 1993). This genetic variance instigates diverse hormonal activity between sexes, and these combined processes cause differences in brain development and resulting behavior patterns. Some notable findings (Kimura, 2002; Kreeger, 2002):

- Men typically have larger brains than women do, but the female brain is more densely organized, which facilitates thought processing.
- Part of the anterior hypothalamus gland, a tiny structure at the base of the brain that regulates reproduction, is larger in men than in women. Variations in the size of the hypothalamus gland may relate to sexual identity, suggesting a biological link to sexual orientation and gender identity.
- Although intellectual differences between sexes are not definitive, researchers have found differences when studies consider specific patterns of functioning and ability. For example, in laboratory studies men typically outperform women on spatial tasks, mathematical reasoning, targeting moving objects, and navigation through a maze. Women, on average, outperform men on measurements such as word recall, verbal fluency, matching items, object memory, and precision manual tasks. Some cognitive and skill differences have been found between young girls and boys as early as 3 years old, leading to increased speculation of hormonal contributions.
- Hormonal deprivation or overstimulation influences sex development and related functioning. For example, production of abnormally large quantities of adrenal an-

drogens in girls might result in play with toys and activities typically associated with masculinity in U.S. culture.
- Studies continue to find a relationship between sex-based differences and vulnerability to particular autoimmune diseases. For example, rheumatoid arthritis tends to occur more frequently in women.

The findings summarized above are examples of some scientific discoveries that *suggest* biological sex differences (Kimura, 2002; Kreeger, 2002). Much more research is required to make firm conclusions. Just as researchers are finding no meaningful genetic differences between racial groups yet more significant variance within groups, similar results emerge from between sex studies. As Kimura (2002) summarized, "On the whole, variation between men and women tends to be smaller than deviations within each sex, but very large differences between the groups do exist—in men's high level of visual-spatial targeting ability, for one" (p. 2).

The social consequences of research findings on sex differences play out in legislative arenas, courtrooms, pharmaceutical companies, and other decision-making venues. Scientific and medical discoveries regarding sex differences influence public perception and have implications for laws passed, court decisions rendered, drugs manufactured and marketed, and a host of other social, legal, and economic choices. Often, scientific findings and conclusions influence perceptions and decisions that are either favorable or unfavorable to women or men. Offering one historical example, Robinson (2005) noted, "Menstruation has been perceived of as an impediment and an illness, and menopause has been labeled a disease and a social problem" (p. 214).

What do these research findings mean for how counselors and human service workers might help clients? First, professional helpers might keep in mind that research of biological differences are similar to other types of group studies and thereby illustrate variance of findings across the group. Therefore, practitioners cannot apply group results with precision to individual clients because they do not know exactly where on the spectrum of statistical variance a particular client might fall. For example, if a study verifies that men, on average, perform differently than women on a spatial relationship test, this conclusion is made from variances in mean scores on the test. However, some women in the study might have scored significantly higher than some male subjects did. Therefore, the range of scores for women subjects overlaps the range of scores for men in the study, even though the mean scores between the two groups statistically are significantly different. Consequently, where a female client falls in the spectrum of spatial relationship scores cannot be certain unless her test results are available and compared with the overall population. Generalizing the results of one study or a group of studies to a particular female or male client could be an error that does disservice to the client. The potential for this type of error exists when counselors generalize research findings to any of their clients.

Biological differences are only one of numerous variables that contribute to human development and functioning. Environmental influences, family factors, cultural traditions, and individual perceptions are among the variables that combine with biology to produce a functioning human being. Understanding the role that all these factors play helps us move from knowledge and awareness about biological sex to comprehension of gender differences and gender roles in society.

Gender

Use of the terms *sex* and *gender* is often inconsistent in both popular and scientific literature. The greatest confusion comes from the synonymous use of these terms by authors from all areas of literature, government agencies, and scientific study. This confusion inhibits understanding of important theoretical assumptions as well as scientific findings, and equally important, causes misunderstanding and disagreement among legislators, policy makers, and the public about vital social and cultural issues. This text uses the term *sex* to indicate biological identity as either female or male. In contrast, *gender* refers to people's self-beliefs and representations of themselves as female or male, or how society responds to people's depiction of themselves. To assess your understanding of the terms, complete Exercise 5.1 "The Gender Quiz" and compare your responses to those of other classmates.

The sex of a newborn may be determined biologically, but how parents, grandparents, other relatives, and society respond and assign value to one sex or another has tremendous impact on self-concept development. Thanks to the development of sophisticated medical technology, expectant parents are now able to identify biological sex before birth. Sonograms using ultrasound technology (sonography) allow visual identification with good, but not absolute, reliability during the first trimester of pregnancy.

The social implications of these procedures, current and future, are that a newborn child enters a world that is already prepared for a particular sex based on common cultural traditions and beliefs. For example, when traditional-thinking parents-to-be in the United States find out their child will be a girl, they might cover the nursery in pink or other pastels. The parents would decorate the room with beautiful curtains, lovely dolls, and cuddly stuffed animals. In contrast, another set of parents might want to "liberate" their daughter from traditional beliefs. They paint the nursery with vibrant colors and fill it with artifacts, playthings, and visual images that could appeal to children of either sex. In both situations,

Exercise 5.1

The Gender Quiz

Instructions: Mark each statement True or False. Compare your responses to those of other classmates.

_____ **1.** After the birth of a newborn, it is appropriate (and accurate) to ask the proud parents about its gender.
_____ **2.** As a term, *sex* has dichotomous meaning.
_____ **3.** The terms *gender* and *sex* are synonymous.
_____ **4.** The sex of a newborn male is masculine.
_____ **5.** People have only one of two possible *gender* orientations, so it is a dichotomous concept.
_____ **6.** A person's *sex* always conforms to societal gender interpretations.
_____ **7.** To be psychologically healthy, males must identify with the masculine gender and females must identify with the feminine gender.
_____ **8.** Other animal species also identify by *gender.*
_____ **9.** *Gender* is a given trait rarely influenced by experience.
_____ **10.** It is appropriate to use the term *sex* when referring to a person as either masculine or feminine.

Exercise 5.2

Gender Role Development

Interview your parents or a close relative who has known you since birth. Ask them about your development as a male or female. Ask them about masculine and feminine roles you adopted or that you exhibited in early childhood. What contributions did they make toward your gender role development? How do their recollections balance or merge with the way you perceive your gender roles today?

---

each set of parents takes steps to begin influencing their daughter's perception of biological sex and gender roles that she might adopt in life.

As part of your development as a healthy and competent professional helper, it is appropriate to consider how your parents' behavior may have affected your gender identity. Complete Exercise 5.2 as part of this journey.

As noted, gender is a combination of biological sex and social construction. Ridley (1999) concluded, "The brain is an organ with innate gender. The evidence from the genome, from imprinted genes and genes for sex-linked behaviours, now points to the same conclusion" (p. 218). In sum, we must consider both nature and nurture when contemplating gender roles. The nurturing side of this issue includes cultural influences important to the dynamics of helping relationships with clients.

Gender and Culture

Since the dawn of humankind, the formation of social groups, the establishment of societal customs, and the development of countless cultures across the globe, people and societies have manifested gender differences. As noted, this process has been a combined influence of biological sex differences and cultural beliefs passed down generation after generation. In prehistoric times, it may not have been accidental that men were the hunters and women the gatherers. Yet, sex differences in contemporary society are rivaled by cultural influences on male and female role development and subsequently on each individual's identity.

In their examination of the relationship between gender and culture, Davenport and Yurich (1991) noted, "some generalizations can be made transculturally" (p. 64). For example, across most cultures women are the caregivers and exhibit characteristics of gentleness, nurturing, and dependence. In contrast, transcultural expectations of men generally are that they will be in control, powerful, and sexually dominant. As Davenport and Yurich (1991) indicated, these expectations influence the emerging *self* of both genders and consist of both negative and positive attributes. They wrote, "The costs of such superimposed, arbitrary structure are that the structure not only rules out certain potentialities as nonlegitimate but also sets as requisites to esteem certain qualities and behaviors that are not possible or even desirable for all people to attain" (Davenport & Yurich, 1991, p. 64).

As an example of social structure that sets requirements for behaviors, consider the power of communication in society and how men and women as public speakers were viewed from the birth of America to the present-day United States. In this instance, we have come light years in changing cultural beliefs and bridging the equality gap between women and men. However, it was not always this way. From colonial days when people ridiculed, shunned, and banned from town women who communicated their opinions in public to present-day institutions where women hold high public office, are celebrity broadcasters and noted orators, we have witnessed significant change (Borisoff & Merrill, 1992). Nevertheless, stereotypical views about communication styles and gender differences persist. For example, a common view is, "Unlike the women activists . . . the *stereotypically* feminine speaker is soft spoken, self-effacing, and compliant. More emotional than logical, she is prone to be disorganized and subjective" (Borisoff & Merrill, 1992, p. 9). In contrast, the masculine stereotype "is that of a speaker who is direct, confrontative, forceful and logical; the few well-chosen words are focused on making a particular point" (Borisoff & Merrill, 1992, p. 13).

Stereotypic views of gender differences are not unique to U.S. society. Counselors and human service professionals understand how various cultural groups perceive gender differences and the impact those beliefs might have on male and female clients and on helping relationships. For illustrative purposes, the following paragraphs describe some common (and in some cases, stereotypical) beliefs about different cultural groups. *For students learning this information for the first time, caution is warranted about applying these beliefs to particular members of identified cultural groups. These are only a sample of beliefs published in the literature that may or may not be applicable to individual clients or other persons who happen to identify with a particular culture.*

African American culture traditionally has viewed women equal in status with men. This is in contrast with the patriarchal structure that historically existed in African cultures where a common view was that women were inferior to men. One consequence of the American slave trade was to diminish this patriarchal structure, placing men and women on an equal yet powerless footing. According to Davenport and Yurich (1991), the oppressive conditions of slavery for African American men and women dismissed "any illusions they had that men were superior to and/or capable of protecting women" (p. 68). An outgrowth of such oppression is that American Black women have cultivated a history of independence, working outside the home while at the same time maintaining leadership of the family. African American females tend to include a multitude of roles in the process of developing their self-identity, and these roles frequently involve work and family (Porter, 2000a). A stereotypical view of African American women, however, is that because of their ability to handle so many tasks, they do not need support or assistance (Harrison, 1989). As Porter (2000a) emphasized, the perpetuation of this stereotype and individual internalization of the impression of a strong self-sufficient woman fails "to acknowledge and recognize the stress it engenders resulting from the tremendous amount of energy required to live up to such standards" (p. 189).

High unemployment rates and lower educational achievement among Black males have had historic effect. In the decades since slavery ended in the United States, the outcomes of this enormous social tragedy have continued to influence African American male status. Largely, the negative effects on male roles can be attributed, in part, to continued economic oppression and denied access to equal educational opportunity. Such an outcome leads many African American men to feel marginalized in trying to overcome obstacles and provide for their families (Brooks, Haskins, & Kehe, 2004).

Historic discrimination and oppression has in essence rebuffed many African American males from taking advantage of educational opportunity, achieving gainful employment, and ultimately sharing power with others in society. In contrast, the independence claimed by many Black women has encouraged entry into educational arenas that often leads to higher employment opportunity. Some evidence suggests that at the turn of the twenty-first century African American women in general were more motivated to enter and complete college than African American males (Cokley, 2001). Consequently, stereotypical views perpetuate the depiction of self-sufficient African American women as opposed to "Black men who are caricatured as shiftless and irresponsible" (Davenport & Yurich, 1991, p. 69). At the same time, some studies indicate that African American men report higher levels of self-worth than their female counterparts and also attach greater significance to spirituality and religious behavior (Parker, Ortega, & Hill, 1999).

Today, educational achievement of both African American men and women is opening economic pathways and employment opportunities that allow them to elevate themselves and their families. Nevertheless, the gap between White and Black educational attainment and economic power in American society continues to be a significant barrier. Unintentional and intentional practices in schools and society in general contribute to this challenge. In 1987, Sadker and Sadker wrote in their classic work about the *hidden curriculum* that schools send messages, perhaps unintended but powerful, to students about roles their gender and/or race *should* take. Nearly twenty years later, stories and pictures in readers, textbooks, and other media used for instruction frequently offer hidden messages that discourage or encourage particular behaviors based on race or gender. Efforts to eradicate such unintentional messages continue, but schools and publishers need to do much more.

Regarding gender differences, White culture in the United States has moved through countless transitions over the decades. Still, some stereotypic views persist, and as social and political pendulums swing back and forth, variations of old themes reemerge. For example, the twenty-first century has included perspectives between the "career woman" and the "stay-at-home mom." At the same time, uncertain economic conditions, changing legal perspectives, and advanced career opportunities have created the "househusband," "single dad," and "stay-at-home dad" phenomena. These changing patterns and views will likely contribute to identity dilemmas for both female and male clients in the mental health and human service arenas.

Porter (2000a) noted that the plight of *Native American* women in comparison to their male counterparts is their "invisibility" (p. 189). Yet, women of Native American heritage suffer the same poverty, lower education, and physical and mental health issues that men do. Historic trauma and unresolved grief among Native Americans have contributed to social and personal problems "such as alcoholism, suicide, homicide, domestic violence, child abuse, and negative career ideation" (Trimble & Thurman, 2002, p. 56). These mental health and social issues are shared by both men and women. In learning and understanding about gender differences among Native Americans, counselors and other professional helpers note the multiple identities existing among people of various heritage. Similar to the number of cultures that comprise Asian or Pacific Islander identities, "a Native individual's multiple identities can be influenced by that individual's tribal lifeways and thoughtways, which may be at variance with conventional expectations and proscriptions" (Trimble & Thurman, 2002, p. 56). Garrett (1995) reported that the U.S. government recognizes over 500 tribes with more than 250 languages and many nations. Because language provides a foundation for expressing cultural beliefs, it is the platform upon which communities describe, accept, and reject gender issues and sexual behaviors. Therefore, gender and sexual differences may be influenced by multiple factors including language that counselors and human service providers might not apply consistently or with certainty across Native American groups.

Porter (2000a) mentioned some historic gender differences across Native American groups. She noted that before European explorers and settlers arrived, Native American women held positions of authority in their families, had considerable power in their tribes, and owned and cultivated land that they inherited from their mothers. The Europeans, according to Porter (2000a), imposed paternalistic and patriarchal structures, which caused Native American women to lose power and status. This legacy regrettably continues in many instances, contributing to the social and cultural outlook of Native American women.

Asian women face the stereotypic view of being passive, shy, and detached. A common perspective is that women of Asian heritage defer to male authority, and this view, according to Bradshaw (1994), is perpetuated and accepted among Asian cultures. Zane, Morton, Chu, and Lin (2004) noted, "Although there is a trend towards increasing gender equality, Asian cultures tend to encourage men and women to hold different responsibilities and to abide by rules of conduct that emphasize social stability over individual rights" (p. 199).

The challenge of identifying gender differences in Asian groups is complicated by the number of various cultures categorized as either Asian or Pacific Islander. Still, the literature notes that large numbers of Asian and Pacific Islander women face the stress of acculturation to American society while taking menial jobs to provide financial support for their family. This new marital role frequently meets with disapproval from Asian or Pacific Islander men who view their newly acquired household chores as demeaning and insulting to the masculine role (Sandu, Leung, & Tang, 2003).

Among *Arab* cultures, some gender roles are commonly misinterpreted (Erickson & Al-Timimi, 2004). For example, although Arab men are generally head of the house, women control their own money and property, giving them an important source of influence. In Arab families, women's influence in decision-making processes usually is done privately, presenting a contrasting public view of more passive behavior. Erickson & Al-Timimi (2004) observed that Americans often misinterpret this difference between private influence and public persona as Arab women being overly dominated and oppressed by men. Although some Arab women have legitimate complaints about gender roles and differences, Erickson and Al-Timimi continued, "Arab women's status varies considerably with socioeconomic background and religious conservatism" (2004, p. 241), a pattern similar to American culture.

Earlier in this section, information about Native American cultures noted how the variance of language might influence attitudes and behaviors about sexual identity and behavior. Language influences these processes in all cultures, and is particularly notable among Spanish-speaking cultures. *Machismo, hembrismo,* and *marianísmo* are beliefs of Latino cultures that illustrate gender role differences. Sometimes misinterpreted as male sexual dominance, *machismo* more accurately means "men's prescribed role as breadwinner, reliable father and spouse, and protector of the family" (Arredondo & Perez, 2003, p. 123). Finding roots in the Catholic belief of the Blessed Virgin Mary, *marianísmo* holds that women should demonstrate caring, nurture their families, and lead virtuous lives.

Hembrismo presents the expectation that women fulfill a multitude of roles in and out of the home (Gloria, Ruiz, & Castillo, 2004). Sometimes, adherence to these values is viewed as submissive and passive behavior, which causes conflict for Latinas who attempt to acculturate to American values.

Bacigalupe (2000) emphasized that language plays an important role in defining gender issues for Spanish-speaking cultures. "We are unavoidably immersed in the world of gender characterized by oppositional terms for male and female: *el/ella, eso/esa, el/la*" (Bacigalupe, 2000, p. 34). To make this more challenging, Spanish language applies gender terms to inanimate objects and abstract concepts as well as to people and animals. Bacigalupe (2000) explains, "the ocean and the sky are masculine . . . the earth and writing are feminine" (p. 34). At the same time, there are no terms to define homosexual lifestyles, which emphasizes a dichotomous sexual world "that may preclude the realities of Latino gays in families and couples" (p. 34).

In addition to what we have learned about gender differences by studying various cultures, research continues to discover behavioral differences between genders. These findings offer general views that might be helpful in understanding male and female client behavior, particularly self-concept development.

Gender and Identity

If gender role is a product of societal expectation and cultural tradition, then how individuals perceive these factors, incorporate them into their *self*-view and ultimately their worldview, and act upon this understanding defines their interpretation of feminine and masculine roles. More important, this unique perceptual process helps each person establish a gender identity. All the factors considered thus far in this chapter—biological sex, societal norms, cultural influence, and others—combine with a person's experiences and unique interpretation of those experiences to reach conclusions about gender roles.

Psychological studies have found that the personal conclusions drawn about gender roles are not static (Papalia & Olds, 1992). Rather, they change as persons move through developmental stages and as societal changes occur. For example, researchers have noted that as girls move through adolescence they often exhibit changes in self-confidence and self-worth. Some studies have shown that adolescent girls show a decline in self-esteem. If true, this finding might be explained by gender phenomena, biological influences, or a combination of factors. At the same time, the biological differences between girls and boys, such as structural differences in brain size and functioning and dissimilar hormonal activity, help explain, in part, various cognitive functioning, emotional and physical expression, and problem-solving styles (Papalia & Olds, 1992).

Two social identifiers that interact with a person's decision about gender role are the terms *masculine* and *feminine.* Generally, masculine behaviors and traits are associated with males and feminine characteristics with females. Depending on cultural beliefs and traditions, societies place different values on *femininity* and *masculinity,* and often it is the masculine gender and the male sex that gains preference. As Robinson (2005) explained, "Gender is a status characteristic that manifests in multiple ways throughout society. Males tend to enter into the world as the preferred sex" (p. 151). Although American society has experienced significant change in gender role differences in recent years, many indicators point to continued disparities between men and women, which supports the notion that being male is preferable. As an example, the significant difference between pay for men and women who perform essentially the same work continues across the labor force and in various professions.

Masculine and feminine characteristics are not absolute or definitive qualities. We view these traits on a continuum of characteristics that, at the same time, are influenced by particular situations. Some men, for example, might exhibit a range of emotional expression depending on the circumstance. It is possible, therefore, that an American man might express sincerity and sentimental feelings, typically identified in western culture as more feminine than masculine characteristics, while mourning the loss of a parent. Soon after, this same man might demonstrate competitiveness, dominance, or other masculine traits as the family seeks leadership to make plans for the future. Likewise, females also are capable of incorporating a range of feminine and masculine responses to various situations. Sometimes, a women's use of masculine qualities to help in career advancement is greeted by disparaging remarks, such as "She acts like a man." Similarly, men who embrace feminine qualities are "sissies" or called other unkind names by people who experience discomfort with men who express emotion openly or demonstrate other qualities commonly identified as being more feminine than masculine.

How a person processes social, psychological, and biological factors into formulating a gender identity is a significant part of the developing self-concept. Return to Figure 2.2 presented in Chapter 2, which explains the influence of society and culture on the developing self-concept. Through this figure, we might see how gender identity contributes to *self*-concept development. The diagram illustrates several social and cultural factors and perceptions, including gender, which, depending on their proximity to "My Self," influence a person's *self*-view and, ultimately, the choices related to self-identity. If we adapt that diagram to focus on gender identity and the influence of biological sex, the result might look like Figure 5.1. As with the original diagram (Figure 2.2), the proximity of perceptions and beliefs (the smaller spirals) to the core of the self-concept ("My Self") indicates the power and influence they have. Use Figure 5.1 to complete Exercise 5.3.

Ultimately, a person's perception about sex, gender roles, and masculine and feminine characteristics interact with her or his biological makeup to influence decisions about sexuality and acceptance of one's sexual orientation. This is a momentous process with implications for self-concept development, social acceptance, and cultural identification.

Sexual Orientation Identity

Every day we learn new scientific research about biological factors that contribute to human behavior. Few behaviors receive more interest, or are more hotly debated in the United States, than those that relate to sexual preference and sexual orientation identity (LeVay & Hamer, 1994; Myers, 2004; Stein, 1999).

Over the years, various theories have attempted to link sexual orientation to mental fitness, family structure and constellations, biological factors such as genetic difference or hormonal imbalance, and unintended learning due to experiences or encounters with

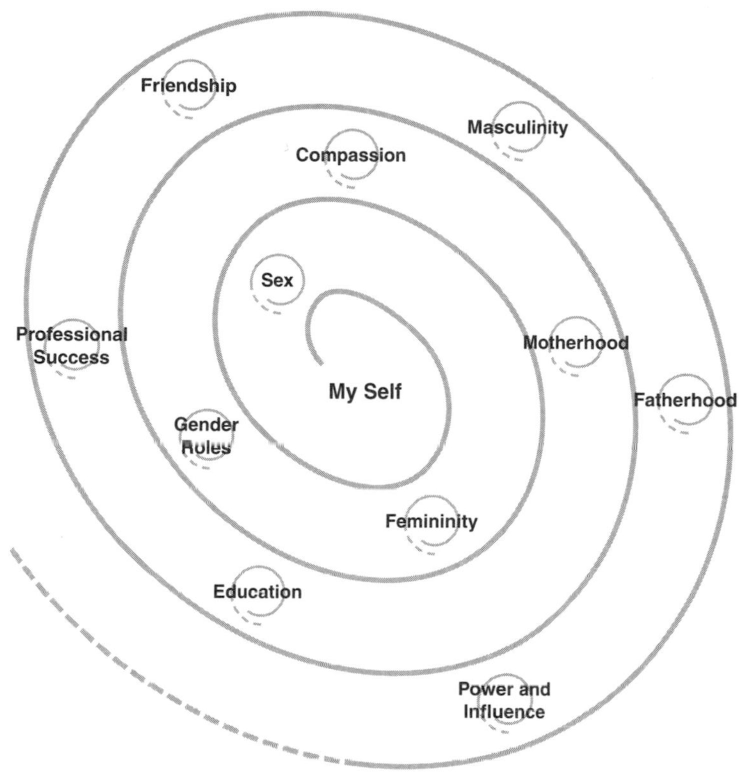

FIGURE 5.1 ***Influence of Sex and Gender Identity on the Self-Concept***

homosexual behavior. Despite volumes of theoretical literature and research reports, no single idea has emerged with a definitive explanation, and no scientific research has produced findings that demonstrate with certainty any specific environmental influences as the determining factors in sexual orientation identity. This lack of certainty is significant because of the debate about helping gay, lesbian, and bisexual people change their sexual orientation and the stress, guilt, and loss that parents and families experience when a child, sibling, or parent comes out. From all the research over the past fifty years and more, no one can say what or how environmental factors influence sexual orientation (Myers, 2004).

Exercise 5.3

Review Figure 5.1. As a counselor or human service professional who might be working with a client exhibiting this self-concept profile, what conclusions would you draw and how would you proceed to help this client if the identified concern is gender confusion? Share your ideas in class discussion.

Theories and Research Findings

The oldest theory, one that related homosexuality to mental illness, was debunked following a classic study by Hooker in 1957. Her study found no support for the belief that homosexuality was linked to mental illness. Hooker's findings, followed by those of other researchers who reached similar conclusions, propelled changes in public opinion and policy, and eventually compelled the American Psychiatric Association (APA) to change its classification of homosexuality as a mental disorder. Today, the APA's latest edition of the *Diagnostic and Statistical Manual of Mental Disorders* (DSM IV-TR) makes no mention of homosexuality (neither gay nor lesbian terms appear in the manual) as a mental disorder to treat (American Psychiatric Association, 2000).

So far, no definitive scientific study has linked sexual orientation to family structure or chance learning. Some preliminary findings suggest a possible link to genetic and hormonal factors, but these results are tentative and, like environmental factors, strongly debated within and outside the scientific community. Yet, continuing research seems to verify a relationship among various biological factors and sexual orientation identity.

Authors often cite the work of LeVay and Hamer to support a biological link to sexual orientation (LeVay, 1993; LeVay & Hamer, 1994). Their initial finding came from LeVay's examination of brain cell clusters taken from sections of the anterior hypothalamus of heterosexual and homosexual people who had died. He discovered that the cell clusters of heterosexual men were consistently larger than they were for women and homosexual men (Myers, 2004). Although critics have noted that some of LeVay's subjects had died of AIDS, which might have affected their brains, subsequent studies of both animal and human subjects have supported the hypothesis that some parts of the brains in heterosexual and homosexual men differ in size (Allen & Gorski, 1992; Myers, 2004).

Scientific studies also suggest that genetics may have a role in sexual orientation. This speculation generally comes from studies of twins, both identical and fraternal, where one or both of the twins were homosexual. Similarly, studies of hormonal activity during the middle trimester of pregnancy indicate some influence of a person's disposition to be attracted to one sex over another (Myers, 2004).

As noted, scientific findings that indicate a possible link to biological factors and sexual orientation are not without critics or controversy. Some researchers, such as Stein (1999), debate whether sexual orientation is simply an "either-or" phenomenon, meaning that it is essentially binary or bipolar in nature. Critics also note that sexual orientation is more complex and even inclusive than some biological researchers might believe.

Today, the general view among researchers and practitioners in the field is that sexual orientation is the outcome of a complex process of interacting biological, social, and personal factors. The process of being heterosexual or homosexual, therefore, is influenced by many variables. Bem (2000) suggested that although biological research seems to overwhelm current literature and findings about sexual orientation identity, developmental understanding of how these factors interact with social and cultural experiences helps to comprehend this vital aspect of the human condition. As the helping professions move toward greater understanding, clear terminology will be helpful.

Terminology

Several terms describe sexual orientation and attitudes about it. *Heterosexuality* is the orientation of being attracted to the opposite sex (female–male) for physical and emotional

FIGURE 5.2 ***An Illustration of Sexual Orientation as a Continuum***

satisfaction. *Homosexuality* is the orientation of being attracted to the same sex (male–male; female–female) for physical and emotional satisfaction. *Bisexuality* is an orientation that includes attraction to both sexes. Robinson (2005) suggested that these categories of sexuality orientation might be on a continuum as illustrated in Figure 5.2. One problem with this illustration is that it seems to define sexual orientation as an absolute quality or condition in every person.

Another perspective might be that sexual orientation results from the multiple factors alluded to earlier, and is guided or influenced by situational and environmental events. Such a perspective might illustrate sexual orientation identity as consisting of overlapping constructs with one dominant point of reference. Figure 5.3 attempts to illustrate this alternate perspective using circles and overlapping areas to denote three interrelated orientations. In this diagram, the size of a particular circle or area represents its prevalence in the person's sexual identity. The illustrations in Figure 5.3 show two clients (A and B) with different sexual orientations. Client A leads a mostly heterosexual lifestyle, yet has strong homosexual leanings, with subsequently bisexual interests. Client B is predominantly homosexual with virtually no bisexuality and limited heterosexual interest.

Among members of the human species, the common orientation is to be heterosexual. Regrettably, this reality too frequently translates into other orientations being described as sinful, unnatural, or disturbed. Some terms that relate to this type of absolute thinking include heterosexism and homophobia. *Heterosexism* is the perception that all persons are heterosexual in their orientation. Therefore, it is the preferred and superior lifestyle. Robinson (2005) noted, "Heterosexism is institutionalized through religion, education, and the media" (p. 188). Heterosexism denies value for other forms of sexual orientation and desire.

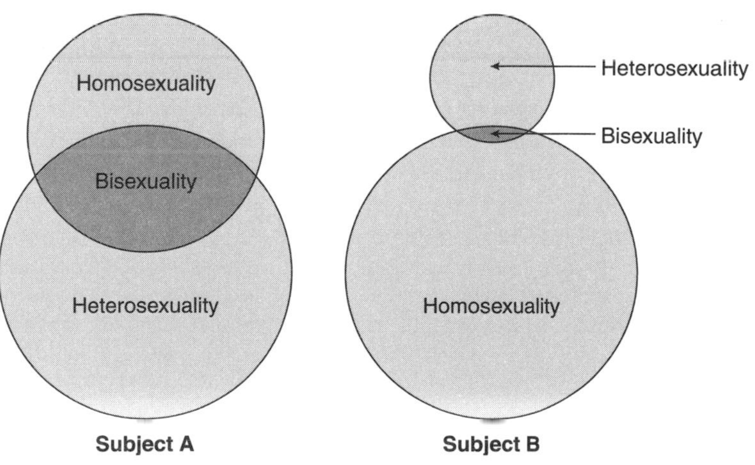

FIGURE 5.3 ***Illustrations of Sexual Orientation as Multiple Perspectives***

Homophobia is a relatively new term in the psychological arena of understanding sexual orientation. People described as homophobic express irrational fears about people who exhibit signs of accepting or using behaviors related to same-sex forms of sexual desire and orientation. Because heterosexism and homophobia have had such devastating effects on people with divergent sexual orientations, new terms have emerged, particularly during the feminist movement, to describe and differentiate sexual preferences and orientations (Robinson, 2005). As an example, *lesbian* (derived from the Greek island of Lesbos where the poet Sappho wrote verses about women) is often preferred by homosexual women to describe their lifestyle.

Sexual Orientation Identity and Development Models

Typically, heterosexual people do not think much about their sexual identity or development due to societal assumptions about "normal" behavior (Fassinger, 2000). Nevertheless, the early work of Sigmund Freud (1946) and Erik Erikson (1968) among others either relegated same-sex behaviors to unhealthy lifestyles or ignored them altogether. More recently, some researchers and theorists, such as Eliason (1995) and Sullivan (1998), have outlined stages and processes to describe heterosexual orientation identity. As with other aspects of *self*-identity, the process of recognizing and accepting one's sexual orientation has attributes and behaviors that can be understood by using stages of development. Building on earlier models and research, Worthington, Savoy, Dillon, and Vernaglia (2002) proposed a multidimensional model of heterosexual identity development that considers combined biological, psychological, and social influences. The model

> distinguishes two parallel, reciprocal processes: (a) an individual sexual identity process involving recognition and acceptance of, and identification with, one's sexual needs, values, sexual orientation and preferences for activities, partner characteristics, and modes of sexual expression and (b) a social identity process involving the recognition of oneself as a member of a group of individuals with similar sexual identities . . . and attitudes toward sexual minorities. (p. 510)

Six biopsychosocial influences in heterosexual identity development described by Worthington and colleagues (2002) include (1) biology, (2) systemic homonegativity, sexual prejudice, and privilege, (3) culture, (4) microsocial context, (5) religious orientation, and (6) gender norms and socialization. At the same time, this model considers multiple dimensions within the two processes of *individual identity* and *social identity* mentioned earlier. Dimensions in the individual identity process are:

> (a) identification and awareness of one's sexual needs, (b) adoption of personal sexual values, (c) awareness of preferred sexual activities, (d) awareness of preferred characteristics of sexual partners, (e) awareness of preferred modes of sexual expression, and (f) recognition and identification with sexual orientation. (Worthington et al., 2002, p. 512)

Dimensions in the social identity process include (1) group membership identity and (2) attitudes toward sexual minorities. Furthermore, this model suggests that individual and social identity process these dimensions according to five statuses or stages experienced by the person: (a) unexplored commitment, (b) active exploration, (c) diffusion, (d) deepening and commitment, and (e) synthesis. According to the authors, "the model should be thought of as flexible, fluid descriptions of statuses that people may pass through as they develop their sexual identity" (Worthington et al., 2002, p. 512). Figure 5.4 illustrates the parallel processes, biopsychosocial influences, dimensions, and statuses of the multidimensional model of heterosexual orientation identity (Worthington et al., 2002).

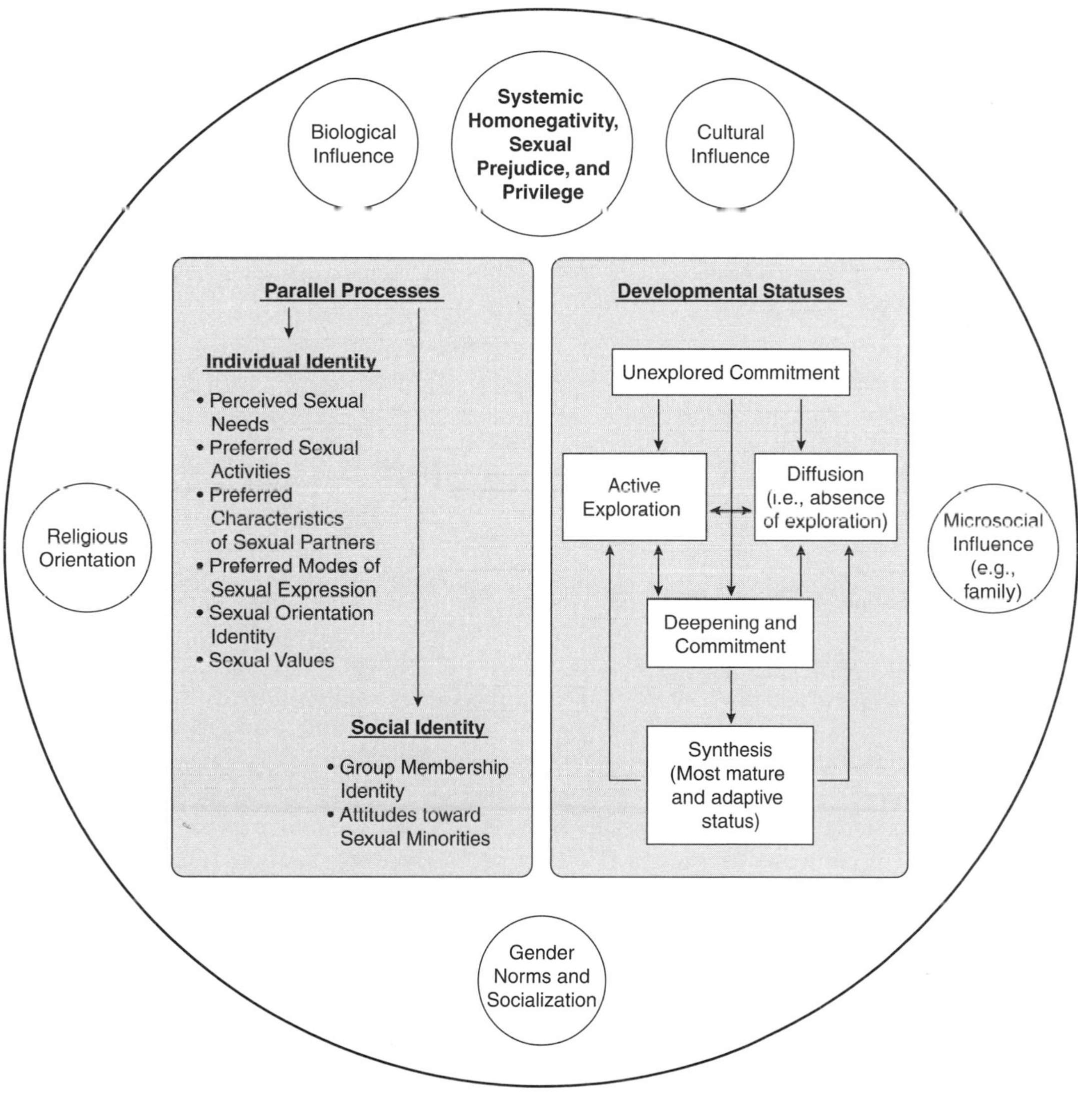

FIGURE 5.4 ***Multidimensional Model of Heterosexual Orientation Identity***

Source: Adapted from Worthington, R. L., Savoy, H. B., Dillon, F. R., & Vernaglia, E. R. (2002). Heterosexual identity development: A mutidimensional model of individual and social identity. *The Counseling Psychologist, 30,* 496–531.

Persons who have *come out*—meaning that they have accepted and announced their homosexuality—identify themselves as *gay,* and some developmental models of homosexual orientation identity have appeared in the literature over the past several decades. Cass's (1979, 1984) model of gay identity formation is one (Baruth & Manning, 1999; Robinson, 2005). According to this model, a person generally processes six stages of development. Some people, however, remain stuck at particular stages, while others regress to earlier stages or skip stages to move to new levels of understanding and accepting their sexual orientation and identity. Other models of sexual identity also use stage theory, and three examples are briefly presented here:

Coleman's Model (1982). This is a five-stage model that presents social pressures inherent in the different stages of development. The stages include pre-coming out, coming out, exploration, first relationships, and integration.

Morales's Model (1989). A five-stage model, this theory suggests an identity process for racial and ethnic minorities who are also gay or lesbian persons. The stages include denial of conflicts, bisexual versus gay/lesbian, conflicts in allegiances, establishing priorities in allegiance, and integrating various communities.

Troiden's Model (1989). This theory suggests a four-stage model that includes sensitization, identity confusion, identity assumption, and commitment.

In addition to general models of homosexual identity development mentioned above, some theorists have presented stage models specifically for understanding lesbian development (Falco, 1991; McCarn & Fassinger, 1996; Sophie, 1985). The following descriptions offer brief summaries of stages of homosexual identity development as gleaned from various models presented or mentioned above. It is a composite view identifying five possible stages of development.

Awareness and Confusion. A person moves into initial stages of sexual development with many unanswered questions about his or her sexuality. However, information about heterosexuality and homosexuality seems pertinent to the individual. As this information becomes more personally relevant, the individual faces increasing confusion and a lack of congruency in life. Some behaviors associated with this stage of development might be inhibition, denial, and expression of innocence regarding certain homosexual-type encounters. For example, a person might disavow a particular homosexual encounter or experience by redefining the behavior within the context it was exhibited. Robinson (2005) offered these examples of such rationalization: "I was just experimenting," and "It was an accident" (p. 194). Other behavior observed during early stages might be serious inquiry into homosexuality as an initial step to learn about sexual orientation. Such behavior might move the person toward the next stage of development.

Identity Comparison and Group Association. At this stage, the person begins to explore the possibility of being gay. He or she moves from self-criticism and denial toward dealing with social isolation, alienation, and hostility from family members, peers, and associates. The person recognizes the existence of varying sexual orientations and might begin associating with gay or lesbian people. At the same time, the person faces an uncertain future by giving up a heterosexual lifestyle, which encompasses many traditions including marriage and raising a family.

Tolerance and Group Identification. The person comes to accept the likelihood that he or she is a homosexual and begins to appreciate the challenge of satisfying personal, social, and sexual desires. The person also begins to seek relationships with other gay/lesbian people and moves closer to the gay community for support, camaraderie, and opportunity for intimate relationships.

Identity Acceptance. At this stage of development, gay and lesbian people move from simple tolerance of their homosexuality to genuine acceptance of their sexual orientation. At the same time, persons increase their association with other gays and lesbians and form new attitudes about homosexuality. In some instances, gay persons might withdraw from their relationships and associations with heterosexual people due to the potential stress of facing homophobic attitudes and reactions.

Sexual Satisfaction and Integration. Models of gay/lesbian identification typically indicate the last stage of development is one of achieving self-knowledge and self-satisfaction with one's sexual orientation. Exhibiting pride in the legitimacy of various sexual orientations increases, and combating dichotomous, stereotypical views of sexual orientation helps to synthesize one's identity. At the same time, the gay/lesbian person at this stage of development recognizes that not all heterosexual people are anti-gay. Awareness that many nongays are genuinely accepting of gay lifestyles and actively support the rights of people with different sexual orientations is achieved.

This chapter has presented theoretical perspectives and research findings related to sex, gender, and sexuality as additional social and cultural foundational aspects important to counselors and other helping professionals. As do previous chapters of this text, it concludes with a summary of implications of these perspectives and findings for helping relationships with clients of varied backgrounds.

Counseling Inferences

As with competent practice when working with clients of diverse racial and ethnic backgrounds, successful helpers approach gender issues and sexual identity concerns from a posture of understanding, awareness, and knowledge. A first step is to know one's own inner thoughts, attitudes, biases, and other personal aspects related to gender and gender roles. Examination of or reflection about one's development from childhood into adulthood, including influential family attitudes and biases, is an appropriate place to start. Rigid views of male and female roles or feminine and masculine characteristics could inhibit a counselor of other professional from being an effective helper with clients who do not meet those standards. Understanding the views that guide beliefs and actions is also an essential step. Likewise, taking action to attack and alter misguided notions that might inhibit the formation of healthy, productive helping relationships is paramount to becoming a proficient practitioner who can assist a wide range of clients.

Reflection and understanding of one's attitudes about gender issues and roles is complemented by ongoing study and informed knowledge of research findings about sex differences. This text barely scratches the surface of this issue. More informed study is required. Although counselors and other professional helpers are not biological scientists, it is nevertheless important to stay abreast of pertinent research findings, so they are better informed to answer clients' questions and offer appropriate resources for further client inquiry.

The combined understanding of attitudes about gender and gender roles and knowing about general scientific findings allows professional helpers to appreciate more fully the dynamics between counselors and clients of same and different sexes. Early unchallenged learning and current attitudes and knowledge interact dynamically to influence a counselor's behaviors within every helping relationship. Similarly, a client's background is a fundamental factor in understanding reactions to a helper's verbal and nonverbal behaviors. Considering all this, the final implication according to many authorities and researchers is how accurately and genuinely a counselor or other helper demonstrates empathic understanding toward each client (Robinson, 2005). This factor—empathy—seems to cross all configurations of same-sex and different-sex helping relationships.

Inferences for working with clients who are dealing with issues of sexual orientation begin with the similar refrains of understanding one's beliefs and attitudes about heterosexual and homosexual behavior. At the same time, counselors and other helpers must be aware of, and comfortable with, their own sexuality. It is hard to imagine a professional who has not moved beyond the entry stages of his or her own sexual identity being successful in helping a young man or woman process feelings, awareness, acknowledgment, and acceptance of his or her sexual development.

The following are some additional thoughts about working with clients about their sexual orientation or sexuality:

- Create a safe and accepting relationship where clients feel secure to share intimate thoughts and feelings.
- Acknowledge clients' confusion about sexual identity and encourage them to explore that confusion as well as their fears and misconceptions about homosexuality.
- When clients acknowledge their homosexuality, help them work through the potential loss of relationships with heterosexual family members and friends, who might be intolerant of their coming out. Grief accompanies all loss in life, but through counseling and other interventions, clients can learn to accept unwanted changes by celebrating new beginnings.
- Prepare homosexual clients for the challenges they will face in a society that remains largely intolerant of different sexual orientations. This reality cuts across many cultural groups and nationalities. Search for strategies to help these clients achieve beneficial social experiences.
- Encourage all clients to create healthy relationships with people of different genders, diverse views of gender roles, and varied sexual orientations. Actively support community programs and other systems that benefit gays and lesbians in overcoming social barriers and fighting injustice.

As noted in this chapter, sex, gender, and sexual orientation identity are important factors in understanding self-concept development. These essential characteristics, particularly gender, are influenced by family and culture, which the next chapter considers.

6

Family, Culture, and Self-Concept Development

A common characteristic among different societies and cultural groups is that children are born into families. Barring tragic circumstances, a newborn's family usually consists of at least a birth mother. Often, families include other relatives such as fathers, possibly siblings, grandparents, aunts, uncles, and others. Cultural variation influences family structure across the globe, but a child's entry into this world assuredly includes membership and involvement with some identified group. As Baldwin (1993) noted, "Even the most incorrigible maverick has to be born somewhere. He may leave the group that produced him—he may be forced to—but nothing will efface his origins, the marks of which he carries with him everywhere" (p. 10).

Each society and culture places particular importance and significance on unique family beliefs and traditions. Variation in family structure and traditional roles of mothers and fathers, as well as roles of extended family members, are as numerous as world cultures themselves. For example, the United States prides itself on "family values." Yet, when compared with global cultures these values are often juxtaposed to other commonly held worldviews. As one example, Walsh (2003) explained, "In many cultures, it is still expected that a brother will marry the widow of a deceased husband" to carry on the family name and heritage (p. 11). Differences in aspects of childrearing also exist. Helms and Cook (1999) observed that psychodynamic theories of development used by professional counselors and other therapists rely on mostly individualistic views and "an invariant age-appropriate sequence of development" (p. 142). Furthermore, they noted that research across global cultures indicates many cultures "do not traverse the lifespan in the same manner" suggested by psychodynamic views and stage theories (p. 142). Two examples cited by Helms and Cook (1999) are reports from Chinese and West Indian graduate students that toilet training of children is not a major developmental issue as it sometimes appears in American culture, as well as information that some African newborns are weaned from breast feeding three months earlier than observed in typical Anglo-American families (Triandis, 1994). Consequently, what many Americans often perceive as "normal" in their view of family structure and function is different from what other cultures and societies might accept. Likewise, what other cultures accept as normal in family descriptions and processes vary as much as the number of cultures observed across the globe.

Exercise 6.1

Searching for Families

Instructions: Review the list of group structures and mark those you believe constitute a family. Be prepared to give your rationale for including or excluding particular structures.

Group	*Family* (Yes or No)
Unrelated teenage boys living in a group home with a house parent	________
A gay couple and the son of one partner	________
Children living in an orphanage	________
Orphaned sisters and brothers living in the same house without older adult supervision	________
Orphaned sisters and brothers living in different houses	________
A runaway teenage girl living with two lesbians	________
A grandmother and two of her grandchildren with other unrelated children in the home	________
Two elderly unmarried people living together	________

Cultural and ethnic beliefs are influential factors in family processes and subsequently in a person's self-concept development. These beliefs provide congruency of social order. Families communicate these values, passing them down to each new member throughout the history of the society, culture, and ethnic group to which the family belongs and associates. At the same time, cultural and ethnic groups affirm certain values about families, thus reinforcing what families teach. In McGoldrick's (2003) words, "Ethnicity refers to a group's common ancestry through which its individuals have evolved shared values and customs. It is deeply tied to the family through which its is transmitted over generations, and it is reinforced—and at times invalidated—by the surrounding community" (p. 236). Exercise 6.1 presents several group structures to consider and decide whether they meet your definition of family.

Appreciating and knowing your cultural values regarding family structure, beliefs, and traditions are significant to understanding your self-concept development. By the same token, knowledge and understanding of dissimilar cultural beliefs about family structure and function provide a starting point to learn about the diverse views various clients might bring to counseling and other helping relationships. This chapter explores family structure and function as social and cultural foundations of *self*-development and ultimately of counseling and human services. As with earlier chapters, this chapter examines family as a foundational influence within the context of culture and self-concept theory. We begin with a discussion of family structure.

Family Structure

When we consider family structure, cultural influence plays an important role in deciding what is typical or normal. Often, the standard used in the United States and other Western cultures is a traditional description of mother and father as authority figures who guide their children by setting appropriate example regarding gender roles, sexual relationships, work ethic, religious practice, and other behavior. This yardstick for measuring family structure, however, does not hold up across global cultures. As Helms and Cook (1999) indicated, a single standard no longer satisfies the complexity and variance of family structures in the United States. For example, they pointed to earlier authors, such as Tafoya (1989) and Boyd-Franklin (1989), who highlighted aspects of Native American, African American, and West Indian families that differ from what some people mistakenly refer to as traditional family structure and values. As such, multigenerational families, non-kin boarders, children living with relatives outside their birth family, and other facets of family structure exist in various cultures around the world as well as within the United States and other Western societies.

In attempting to convey what is typical or normal family structure, Walsh (2003) noted, "definitions of normality are socially constructed, influenced by subjective world-views and by the larger culture" (p. 4). Therefore, acceptable family features, as with other social and cultural factors that influence self-concept development, are largely determined by cultures, particularly by dominant groups within societies. Consequently, as individuals within cultures develop *self*-views and incorporate them into a broader worldview, they accept the notion of a "normal family structure" based on a conceptualization of *family* rooted in their social and personal belief systems.

What do we know about family structure, particularly in the United States? Review of literature and research indicates a variety of family structures comprised of different factors (Gladding, 2002; Hetherington & Kelly, 2002; Midgley & Hughes, 1997; Papalia & Olds, 1992; Reynolds, 2005; Robinson, 2005; Walsh, 2003). In addition, data about other social trends indicate ongoing change related to family structure. The following is a sample of findings:

- In twenty-first century United States, dual earners comprise over two-thirds of all two-parent families. Less than 20 percent of U.S. families fit the traditional image of husband as the sole wage earner.
- During the past 20 years, the number of single adults has nearly doubled. In the mid-1990s, over 24 million people in the United States lived alone, and the forecast is for that number to increase to more than 30 million by the end of this decade.
- Single-parent families are more common today. The divorce rate escalated in the 1970s with about 50 percent of marriages breaking up. Although that rate shows some signs of stabilizing, single parents manage approximately one-third of the households in the United States.
- Although research findings are inconsistent, it appears that an overwhelming majority of children from divorced families do fairly well in their development.
- Single mothers lead 25 percent of all U.S. households, with over half of African American families headed by single mothers.
- Remarried families, including stepfamilies, merged families, blended families, and other forms of remarriages, have become the "norm" in U.S. society. Three out of four people who divorce eventually will remarry.
- Today's young couples are postponing marriage and childrearing. Cohabitation among young couples before they marry exists more than 50 percent of the time. Yet, such couples are more likely to divorce than couples that do not cohabitate before marriage.

- Although the United States remains a leader in teenage pregnancy, the rate has declined in recent years. A disproportionate number of pregnant teens comes from disenfranchised, impoverished, and minority populations. About 90 percent of pregnant teenagers initially choose to keep their babies. Yet, the demands of parenting and harsh economic realities often prove so pressing that these young parents often are overwhelmed, and the child eventually enters a state's foster care system.
- Adoptive families are on the rise as are same-sex families. Data suggest that gay and lesbian partners have more education and higher income than heterosexual couples.
- Grandparents are frequently the primary caregivers for young children.
- No shortage of myths exists about the ideal family life or the best family structure.
- In family counseling and therapy, the terms *functional* and *dysfunctional* have replaced *normal* and *abnormal* to describe family structure and relationships.
- Socioeconomic factors continue to have tremendous impact on diverse cultures and family structure. Economically impoverished families tend to be larger, maternally led, and rely on assistance from relatives. In contrast, affluent families tend to be smaller, are led by educated and/or professional parents, and frequently rely on hired help to care for children and manage the home.

The factors listed above are a few examples of the conditions and characteristics that affect family structure and function. To appreciate how these factors influence family life and individual *self*-development, it may be helpful to examine your own family structure. Exercise 6.2 asks a series of questions. Answer them as honestly as you are able, and if comfortable, share your responses with a classmate.

Numerous cultural values such as time orientation, relationship with the environment, personal relationships, views about the nature of humankind, and preferred modes

Exercise 6.2

My Family

Instructions: Respond to as many questions as you are able to answer. When finished, share and compare your responses with a classmate. In the larger group, discuss the different structures and their impact on self-development that emerged from this exercise.

1. When you were born, who was already in your family?
2. How old were your parents when you were born?
3. If you have siblings, where is your position among them?
4. When you were born, had either of your parents been married before? Do you have half- or step-siblings?
5. Did any changes in family structure occur after you were born? If so, what and when?
6. Who was (were) the wage earner(s) in your family?
7. When you were born, what was the physical and emotional health of your parents?
8. What role does religion or spirituality play in your family?
9. Name at least three values/beliefs that you hold today and can attribute to your family.
10. Growing up, what do you recall about the wealth and comfort of your family?

of functioning are essential values for counselors and other professional helpers to consider and understand about themselves and families who seek services. The next section summarizes some familiar differences across cultural and ethnic groups.

Family and Culture

According to Steigerwald (2003), "The family is the vehicle that both carries culture forward to the next generation and teaches values, prejudices, worldviews, and cultural identity" (p. 213). Therefore, a person's consideration of many of the identity variables presented thus far in this text is greatly influenced by family attitudes, beliefs, and biases. As people perceive events, experience circumstances, and screen these experiences in forming conclusions about their self-view and worldview, family influence acts as an important filter in the screening process. The degree to which a person accepts or rejects the influence of family contributes to the harmony or tension with family life and to the ease with which a person moves through developmental processes. Diverse clients as well as clients from the dominant culture deal with the reality of family influence.

The United States consists of seemingly countless cultural groups, each of which has differences in family structure and/or functioning. This section attempts to provide a brief summary of differences noted in the literature about various family groups. When considering racial, gender, or ethnic differences reported in the literature, counselors, human service professionals, and other helpers are cautious not to generalize findings too precisely for particular clients simply because they come from certain cultural or ethnic groups. These summaries offer a general understanding of how family structure and function might vary across diverse populations. Individual clients who have a particular national, cultural, or ethnic heritage may or may not reflect these generalized findings.

The cultures highlighted here do not give just coverage to the diverse global cultures and families that exist throughout the United States and world. Variations found among European American families, for example, such as those with Italian, Greek, German, Spanish, Norwegian, Hungarian, Polish, or other heritage, could not be given fair treatment in this brief summary. Similarly, Asian American families include a wide variance of nationalities and cultures such as Cambodian, Chinese, Japanese, Asian Indian, Korean, Vietnamese, and Pacific Islander. In addition, the family differences found within identified cultural groups may be as significant, if not more so, than differences between groups. We cannot overemphasize this point. *Generalization across cultural groups is risky and, at best, only provides a starting point to ask clients to disclose perceptions about their heritage, background, and family life.* With this caveat in mind, the following sections briefly consider the following family groups: African American, Arab American, Asian American, European American, Jewish American, Latino/Hispanic American, and Native American families.

African American Families

Diversity of structure, customs, and traditions within African American families is probably as great as any common thread we might find among them. Nevertheless, one similarity that many African American families continue to share is the heritage of slavery that brought their ancestors to the United States by force, and a dark skin tone that differentiates them from the dominant White society (Gladding, 2002). These two factors have contributed to historic racial discrimination faced by most if not all Black families and to related social and economic disadvantages placed on them.

A common characteristic of African American families reported in the literature is frequent occurrence of female-led households (Wilson, Kohn, & Lee, 2000). Also, multigenerational families are common and often a response to economic challenges. Multilayered families frequently include members who are not necessarily blood relatives, but they offer extended family structures that permit "an elastic kinship-based exchange network that may last a lifetime" (Robinson, 2005, p. 240). This type of extended family structure reflects in some ways the slave heritage of establishing networks of support to survive, communicate, educate, and nurture related and unrelated members of the community.

Social and economic changes have had a profound effect on the African American family. On one hand, the success of the civil rights movement of the 1960s led to educational and employment opportunities for some, which provided increased choices in housing and other opportunities for upward social mobility. On the other hand, however, a large segment of the African American community continues to face oppressive poverty and continuing racism that inhibit them from taking advantage of these new-found opportunities (Gladding, 2002). High birth rates among single women, a large number of failed marriages, exposure to violent crimes, particularly physical assaults and male homicides, are other factors that have a negative impact on African American families (Robinson, 2005; Wilson, Kohn, & Lee, 2000). Still, countless accounts exist of African American families that have survived and flourished despite oppressive circumstances. As one example, Muhyiddin Shakoor, a counselor educator and family therapist, revealed in his biographical summary, "My sister, brother, and I always stood out because of how we were raised. We were poor in terms of dollars, rich inside ourselves. We were always clean and cared for and told that any one of us could be the pride of the entire nation of black people or even the entire human race" (DeLucia-Waack & Donigian, 2004, p. 80).

Strengths of African American families begin with the kinship bonds of sisterhood and brotherhood that include, as noted earlier, both unrelated and related members. Spirituality and strong religious affiliation and participation are also important characteristics. African American families look toward their churches for social resources and support as well as spiritual guidance. Another legacy of slavery in African American families is their adaptability across different roles without regard to traditional gender roles embraced by the dominant culture. In addition, cooperation and collaboration, motivation to achieve, work orientation, and attitudes about nurturing children are other strengths noted in the research of African American families (Gladding, 2002).

Arab American Families

Families of Arab heritage migrate to the United States from many parts of the world and represent a multiracial and multiethnic group with some common cultural identities and similar language. As Erickson and Al-Timimi (2004) observed, "Arab countries are those that share a common culture and speak Arabic as a primary language" (p. 235). These countries occupy areas referred to as the Arabian peninsula, the Middle East, and Maghreb (or Magrib) (Hejleh, 2003).

Erickson and Al-Timimi (2004) noted three separate waves of Arab migration to the United States, each having its own distinct characteristics, and reflecting particular cultural experiences. From the late 1800s to the beginning of World War I, Arab immigrants came from the areas now known as the countries of Syria and Lebanon. Consisting of mostly Christians who were merchants and farmers, these people moved to cities in the Northeastern and Midwestern areas of the United States After the state of Israel formed in 1948, another movement found many Palestinian refugees and other Arab immigrants also coming to urban areas of this country. A third wave began after the Arab-Israeli war ended in 1967 and it continues to the present day. This movement includes more Muslim people who have migrated across the United States settling into towns and cities from coast to coast. According to Erickson and Al-Timimi (2004), "Immigrants in the third wave have experienced a more negative reception and have assimilated into mainstream society less than those of the previous waves" (p. 235).

Although the heterogeneity of Arab Americans is understood from their broad regional representation, some common family values exist. As in other cultures, the family is central to a person's development, with honor and respect holding high value. Putting family welfare over individual interests is expected, and work, educational achievement, frugality, and conservative values reflect positively on the family. Extended family structure is an important aspect of Arab cultures and family influence on individual members is lifelong (Abraham, 1995). Financial and moral support for the eldest child is common through school and into the start of a career. Afterward, the eldest child supports the next sibling, and this process of one helping the next continues through the youngest in the family. Grown children have responsibility for caring for their parents and elderly relatives (Abudabbeh & Nydell, 1993). Erickson and Timimi (2004) summarized many other characteristics of Arab American families from a wide number of sources. The following paragraphs describe characteristics pertaining to marriage, family ties, and parenting.

Marriage. Arranged marriages remain common among Arab cultures, but Islamic beliefs allow women to decline potential mates proposed by their families (Abraham, 1995; Abudabbeh, 1996). Family reputation and social status are important variables in proposing marriage partners, and finding a good match along religious affiliation, educational attainment, family reputation, and social status is the goal. Social interaction between males and females is often limited, so using community sources to verify potential marriage partners is common.

Family Ties. As noted, family ties are strong and last a lifetime. Commitment to family supersedes all others, including personal goals such as career development. Separation from family can be very difficult and bring on severe loneliness (Jackson, 1997). After children marry, they often continue to rely on their family for emotional support, sometimes more so than they depend on their spouse (Abudabbeh & Nydell, 1993).

Parenting. Arab parents tend to use authoritarian methods of child-rearing and maintain high expectations for their children, which include adherence to traditional practices and customs followed by the family. Parental influence over every aspect of a child's development from childhood friendships through dating and career choices is the norm and parents will voice strong opposition and disapproval about choices contrary to family wishes and values.

Among Arab Americans who follow the teachings of Islam, not only is family a fundamental unit of society, but also women hold an essential role (Roald, 2001). As such, in Arab American families men, women, and children work together for the common good and protection of all family members. Roald (2001) explained, "The importance for men and women of staying together is rooted in my conviction that in much research and thought about 'male' versus 'female', there is a tendency to forget the third party which is the child. In order to build a sound family and sound society all parts have to fulfill their duties and thereby obtain their rights" (p. xi). At the same time, Islamic law and other sources emphasize the prominent position of family life, and "the Muslim woman has been regarded as the most essential member of the family, the protection of women's traditional role has been one of the main topics of Islamist literature, particularly from the early nineteenth century" (Roald, 2001, p. xi).

Among followers of Islam and researchers of this religion, an understanding of the roles of family and various family members is a challenge. In large part, this challenge comes from the various interpretations of the *hadiths,* narratives that relate the deeds and utterances of the Prophet, Mohammed. Due to different interpretations of these narratives, various meaning is often derived about a wife's obedience to husband, men as caretakers of women, physical punishment of women, and division of labor (Roald, 2001). "The greatest challenge Muslims face in a changing world is, in my view, to find ways of dealing with the vast hadith literature. How should hadiths be understood? . . . The new age of Muslims, I predict, promises a new vision with regard to many aspects of its creed—especially with respect to women" (Roald, 2001, p. 302).

Asian American Families

As noted in an earlier chapter of this text, grouping Asian cultures under one heading is unfair at best. So many variations exist among Asian groups, including Pacific Islanders, revealing wide differences in language, heritage, and economic power. Despite the range of nationalities and cultures, literature and research provide consistent (and perhaps stereotypical) views of shared cultural and family values for Asian Americans. These values include general respect for elders, family loyalty and extended support, and high value on education (Olson, 2000). In addition, Asian American families tend to emphasize hierarchical relationships, self-discipline, family over individual needs, connectedness of relationships, social etiquette, modesty, patience, emotional restraint, spirituality, and harmonious living (DeLucia-Waack & Donigian, 2004; Gladding, 2002; Wilson, Kohn, & Lee, 2000).

Traditional Asian families typically show extended groups with fathers usually assuming leadership roles. Sometimes sons are more honored and valued than daughters (Ho, 1987). Respect and honor to the family is paramount such that deviant behavior, academic failure, poor work habits, and other misdeeds bring shame on the entire family. Three dominant relationships stressed within traditional Asian families are father–son, husband–wife, and elder–younger sibling relationships. Strong feelings of authority and obligation define all these relationships. As Daya Sandhu, an Asian Indian and counselor educator, wrote of his family, "My father's authority is absolute even now when he is 83 years old. . . . Communication patterns have always been vertical from top to bottom. . . . Even at age 58, I have not dared to confront my father" (DeLucia-Waack & Donigian, 2004, p. 77).

Some research suggests differences in how Asian American families process difficult problems and challenging situations. Emotional restraint and pragmatic problem-solving strategies are more often the norm than are confrontation and exploration of feelings. Individual family members suppress their emotions to gain harmony and mediate or negotiate solutions, which Asian Americans consider more important to family functioning than open expression of feelings (Wilson, Kohn, & Lee, 2000).

For Asian families who migrate to the United States, some changes in traditional views and values take place. As subsequent generations of Asian Americans move into mainstream society, there may be a shift in family function and values. The mobility of American society has meant that many families have moved apart, including Asian American families (Gladding, 2002). Such changes have had an impact on the traditional values of obedience and family loyalty with corresponding and increasing focus on individual needs and development. At the same time, Asian families have had to deal with a rise in deviant behaviors including drug and alcohol abuse as well as relationship issues such as interracial marriages (Mercado, 2000; Wang, 1994).

Changes in traditional family beliefs have implications for counseling issues and concerns of self-concept development and cultural identity for many Asian Americans. The former choices of finding a satisfactory place in American society by either retaining one's ethnic culture, family, and community or shunning one's ethnicity by adopting the culture, values, and viewpoints of the dominant Anglo-American group are no longer the only options. Spickard (2000) highlighted the increasing trend of people with mixed heritage of Asian, American, or other ancestry choosing to process and embrace multiple identities. The research suggests that "the choice of a biracial identity is, for most mixed people, a healthier one than being forced to make an artificial choice" (Spickard, 2000, p. 265). Family support in this process is essential.

European American Families

People identified in the literature as having European background claim heritage from several countries spanning the British Isles through Central and Eastern Europe. Some of the countries include Albania, Armenia, Belarus, Czech Republic, Denmark, England, Estonia, Finland, France, Germany, Greece, Hungary, Ireland, Italy, Norway, Poland, Russia, Scotland, Spain, and Turkey to name a few. Reflected in these many nationalities is a wide span of language, customs, cultural beliefs, religions, and family structures and functions. Therefore, when we use the term *European American,* it encompasses a large group of people and numerous cultures. Such diversity, as with the other groups presented in this section, makes generalizing about European American families a risky process.

In a period of U.S. history from the early 1800s to the early to mid 1900s, millions of people migrated to America. At the start of this migration, most immigrants to the United States came from western and northern Europe, but later, Italian families and other southern European groups arrived. After World War II, German and Polish immigration increased significantly. Since the end of the twentieth century, the fall of communism in the former Soviet Union, and the rebellion and conflict in parts of eastern Europe, increased migration from Russia and other republics that were once part of the Soviet Union as well as from war-torn regions of eastern Europe has occurred (Baruth & Manning, 1999; Richmond, 2003).

Richmond (2003) stated that each European group that came to the United States during all the years of immigration up to the present day "sought to integrate within the American culture . . . but it was not easy" (p. 135). New immigrants faced the wrath of settlers who came before them. People who arrived in search of a better life in what they thought was a land of plenty often found themselves without suitable housing, impoverished, and shunned by mainstream society. "Prejudice against each new nationality ran rampant" (Richmond, 2003, p. 136).

While difficult to give uniform descriptions of European American families, some traditional beliefs cross an array of cultures and nationalities. For example, Baruth and Manning (1999) noted common beliefs such as "preference being shown to boys, expectations for girls to perform household duties, and expectations of both genders to show strong support and concern for the family" (p. 221). At the same time the authors observed, "the success or welfare of the family is more important than the welfare of the individual" and children follow commands of authority figures (p. 221). Other values often attributed to European Americans include independence, exploration, and self-control. However, variance among families of European ancestry precludes any clear description of common family values, particularly ones that are maintained after families settle in the United States and begin adapting and adjusting to American culture.

Because the diversity of European American families is broad, counselors and other professional helpers consider several factors when working with individuals or families. Some factors might include the following (Baruth & Manning, 1999; Richmond, 2003):

- How recently the family or individual immigrated to the United States
- Number of generations the family has lived in the United States
- How closely the individual or family identifies with and practices cultural/ethnic traditions
- Language spoken at home
- Attitudes about *self*-development, minority groups, cultural heritage, religious beliefs, and other values that influence gender roles and family living

Jewish American Families

In a critique of the counseling profession's relationship with Jewish counselors, Weinrach (2002) wrote, "Jews, especially in America, by all outward appearances, have thrived and been exempt from many of the stressors associated with minority status. As with other minorities, their problems are rooted, in part, in oppression, although Jews in twenty-first century America typically do not encounter oppression in ways similar to some other minority groups" (p. 300). However, Jews were one of the earliest groups to experience religious discrimination in the new colonies due to an English law passed in 1250 that banned them from British land (Richmond, 2003). In the mid-1600s, a persuasive Dutch rabbi convinced the British government to allow Jews to settle in the New World, in part for religious reasons but also to capitalize on the knowledge of Jewish merchants to build commerce with the emerging colonies. As Richmond (2003) recounted, Jewish families settled in Boston, Massachusetts; Newport, Rhode Island; and New Amsterdam, which became New York City after the British takeover from the Dutch.

Early Jewish American families had historical roots in Spain and Portugal, starting congregations from New England to Charleston, South Carolina. During this period and through the revolutionary war, many prominent Jewish families established themselves in America (Richmond, 2003). In the 1800s, with anti-Semitism escalating in Europe, particularly in Germany, many Jewish families migrated to the United States. The newly arrived German Jews did not have the economic status of colonial Jewish settlers, and neither did the other Jews of the larger society accept them. Nevertheless, by establishing themselves as dealers and sellers of clothing, jewelry, and household wares, these merchants began to build a culture for themselves in America. Richmond (2003) reported that although these peddlers did not make much money, they started businesses that later "would emerge as department stores such as Macy's, Bloomingdale's, and the Hecht Company" (p. 137). Still, there was friction between their form of Judaism and the Orthodox Jews.

In the mid-1800s and through the early 1900s, another wave of Jewish immigrants came from Eastern Europe, particularly from war-torn countries such as Lithuania, Latvia, Poland, Romania, and Russia. These immigrants were poorer than the earlier two waves of Jewish settlers, spoke Yiddish, a different language, and came to the U.S. in greater number than either the Spanish or German Jews migration. During the later 1900s and into this twenty-first century, Jewish families migrated from the former Soviet Union. This migration resulted from a poor economic situation after the fall of communism and increasing anti-Semitism in Russia (Baruth & Manning, 1999).

Today, Jewish American families represent these various eras of immigration to the United States. Although many differences exist among these groups, their common bond is a flight from anti-Semitism and religious persecution. Tragically, what united the ancestors of the first three groups of immigrant Jews in the 1900s was the horrific Holocaust against all Jewish people by Adolf Hitler and the German Nazis. As Weinrach (2002) noted, however, this attempt at extermination "was only one recent chapter in a long history of malice, or worse, toward Jews" (p. 302). He recounted numerous events throughout the ages that "have marked the world's hatred of Jews" (p. 302), including enslavement, destruction of temples, expulsion from various countries, and countless executions and massacres throughout Europe and the Middle East. It is this history of exclusion, expulsion, and execution that influences Jewish family life today.

The combined legacy of anti-Semitism and common stereotypic behavior and attitudes of people toward Jews has an impact on family function as well as individual development. At the same time, Jewish American traditions and practices have been affected by generational differences, interfaith marriage, and family mobility among other factors (Hartman & Hartman, 1999). Although the range of Jewish American beliefs and customs is broad, some characteristics of typical Jewish identity include the following:

- A sense of belonging and attachment to Jewish people and a differentiation from non-Jews.
- Informal and formal association and interaction among Jewish friends, associates, and other social networks. These networks and associations share characteristics common to extended families of other cultural groups.
- A shared history of rejection, exclusion, oppression, and extermination.

- Use of distinctive languages in religious ceremonies and social interactions (e.g., Yiddish or revived Hebrew).
- Attention to the importance of kosher food in family traditions and religious beliefs.
- Emphasis on education in personal development.
- Use of humor in understanding and dealing with life's events.

Jewish American families reflect the diversity of differences found across various forms of Jewish faith. Marriage as an institution is highly regarded, and parental roles of both father and mother are important. Orthodox traditions place the father as the head of the family, but in both popular literature and media, the Jewish mother is often portrayed as a dominant family figure. In daily functions, however, gender roles appear to be equitable in typical Jewish families and communities. Cynthia Kolader, a professor of counseling psychology, recalled, "As I grew up, both of my parents were involved in my life. We had family dinners almost nightly; my mom cooked, and my dad cleaned up" (DeLucia-Waack & Donigian, 2004, p. 66).

Latino/Hispanic Families

As a rapidly rising population and culture within the United States, the Latino/Hispanic population could reach over 80 million people within the next half century (Flores, 2000a). People of Latino heritage who trace their roots to Spanish-speaking countries of the Americas, including Puerto Rico, or who have origins among Hispanic people of the United States whose ancestors were either Spanish or Mexican, are establishing families and joining communities throughout the country. As with other cultural groups considered in this chapter, people of Latino/Hispanic backgrounds express wide diversity of beliefs and values about family structure and function. Some generalizations, nevertheless, are reported in the literature (Gladding, 2002; Robinson, 2005; Wilson, Kohn, & Lee, 2000).

Extended families are typical in Latino/Hispanic culture, including relatives beyond the immediate family. These extended family members usually live nearby each other, but not necessarily in the same household (Wilson, Kohn, & Lee, 2000). Gonzalez (1997) and others have pointed to a rise in mother-only households. Often, traditional views of self-development maintain that *self*-interests are subjugated to the needs and welfare of the family (Robinson, 2005). Family members willingly sacrifice for the good of the family. However, Latino/Hispanic people and families with nontraditional perspectives, or who have acculturated into the mainstream, dominant culture, might not follow this collective philosophy.

Personal identity within Latino/Hispanic families is influenced by immediate and extended members who teach traditional values related to dignity, pride, self-reliance, trust, intimacy, and respect (Gladding, 2002). At the same time, positive individual identity is associated with inner strength, determination, and will power to have and maintain self-control. People without these values are perceived as weak and unable to muster the strength to withstand stressful events or take control of their lives (Robinson, 2005).

Personalism *(personalismo)* is an important concept in Latino/Hispanic culture that is fundamental to understanding interaction among family members and the community. Created in response to a social and cultural caste system in Latin America, personalism means a "sense of uniqueness and personal goodness" established as a "group norm that emphasizes that relationship information must be established before a task can be accomplished" (Flores, 2000b, p. 7). As such, the concept of *personalismo* includes the attributes of respect and dignity, which when apparent within the person, allows the family or community to assign appropriate tasks. Therefore, *personalismo* is the establishment of trustful relationships, which in turn determines the nature of tasks assigned to individuals (Flores, 2000b). Application of this concept differs from Western perspectives that value tasks first followed by relationships. The work ethic of dominant U.S. culture, for example, values "the accomplishment of a task, not the person's goodness" (Flores, 2000b, p. 7). In contrast, Latino/Hispanic families and communities first accept the person as a trustworthy and respectful member before assigning appropriate tasks and responsibilities. For Latin American immigrants to the United States, therefore, learning that relationships are not essential or required for assignment of tasks and responsibilities is an important acculturation process (Flores, 2000b). Of course, not all Latinos/Hispanics value relationships more than or before accomplishments.

Other social factors such as discrimination, unemployment, poverty, and higher birth rates have an impact on family function and dysfunction among Latino/Hispanic communities. Although the overall socioeconomic wealth and status of Latino/Hispanic families might be improving, a high percentage continues to live in poverty compared to other groups (Flores, 2000b). In addition, they have a higher unemployment rate and lower educational achievement, which contribute to higher family stress and dysfunction.

Native American Families

With over 2 million Native Americans, including Alaskan Eskimos and Aleuts, in the United States, there are more than 500 government-recognized tribes (Herring, 1991). Though diverse in their beliefs and values, these tribes typically follow traditions that embrace a philosophy of cooperation, harmony with nature, sharing, and respect for family (Gladding, 2002). As with other cultures mentioned in this section, Native American groups often value an extended family structure. This belief relates to extreme hardships and difficult experiences by Native Americans caused by U.S. government action that fragmented families and placed children and other family members in foster homes, boarding houses, and other locations. The impact of these experiences on personal identity development and extended family relationships for many Native Americans has been devastating (Gladding, 2002; Herring 1991).

Tribal identity and respect for their culture remain strong aspects of Native American families. In addition, respect for elders, adherence to collective and democratic processes, and regard for land and nature are important values. Similarly, children are valued members of the family and community, which highlights again the devastation of past government action that took children from their families and placed them in federal boarding schools (Wilson, Kohn, & Lee, 2000).

Native American families face many contemporary challenges, including physical and mental heath problems, suicide, alcoholism, juvenile delinquency, violence, and child abuse/neglect. Regrettably, mental health and other community services have not responded adequately to the needs of Native American families, often because mental health practitioners and other providers minimize or ignore important cultural traditions and beliefs in the process (LaFromboise, 1988; LaFromboise, Trimble, & Mohatt, 1990).

Many Native American beliefs, such as shared responsibility, expand across the extended family and include the larger community. This has significant importance for individual self-development. For example, Robinson (2005) observed "shared responsibility includes food, shelter, automobiles, and all available services, including child care . . . [and as] a result of an extended concept of self, the community is enabled to enforce values and to serve as a source of standards" (p. 238). Consequently, individual personal identity and self-concept development relate closely to family, community, and tribal customs and beliefs.

The preceding sections offer thumbnail sketches of various family groups. For counselors and other professional helpers who work with diverse client groups representing different ethnic and family backgrounds, it might be valuable to assess and understand their own family heritage. Such understanding provides a foundation from which to empathize with clients experiencing internal or external cultural conflict. In addition, it avoids overgeneralization about particular nationalities, cultures, and family traditions, structures, and functions. Exercise 6.3 offers an opportunity to evaluate your family background from a cultural/ethnic perspective.

The factors mentioned thus far in this chapter emphasize common aspects of family structure and functioning found within and sometimes across various cultural and ethnic groups. The previous sections devoted attention to the influence of family and culture in a person's development and in the collective beliefs promulgated by and within particular groups. General aspects of family functioning across diverse groups and cultures were examined. Next, this chapter briefly considers the closeness of *family and community ties,* and how such perceptions might influence different clients, regardless of their cultural background.

Exercise 6.3

Assessing My Family Background and Experience

1. What cultural/ethnic factors make my family different from others I know?
2. What are important differences between my family and other families within my cultural/ethnic group?
3. What role does skin color/tone play in my family heritage and functioning?
4. What role do religious beliefs or spirituality have in my family?
5. When did my ancestors come to America, and what bearing does that event have on my family today?
6. What historical events have influenced my family life and heritage?
7. What important family beliefs do I hold?
8. What important family beliefs do I no longer follow?
9. What experiences have influenced my decisions to follow or not follow particular family beliefs?
10. What influences have social status and economic class had on my family and my identity?

Family and Community Ties

Clients who seek assistance from counselors and other professional helpers often express conflicting views with those of other family members. With clients from cultures that place great emphasis on family cohesiveness and loyalty, these conflicts can be most stressful and overwhelming. In working with such clients, counselors are particularly diligent to monitor their personal beliefs about family, connectedness, and related values, and refrain from injecting their biases about family ties or family interference in the counseling relationship. The ultimate goal is to help clients process their beliefs and goals within an appropriate cultural context and make decisions that can bring resolution to the conflict while maintaining respect for family and culture. Often, inclusion of families in the process can help to retain beneficial families ties while assisting the client with important life decisions.

Refugees and immigrants are two groups that face many challenges to traditional family functions and relationships. Bemak and Chung (2002) noted that family relocation often affects child-rearing practices, decreases adherence to traditional family values by youth who are acculturating to a new society, accelerates parental loss of authority, and introduces new cultural mores and behaviors related to dating, marriage, and other phenomena that threaten parental roles and family functioning. At the same time, young people of diverse cultures whose families have immigrated or relocated "may witness the transformation of their parents from previously autonomous and culturally competent caretakers to depressed, overwhelmed, and dependent individuals" (Bemak & Chung, 2002, p. 219). Such observations might damage children's confidence in and respect for their parents' judgment.

Counselors and human service providers who work with clients from cultures that historically have held high regard for close family ties and cohesiveness among extended family members are careful about understanding and managing the family dynamics that might change as a result of clients' decisions. It is often impossible to undo changes in these dynamics once clients make life-altering decisions, particularly those contrary to family wishes. Helping clients understand the serious impact that their decisions might have on future family relationships and how that might conflict with values they still hold close is an essential part of the helping process.

Beyond family ties, culturally diverse clients might also need to consider how their decisions will affect relationships within their ethnic community and communities of the dominant culture. As people develop, they interact with their family and a larger society. They also form associations and relationships within a given community. Sometimes, these communities are small, rural towns, while other times they are neighborhoods within larger urban cities or suburbs of cities. Communities also take forms designated by particular cultures. For example, among Native Americans, communities are known as nations, societies, and tribes. In addition, communities exist through places of worship, such as mosques, synagogues and churches, or within institutions such as schools, universities, and manufacturing plants where people study, work, belong to professional associations, hold membership in fraternities or sororities, and join labor unions among other communal activities. These different forms of community provide venues for people to observe behaviors, listen to opinions, and learn about customs and traditions that they filter through a unique perceptual framework drawing conclusions that contribute to their personal development.

People of diverse cultures tend to live, work, and congregate in communities that share similar beliefs, values, and customs. This phenomenon is commonplace in U.S. society. In towns and cities across the country, we find people living in particular communities where their culture dominates the lifestyle. Areas in large cities, such as those known as "Chinatown" or "Little Italy," illustrate this bond among people from diverse cultures, but smaller towns as well consist of neighborhoods that take on distinct cultural appearances.

Communities have an important influence on human development. Sometimes this influence is positive and sometimes it is not. In communities that protect people, teach cultural history, customs, and traditions, and nurture their members to acculturate into the larger society in appropriate ways, healthy development is likely. These communities are highly regarded by the larger society that respects and celebrates their diversity while including them in decision-making processes for society as a whole.

Unfortunately, some communities and neighborhoods do not receive equal treatment within the larger society. Neglected in terms of protection, resources, and equal participation in governing processes, they often show severe signs of physical and human deterioration, have high crime rates, and are fearful places for both the residents and people from outside the area. These types of communities also have an impact on the development of their residents and depending on the level of deterioration and crime, can have devastating effects on families and individual development.

Exercise 6.4 asks about the communities where you grew up and where you live today. In addition, it asks that you reflect on aspects of the community (past and present) that have had an impact on your self-development and worldview.

Exercise 6.4

Instructions: Describe the community where you grew up (e.g., the neighborhood, housing development, apartment complex, etc.). List cultural aspects of the community that had a positive influence on your development and then list any negative aspects of the community that you recall. Repeat this exercise for the community in which you live today and make comparisons.

Childhood Community	***Cultural Factors***	***Negative Factors***
____________________	____________________	____________________
	____________________	____________________
	____________________	____________________
Present Community	***Cultural Factors***	***Negative Factors***
____________________	____________________	____________________
	____________________	____________________
	____________________	____________________

Counseling Inferences

Understanding family background and cultural heritage is a first step in developing empathic understanding for others, particularly for clients whose families are different from yours. This chapter explored the influence of family in terms of structure, traditions, socioeconomic status, and other factors on the emerging *self.* When working with individual clients or families from diverse cultures, many of the principles noted in earlier chapters pertain. Certainly, counselors and therapists who work with diverse families want to understand how their worldviews, particularly as related to family structure and function, language, religious traditions and beliefs, gender roles, and social class, might affect helping relationships and the ability to be effective practitioners.

A next step is to learn from the client's perspective how family influence has affected his or her self-development. An adaptation of Exercise 6.3 might be a helpful assessment to use in learning about a client's family background and heritage. Learning about the client's perspective and how she or he has retained or rejected certain family values is essential in understanding the client's worldview. As seen in this chapter, many different values interact within families and across cultures in various ways. For example, religious and spiritual beliefs and traditions of African American, Arab American, Hispanic/Latino, Native American, and Jewish American families, to list just a few, play a significant role in family life and individual development.

Frequently, the inner conflict people have in their *self*-development results from consternation and disagreement with family members about beliefs, customs, and traditions that the individual no longer embraces. In the United States, every cultural group experiences these conflicts as new generations acculturate into the larger society. Counselors and other professionals who help diverse individuals and their families reconcile these conflicts by establishing safe, comfortable, and trusting relationships without imposing their views and values in the process have a chance at being successful.

Family factors are important cultural influences that play a role in the self-concept development of the individual. As noted in this chapter, such influences are tempered and altered, depending on adherence by the individual to particular beliefs and values. Generational differences, family mobility, and the influence of the dominant culture through education, media, and other forces have an impact on the degree to which each person follows family traditions.

Another factor related to identity formation is a person's physical *self,* which interacts with sex, gender, and orientation as discussed in Chapter 5. At the same time, physical ability, disability, appearance, and image are culturally and socially influenced. The next chapter considers how physical attributes merge with social and cultural constructs to influence self-concept development across groups and genders.

7

Ability, Attractiveness, Aging, and Self-Image

Chapters 3 and 4 discussed racial and ethnic characteristics as social status variables, and presented several identity models that attempt to explain the relationship of these characteristics with self-development. As such, they focused, in part, on skin color and noticeable physical traits related to personal appearance and the subsequent social judgments that might come from these factors. This chapter also considers physical appearance, but in the context of what society promotes as being most able, agile, and attractive. In addition, it discusses aspects of physical ability and attractiveness in terms of their impact on the emerging self-concept.

Physical development is an essential and lifelong characteristic of human development, and as such, influences self-identity throughout the life span. Optimally, physically fit people use whatever attributes they have to create a lifestyle and participate in activities that they value and ultimately give them self-worth. Physical fitness, however, does not mean that people excel physically in all aspects of their lives. Rather, in a social/cultural context, it means using physical traits and skills available to live as full a life as possible without discrimination or exclusion from activities that enable every person to reach desired goals. That is the ideal. In practice, however, individuals, societies, and cultures sometimes convey messages saying that only people who are the most able, the most fit, are worthy of a full and worthwhile life.

Societies often create social constructs, promote belief systems, and foster faddish behaviors that persuade individuals, subcultures, and other groups about physical ability, body image, and youthfulness (Sparkes, 1997). In an issue of a popular news magazine, the cover-story headline read, "Vigorous Bodies, Positive Feelings." The articles comprising this volume actually provided useful information for healthful living. The smaller subtitle read, "A special issue on men's health," but the main title was the *grabber.* People who attain vigorous bodies might have positive feelings as the headline purports, but is the converse necessarily true? Do less vigorous people have less positive feelings? If we judge only by the content of advertisements in popular magazines and on television, the answer might be yes.

The power of media, "pop up" messages on the Internet, and a constant barrage of advertising on television, radio, and in magazines, inundate people with pictures and slogans telling them to look different, become more attractive, and build their bodies for their lives to be more fulfilled. This advertising blitz has been most apparent in the United States since the early twentieth century. In later decades, other Western countries became active participants in this cultural phenomenon. Now, during this twenty-first century, as the global economy expands and communication systems instantaneously connect people and societies across the world, we might expect other countries and cultures to be influenced by or to create new messages, selling products for changing physical appearance, increasing strength and agility, or altering physical characteristics that purportedly will bring added life satisfaction.

How societies and cultures view physical appearance and ability, and subsequently act on those perspectives, is another aspect of the social and cultural foundations that influence individual self-concept development as well as collective views of a society. These views are as divergent as the global cultures that form them. For example, in her treatise on the Moors of the Sahara desert, Popenoe (2004) noted that for Azawagh Arab women "the ideal of female beauty for centuries has been to be as fat as possible. Girls are fattened on milk and porridge for several years leading up to puberty to attain the full, abundant, luscious look that is admired by men and women alike, and that is considered sexually desirable" (p. 1). This revelation offers a differing view from Western cultures, which promote media advertising and male fantasy of beauty ideals often resulting in the oppression of women and escalation of eating disorders (Atlas, Smith, Hohlstein, McCarthy, & Kroll, 2002; Davis, 1997). Cultural influences in matters of physical ability and attractiveness are powerful and deeply rooted. As Popenoe (2004) argued, "these ideals persist not primarily because of their imposition by a powerful few or by forces extrinsic to the individuals held in their sway, but because they are deeply embedded in wider cultural values and social structures that we are all party to" (p. 1).

As noted, this chapter considers physical ability and attractiveness as well as issues of discrimination, exclusion, and oppression in society related to physical appearance and ability. Most important for this text is the notion that physical aspects of people's development have implications across cultures and societal groups, within families, and for individuals. These physical aspects include ableism, disability, self-image, and aging. Before considering these factors, some general information about physical development, body type, and self-image begins the chapter.

Physical Development and Self-Image

Social constructionist theory suggests that the *body* has been defined and symbolized in different ways through the ages. For example, over time the human body has been referred to as a temple, a host, a machine, and the *self,* among other terms. "This being the case, it is interesting to note that the constructions of the body in the 20th century have been dominated by notions of the *mechanical body* and the *body beautiful*" (Sparkes, 1997, p. 87). Now in this twenty-first century, as the United States continues its journey of becoming a pluralistic, multicultural society, it is unlikely that consensus about the definitive human body will occur "since constructions will reflect the values not only of the culture, but also of the subculture and of specific individuals" (Sparkes, 1997, p. 88).

People derive meaning about their bodies within a cultural context. In this developmental process, they learn about the importance and value assigned to the body and to certain types of bodies. This learning occurs at the same time the *self* is developing, and therefore, values placed on physical definition and form influence the internal belief system in much the same way as other cultural traditions do. Consequently, each person decides about his or her body based on learned cultural beliefs passed down from generation to generation, and these decisions are influenced and altered by contemporary trends in particular cultures.

Decisions people make about their physical *self* incorporate a range of beliefs involving athleticism, masculinity, femininity, healthful living, lifestyles, and youthfulness among others. "At the heart of these [beliefs] lies the dominant ideology of individualism that pervades Western cultures. It works as a system of beliefs that is central to the process of producing meanings and ideas in our society relating to issues such as the body, health, wealth, and poverty" (Sparkes, 1997, p. 90). Within the individualistic framework, then, there is a power to self regulate according to social norms. In the United States, this self-regulation takes its form as attempts at being slim, trim, and in shape, and people who do not conform simply *choose* not to do so. Although individual responsibility for healthy living is an important life concept, such overemphasis on personal commitment to socially constructed values related to body image and lifestyle might have dangerous implications.

Body Stereotypes

During the twentieth century, U.S. researchers attempted to associate physical body shapes with certain personality types (Kretschmer, 1925; Sheldon, 1954). Hamachek (1992) recounted that Sheldon's work (1954) was "the last major effort to develop a method of classifying personality on the basis of physical characteristics" (p. 160). In it, Sheldon (1954) proposed a continuum of classified body types featuring *ectomorphic* (tall, thin), *mesomorphic* (athletic, muscular), and *endomorphic* (heavy, rotund). Although his system of classifying and rating body types was generally accepted, Sheldon (1954) was criticized for his attempt to assign particular personality or psychological traits to specific body shapes (Hamachek, 1992). Such systems of "somatotizing" people based on their physiques are flawed because of overgeneralization and oversimplification of *self*-development. Hamachek (1992) noted, "there *are* relationships between certain body types and personality, but they are neither as direct nor as simple as physical type theories would have us believe" (p. 161). Nevertheless, stereotypical perceptions of various body types as well as variations of physical maturation relate certain personal characteristics to these phenomena (Blaine, 2002; Emmons, 1992; Gillett & White, 1992; Hamachek, 1992). These stereotypes, as noted earlier, are socially defined and culturally perpetuated.

As mentioned, Hamachek (1992) delineated stereotypic perspectives supported by research across three general body types. Generally, research findings have aligned stereotypic perspectives of male body types with the following sample of traits:

Mesomorphic (muscular, firm): Strong, athletic, lean, energetic, viral, competitive, self-reliant, adventuresome, and prone to exercise.
Endomorphic (tall, thin): Quiet, private, determined, anxious, stubborn, studious, and sensitive to pain.

> *Ectomorphic* (heavy, rounded): Friendly, good-natured, agreeable, indulgent, sympathetic, weak, and food loving. (Hamachek, 1992; Robinson, 2005)

The above traits associated with different body types are a sample of stereotypic descriptions and not an exhaustive list. Most important, they are *stereotypical* views not *scientifically validated* characteristics. As such, they are perceptions created and constructed by society, perpetuated in literature, television, and advertising, and woven into the cultural fabric of daily life, especially in the United States.

Physical stereotypes influence self-concept development starting at an early age. Research of elementary-school-age children in the 1960s and 1970s showed that at that time, boys and girls agreed with assignment of certain characteristics to particular body types, and this finding paralleled research with adult perceptions of young children's physiques and personal traits (Hamachek, 1992). These early findings of stereotypical views appear to be consistent with today's culture as indicated by Western obsession with ideal body image, weight, and attractiveness (Bissell, 2002; Johnson & Petrie, 1995; Robinson, 2005). Such stereotypic views perpetuate body images that might lead individuals whose bodies do not mirror society's perfect torso to choose unhealthy lifestyles in trying to reach an unrealistic goal, or to develop inferior self-concepts in terms of their physical appearance. In contrast, people who come closer to fitting the ideal body image propagated by the prevailing culture might find they gain social acceptance and other advantages unavailable to others. In either case, the outcomes are related, in large part, to cultural myths about body image.

Body Image and Self-Concept Development

According to Davis (1997), "*body image*—that is, the manner in which we view our body and the mental representation we have of it—forms an integral part of our body esteem and overall self-worth" (p. 145). She continued, "the preeminent factor in the formulation of the attitudes we hold about our physical self, as least during most of our lives, is the degree to which it conforms to the cultural ideals of beauty and sexual attractiveness" (p. 146). People incorporate these cultural ideals, as with other societal and cultural values, into their self-concepts through complex perceptual processes that help them create private belief systems. At this point, you might return to the self-concept diagrams in Chapter 2 (Figures 2.1, 2.2, and 2.3), and use them to examine and understand your own beliefs about body image. In addition, Exercise 7.1 invites you to consider beliefs about yourself as well as beliefs about other body images.

As you complete Exercise 7.1, consider which statements tend to perpetuate cultural stereotypic views. Do you recognize gender differences in any of these views or in your beliefs about body image? Davis (1997) noted a significant difference in the number of studies of women and body image versus men and body image. In recent years, however, there is some indication that men in the United States have become more bodily conscious. For example, Robinson (2005) observed that trends in advertising indicate a greater emphasis on male sexuality and a muscular build, which might influence increased male attention to body image.

Racial beliefs and identity also may influence body image. Some research has shown that White women tend to suffer more from eating disorders than Black women, and they

Exercise 7.1

A Dozen Beliefs about Body Image

Instructions: Consider each of the statements in this exercise and reflect on your responses. Assess how these beliefs might influence your self-concept. Discuss with a friend or classmate.

1. I am generally satisfied with my body.
2. If I could change anything about my body, it would be __________.
3. I feel under great pressure to change my appearance.
4. Body image makes little difference in terms of my attraction to people.
5. I often wonder why very heavyweight people do not lose weight.
6. I often wonder if thin people are anorexic or bulimic.
7. Most beautiful people probably have had cosmetic surgery or other medical treatment.
8. Race, culture, and ethnicity are influential factors when considering body image.
9. I have more difficulty dealing with heavy women than I do with heavy men.
10. A thin woman might be beautiful, but a thin man probably needs to gain weight.
11. Muscular men are attractive; muscular women are a turnoff.
12. I am greatly influenced by advertisements about weight loss or bodybuilding.

---

also indicate lower levels of body satisfaction (Crago, Shisslak, & Estes, 1996; Henriques, Calhoun, & Cann, 1996; Striegel-Moore, Schreiber, Lo, Crawford, Obarzanek, & Rodin, 2000). However, other studies tend to indicate more similarity in perceptions and claim that socioeconomic status (SES) could be a mitigating factor. For example, a study of college women's eating and dieting expectancies, bulimic symptoms, and dietary restraint or lack of restraint generally found no differences across races regarding perceptions about thinness and dieting expectations. However, African American females in this study indicated fewer risk factors and fewer symptoms (Atlas et al., 2002). At the same time, African American women of higher SES may tend to be more similar in their views to White women (Davis, 1997). Likewise, perceptual differences between White women and women of other heritage, such as Asian American, may be diminishing in the United States.

Blaine (2002) posited that social stereotypes about body image are based on belief systems that place great responsibility on individuals to be in charge of their life choices and outcomes, including those related to body weight and appearance. For example, heavy people are generally perceived as being irresponsible about controlling their weight, and therefore, they often elicit emotional reactions that include fear, pity, repulsion, and hostility (Blaine, 2002; Crandall, 1994; Crandall & Martinez, 1996). As such, the processes related to forming an individual's belief system about body image are also the processes that help define that person's views of acceptable and desired body types for others. These processes combine individualistic philosophies of the person and society with collectivistic views propagated by culture. What is the best body image for the individual to attain in order to be accepted, and perhaps revered, by the larger group? Media is often the vehicle that defines "best" body image in society.

Media

Research continues to indicate that media has a powerful effect on body image for the general population in the United States. (Blaine, 2002). Bryant and Zillman (2002) noted that research results demonstrate how television programs and advertising reflect and perpetuate social beliefs and cultural values, and the significant impact television viewing has on people. In doing so, the media plays a role in not only in reflecting societal values but in helping to create and mold values. In a meta-analysis of 25 research studies, Groesz, Levine, and Murnen (2002) found that negative body images were more likely to occur after viewing media images of the "slender ideal" than they were after viewing images of inanimate objects, average-sized models, or plus-sized models. The authors noted that this negative effect was more pronounced for subjects under the age of 19 and who were more susceptible to the popular notion of thinness.

These findings confirm the power of media to convey social values, particularly about physical appearance and attractiveness. At the same time, these messages perpetuate mythical ideal body images that bring to surface negative feelings related to body dissatisfaction (Groesz et al., 2002). Yet, according to Blaine (2002), we cannot entirely blame the media, which gives the populace what it consistently embraces. If this speculation is true, we might expect the media to change its focus as society and the dominant culture alter perceptions and belief systems about body image.

Related to attractive physical appearance is the concept of physical ability. U.S. culture values physical beauty and the slender ideal with much the same attention given to physical ability and agility. The next section considers societal notions of ability and disability and relates them to prejudices and discriminatory practices known as *ableism.*

Ableism and Disability

Throughout history and across societies and cultures, people with less than optimal physical, mental, and emotional abilities have faced discriminatory practices. Crippled, diseased, and intellectually impaired people routinely have been shunned at best and discarded at worst, even by the most civilized of societies. In the United States, the extraordinary focus on individual responsibility and independent functioning often translates into excessive emphasis on physical fitness and ability (Robinson, 2005). These perceptions, regardless of the society or culture embracing them, form an overarching belief system called *ableism,* which affects social, educational, political, and personal dimensions of human functioning. Hehir (2002) noted that as a belief system, *ableism* shares history with common forms of oppression and discrimination that, as Overboe (1999), Smith (2001), and Weeber (1999) described, rival racist, sexist, and homophobic mentalities.

Ableism (also called able-body-ism) is "a pervasive system of discrimination and exclusion that oppresses people who have mental, emotional and physical disabilities. . . . Deeply rooted beliefs about health, productivity, beauty, and the value of human life, perpetuated by the public and private media, combine to create an environment that is often hostile to those whose physical, mental, cognitive, and sensory abilities" (Rauscher & McClintock, 1996, p. 198). Hehir (2002) listed several widely accepted beliefs that launch an unchallenged ableist perspective. We adapt and expand his list here.

It is better to

- Walk than to roll or crawl.
- Speak than to sign.
- Walk independently than to use mechanical transportation or other devices for support.
- Read print than to read Braille.
- Read printed material than to listen to audio presentations.
- Associate with physically abled people rather than with disabled people.
- Spell independently than to use a spell-check device.
- Perform mathematical computations than to use a calculator.
- Appreciate great art through vision than to hear an expert describe it.
- Use formal handwriting to express personal feelings than to type messages.

In reviewing the list above, consider your reactions to the statements. Exercise 7.2 provides an opportunity to examine your beliefs about these notions.

Exercise 7.2

Ableist Beliefs

Instructions: Read each of the statements and circle the number to show whether you agree, disagree, or are unsure. When finished, tally the total score to see how close it comes to an "ableist" perspective (scores of 11 and higher might be suspicious).

Scale: D—Disagree; U—Unsure; A—Agree

	D	*U*	*A*
1. Society should do as much as possible to accommodate people with physical disabilities.	3	1	0
2. Schools should allow all types of technology (e.g., computers, calculators, hearing devices, etc.) when assessing students in achievement and ability.	3	1	0
3. I am comfortable associating with people who have severe physical disabilities.	3	1	0
4. Physically disabled persons have the right to access all public places and institutions.	3	1	0
5. All deaf people should have cochlear implants so they can hear.	0	1	3
6. American Sign Language should be the choice of communication for all deaf people rather than trying to learn how to speak.	0	1	3
7. Verbal communication is always the most succinct and effective way to send and receive messages.	0	1	3
8. Physically disabled people, regardless of their challenges, should be encouraged, supported, and accommodated in every way possible to help them live a full and productive lives.	0	1	3
9. The government is not responsible for providing physical structures, technological devices, or other accommodations to help people who cannot help themselves.	0	1	3
10. People who cannot care for themselves are the responsibility of their family or private care institutions.	0	1	3

Total Score: ___________

Even when society has best intentions to help people with disabilities, sometimes it sends messages that appear incongruent with the care intended. For example, Hehir (2002) observed that *ableist* assumptions are apparent when schools and other institutions "focus inordinately on the characteristics of their disability to the exclusion of all else, when changing disability becomes the overriding focus of service providers and, at times, parents" (Ableism and Schooling section, section 5). Inherent in a seemingly noble attempt to rid people of physical challenges is the unspoken message that their disability is a negative and tragic characteristic of their *self.* Such a posture or stance conveys ever so subtly a social dysfunction and cultural prejudice (you might revisit item #8 in Exercise 7.2).

Shapiro (1994) described several examples of this type of unintentional message of despair in his narratives about the poster children of the muscular dystrophy telethons. His references to these poster children as "Tiny Tims" and "supercrips" offered the perspective that such attempts at advertising charitable events to assist in otherwise noble causes might be viewed contrarily, portraying disabled children as dependent, needy, and damaged goods. Although well meaning, these portrayals perpetuate ableist assumptions and corresponding cultural prejudices that devalue people as they are by saying, "When society finds a cure, or fixes this abnormality, then you and others like you will be complete in your personhood."

In U.S. culture, being able-bodied is so highly valued that anyone with physical deficiencies or differences faces seemingly insurmountable challenges. As noted earlier, learning differences and difficulties lead to stereotyping and labeling in our educational systems. Counselors and human service providers have a responsibility to counteract societal assumptions and cultural prejudices that inhibit development of all clients, regardless of the diverse characteristics that they bring to the helping relationship.

Many clients exhibit aspects of diversity not only by their racial or cultural identity, but also by their physical or learning disabilities. The discrimination and prejudice that physically disabled and learning disabled people face are similar in form and function to the biases faced by other diverse clients. Helping clients to deal with the dominant society's reactions to their physical or educational conditions is an important service of professional helpers. At the same time, disabled clients have to handle their physical or other challenges within the context of cultural stereotypes related to identity factors such as gender and social class. For example, Robinson (2005) observed, "In a society where masculinity is often equated with virility, strength, sexuality, and self-reliance, it is understandable how men with physical disabilities can be perceived as a contraindication to hegemonic masculinity" (p. 218).

As with all clients, the goal when assisting and counseling disabled people is to help them find and choose a direction in life that brings satisfaction and feelings of self-worth. At the same time, counselors and other professionals want to encourage clients to look beyond their limitations and actively reach out to help other people (Schmidt, 2002). As a counselor educator, this author has been fortunate to meet many people from diverse backgrounds who faced a variety of personal, physical, and educational challenges as they pursued a master's degree in counseling. Yet, all these people graduated as counselors with the hope of helping others make better lives for themselves. Regardless of the limitations these counselors may have initially experienced or perceived for themselves, their ability to see beyond those imperfections enabled them to envision a bright future. One man was profoundly deaf and his story offers an example of how a person can move to higher levels of functioning by dismissing critics who narrowly define capabilities necessary to perform at some preconceived level of satisfaction. His story (Narrative 7.1) illustrates an understanding of this challenge and how counselors and other human service professionals use this understanding to help their clients.

NARRATIVE 7.1 • *Listening* beyond the Details

Growing up I was very active in sports. I boxed, played football and baseball, and was an avid surfer. I feel lucky that I was able to continue all those activities after losing my hearing at the age of 13 to spinal meningitis.

As a counselor, one of my biggest regrets was a job I left after four years because a few co-workers held great animosity and contempt toward me. Unfortunately, I eventually came to feel the same way about them, so it was time to leave. Never before had I experienced people feeling that way about me, and even after I made several attempts to establish working relationships, the situation did not improve. I admit it did hurt.

In addition to the animosity and contempt I experienced, another difficult part of the job was my apparent lack of interest in details contrasted by greater fascination with abstract concepts in counseling relationships. I attribute this, in part, to my loss of hearing, because since that near-death experience, I have never been able to focus on superficial details of life. I tend to be more interested in the colors and flavors, the feelings and thoughts, of life. Some of this may have to do with my being deaf and how I experience the world around me. The implication of all this is that as a counselor, I try to help clients dig deeper into the superficiality of their lives and examine their concerns, pain, and suffering within a bigger picture, whatever that may be to them.

Hehir (2002) presented several recommendations to help educational institutions take positive action in helping students understand the dynamics of disabilities within the context of diversity. Counselors, human service workers, and other social activists may find the following adaptation of some of his suggestions useful in formulating strategies and services for clients.

Include disability as part of all diversity initiatives. This text embraces a broad definition of diversity in helping professionals identify with their clients the personal, social, and cultural obstacles and barriers to development. Most important in this recommendation is to address disabilities in a genuine and candid manner without patronizing clients, referring to their disability in stereotypical terms, or assuming an ableist posture. At the same time, helping professionals can take a proactive role that encourages social, educational, and political changes, thereby diminishing able-bodied assumptions while advocating optimal access and development for all people.

Actively help disabled clients to acquire and use physical skills and alternate modes of communication effectively and efficiently. Disabled clients and able-bodied clients are not the same, anymore than other clients are the same. For this reason, it is important that professionals not approach disabled clients with the intent to help them adapt and cope in the same way they expect other clients to adjust. This is not to say that disabled clients can not perform in ways similar to other clients, but by approaching them with a singular intent, counselors and other helpers might overlook other strategies that have the potential to broaden modes of communication, learning, and problem-solving.

Advocate for equity while maintaining the uniqueness of the person. It may seem like a contradiction to advocate that all clients be treated equitably while maintaining that differences do exist. Yet, this is the challenge for helpers who work across cultural groups, including disabled persons. Services provided to disabled people must help them gain access to educational, commercial, career, political, and other aspects of society, but not at the expense of sacrificing the unique qualities and traits they bring to the table. Therefore, services should be delivered at the same level of expertise and proficiency of services rendered to all other clients. They also should present the same challenges and opportunities. The only difference in the helping process is in the accommodations made to recognize clients' disabilities and enable them equal likelihood for success.

Worry less about what you can "do for" clients and focus more on the results you can accomplish together. In recent years, various federal legislation and initiatives in the United States have raised awareness about the needs of disabled people. Consequently, we have seen an increase of educational, career, and social services for a wider population (U.S. Department of Education, 2000). One result of this expansion of services is that occasionally, professionals help by "doing for" people what they are perfectly capable of doing for themselves. Purkey and Schmidt (1996) contrasted this helping perspective with a "doing with" stance, which seems more compatible with the notions of acceptance and positive regard, commonly recognized as core conditions of helping.

An essential aspect of this "doing with" stance is advocating inclusion for disabled clients. Ableism is a strong force to battle in this process, but caring counselors and other helping professionals do more than advise and counsel clients. They also actively seek out injustices and marshal services to combat discriminatory policies and programs. Through processes of involvement and education, professionals and their clients can help nondisabled people raise their awareness and become more accepting of disabled persons.

Cultivate high expectation and develop appropriate measures of success. Hehir (2002) emphasized that one of the most debilitating beliefs of able-body-ism is that disabled people lack the capability to succeed. Disabled clients often resist change in ways similar to other clients. As noted in Chapter 2, the self-concept is relatively stable and most people do not readily change. Therefore, counselors and other helpers must not fall prey to a false assumption of incapability, but rather set high standards and expectations for all their clients. At the same time, they help clients set reasonable goals and create appropriate measures of success in tracking progress through the helping relationship. In a later chapter, we will consider assessment issues in more detail.

Promoting universal design is for the common good. The concept of universal design, according to Hehir (2002), was first applied to architecture, and now with the legal support of the American with Disabilities Act (ADA), has been more broadly applied. As a result, it is common to find automatic door openers, accessible toilets, ramps, and lighted alarm systems in new and renovated buildings, all of which complement ringing bells at intersections of streets and sidewalks. Captioning devices on new televisions and computer-screen readers of digital text are also becoming more commonplace. "Universal design allows for access without extraordinary means and is based on the assumption that disabled people are numerous and should be able to lead regular lives" (Hehir, 2002, Toward Ending Ableism in Education section, ¶ 19).

Hehir (2002) mentioned the benefits of universal designs for the broader society. He noted how people pushing baby carriages or other carts and wagons appreciate sidewalk curb cuts. Likewise, closed captioning in noisy sports bars and restaurants helps hearing patrons keep up with the action while they enjoy a beverage or meal or socialize with their friends. Of course, these unintended uses are not justification for providing them. Hehir (2002) illustrated them simply to acknowledge their universality. Nevertheless, the common use of technical devices and architectural adjustments might help sensitize nondisabled people and raise their level of awareness and understanding of the needs of everyone in society.

Another aspect of physical disability comes naturally through the aging process. How societies view aging and create social constructions that accept or reject and ignore or revere older people is another dimension of physical appearance, ability, and disability. The next section of this chapter considers the process of aging, ageist attitudes, and self-concept development.

Aging and Ageism

This chapter has presented various factors related to physical attractiveness, ability, and body image that interact with personal perceptions and influence individual behavior and *self*-concept development. As social constructions, these factors all have in common some degree of choice on the part of the developing person. The factors themselves are external interpretations of a person's physical appearance and ability based on social beliefs and values. Ultimately, however, each individual internalizes these socially constructed attitudes and accepts or rejects them into his or her private logic, creating a corresponding self-view. As noted in this text, these choices are most often an outcome of countless perceptions, filtered and processed through each person's unique cognitive structure, from birth until death.

Unlike previously mentioned factors—physical appearance, ability, and body image—aging is natural process for everyone. All people experience it; no one escapes it. From the moment of conception, human beings begin the aging process and eventually they die, for that too is a given. Regarding the absolute quality of aging, you might wonder why this factor is important in a chapter about physical appearance and ability. Of equal concern might be how aging relates to social and cultural foundations of counseling and human services. Aging is a social factor not because of any choice people have regarding whether or not they will get older, but because of choices they and society make about aging, social conditions that impede or enhance the process, and values, beliefs, and behaviors that society associates with both aging and dying.

Medical science and technological invention continue to extend life expectancy across populations in the United States. and globally. National data indicate that people born in 2001 can expect to live an average of 77.2 years, an increase of 1.7 years from a decade before (National Center for Health Statistics, 2003). At the same time, projections are that life expectancy will continue to increase across groups, with the highest estimates reaching above 90 years old on average for both men and women by the end of the twenty first century. Among all these estimates, females will continue to outlive men on average across all racial groups (National Projections Program, 2000).

"Baby Boomers" (people born between 1946 and 1964) and those over the age of 80 combine to form one of the fastest growing groups in U.S. population, and this has numerous implications for health care, leisure programs, social services, and mental health services for individuals and families (Woodard & Komives, 2003). In addition, this aging population will have an effect on career and other life decisions that will have ramifications on the traditional three-phased view of life experiences: education, career, and retirement. In the future, we might expect these phases to become cyclical, meaning that people might complete one career, return to the education phase for new training and preparation to reenter the work force in another capacity, such as a totally different full-time career or a part-time job while enjoying semi-retirement (Gysbers, 1996).

Common Stressors and Cultural Factors

As the average lifespan increases, society, families, and individuals will experience more pressure to cope with the aging process. Multiple challenges will emerge as personal desires, medical requirements, social changes, cultural values, economic disparity, political forces, and other factors interact in this arena. Among these factors are the inevitable physical and medical services that will be required due to longer life expectancy. In addition, the availability of social activities, likelihood of family and generational interaction, opportunity for educational endeavors, and access to counseling and other human services to deal with stressors related to aging will determine the quality of life people can expect in their later years.

Some common stressors associated with aging populations include the grief resulting from the death of one's spouse, health changes and chronic illness, loss of control in life decisions, family conflicts, vulnerability to crime and political pressures, lack of transportation and reliance on family members or others, and financial pressures. How individuals perceive these conditions and the ability they have to take an active and decisive role in handling different issues are measures of healthful living.

Cultural factors that may influence how persons handle these issues include attitudes about and toward older family members. Over the years, volumes of studies of different cultures have found that "pursuing a culturally sensitive examination of the well-being of the elderly is a quite complex task" (Sokolovsky & Vesperi, 1991). Tradition, custom, and personal perception intermingle to create this complexity, which then becomes magnified by status variables such as gender, race, urban or rural identification, and social class.

Of all the factors that influence a person's perception of aging, poverty is one of the most debilitating. It interacts with most, if not all, of the major issues surrounding the aging process mentioned earlier in this section. For example, medical requirements are most stressful when the costs prohibit meaningful and necessary care. In 2002, 5.8 million people over the age of 55 were below the poverty level in the United States. "Older women, in general, had a higher poverty rate than older men—10.3 percent and 8.4 percent for those 55 to 64, compared with 12.4 percent and 7.0 percent among those 65 and over" (Smith, 2003, p. 4). As might be expected, the poverty gap between groups based on racial identification indicates that about four times the number of Black elderly couples are poor compared to elderly White couples (Henderson, 1993). We will consider socioeconomic conditions, including poverty, and their influence on self-concept development in greater depth in Chapter 9.

Exercise 7.3

About Aging and Dying

Instructions: Try using this exercise in three ways. First, consider the questions, giving thoughtful responses from your perspective. Second, use similar questions to interview an older person, preferably someone whom you do not know very well. Third, compare responses from the first two administrations of the exercise with responses that classmates compile.

1. How do you perceive younger people in today's society?
2. How do you perceive older people in today's society?
3. What cultural aspects or beliefs have influenced your perceptions about youth and aging?
4. What experiences have you had in working with or associating with older people? How have those experiences influenced your perceptions of aging?
5. What steps have you taken, if any, to lessen the impact of the aging process on yourself? (e.g., eating habits, exercise, social involvement, educational pursuits, leisure activity, medical intervention, etc.).
6. How long you would like to live? How do you see yourself spending the last years of life?
7. What do you think about mortality? What feelings emerge as you think about aging and dying?
8. What experiences with death have you had, and what impact have they had on your development?
9. What challenges do you foresee as you continue to age? How do you expect to handle these challenges?
10. What positive factors do you relate with aging?

To understand how personal perceptions of aging interact with social and cultural factors, it is helpful to appreciate your own perceptions and beliefs about getting older and about dying. Exercise 7.3 asks you to assess some self-perceptions and personal beliefs about both processes.

Cultural differences exist in how various societies view aging and older people. At the same time, there may be equally as many myths about these cultural differences. For example, "[the perspective] that the old are devalued here in America and venerated in other societies is oversimplified" (Cruikshank, 2003, p. 9). Sometimes, professed beliefs by a society do not necessarily reflect actual practices. All the factors mentioned previously in this section are contributing elements across cultures about how older members are treated. Affluence, racial identity, sex, political power, and other variables have tremendous influence on aging and how society perceives and treats older people, regardless of culture or nationality.

Physical Appearance, Ability, and Disability

In U.S. society, youthfulness is desired and admired, often at the expense of aging members of society. At the same time, because the aging process is inevitable, everyone who lives a long life can expect to experience bodily decline, less resistance to illnesses, more frequent and unexplained aches and pains, and less stamina and agility to perform common physical tasks that presented no problem in younger years. Yet, prejudicial beliefs about old people being sick and disabled are for the most part more myth than fact

(Palmore, 1990). The facts are that over three-quarters of people the age of 65 and older are healthy and able to perform normal day-to-day activities. At the same time, while older people do tend to have chronic illnesses, they also have fewer acute sicknesses, fewer home injuries, and fewer automobile accidents than younger people do (Robinson, 1994).

Some older people become preoccupied with the decline in physical appearance and ability, yet others take it in stride and continue to enjoy life to its fullest. In such cases, the same perceptual processes and conclusions about self-development that helped a person cope with other life transitions or setbacks are influential in deciding whether to view aging in a positive or negative light.

Other stereotypic views include the notion that older people decline in physical appearance and beauty and lose their mental capabilities. In the United States, the association of aging with declining beauty is more apparent than in other cultures. For example, Japanese culture views signs of aging as an indication of maturity, wisdom, and years of service to the community (Robinson, 1994). Facts about mental decline suggest that while old people tend to slow down in their reaction time and might take longer to learn new things, most hold on to their mental capabilities at a normal level of functioning (Robinson, 1994).

Depression is often commonly, but mistakenly, associated with aging. Studies indicate that severe forms of depression are less likely among older populations than among younger people. Nevertheless, considering the various mental illnesses that affect all different populations, depression is one of the most common found in elderly populations (Robinson, 1994). Some research has indicated a relationship among a physical self-image, perception of physical status, and depression (Davis-Berman, 1990). Overall, the findings place greater emphasis on physical self-efficacy than on objective physical status variables (i.e., physical problems, number of visits to physicians, and overall levels of health and physical activity) as a predictor of depressive symptoms.

Understanding stereotypic views of aging, physical appearance, and ability is important to becoming an effective helper, particularly one who might work with clients from aging populations. Exercise 7.4 asks you to explore some of your beliefs about aging, attractiveness, and ability.

How people perceive factors associated with aging and subsequently act upon their perceptions relates to the notions of individualism and collectivism explained in earlier chapters. On one hand, older citizens may be successful and satisfied with the aging process to the extent that they maintain a degree of self-reliance. On the other hand, pure individualism is probably not realistic for most people in the latter stages of life. Therefore, understanding the limitations one has as an elder and relying more on family and community softens an individualistic stance and recognizes the power of collective support in the process (Cruikshank, 2003). However, when social constructions force negative perceptions on people who are making educational, career, and other life decisions, another oppressive and discriminatory factor, called ageism, raises its ugly head (Cruikshank, 2003; Seabrook, 2003).

Ageism

Butler (1969), the first director of the National Institute on Aging, is credited with coining the term "ageism" (Robinson, 1994; Woolf, 1998). Early definitions aligned ageism with other forms of discrimination such as sexism and racism, citing it as systematic and stereo-

Exercise 7.4

Ageless Beauty

Instructions: Consider each of the statements and questions, and assess where you stand in terms of these views.

1. Descriptions of old people include *forgetful, childlike, helpless, wrinkled, bald, gray-haired, awkward,* and *slow.*
2. What age will you be when you are *old*?
3. What does the phrase "aging well" mean? How would you describe a person who is *aging well*?
4. Now that you have described *aging well,* how would you describe a person who is *aging poorly*?
5. Can you think of old people who are beautiful? What characteristics give them such beauty?
6. Should old people have certain privileges due to their age? If so, what might these privileges be?
7. Should old people have certain restrictions due to their age? If so, what are they?
8. As you think about aging, what concerns, fears, or apprehensions do you have? What hopes and aspirations do you have?
9. When you consider sexual attractiveness, how does aging influence your thinking?
10. As you learn about aging and culturally diverse clients, do any views about old people change?

---

typic prejudice against people simply because they were old. Contemporary definitions are inclusive of all age groups (Palmore, 1990), meaning that ageism does not apply only to older people. However, in this section we limit our discussion of ageism as it applies to the notions of physical appearance and ability of old people.

Some stereotypic views of old people in U.S. society include notions that older people

- Often forget names and other information because they are senile or disoriented.
- Are cranky or irascible even when sharing legitimate concerns.
- Are physically frail and incapable when unsure of their footing or appear to falter momentarily.
- Should accept the fact that they are old and, because of their age, are no longer energetic and essential producers in society.
- Behave inappropriately when they demonstrate normal physical affection to another person or express healthy sexual feelings (dirty old man syndrome).

Such stereotypic views create an atmosphere conducive to ageism. Many more could be added to the list. The National Institute on Aging (NIA) offered a 20-item true-and-false quiz to test people's "Aging IQ" (Robinson, 1994) and, more recently, revised this questionnaire into an informational booklet (National Institute on Aging, 2003). Exercise 7.5 provides an adaptation of this information, followed by the answers.

As with other discriminatory and oppressive belief systems, people learn ageism early in life and continue to fuel these misguided beliefs through misunderstanding, misinformation, fear of the unknown, and ignorance. Similar to sexism, racism, and other beliefs that reflect prejudice against particular individuals or groups in society, ageism also consists of language and terms created to perpetuate negative notions about old people. We

Exercise 7.5

Your Aging IQ

Instructions: Answer True or False:

________ **1.** More women than men survive to old age.
________ **2.** Intelligence declines with age.
________ **3.** Most old people have little interest in or ability to perform sexual acts.
________ **4.** If you live long enough, you will become senile.
________ **5.** At least half of all old people live in nursing homes.
________ **6.** Old automobile drivers have more accidents than younger drivers do.
________ **7.** Old people tend to become more religious with age.
________ **8.** Old people need calcium in their diet as do young children.
________ **9.** Families in the U.S. tend to abandon their older members.
________ **10.** Depression is a leading problem among old people, more so than for young people.
________ **11.** African Americans have about the same life expectancy as White Americans.
________ **12.** On average, women in the U.S. tend to live about four years longer than men do.
________ **13.** Most old people in the U.S. are lonely and socially isolated.
________ **14.** All five senses decline with age.
________ **15.** As with physical changes that occur with aging, personality also changes with age.
________ **16.** Loss of hearing is one of the most chronic conditions for old people.
________ **17.** It is natural of old people to withdraw from active community life in advanced years.
________ **18.** Young people have more acute illnesses than older people do.
________ **19.** Among all adult groups, older populations have a higher incidence of poverty.
________ **20.** Older adults are a group at most risk for committing suicide.
________ **21.** The older a person becomes, the less sleep he or she needs.

Answers:

True **1.** More women than men survive to old age. [*On average in the 1990s, women outlived men by about 8 years.*]

False **2.** Intelligence declines with age. [*For some, learning processes might slow, but overall intellectual ability remains.*]

False **3.** Most old people have little interest in or ability to perform sexual acts.

False **4.** If you live long enough, you will become senile. [*Among the oldest living adults, only about 25 percent might develop Alzheimer's or other debilitating disease.*]

False **5.** At least a quarter of all old people live in nursing homes. [*Estimates are closer to 10% to 15%, but these figures might change as more alternative residential care facilities emerge and life span increases.*]

False **6.** Old automobile drivers have more accidents than younger drivers do.

False **7.** Old people tend to become more religious with age. [*Generational differences exist, but they may be due more to current events and contemporary values than to the aging process.*]

True **8.** Old people need calcium in their diet as do young children. [*Current health advice advocates intake of calcium, particularly for women, whose risk for osteoporosis increases after menopause.*]

False **9.** Families in the U.S. tend to abandon their older members. [*In the United States, the family remains the primary caretaker of older adults.*]

False **10.** Depression is a leading problem among old people, more so than for young people. [*However, depression is a serious mental issue for old people as it is for other age groups.*]

True/False **11.** African Americans have about the same life expectancy as White Americans. [*Although the average life span for African Americans was about six years less than that of White Americans in the 1990s, African Americans who lived beyond the age of 80 tend to live longer than their White counterparts. As all U.S. residents gain equitable access to employment, health care services, and other societal benefits, we might expect life expectancy differences to disappear.*]

False **12.** On average, women in the U.S. tend to live about four years longer than men do. [*In the 1990s, women tended to live about six years longer than men.*]

False **13.** Most old people in the U.S. are lonely and socially isolated. [*Studies indicate that the overwhelming majority of old people report they are rarely lonely, nor do they identify loneliness as a major problem.*]

True **14.** All five senses decline with age. [*However, the extent of such decline varies greatly among individuals.*]

False **15.** As with physical changes that occur with aging, personality also changes with age.

True **16.** Loss of hearing is one of the most chronic conditions for old people. [*Arthritis and heart disease are the other more common conditions.*]

False **17.** It is natural of old people to withdraw from active community life in advanced years. [*Although this view was once used to explain decreasing activity for some older adults, recent research and new theories point to a variety of explanations for this phenomenon.*]

True **18.** Young people have more acute illnesses than older people do.

True **19.** Among all adult groups, older populations have a higher incidence of poverty.

True **20.** As a group, older adults are at most risk for committing suicide. [*In the U.S., adults age 65 and older have a 50% higher rate of suicide than the general population.*]

False **21.** The older a person becomes, the less sleep is needed. [*Although sleeps patterns might change with age, the total amount of sleep an individual requires varies little.*]

(Adapted from "What's Your Aging IQ?" (Robinson, 1994; National Institute on Aging, 2003)

---

find such language in everyday conversation, in the media, and in jokes told about aging and old people (Woolf, 1998). As examples, terms and phrases such as "crotchety," "old fogy," "old maid," "old goat," and "over the hill" are commonplace. When accepted by the dominant group (i.e., younger people), these terms and phrases become part of a culture that denies old people respectful treatment and, consequently, creates an atmosphere in which all people, young and old alike, accept the negative images conveyed by society. Such consequences risk increase in shame, withdrawal, and loss of self-esteem among old people who, if treated more respectfully, would live more productive and satisfying lives during their later years. This result detracts from a humane society as it dehumanizes and objectifies its older members (Robinson, 1994). In earlier exercises, you assessed some perspectives and knowledge about aging and old people. Exercise 7.6 invites you to examine contemporary media and the depiction of people.

As with defeating other prejudices, society can combat ageism by attacking the systems and institutions that perpetuate it. Counselors and human service professionals help in this effort by becoming socially active with groups and initiatives that monitor educational programs, media, business and government institutions, and human service systems to eliminate ageist attitudes and policies (Rodeheaver, 1990). Education is an important

Exercise 7.6

Print Media Assessment

Instructions: Find a popular magazine for a wide audience. Avoid selecting a magazine that targets a specific group or activity such as teens, men's sports, or retired people. Choose one that has broad appeal, such as news and lifestyle magazines. Look at the magazine you select, review each advertisement carefully, and answer the questions below.

1. How many ads did you review?
2. In all the ads, how many old adults did you see? What percent of the total ads featured older people?
3. If you found some ads featuring old people, what were they doing in the ads?
4. As you review these ads with old people, what conclusions do you draw about the messages being conveyed? Are there hidden messages as well as overt messages?

---

part of this process, beginning with young children in schools. It is not simply a matter of eliminating negative attitudes, but also includes active encouragement, highlighting positive aspects of aging and the contributions older adults make to society.

Counseling Inferences

The introductory chapters of this text emphasized the interaction of *self* with society in the process of human development. Similarly, this chapter presented several social factors that have potential impact on self-concept development in the context of physical appearance, body image, ability or disability, and aging. The success counselors and other helping professionals have in assisting clients with feelings about physical appearance, abilities, or the process of aging is contingent, in part, on the stereotypic beliefs these professionals have about beauty, body image, disabilities, and old age. In addition, the knowledge professionals have about accurate facts related to these concepts helps determine their proficiency. Accurate information and knowledge of research findings helps to combat stereotypic views for both helpers and clients. Effective use of appropriate skills and interventions is only possible with an informed knowledge base.

As noted in other chapters of this text, specialized training and appreciation of one's limitations as a helping professional are also important considerations, particularly when assisting clients with eating disorders, severe disabilities, or serious issues related to aging. Counselors and human service providers who have large clientele with such concerns want to be highly versed in current knowledge and proficient with viable interventions to provide dependable assistance.

In addition to knowledge and skill for individual and group counseling or other interventions, professionals can become active in their communities to combat stereotypic views and institutional prejudices that spread falsehoods about physical disabilities, the perfect body, and aging. The perpetuation of such beliefs is detrimental to a healthy society. Therefore, active participation in education programs, information dissemination, and other initiatives can foster healthier perspectives and lifestyles for all citizens.

8

Spirituality, Religion, and Self-Concept Development

Spirituality and religious beliefs provide personal avenues for people and groups to construct meaning and purpose in life. These personal avenues are greatly influenced by social and cultural traditions, family values and customs, and individual experiences. This chapter explores the influence of spirituality and religion on cultures, individual development, and collective views. Before that exploration, we begin with an examination of spirituality and religion in a historical context.

Historical Considerations

Famed Irish author Jonathan Swift, most noted for his acclaimed work *Gulliver's Travels,* once wrote, "We have just religion enough to make us hate, but not enough to make us love one another" (Bartlett, 1992, p. 288). In contrast, American author and philosopher Ralph Waldo Emerson remarked, "Great men are they who see that spiritual is stronger than any material force, that thoughts rule" (Bartlett, 1992, p. 433). These two perspectives reflect historic differences and conflicts that have existed among world cultures, empires, and countries in the name of either spirituality or religion. On one hand, spirituality conveys humankind's search for lasting peace and harmony with nature, while on the other, religious differences have too often accounted for rejection, oppression, hostility, and hatred between and among people who cannot accept divergent views and practices. If present news reports are any indication, there appears no end in sight for this discord in today's world.

Many parts of the globe remain enmeshed in seemingly endless combat, terrorism, or horrific acts of oppression and annihilation, pitting religious groups against one another. In most cases, these conflicts have long histories. The ongoing violence in Northern Ireland between Catholics and Protestants, hatred between Christians and Muslims in war-torn Serbia, political turmoil between Buddhists and the Tamils in Sri Lanka, and conflict across the continent of Africa are only a few of countless religion-oriented hostilities to mention. To be fair, many of these conflicts are founded in political unrest as much as religious differences. Yet, religious animosity often fuels the fires of hostility.

Before the emergence of Christianity, major battles and world conflicts were usually about political differences, territorial expansion, or empire building. The beginning of the eleventh century with the start of the Christian Crusades seemed to alter fundamental reasons for taking up arms and going to war. Before that time, much of Europe consisted of constant political and social conflicts. Following years of strife, a united England came under a single monarchy. France was a montage of small estates and kingdoms frequently at war with one another, and Italy consisted of a network of city-states, constantly invaded by outside forces such as the Normans, Scandinavians who settled in the area of Normandy, France. In reaction to the turmoil, the Roman Catholic pope, Urban II, prohibited fighting from Sunday to Wednesday, and forbade all hostilities involving clergy, women, workers, merchants, and shopkeepers any day of the week. About this same period, Turkish marauders were assailing Christian pilgrims in what was then the Byzantine Empire. Pope Urban II decided to unite the warring factions in Europe and send them on a Crusade to reclaim the Holy Land for the Church. During the Council of Clermont, in France, which brought clergy and many others together, Urban II warned about the Turkish movement and its threat to Europe and Christianity. A powerful speaker, he urged clergy and representatives from European states to build armies, send them to rescue Christians in the East, and reclaim the churches that Moslems had captured and converted to mosques. Pope Urban II put forth the hypothesis that if one Christian region fell, it would not be long before the Vatican would meet the same fate. He invoked the will of God, saying that God would lead the battle, and all who fought and died in His service would receive full absolution of their sins. Indeed, the divine fervor with which Urban II delivered his speech inspired the battle cry *Deus lo volt!* (God wills it!) (Connell, 2001). Thus began the first of many Holy Crusades in 1095—religious campaigns that lasted about 250 years. Since then, the justification of warring in the name of God has filled historical accounts, and continues today in this twenty-first century.

Between the late 1500s and early 1600s, growing divisiveness among Christians throughout Europe, primarily between Protestants and Roman Catholics, led to bloody wars between and within countries. During this hundred-year period, the French fought many civil wars between Roman Catholics and Protestants (called Huguenots), which ended when the *Edict of Nantes* granted religious and political freedom to the Huguenots. Spain, led by a Catholic king, Philip II, spent years stopping Turkish invasions, conquering parts of northern Europe, and defeating Protestant uprisings, such as in the Netherlands and elsewhere. At first reluctant to engage England in battle, Philip II invaded the British Isles with a Spanish Armada of ships in 1588. England defeated this powerful naval force, a momentary military setback for Spain that gave Protestants across Europe hope in their struggle for religious freedom. The Thirty Years' War (1618–1648) continued the religious conflicts of this period, involving nearly every part of Europe. Although largely political in nature, these wars had religious overtones. At the time, the Holy Roman Empire (central Europe from the Mediterranean to the North Sea) consisted of several sovereign states, each with its own political structure and army. These warring states evenly divided between Protestant and Catholic populations. The wars ended with the *Treaty of Westphalia,* which affirmed that each autonomous state within the Holy Roman Empire could decide its own religion. Today, the conflicts found around the globe and within countries continue the religious strife begun centuries ago, but now they include more forms of religions and diverse beliefs than before.

Knowledge of the history of religious conflict contributes to our understanding of the role religion takes as a social and cultural influence in human development, particularly in the construction of *self*-views and related worldviews. Strong emotions play an important role in this developmental process, often due to their historic meaning for particular groups, cultures, and societies. Equally important is an understanding of spirituality, an appreciation of various religious beliefs, and our ability to distinguish between the two.

Defining Spirituality and Religion

MacDonald (2004) provided a historical account of spirituality including its association and relationship with religion and evolving worldviews. He noted that despite efforts by individuals, institutions, and associations (such as the American Counseling Association) to define spirituality it is an "amorphous" term for which it is difficult to identify a single or absolute meaning for everyone (p. 294). The word *spirituality* seems all encompassing as it includes concepts of religious beliefs, human creativity and development, love and compassion, and host of other dimensions that highlight a certain connectedness among human beings.

People tend to define spirituality from an internal perspective. As such, spirituality usually holds personal definition that transcends materialism and moves the person to connect with the vast, extraordinary, and sometimes, unexplainable universe (Baruth & Manning, 1999). Spirituality has both broad and narrow meaning. When narrowly interpreted, spirituality signifies a single part of a person, the spiritual *self.* More broadly, spiritualness describes what it means to be human, the wholeness of person to attain awareness of self and others, and how to use one's awareness to benefit humankind and all of nature (Fukuyama & Sevig, 2002). By having faith in spiritual relationships with the universe and all living things, people are able to cope with day-to-day challenges and find meaning in their lives. For helping professionals, the spiritual dimension of human existence offers opportunity for more complete understanding of the client and his or her self-concept development within the context of cultural experience (Ivey et al., 2002).

We often define religion according to denominational affiliation (e.g., Baptist, Jewish, Lutheran, or Buddhist), and by some measure of religious practice and morality, such as attending worship services and living life according to a specific belief system. As such, a full definition of religion includes social constructs (e.g., indulgences, sacraments, virtue, nirvana, and reincarnation), adherence to specific doctrine (e.g., Hindu scriptures of the *Upanishads* and *Yoga Vasistha,* the Ten Commandments, teachings of the *Koran* [also written as Qur'an], the Ascension of Christ, and infallibility of the Pope), and performance of ritualistic practices (e.g., communion, prayer, meditation, fasting, and worship). People across divergent cultures lead spiritual lives while following particular religious beliefs and adhering to specific practices. Others choose not to follow established religions. Nevertheless, they find value in spiritual principles learned from their culture or through experiences with people from other cultures.

Comparison of Spirituality and Religion

Fukuyama and Sevig (2002) noted that religion comprises organized and institutionalized systems, which offer structure to spirituality by translating doctrine into beliefs and, subsequently, beliefs into religious practice. For example, one common doctrine among world religions is belief in a Divine Spirit, Supreme Being, or Higher Power. This belief seems to have universal acceptance among most world religions. Across varied systems, we find numerous names for deity, including Allah, Brahma, Vishnu, Shiva, Buddha, Christ, Elohim, God, Great Creator, Great Spirit, Jehovah, Jesus, Lord, Messiah, Sri Krishna, and Yahweh among others.

People often define religious and spiritual beliefs by specific and seemingly indisputable values, such as "eternal life" and "God's plan." Occasionally, such strong views might interfere with counseling or other helping relationships. According to Helms and Cook (1999), "Most of the major theoretical therapy orientations have as a goal assisting the client in becoming more self-directed, self-actualized, or self-empowered, whereas most religions or forms of spirituality have as a goal an individual's surrendering of his or her life" (p. 189). However, many people find strength from spiritual beliefs and religious doctrine to make it through life's adversities. Therefore, in working with clients across cultural groups, counselors and other helpers might use these beliefs in collaboration with therapeutic goals rather than as competing forces (Helms & Cook, 1999).

Living a spiritual life means exhibiting genuine elements of caring for oneself, other people, and the universe in mutually beneficial ways. In this sense, spirituality in and of itself may be different from traditional religious faith. People across cultural groups frequently profess strong religious beliefs, such as belief in a deity and celebration of religious holy days. When they complement this faith with an equally important spiritual purpose, they demonstrate unconditional regard for fellow human beings regardless of cultural or religious differences that exist among people. In contrast, when religious fervor is void of spiritual caring for oneself and others, an imbalance occurs. At these times, religious passion might override regard, respect, and tolerance for persons and groups who express contrary religious beliefs. When individual people or groups are unable or refuse to balance religious beliefs with a caring and rational spiritual life, they might resort to destructive and hateful ways of relating to others who hold divergent views. Too frequently, the world has witnessed such imbalance, as evident by the wars and destruction discussed earlier in this chapter. Exercise 8.1 invites you to explore religious and spiritual beliefs, and assess your level of tolerance of divergent views.

Across divergent cultures, we find people that maintain a high level of spiritual purpose in their lives. By doing so, they exemplify the distinction between religious beliefs and spirituality. At the same time, most people are able to see the common ground between these two concepts. Likewise, people who live healthy balanced lives are able to hold strong beliefs about the existence of a divine being or other religious doctrine while accepting spiritual guidance without relinquishing personal responsibility for their day-to-day behavior. Truly spiritual people across cultural groups distinguish between religious fervor and a spiritual life. For example, there is a significant difference between the lives of caring spiritual leaders, such as Mahatma Gandhi, Mother Teresa, Reverend Martin Luther King, and the Dalai Lama, and the lives of destructive fanatics who invoke "God's will" in seeking power without regard for fellow human beings or divergent groups. From the dawn of civilization to this twenty-first century, the world has witnessed acts of revolution or terrorism and responding force, with each side justifying its actions, in part, because of holy guidance, divine blessings, or eternal rewards granted by a higher power.

Exercise 8.1

"Religious and Spiritual Views"

Instructions: React to the statements below. Then pair up with a classmate and compare responses. When you have completed the exercise, reflect on your overall tolerance of divergent religious beliefs and spiritual views.

1. I believe in a Supreme Being and have definite views about this higher power's relationship with me, all of humankind, and the universe.
2. I believe in a higher power, but am uncertain about its function and relationship to humankind, the universe, or me.
3. I hold no particular religious or spiritual views, but believe in leading a good life that benefits me and other people.
4. I accept other people's views of religion and spirituality, but if those views differ from mine, I do not believe they will be "saved" or experience eternal joy after life.
5. I accept other people's views, even though they may differ from mine, and believe what is important is the understanding people have about how religion and spirituality guide their development in life.
6. I believe in life after death and a spiritual force that guides the entire universe.
7. I am uncomfortable when people profess strong religious beliefs in my company, particularly when their beliefs differ from mine.
8. I believe all things in this life are connected somehow, by some power.
9. I believe that the [Bible, Torah, Koran, Upanishads, or other notable document] is the guide that all people must follow to lead a spiritual life.
10. I believe there are basic and universal principles for humankind to follow, which transcend formal religious beliefs.

Often, these conflicts are rooted in cultural differences, including religious beliefs, and a legacy of intolerance, rejection, oppression, and hatred that have characterized hostility among divergent worldviews. Robinson (2005) observed, "Religion and spirituality are conceptualized differently" within various cultures (p. 16). Religious beliefs are associated with affiliation with a particular denomination, sect, or tribe, and by the practice of certain behaviors such as attending services and avoiding "sinful" actions. According to Robinson (2005), "Spirituality is often private and/or internally defined, transcends the tangible, and serves to connect one to the whole (other living organisms and the universe)" (p. 16). The next section of this chapter catalogs some commonly held religious and spiritual beliefs of various cultural groups in America.

Culture-Specific Perspectives

The United States consists of diverse cultural groups with equally as many views about spirituality and religion. The beliefs recorded in the following sections are some frequently registered in professional literature about culture and religions. As cautioned earlier in this text, such information provides generalizations about cultural beliefs, and is not intended to assess or describe specific views and values of individuals who happen to identify with particular groups.

African American. According to Baruth and Manning (1999), "Historically, the church served as a frame of reference for African Americans coping with discrimination resulting from their minority position, and it continues to play a key role in their survival and advancement. The church has been one of few institutions to remain under African American control and relatively free from the influence of the majority culture" (p. 127–128). Members of the African American community affiliate with many denominations, including Islam, various Protestant sects, Catholicism, and others. Services in predominantly Black churches are often celebrations, and members of the congregation are more demonstrative than in predominantly White American churches.

As an institution, the church in the African American community is second only to the family and serves several functions. Typically, the church provides an expressive outlet for release of people's deepest emotions, sometimes with cathartic benefits to people. At the same time, it functions as a status symbol, bestowing recognition to individuals and families often denied by the larger society. Churches can also be refuges and havens from a hostile world and a source of understanding for members searching for fulfillment and meaning in this life and the hereafter (Baruth & Manning, 1999).

African American beliefs follow a *spirituality* that emanates from African tradition, and "suggests that there is a spiritual essence that permeates everything that lives and exists in the universe" (Parham & Brown, 2003, p. 83). It defines the basis of human existence and humanity, and finds its source in divine nature. Another assumption of African heritage is the connectedness of all living things, with humankind at the center of the environment and a divine being as the creator and sustainer of everything in the universe.

Collectivity is an important spiritual concept, as noted earlier in this text. It is the idea that the larger group and not the individual is the most important element, and that each person owes his or her existence to a unit of kinship and social network. Regarding individual development, another spiritual belief is that self-knowledge is a key to healthful living and that people can fully understand humanity only through their comprehension of their relationship with a spiritual force, which guides the entire universe. "Fundamentally then, it is believed that people possess a 'spiritual anatomy' that seeks out opportunities for growth and transformation through the exercise of morally grounded relations with others" (Parham & Brown, 2003, p. 84).

As noted in this brief description, religion is important aspect of African American development. Yet, according to Baruth and Manning (1999), little research has focused on the role religion plays in the development of children in African American communities. Perhaps this is because more focus has been on religious aspects of civil rights, economic leadership, and the quest for the equal opportunity of African Americans in the larger U.S. society. Nevertheless, churches of all dominations are the source of social and spiritual leadership and the center of cultural life in the community—an integral part of African American life.

Asian American. Within the broadly defined Asian American community, several religions are represented and religious rites and ceremonies play an important role (Hanna &

Green, 2004). Although definitive data are not available about which religious affiliations comprise Asian American populations, Le (2003) compiled statistics from a survey of over 50,000 households gathered by the Graduate Center at the City University of New York, and estimated that about 1,760 Asian Americans were included in the sample. Of that group, Le (2003) projected that Catholic (21.1%) and Protestant (9.6%) denominations had the highest percent of Asian American affiliation, and a substantial percent indicated no affiliation or agnostic beliefs (20.2%). The largest Protestant group was Baptist at about 4.6 percent, with the next highest being Methodist at 1.9 percent. Another 5.8 percent of the sample indicated they were Christian, but because participants classified themselves in the survey, it is unclear if these respondents might be Catholic or Protestant in their affiliation. About 9.1 percent of the sample was estimated to be Buddhist, 5.2 percent Muslim, and less than 1 percent Jewish. Le (2003) noted that extrapolation of data did not allow for an estimate of Hindu affiliation because of the small number of Hindu responses in the survey's original results.

Traditional beliefs across Asian cultures maintain a holistic view of spirituality and often explain life and death issues in relationship to karma and reincarnation. Karma is the infallible law of cause and effect, which governs the universe and holds that every action brings consequences (Fukuyama & Sevig, 2002). As Hanna and Green (2004) noted, "morality in Hinduism is not based on the dictates of a deity, but on the well-known idea of 'karma' " (p. 327). Many Eastern religions follow a belief in reincarnation. It is the belief that when a person dies, the physical body decomposes, but the spirit is reborn in another body. Not all the bodies in this process of rebirth are necessarily human form. For this reason, some cultures that believe in reincarnation do not eat the meat of certain animals because they might hold the souls of their ancestors. In addition to following the tenets of karma and reincarnation, some Asian cultures promote intuitive healing processes or folk beliefs.

As seen by the estimates of religious participation by Asian Americans, it appears that a large percentage associates with dominant religions of U.S. society. Catholic and Protestant affiliation comprise about a third of the Asian American population according to these figures. As such, Asian Americans frequently follow mainstream religious beliefs, and for many, attachment to a particular church might help the process of forming communities that support cultural traditions and beliefs (Le, 2003).

Euro-American. As one might expect, religious affiliation among European Americans covers a wide spectrum. Many variables interact and influence a person's spiritual development and religious affiliation over a lifetime. For most Americans of European ancestry, religious adherence depends on geographic location, degree of acculturation, family background, marriage, and other factors. Catholicism, Protestantism, Greek Orthodoxy, Judaism, Islam, and several other denominations are among the religious memberships held by Americans. Sometimes, certain cultural groups, such as Italians and Greeks, demonstrate strong religious beliefs and practices in relationship with family function and community life.

Data about religious affiliation in the United States are in constant flux and come from an array of sources. The U.S. Bureau of the Census collected information from religious organizations until 1936. By law, the Bureau can no longer require information about religious affiliation. However, the *Statistical Abstract of the United States: 2000* (U.S. Bureau of the

Census, 2000b), which compiled data from a variety of sources, listed that religious preferences in 1999 were Protestant (55%), Catholic (28%), Jewish (2%), other (6%), and none (8%). Of this sample, 70 percent indicated membership in churches or synagogues, while 43 percent indicated they had attended a church or synagogue in the last seven days. By comparison, an *American Religious Identification Survey* (Ontario Consultants on Religious Tolerance, 2003) conducted in 2001 found that about 81 percent of respondents affiliated with a specific religion, with 52 percent selecting Protestant and 24.5 percent choosing Catholic. About 14 percent of respondents indicated they did not follow any organized religion. The previous data vary considerably with results of a 2002 USA Today/Gallup Poll that indicated about 50 percent of respondents considered themselves religious, 33 percent considered themselves spiritual but not necessarily religious, and 10 percent were neither spiritual nor religious (Ontario Consultants on Religious Tolerance, 2003).

Despite variance in survey results and other data about religious adherence and affiliation, it appears that a majority of Americans identify with some form of religious belief system. Therefore, we might expect that most European Americans follow religious beliefs and teachings, and these values influence their *self*-development, cultural traditions, and worldviews. At the same time, a significant portion of the population might eschew religious affiliation and instead follow their own spiritual preferences or no preferences at all.

Two religious groups often considered part of Euro-American cultures are the faiths of Judaism and Islam. Because these groups comprise a small percentage of the overall European American population, they are often overlooked in terms of their religious and spiritual impact. Therefore, the next two sections offer brief descriptions of each.

Judaism. As mentioned in an earlier chapter, Jewish heritage is replete with accounts of oppression, hostility, and annihilation. Rosenthal (2001) stated that the continuing mistreatment and rejection of Jews worldwide and the prevalence of anti-Semitism in contemporary society would not disappear. "On the contrary, it was an incurable psychological disease rooted in the unique social, political, and economic position of Jews . . . whose unnatural status inspired in Gentiles fear and revulsion. For this reason, even immigration to other countries that might initially welcome their presence was but a temporary solution. Once the majority felt threatened by Jewish economic competition, anti-Semitism would recur" (Rosenthal, 2001, p. 3). Such a legacy propelled the founding of the state of Israel in 1947, where Jews could "bring about their own self-emancipation" (p. 3), giving them national independence and status among other nations.

The American Jewish community financially and spiritually supported the formation of the Israeli state. Many American Jews today continue to be unflagging supporters of Israel. However, Rosenthal (2001) observed that the diversity of American Jews among other factors has weakened this bond. Perhaps most significant is the shrinking Jewish community itself. Intermarriage is a major force in the decrease of Jewish families. Some data indicate that over half of American Jews marry non-Jews, and relatively few offspring from those marriages marry Jews (Polsky, 2002).

Diversity among Jewish American families, combined with the decreasing proportion of Jews in the United States, has caused consternation within the community. These differences of opinion among people of Jewish faith have sometimes divided families and other groups. Fishman (2000) observed, "Jews sometimes experience these changes not only as a threat to the normative family unit, but also as a threat to Jewish continuity. Communal responses to the current diversity of Jewish households have hardly been dispassionate" (p. 115).

The percentage of Jews in the United States continues to be relatively small in comparison to Catholic and Protestant estimates. Despite these figures, tremendous Jewish contribution to American culture through art, theater, music, publication, humor, psychology, law and social justice, medicine, and countless other efforts is well-documented (Whitfield, 1999). Renowned artists, composers, actors, writers, humorists and satirists, trial attorneys, therapists, and scientists have come from the Jewish community. Weinrach (2003) reminded professional counselors, for example, that many popular theorists have Jewish backgrounds, including Sigmund Freud, Alfred Adler, Albert Ellis, Eric Berne, Fritz Perls, William Glasser, and Donald Meichenbaum among others. At the same time, American Jewish life has been influenced and altered by traditions and popular culture of the larger society. As an example, some American Jewish families participate in Christmas activities of Christian faiths while celebrating Chanukah during the same time of year.

Because American Jewry is so diverse and religious allegiance consists of several groups, it is challenging to delineate standard principles of faith. Nevertheless, from traditional Jewish teachings some fundamental beliefs emerge. These beliefs, sometimes referred to as "Thirteen Articles of Faith" in Jewish prayer books, are the following:

1. A belief in God;
2. The belief that there is only one God;
3. God is incorporeal, i.e., has no physical shape or form;
4. No other god has existed before God;
5. People serve and worship God alone and not symbols or likenesses of Him;
6. Prophets have been sent by God;
7. The prophecy of Moses is superior to all those of other prophets;
8. The Law of Moses (the Torah) was given to the Jewish people by God;
9. The Law of Moses will not be displaced or changed;
10. God knows all and is the Supreme Ruler of the world;
11. God rewards good and punishes evil;
12. A Messiah will eventually come, and people believe in his eventual coming;
13. The coming of the Messiah will bring with it the resurrection of the dead. (Cohen & Mendes-Flohr, 1972)

Regarding Jesus Christ, traditional Jewish thought is that he lived and that many people thought he was the Messiah and followed him. From that following emerged what we know today as Christianity. Some scholars believe the teachings of Jesus and subsequent Christian principles can be interpreted as expressions of Jewish beliefs. At the same time, the revelations of Jesus might be interpreted as prophecy according to Jewish faith (Cohen & Mendes-Flohr, 1972).

Islam. According to some sources, Islam is one of the fastest growing religions in the United States. Followers of Islam are Muslims, sometimes referred to as Moslems. Estimates of the number of Muslims in the United States vary greatly, ranging from 2 to 6 million depending on the source. According to the American Religious Identification Survey of 2001, the national estimate of Muslims is about 2.2 million (Kosmin & Mayer, 2001).

There is frequent confusion about Muslim heritage. In particular, two common myths—that all Muslims are Arabs or that all Arab Americans are Muslim—contribute to uncertainty and misunderstanding about Islam. Some data suggest that most Arab Americans follow a Christian religion, while about 25 percent follow Islam. In addition, with over 1,200 mosques in the United States, about 60 to 65 percent of Muslims indicate they attend a mosque, and the majority of those respondents are male (Kosmin & Mayer, 2001).

Islam follows the teachings of the prophet Muhammad (also spelled Mohammed), born about 570 in Mecca, a trading center in the northwest region of Arabia. His father died before he was born and his mother died when he was a young boy, so he was raised by a grandfather and later an uncle. In adulthood, Muhammad became a trader, married, and fathered two sons and four daughters. After working several years and traveling the region extensively, he began meditating in a cave outside of Mecca. The Islamic belief is that during this time an angel's voice commanded Muhammad to recite a verse proclaiming God as the creator and source of all knowledge. This and subsequent revelations are found in the Qur'an (also spelled Koran), the holy book of Islam, which cites the teachings of *Allah,* the Arabic word for God.

The historic meaning of Mecca to Muslims worldwide is significant. It is the holiest city, located in Saudi Arabia about 50 miles from the Red Sea. Muslims revere the city as the first place created on earth, as well as the place where the Ka'ba was built, surrounded by the great mosque. The Ka'ba is a brick structure that, according to Islam, is the center of the world, and the direction toward which Muslims pray (called the *salat*). Mecca is the center of religious teaching for Islam and the site of a compulsory pilgrimage for all Muslims.

Another important city to Muslims is Jerusalem, located in the state of Israel. It remains a city of much controversy and conflict because of Christian, Jewish, and Muslim reverence and historical significance. For Muslims, Jerusalem is where the Holy House of Allah is located. This mosque, in the heart of Jerusalem, is at the Noble Sanctuary, called Al-Haram al-Sharif, which is an enclosure of land, fountains, gardens, buildings, and domes. Known as the Al-Aqsa Mosque, this celebrated landmark is an important religious symbol to Muslims. The Noble Sanctuary is a significant site in Islamic teaching and religious worship.

As noted, followers of Islam use the Qur'an as their religious doctrine. Some fundamental beliefs of Islam are the following:

1. There is one true God, who has no son, nor shares His divinity with any other deity. No other god exists, and only the true God is deserving of worship.
2. God is the Almighty Creator and sustainer of everything in the universe. He knows all, and all things depend on Him. He is all-powerful and merciful.
3. God is not Jesus and Jesus is not God. Jesus was a mighty messenger sent by God and born of a virgin birth. With God's permission, Jesus healed the sick, cured the blind, and gave life to the dead.
4. God has no human form and all attribution of any human form is rejected.
5. Angels exist. They honor God, and obey Him. The Angel Gabriel gave the Qur'an to Muhammad.
6. God revealed books to His prophets as guidance for all people. Among these books is the Qur'an, which God revealed to Muhammad.

7. God sent several prophets and messengers to help guide humanity. Beginning with Adam and including Abraham, Ishmael, Isaac, Jacob, Moses, Noah, and Jesus, God created these messengers in human form to convey His word.
8. God sent his final message through his last prophet, Muhammad.
9. In the Day of Judgment, God will resurrect all people and judge them according to their beliefs and life deeds.
10. God has given all humans a free will, meaning that every person can choose right or wrong and is responsible for these decisions.
11. Divine Predestination *(Al-Qadar)* is the belief that (a) God knows all things, past, present, and future, (b) He has recorded all that has happened and will happen, (c) What God wills to happen will happen and what He does not will to happen, will not happen.

As noted in Chapter 6 about family and self-concept development, Islamic beliefs have historically viewed significant differences between male and female roles and that some of these views come from interpretations of the Qur'an (Hanna & Green, 2004; Roald, 2001). Hanna and Green (2004) observed, however, that regardless of the apparent ambivalent attitudes towards women found in Islamic doctrine, "we cannot lose sight of the fact that Islam remains a highly spiritual perspective that promotes spiritual values such as benevolence, forgiveness, and personal development" (p. 330). At the same time, these authors noted that socio-political perspectives woven throughout Islamic doctrine not only generate feelings of hostility toward Western beliefs by Muslims, but also invite prejudicial and discriminatory reactions from non-Islamic Americans (Hanna & Green, 2004).

Hispanic and Latino(a). As noted in earlier descriptions of Hispanic and Latino families, religion takes a powerful role in these cultures. "Overall, the church and faith play a crucial role and shape core beliefs, such as (a) the importance of sacrifice, (b) charitability and service to others, and (c) long suffering, even in the face of adversity" (Robinson, 2005, p. 83). For Latino families who immigrate to the United States, spiritual faith and religious beliefs are core values to hold onto as means of surviving the social pressures and economic depravity experienced in their newly adopted country. Urrabazo (2000) commented that survival helps these immigrants to weather initial experiences of an America "without mercy, without justice, without compassion," and eventually come to see a different country where "there is also a lot that is good . . . and that their experience of the shadow side of our society is just that one side" (p. 207). However, Urrabazo (2000) also noted that the contemporary values of U.S. society often clash with those of Latino families. "Given the certitudes of the Latino world, the certitude of God, the certitude of their role in the universe, and purpose of life, the openness of our modern society seems chaotic and without clear direction" (p. 207).

According to Fukuyama and Sevig (2002), spiritual beliefs intermingle with mental and physical illnesses and healing processes in Latino and Hispanic cultures. Catholicism is strong but there are also other forms of religion, such as Santeria, a combination of Catholic and Yoruba (West African) beliefs and practices. In addition, some reports indicate about a quarter of Latinos in the United States follow a Protestant sect (Murray, 2003). Furthermore, some communities incorporate secret religious practices, such as talking with spirits. In these instances, Latinas are sometimes thought to have mystical and psychic powers. Faith healers in some communities practice in consultation with clergy (Fukuyama & Sevig, 2002).

Murray (2003) reported that abandonment of Catholicism among Latinos seems to be a demographic trend. Some data indicates that from first to third generations, over a 10 percent drop in Roman Catholic affiliation occurred (74% to 62%). At the same time, identification with mainline Protestants and evangelical groups increased across the same generations about 15 percent. The prediction is for this trend to continue. Despite the increasing number of Protestants, the vast majority of Latino families in the United States (70%) are Roman Catholic. Although some Latinos leave the Catholic Church, especially among subsequent generations of immigrants, the 70 percent figure has remained stable for the past decade, largely due to increased immigration from Mexico. Regardless of the trends in affiliation, the expectation is for religion to remain an important part of Latino and Hispanic communities (Murray, 2003).

Religious beliefs of the majority of Latino and Hispanic families find basis in their native heritage and the influence of Christian missionaries during the sixteenth century. Although this influence has come largely from the Roman Catholic Church, we also find aspects of African and Asian beliefs among some Latinos (Urrabazo, 2000). Conventional Christian beliefs of Latino/Hispanic people include an overwhelming consensus that Jesus Christ is God and that the Virgin Mary (Our Lady of Guadalupe) is not only the mother of Christ, but their own mother as well. "Many Latinos hold Mary as their ideal. Accordingly, a life of motherhood, devoting oneself to the children is an important role for Latinas" (Urrabazo, 2000, p. 216). At the same time, the canonized saints of the Church are models of encouragement for living a life of integrity and good character (Urrabazo, 2000).

The church in Latino communities is a safe haven where people find comfort and refuge from the dominant society and language. A supportive vehicle, the church offers a familiar environment and, at the same time, provides possible avenues for community involvement. Urrabazo (2000) noted that church involvement "can be an important first step in the acculturation process and in feeling comfortable with being in this country" (p. 218).

Native American. In general, traditional Native American and Alaskan American beliefs encompass spiritual leanings without necessarily including formal religious affiliation. "American Indian and Alaskan Native people believe in a Supreme Creator that is considered both male and female and is in command of the all the elements of existence" (Robinson, 2005, p. 65). Among their spiritual beliefs are a focus on harmony with nature and all things, reverence for the sacredness of the Creator, respect for elders, and a philosophy that sharing is more significant than material matters because everything belongs to Earth. Native Americans believe in the connectedness and purpose among all things (Garrett & Garrett, 1994).

As do other cultural groups in the United States, Native Americans exhibit much diversity among their nations, communities, and tribes. Frequently, published accounts of Native American beliefs do not come from the communities and members themselves. Therefore, many myths exist.

Contemporary Native American beliefs trace their roots to the arrival of the first nomadic people across the Bering Strait from northeast Asia. From these ancestors, oral histories passed down for generations helped Native Americans develop beliefs in spirits, life after death, shamanism, taboos, and ceremonies that constituted various religions. Today, the number of Native American nations and communities and the diversity of beliefs among these groups make the task of describing common threads difficult. Nevertheless, the origin of religious beliefs found in the notions of spirituality and harmony with nature, humility, connectivity among all things, and other values mentioned earlier is apparent (Native American Spirituality, 2003).

The Native American Church, founded in 1918 and known as the Peyote Church, maintains a membership of approximately a quarter million people. The church uses an eclectic array of Native American spiritual rites, Christian beliefs, contemplation, and the peyote cactus plant in sacramental ceremonies as part of religious worship (Native American Spirituality, 2003).

An important spiritual symbol in Native American culture is the circle—representing life cycles and symbolizing the most sacred elements of life. The Circle of Life includes four directions: spirit, nature, body, and mind, and symbolizes the countless circles that embrace all people, exist within everyone, and are the essence of human existence (Garrett & Garrett, 1994).

According to Native American beliefs, failure to handle life challenges, physical illnesses, and mental health problems are consequences of lost harmony and living out of synch with one or more of the four directions of spirit, nature, body, and mind. This conviction demonstrates how a Native American interpretation of spirituality offers a holistic model of healthful living, harmony with nature, and collective community—values that historically and to the present day have been often at odds with the dominant culture and government powers in the United States.

The Native American relationship with Christianity has been one of great ambivalence. The history of oppression and injustice associated with the conversion of these indigenous people by Christian missionaries is indeed one of the tragic tales of the conquered New World. At the same time, the impact of Christianity on Native American culture and religion and the corresponding effect of Native American beliefs on the American conscience about how to live in harmony with the Earth need more attention from researchers and greater understanding by professional and lay persons alike.

The previous sections offer thumbnail sketches of spiritual and religious aspects of various groups in the United States. Reading about these different aspects might enhance your development as an effective counselor, but experiencing these divergent views and beliefs would strengthen it even more. Exercise 8.2 encourages you to expand your cultural experiences and spirituality.

Exercise 8.2

Diverse Religious Encounters

Instructions: Take time to attend a religious or spiritual ceremony that is different from any others you have ever had in your development. Attend services at a synagogue, mosque, church, or other place of worship that is different from your normal practice. Participate in a Native American Powwow, or other cultural experience that has spiritual or religious meaning. After your experience(s), share your thoughts with the class and discuss these questions:

1. What preconceived notions did you have prior to attending this service?
2. What anxieties did you feel in relationship to this experience?
3. What kind of reception did you experience from people attending this service?
4. Upon completing this experience, what feelings and/or observations did you have?

Exercise 8.3

What I Know about Religions of the World

Instructions: Read the list of religions below and write one or two things you know about each. Compare your results with a classmate.

Religion	*Something You Know*
Buddhist	____________________
Sikh	____________________
Hindu	____________________
Jehovah's Witness	____________________
Scientologist	____________________
Mennonite	____________________
Mormon	____________________
Moravian	____________________
Quaker	____________________
Baha'i	____________________
Jainist	____________________

As noted at the beginning of this section, only a few of the major religious groups are mentioned as examples of how religion and culture interconnect. Many other belief systems and cultures are omitted from this discussion, yet as a future counselor or professional helper, you might encounter clients with diverse spiritual views. For example, this section has not considered Amish, Mormon, Jehovah's Witness, Hindu, Sikh, Scientologist, Buddhist, or many other religions of the world. Exercise 8.3 tests your knowledge about some world religions that may not be familiar.

Spirituality and Counseling

Some authorities in counseling believe that spiritual beliefs are an essential component in the helping relationship. Given the array of spiritual and religious beliefs that clients bring with them to counseling and other helping relationships, the question for counselors and human service professionals may not be whether to include spirituality and religious beliefs in helping relationships, but rather how to do it in appropriate and beneficial ways. Ivey and colleagues (2002) suggested that understanding the contribution of spirituality is paramount in successfully handling multicultural encounters in counseling relationships. As emphasized in this text, people have multiple identities, and these include spiritual and religious perception of self and others. Therefore, counseling a broad clientele demands an understanding of how all these identities, for both the client and counselor, interact and influence self-concept development and life choices.

Strong religious beliefs or spirituality sometimes elicits caring behavior, thus influencing counselors and other professional helpers to reach out to people in need. For some helpers, caring is an essential aspect of their spiritual being. Such action may or may not be prompted by strong religious beliefs, but is often guided by an assumption that something connects all people in a meaningful way. As such, spirituality is the cultivation of a life in which helping professionals exhibit genuine caring for people in mutually beneficial ways. This philosophy might not include beliefs in a higher power, but if it does, these beliefs complement a spirituality that exhibits unconditional regard for all people regardless of their religious commitment.

Helms and Cook (1999) noted that many principles found in traditional approaches to counseling have parallel assumptions and philosophical beliefs with world religions. For example, God as the ultimate nurturer or parent who provides unconditional love and forgiveness takes on the image of a helper who demonstrates unconditional positive regard and authenticity within an empathic relationship. Similarly, the power of prayer might have cognitive-behavioral connotations in helping people to form positive images and to use them to diminish obstacles, for achieving a healthy, fulfilled life.

Fukuyama and Sevig (2002) recalled that Sigmund Freud was one theorist who wondered if religious beliefs were negative forces in human development. His view contrasted with those of contemporaries Carl Jung and Alfred Alder, who both contended that religious and spiritual beliefs might benefit the therapeutic relationship and overall human development. In addition, theorists from the humanistic arena promoted the notions of "self-actualization and the fully functioning being, which includes aspects of transcendence and the meaning of life" (p. 276).

Transpersonal approaches to counseling surfaced in the 1960s from the field of humanistic psychology. According to Fukuyama and Sevig (2002), transpersonal assumptions reached for a level of helping beyond understanding of a socially constructed *self* to one of appreciating a higher consciousness and spiritual presence. Transpersonal theorists "suggested that spirituality and the search for meaning are at the center of human existence" (p. 278).

Most cultures have a holistic view of human development with the body, mind, and spirit seen as one entity. In a sense, this perspective is a collective and synergistic belief that maintains the sum of the parts is greater than the whole. From a holistic perspective, professional helpers strive to understand the connectedness and interrelationship of all internal and external elements. In contrast, a strictly individualistic perspective views the person as separate parts, and perceives helping as a narrow focus on broken or damaged elements without regard to their relationship to the whole.

Counseling Inferences

Becoming a competent counselor requires achievement of knowledge, skill, and understanding to work with clients who profess diverse spiritual and religious views. Ivey and colleagues (2002) and Fukuyama and Sevig (2002) listed several competencies related to counselors' spiritual development and understanding. The following is a compilation of their suggestions. Professional helpers who are competent to work with culturally diverse clients are able to

1. Explore their spiritual universe and articulate the meaning that comes from such exploration;

2. Understand and empathize with diverse religious and spiritual expressions and orientations;
3. Understand the limits of their knowledge of spiritual and religious elements manifested in counseling relationships, and use appropriate referral sources to help clients handle these issues;
4. Assess the relevance of spiritual and religious elements in the helping relationship;
5. Use spiritual, transpersonal, and religious beliefs and themes as part of the counseling process to help clients meet personal and professional goals;
6. Articulate the relationship among religious, spiritual, and transpersonal beliefs and practices and their meaning for development over the life span;
7. Describe spiritual/religious beliefs and practices in a cultural context; and
8. Appreciate and understand how spiritual development contributes to overall self-development.

As we close this chapter about religion, spirituality, and their interaction with culture, it is important to reemphasize their influence on *self*-development. People embrace spiritual and religious beliefs depending on various factors in their life. Family, community, and heritage as well as significant experiences and events help people decide about issues of faith and spirituality. How clients process these factors and incorporate religious or spiritual beliefs into their self-concept development, or discard past beliefs, may have meaning in counseling relationships. Equally important, the extent to which counselors and other professional helpers understand their own spiritual existence and religious principles, and the influence these values have on relationships with other people, is a measure of how effective they might be with clients from varied religious and spiritual backgrounds.

9

Social Class and Economic Considerations

This text has presented several socially constructed status variables that interact with individual perceptions as people form their unique *self*-views and ultimately their worldviews. These variables included race, culture, ethnicity, ability, disability, attractiveness, religion, and family among others. A final variable that converges with most if not all of the previously mentioned ones is socioeconomic status (SES), which is the relative ranking by financial wealth of a person, family, or group within a particular society. As with all the other variables, socioeconomic status is a socially constructed symbol. Nevertheless, actual differences in financial wealth and the distribution of wealth within and across social groups exist. The interaction of socioeconomic status with individual self-concept development, and the manner in which society handles its diversity of wealth includes these three aspects: (1) reasons that economic differences occur, (2) the meaning that society assigns to the differences that exist, and (3) how individuals perceive wealth, poverty, and their relative place within society's overall economy.

Socioeconomic status and the related construction called *social class* are as important to identity development as other status variables—race, ethnicity, sex, gender, sexual orientation, and ability—discussed in earlier chapters (McEwen, 2003). Some authors in the counseling and helping professions have noted the omission of social class as a vehicle of oppression (Robinson, 2005) and have argued that by neglecting its importance in the study of discrimination, professions reinforce notions of class oppression and unearned privilege gained simply from wealth and social power (Dill, 1994; hooks, 2000). At the same time, Robinson (2005) optimistically noted that a fresh focus in the counseling literature "addresses race, gender, and class as interconnected constructs" (p. 170).

As a science, economics may not lend much understanding to the notion of how socioeconomic status relates to an emerging self-concept or to a person's worldview. By definition, economics is the science of studying the production, distribution, and consumption of products and services in a society. However, in a presentation of *personalist economics,* O'Boyle (1998) differentiated types of economics. He noted, "Personalist economics centers on the human person as worker and consumer which means that economics necessarily is a moral science" (p. xv). Contrastingly, *conventional economics* focuses on material goods, services, financial wealth, and resources. O'Boyle (1998) continued that the greatest challenge for economists who follow the notion of *personalism* is to resolve contrasting beliefs about personal freedom as the ultimate principle versus the common good as the ultimate principle. This conflict among economic theorists appears similar to the divergent concepts of individualism and collectivism discussed in earlier chapters of this text. Perhaps ideas associated with "personal freedom" align with aspects of individualism, while those related to "the common good" relate more to collectivism.

O'Boyle's (1998) discussion of *personalist economics* devoted attention to many concepts that are important to counselors, human service providers, and other professional helpers who work with diverse clients. These concepts include the notions of justice, charity, belonging, caring, needs, unemployment, physical and mental hardships, poverty, homelessness, criminal behavior, production loss, and redistribution of income. All these concepts have potential impact on individual development and socially constructed statuses.

In this chapter, we explore social class and socioeconomic status as two related variables that influence self-concept development. Both are worthwhile factors to consider when working with diverse populations. In addition to these general factors, this chapter also focuses on specific aspects of classism, poverty, and affluence; how they interact in the process of self-concept development, and how individuals relate to the larger community and society to which they belong.

Socioeconomic Status and Social Class

Income, wealth, and resulting socioeconomic status are factors that influence individual identity as well as family structure and functioning (Aponte & Crouch, 2000; Gladding, 2002; Robinson, 2005). In addition to income and wealth, education and career status are related variables that contribute to socioeconomic status (SES). Although social and cultural research and literature in counseling and other helping professions focus on important variables such as race, ethnicity, and gender, SES and social class have only recently begun to receive attention (Liu & Pope-Davis, 2004). The profession's neglect of social class while affording race, ethnicity, and gender more attention as identity variables is noteworthy. As Robinson (2005) indicated, "Race, gender, ability and disability, and class converge and affect the discourses about the ways people engage in self-definition" (p. 172).

Social class is a common identifier found in everyday descriptors. For example, the expressions "lower class," "working class," "middle class," and "upper class" are part of the U.S. lexicon used to describe people we know and with whom we work. These class groups are representations of various levels of socioeconomic status (SES). As populations expand and fewer levels of stratification satisfy our seemingly insatiable need to classify people, we add descriptors such as "lower middle class" and "upper middle class" with the false hope that these added dimensions will describe individuals and groups more precisely. At the same time, researchers and practitioners use similar terms to group subjects and clients. All these instances of grouping and identifying social classes include assumptions, biases, and prejudices commonly found in most systems of stratification. However, terminology in and of itself does not explain social class—what it is and why it exists.

Some people reject the notion of social class and view the democratic culture espoused by many people in America as fostering a classless society. However, Langston

Exercise 9.1

Classist Myths

Instructions: Read the statements below and reflect on your beliefs about each. Discuss with a classmate or in a group.

1. Being born with a *silver spoon* in one's mouth does not mean a person will have greater advantages than less affluent people.
2. There are plenty of jobs advertised and available, so no person has an excuse to be unemployed in the United States.
3. Poor people who succeed are able to "pull themselves up by their bootstraps," and that kind of perseverance and self-reliance is all anyone needs to improve his or her life.
4. As helping professionals, counselors and human service providers are not biased by their clients' social class.
5. The problem with most poor people is that they do not live within their means because they are impulsive and unable to delay gratification.
6. People who are not willing to learn how to speak and write according to Standard English cannot expect to move up in class.
7. Race, ethnicity, and gender have little relationship to social class in the United States. Money above all else rules.
8. Poor people who have more children than they can afford are socially irresponsible.
9. All individuals have the power to advance their social class by taking advantage of educational opportunities.
10. Counselors and other helpers who have experienced and overcome poverty are more likely to inspire clients from impoverished backgrounds.

(2001) called the notion of a classless society a myth perpetuated by misguided beliefs in the power of self-reliance, personal ambition, and individual intelligence. In and of themselves, these qualities are important values, but the belief that everyone in the United States has equal opportunity and advantage to succeed using these traits is widely overstated. Exercise 9.1 offers some common phrases and thoughts about social class and personal success. See what you think about the statements in this exercise.

According to Liu and Pope-Davis (2004), social class exists because of "the inequalities that arise between people when individuals understand the economic expectations of their environment and behave to meet these demands" (pp. 298–97). As such, in constructing self-views and subsequent worldviews, people include aspects of the economic environment, which gives meaning to their "class" as well as other classes, and allows them to function in an identified social group. Because people construct self-views by drawing perceptual conclusions, as proposed throughout this text, some people might make different interpretations for themselves than commonly held beliefs about their particular social class. Otherwise, how would we explain members of one social class intentionally moving to a higher or lower level in the course of a lifetime? For example, a young woman from an impoverished family might reject the descriptor of "lower class" for herself and aspire to achieve educational status or other attributes that elevate her to a higher social class. In contrast, another person, born into affluence, might choose a life of humble means and austere surroundings.

Herring (1999) recalled how the lack of financial resources during his formative years and corresponding classism affected the development of himself and fellow classmates. "During my public school years," he wrote, "discriminatory experiences were based entirely on social class. The students from the mill village were looked down on by teachers and students alike" (Herring, 1999, p. 26). Nevertheless, in his narrative Herring (1999) also noted that individual differences enabled him to overcome the classist oppression of his community, even though these accomplishments contradicted his perceived social class. While most of his schoolmates remained in low-paying career tracks, taking jobs after completing or dropping out of school that "continued their family's cycle of low economics and dysfunctional social interactions," Herring was able to "escape the cycle through sheer determination and by presenting a maverick persona—meaning I attempted things that students from my SES and part of town were not expected to do" (Herring, 1999, p. 26). This recollection by Herring is an example of how individual beliefs, nurtured by family and community, can overcome socially constructed negative status variables to create a successful and productive life.

Simply attaining or losing wealth to move from one class to another is not the only aspect in understanding social class phenomena. As a construct, social class has contextual meaning. Therefore, moving up or down in social class means more than acquiring or losing wealth. Other variables need consideration and examination. For example, geographic location may be a mitigating factor in determining social class of a family. If a family living in the United States with a certain amount of wealth moves to Mexico, its social status, based on affluence, might change. Similarly, a family from upstate New York that moves to Southern California might realize a status change simply by its relocation. Exercise 9.2 asks you to consider personal perceptions and experiences related to social class.

Based on the discussion thus far, we have learned that class association and identification are influenced by many variables including wealth, education, location, and membership in other social group, such as family. Furthermore, these variables contribute to an

Exercise 9.2

Perceptions and Experiences Related to Social Class

Instructions: Consider each of the statements and reflect on perceptions and/or experiences that have influenced your views and feelings about social class. Share your thoughts in a group discussion.

1. I have experienced poverty during my lifetime.
2. I constantly strive to move to a higher social class.
3. Being around poor people makes me uncomfortable.
4. Being around wealthy people makes me uncomfortable.
5. Money (financial wealth) is important to me.
6. I often evaluate people based on their likely social class.
7. Most of my friends are in the same social class as I am.
8. As a group, my friends comprise a range of social classes.
9. I believe that all people have equal opportunity to gain as much wealth as they want.
10. I have never experienced a time when I did not have sufficient money to do what I wanted to do.

identification system of social class that is essentially artificial and discriminatory. It promotes classist attitudes that enable people to maintain or elevate their status while keeping others in theirs. Understanding the concept of classism is as important to counselors, human service specialists, and other helping professionals as is racism, sexism, or other belief systems that perpetuate discrimination and oppression of individuals and groups. In the next section, we consider the concept of classism.

Classism

Liu and Pope-Davis (2004) noted that people at all socioeconomic levels express class attitudes within their respective families, groups, neighborhoods, institutions, and other environments. Such attitudes establish a strategy of classism, "which people use sometimes to maximize their opportunities to accumulate the valued capital within their economic culture" (Liu & Pope-Davis, 2004, p. 300). Four suggested levels of classism include

Downward Classism—Prejudice and discrimination towards individuals and groups thought to be lower in social status.

Upward Classism—Prejudicial attitudes towards people thought to be in a higher social group.

Lateral Classism—Attitudes and behaviors that attempt to reshape or reeducate a member of a social class who has developed a divergent social worldview from the group's mainstream beliefs.

Internalized Classism—Feelings of failure, depression, anger, despair, or frustration that result from a person's inability to produce or attain sufficient wealth or otherwise meet the demands and expectations of the economic culture.

These proposed forms of classism might be helpful in understanding clients' perceptions relative to their social class. We will revisit the construct of socioeconomic classism and its relationship with *self*-development in the next section. Here, we consider how perceptions of social class might explain family and community attitudes and influences that relate to clients' concerns.

In an earlier chapter, this text noted varied family structures that exist in U.S. society and around the world. In many instances, family structure contributes to or inhibits the economic health of families and the subsequent socioeconomic identity of family members. Furthermore, decisions made by the family to address economic conditions often have implications for gender roles, educational goals, and other status variables. As families process these decisions and succeed or fail to meet economic expectations of their social group, attitudes and behaviors associated with different forms of classism emerge. When embraced by individual family members, these attitudes and behaviors establish classist prejudices and discriminatory practices that define families, cultures, and societies. However, when families do not accept classist attitudes embraced by the larger culture, they put themselves at risk of alienation and exclusion. In either case, counselors or other helping professionals can be more effective in helping clients deal with these family issues by understanding the dynamics of various forms of classism and their effects on self-concept development.

Of all social class identifiers, none has more debilitating effects than poverty. Because of its implications for disadvantaged and oppressed groups, we pay particular attention to poverty and its relationship to family structure and function.

Poverty

This text has compared individualism and collectivism as two contrary or competing perspectives related to social and cultural foundations of counseling. In the United States, both of these views are represented across various cultural and ethnic groups. Ironically, basic principles of each perspective—individual responsibility and social equality—are threatened by the disparity of wealth across segments of the population. Poverty has a devastating effect on an individual's self-concept and on a group or family's access to social, political, and educational benefits, which in contrast are realized more often by people who are financially fortunate or privileged. Consequently, many worthwhile initiatives, such as counseling services to help families and individuals meet personal, social, and career challenges, may be futile without an understanding of how socioeconomic status intercedes or interferes as a significant variable in the process of self-concept development.

Research has indicated a relationship between brain development in early childhood and family poverty (Shore, 1997). In the United States during the late 1990s, about 2.5 million children lived in poverty and, therefore, faced a greater risk of delayed or injured brain development (National Center for Children in Poverty, 1999). Although many poor children are able to overcome impoverished circumstances and lead healthy and successful lives, research studies indicate that early childhood is a period when brain growth and development is greatly influenced by environmental stimuli, which are created, enhanced, and sustained by family socioeconomic status (National Center for Children in Poverty, 1999). Some factors produced by impoverished conditions that subsequently have a serious negative impact on brain development include inadequate nutrition during formative years; substance abuse during and after pregnancy; maternal depression; exposure to environmental toxins; physical, mental, and emotional abuse; and lack of quality daily care that allows healthy social interaction (National Center for Children in Poverty, 1999).

The possible link between brain development and poverty is given additional credibility from studies of learning in children. For example, Roseberry-McKibben (2001) noted the impact of low SES on children's language development and related educational success. Likewise, a study of kindergarten students indicated a positive correlation of academic achievement with socioeconomic status (Jacobson, 2002). Sometimes, studies have shown that poverty relates to indirect factors that might inhibit learning. For example, Gould and Gould (2003) noted that "undetected and uncorrected vision problems" among school-age children, particularly from impoverished families, have an impact on learning (p. 324).

Health considerations for the population at large present another equity issue related to socioeconomic status. In addition, SES often interacts with other status variables, such as race, in creating disparate health services for the general public. As an example, Freeman (2004) noted the relationship that exists among poverty, race, and SES in treating cancer patients. Reports from 1989 by the American Cancer Society and more recently by the U.S. Institute of Medicine indicate that poor people, and particularly African Americans, are least likely to obtain the most aggressive and curative types of cancer treatment (Freeman, 2004).

A widening economic gap divides the United States. Census figures from 2002 indicate that almost 10 percent of all families lived in poverty, about 7.2 million families. Of this group, 26.5 percent of all female-headed households were below the poverty level compared to 5.3 percent of married-couple families (Institute for Research on Poverty, 2003). The overall wealth of the country has improved over past decades, as indicated by the decline in percentage of citizens living in poverty. Nevertheless, many subgroups continue to suffer higher than average levels of poverty, and often the families suffering the most are from historically oppressed and discriminated groups. For example, in 2002 over 20 percent of all African American families and nearly 20 percent of all Latino families were impoverished economically, while 7.8 percent of all White families and 7.4 percent of all Asian families were below the poverty level (U.S. Bureau of the Census, 2003). As a result of poverty, a high percentage of African American and Latino children suffer from poor nutrition, lack of heath care, and other deficiencies that inhibit educational development (Howe, 1991).

In 2001, the Joint Center for Poverty Research noted that during the economic expansion and growth experienced by this country in the 1990s, differences continued between rural and urban populations. Poverty rates increased more in metropolitan areas, but over 14 percent of the people who lived in nonmetropolitan areas were poor. At the same time, fewer job opportunities and higher unemployment rates for single-mother families were found in rural areas (Institute for Research on Poverty, 2001). These findings have implications for professional counselors and other helpers who work in both urban and rural areas. Great disparity in economic wealth divides a population and makes it difficult to bring diverse groups together in working toward important social goals such as equal mental health services for all citizens.

A large portion of U.S. society does not experience extreme poverty during a lifetime. Probably, students reading this text who are in either undergraduate or graduate study for degrees in counseling or another helping profession do not live in extreme poverty, for if they did, they probably would be unable to pay tuition for school. This does not mean that financial obligations for all students are easy to fulfill. Many students struggle financially to meet their daily expenses and pay costs of their education. Nevertheless, extreme poverty is another thing altogether. In certain instances, however, even affluent people find themselves without cash or strapped for funds temporarily. Exercise 9.3 helps you process this possibility and to reflect on the feelings you may have experienced when low on funds.

Socioeconomic status and social class are important factors to consider when working with clients from diverse groups. As the exercises in this section have tried to illustrate, what may be most important is how individual people perceive their social status and incorporate beliefs about it into their self-concept development. The next section considers factors that relate to SES and self-concept development.

Exercise 9.3

Nobody Knows You When You're Down and Out

Instructions: Think of a time or a circumstance when you were low on funds, out of cash, or had a loan application turned down or a credit card rejected. Reflect on that experience by answering the following questions or statements and sharing with another classmate or group.

1. What was the situation, and what were you trying to buy or pay for?
2. Who else was involved in the transaction (e.g., store clerk, banker, friend, family member)?
3. Recall your immediate feelings. What did you do?
4. What reactions did you observe from other people involved in the transaction?
5. Have you done anything in your routine to avoid this type of experience again?

SES and Self-Concept Development

The previous section reviews how socioeconomic status interacts and relates to classism in society. It also reveals statistics that describe the extent of poverty in the United States across diverse cultural groups. In this section, we examine this status variable as it affects personal and *self*-development within society. In particular, this section reviews affluence and poverty across cultures, reflects on the relationship among SES, gender, race, marital status, and lastly, connects SES with the stress that many clients bring to helping relationships. First, we consider the notions of affluence and poverty in general.

Affluence and Poverty

The idea that affluence and poverty have an effect on *self*-development may seem self-evident, but as noted in the first part of this chapter, they are important concepts to explore in gaining an understanding of how people interact within society from a socioeconomic perspective. It might seem obvious that economic comfort is better than economic discomfort for people across cultural groups. As the old saying goes, "I've been rich and I've been poor, and rich is much better!" Yet, affluence in and of itself does not guarantee healthy *self*-development or happiness. News reports and other sources have indicated that American culture continues to focus on the accumulation of wealth while at the same time living a comfortable to luxurious lifestyle (Asnes, 2003). For the average American, more disposable income is required for basic and necessary expenses, such as food, while at the same time the cost of many items once thought to be luxuries has declined. This is particularly true among electronic appliances and equipment such as televisions, recorders, and computers. The ability to purchase goods that improves lifestyle may help enhance self-image and perhaps a person's overall life satisfaction. One survey, for example, found that among affluent respondents (median household income of $121,000), 84 percent agreed that while money may not buy happiness, it certainly does help (Asnes, 2003). In contrast, only 16 percent of the sample disagreed with the statement.

Affluence in America is becoming more available to members of diverse cultural groups, and projected growth in buying power is greater for minority populations than the majority population (Wentz, 2003). Evidence of increased buying power exists among targeted advertising audiences. For example, growth of the Hispanic advertising market has exploded in recent years, with reports indicating that over 1.2 million Hispanic/Latino households claim incomes of $75,000 and higher. Language appears to be an important variable in this phenomenon, with bilingual families making greater economic strides. At the same time, many Latino and Hispanic people are reestablishing their cultural roots by signing up for Spanish lessons (Wentz, 2003).

African Americans have shown a decline in their overall poverty rate and an increase in economic progress since the 1960s. The average per capita income for African Americans from 1990 to 2000 rose 64 percent in comparison to 55 percent growth for the total population. Still, because a large portion of the Black population is unemployed or employed in marginal low-paying jobs, they are vulnerable to the ebb and flow of the national economy. African American families often suffer unemployment at greater rates than the rest of the population in the best of times, and with economic downturns, their suffering typically increases. Despite growth in overall income, in 2000, poverty continued to be a shackle that strapped 22.5 percent of African Americans compared with only 11.3 percent of the total population (Lewis & Benet, 2003).

Fewer children across cultural groups are living in poverty compared to a decade ago. Yet, the growth in the number of families headed by single parents continues to be a factor that contributes to child poverty (Toppo, 2003). This phenomenon, perhaps more than any other, points to the combination of gender, race, and marital status as an influential factor in the study of affluence and poverty.

Gender, Race, and Marital Status

An abundance of research indicates that women across cultures in American society earn less income than men do, and this holds true when men and women hold the same jobs with similar levels of experience. In addition, females lead most single-parent families, and as noted above, these families have a high incidence of poverty. Therefore, single motherhood is a negative factor when considering socioeconomic status as a variable that contributes to self-concept development.

Race is also a convergent factor in this formula. For example, Robinson (2005) noted that factors such as high unemployment, job loss, and extraordinary indebtedness are stressors that debilitate African American men disproportionately in achieving economic power and self-fulfillment as providers for their families. In a sense, many Black men suffer from not only the legacy oppression and discrimination in America, but they also constantly fight the economic realities that plague workers most often placed at the lowest rungs of job market. Racism, both intentional and unintentional, plays a major role in this phenomenon. Still, some progress has occurred, with more African American men and women obtaining college degrees and nearly 50 percent of Black families owning homes (Lewis & Benet, 2003).

Stress

All the socioeconomic conditions discussed in preceding sections of this chapter contribute to stressful relationships in people's lives. At the same time, life's stressors frequently become mitigating factors in people's decisions to choose behaviors that are unproductive and sometimes destructive. For diverse people attempting to acculturate into a new society while at the same time dealing with family relationships, job and employment issues, financial problems, and the day-to-day challenges that affect most everyone, these stressors might seem insurmountable. At times, they may be so great that the person perceives no alternative but to fight against the system, withdraw from family and society, or turn to self-destructive behaviors as a means of escaping discrimination and humiliation.

For most people, stress is a normal part of living, and to a degree, some stress can be a motivating factor in challenging people to set goals and move forward in their lives. Without some stress and challenges, people might become complacent and even stagnant in their development. Contrastingly, groups that have been historically oppressed and excluded from the benefits enjoyed by the larger society, or who have migrated from ravaged, worn-torn parts of the globe, often experience stress that takes on traumatic proportion and effect. In the first instance, people who feel disenfranchised from mainstream society might become exhausted trying to use socially acceptable, legal, and peaceful means of dealing with stress, especially financial stress. If so, their exhaustion could lead to frustration and anger that propels them to acts of desperation, hostility, and sometimes violence. Similarly, immigrants who come to a new culture from countries where they left persecution or the trauma of war often bring intense stress with them as they face challenges that come with the start of a new life in an unfamiliar land.

Even under the best of circumstances when people move to a new culture, whether within their own country or to an entirely new country, they experience emotional highs and lows as they adjust to new surroundings, languages (or dialects and phrases), jobs, schools, places of worship, economic challenges, and other factors related to the move. People react differently to changes in time orientation, unfamiliar foods, different accommodations, job expectations, school schedules and regulations, new currency, shopping customs, transportation availability, and a host of other changes that add stress beyond those normally expected from a move. Add financial challenges to this formula and you compound the difficulties. Such stress might manifest itself as homesickness, depression, withdrawal, hostility, or other reactions.

Counselors, human service providers, and other professional helpers are cognizant of the stressors affecting daily lives as well as residue of stressful events left behind in their former country or region. At the same time, professional helpers are aware of how they might react to the stress experienced by their clients. Exercise 9.4 is a virtual reality list to assess how you might fare in a move to new situation.

In addition to understanding social and economic factors that contribute to stress, helpers also need to differentiate between interpersonal and intra-personal stress presented

Exercise 9.4

New Cultural Experiences

Instructions: Read the list of changes that might affect how you feel and operate in daily life. Assume these changes are a result of moving to another region or country. In the right-hand column, assign a number from 1 to 5 indicating the level of stress each change would mean for you (1=lowest). Discuss and compare your assessment with other classmates.

Change	*Stress Level*
Eating unfamiliar foods	______
Learning a new language (or phrases)	______
Learning a new currency	______
Being away from home	______
Wearing unfamiliar types of clothing	______
Bathing or showering less frequently	______
Having less access to transportation	______
Losing money or having less money	______
Being unfamiliar with habits and customs	______
Attending a different place of worship	______
Sharing living quarters or having less space	______
Doing with less sleep	______
Dealing with different noises	______
Eating meals on a new schedule	______

by clients. Interpersonal stress occurs through interactions with family members, associates such as a new boss and co-workers, and people in day-to-day relationships such as shoppers, clerks, police officers, bus drivers, and countless others. Of course, it is not only the interactions themselves with this multitude of people, but also the individual's perceptions about these interactions. For this reason, two different people might experience the same situation, such as an approach by a police officer, each perceiving it differently, and drawing opposite conclusions that result in opposite behaviors. In one case, a person might see the police officer as an ally and in the other as an enemy or threat. Similarly, people from diverse social classes relate to financial officers and bank managers from different perspectives.

Intra-personal stress comes from the inner behaviors and emotions of the person. It is the culmination of thoughts and feelings a person has about herself or himself relative to either a specific event or a more global perspective of life in general. As such, intra-personal stress results from the private logic of the individual and how each person uses this logic to evaluate events and life in positive or negative ways.

As noted earlier, some stress might prove healthy in motivating a person to make changes, set goals, and achieve objectives toward a better life. This might be true for both interpersonal and intra-personal forms of stress. When either form, however, reaches levels where people are incapacitated or thwarted in their development, counseling or other professional help might be necessary. Through counseling or other intervention, clients might learn coping behaviors, such as relaxation exercises, to better handle stressful situations. In the case of socioeconomic stress, coping behaviors might include gaining information about educational, vocational, and other services that might help people set reasonable goals to achieve financial security.

The previous sections of this chapter present information to understand the multifaceted relationship among various status variables and social class. Equally important is the notion that each client seeking assistance from a professional helper defines these variables and assigns them particular value according to his or her unique perceptual lens and subsequent *self*-view. As such, a client who lacks financial wealth might nevertheless perceive herself as holding high social status. In contrast, a financially wealthy client might perceive himself as destitute. Understanding the unique process of self-creation and self-definition is essential in helping clients make appropriate social, personal, educational, and career decisions.

Counseling Inferences

A significant aspect of self-concept development is the interaction of the person with society. This chapter presented social factors related to socioeconomic status and social class that might have an impact on people's individual development as well as how they function in society in general. How counselors and other helping professionals assist clients in handling any or all of these factors is dependent on the knowledge they have about facts and issues related to socioeconomic conditions, trends, and individual behaviors and their self-understanding of social class.

Helping clients to work through various social factors that impede *self*-development or damage personal relationships must also take into account cultural beliefs and differences. As noted in other chapters, the focus of this text is on social and cultural foundations that relate to and affect counseling relationships. When working with clients who exhibit behaviors or face challenges related to any of the variables presented in this chapter, successful counselors learn about family and cultural background to help clients work through issues within an appropriate context. Ignoring ethnic or cultural factors places the *helper* at risk of encapsulation, which inhibits empathic understanding and limits the likelihood of successful helping relationships.

As with all the other status variables presented in this text, socioeconomic status and social class must be explored and understood by counselors or other professional helpers if they expect to be effective with clients across cultural groups. The starting point for such exploration and understanding is to self-examine and self-reflect about your perceptions and beliefs regarding these socially constructed variables. At the same time, sensitivity about how clients might perceive you, and your social class, is also important in establishing credible helping relationships. Often, class biases are unknown to counselors and other helpers who have them. Sometimes, biases are inherent in the mental health system or counseling services as they are designed. For example, a public counseling service that only offers daytime hours unintentionally neglects a large portion of the community who, due to work schedules, could only participate during evening hours. Missing work and pay could present a tremendous financial strain that would be unrelieved by any counseling service. Similarly, the cost of services might be prohibitive for some clients.

Few professional counselors are equipped or prepared to handle any or all issues that clients might bring to the helping relationship. Helpers might require expertise for many of the social factors covered in this chapter and throughout the text. Knowing your limitations, seeking additional knowledge and skill, or referring clients to more appropriate sources for assistance are essential ingredients in being an intentionally effective counselor (Schmidt, 2002). In terms of socioeconomic status, counselors and other helpers can search for informed financial sources to provide clients with accurate information about savings plans, loans, employment opportunities, retirement plans, educational programs, and a host of other resources to enable clients to make informed decisions.

Because of socioeconomic realities, counselors and other human service professionals take action beyond their own self-understanding and the immediate services they offer clients. They become socially and professionally active in helping communities provide broad-based services to a wide audience of clients. Narrative 9.1 tells about Bayview, Virginia, and the story of people who proactively took charge of their town. In the next chapter, we will explore this notion further by considering advocacy, conflict resolution, and social justice.

NARRATIVE 9.1 • *The Revival of Bayview, Virginia*

CBS News and the TV show *60 Minutes* have reported about how a 300-year-old community, Bayview, Virginia, and one of its residents, Alice Coles, mustered political action and public involvement to change the course of a town.

In the 1990s, Bayview was a forgotten town in the eastern shore farmland of Virginia. Comprised of run-down shacks that rented for about $30 a month, this community had been home to African Americans for decades. Now impoverished, these once proud residents lived in substandard dwellings without indoor plumbing and with hazardous electrical wiring. According to Alice Coles, who lived in Bayview most of her life, the houses had no designated kitchen, because no plumbing or electrical appliances gave any particular room that distinction.

In 1995, the state of Virginia began deliberating the possibility of putting a maximum-security prison in the middle of the town. Coles, at that time a middle-aged single mother making less than minimum wage as a crab picker, began her crusade against the government's plan. With a small band of community members, she founded The Bayview Citizens for Social Justice and proceeded to lobby for better conditions in the town and against the prison being built in their community. Through their efforts, the group learned about lobbying, politics, and non-profit organizational status. They eventually recruited Maurice Cox, an architect and college professor, to help them design a new vision for Bayview. After much effort to clean up the town, politicians and government officials began to pay attention. The state started to commit money for projects, and overall Bayview raised about $10 million from various state, federal, and private sources.

By 2004, several new houses were constructed for families to leave their shacks and begin new lives. The new prison had not been built in Bayview, but a new community center was on the drawing board. Plans were to help the community continue to realize its dream of restoring pride in its heritage. All this became possible because of a few people's desire to make positive changes, seek the financial resources to restore a community, and take political action to prevent the loss of their town.

More details about this story can be found through the following resources:

Alice Coles of Bayview. (July 18, 2004). CBSNews.com (*http://www.cbsnews.com/stories/2003/11/26/60minutes/main585793.shtml).*

This black soil: A story of resistance and rebirth. (2004). Bullfrog films. (*http://www.bullfrogfilms.com/catalog.this.html).* A 58-minute color film for grades 10 through adults.

The previous six chapters of this text have explored several social and cultural factors that influence self-concept development. These factors include race, ethnicity, sex, gender, sexual orientation, physical ability and disability, attractiveness and body image, family background, religion and spirituality, and social class. Each of these factors assumes value, either negative or positive, assigned by society and cultural groups within society. Those assigned values convey particular status to individuals depending on the factors involved and the degree to which individuals possess or lack these characteristics. Such assigned statuses contribute to diversity within particular groups, both intentionally and unintentionally. The challenge for counselors, human service providers, and other helping professionals is to understand existing diversity issues created by socially constructed statuses, recognize societal bias and prejudice that contribute to these statuses, and appreciate the oppression, discrimination, negligence, and exclusion that result from the application of these statuses in social programs, educational institutions, legal procedures, and other aspects of society.

At the end of each chapter, this text has presented inferences about these social/cultural statuses for counseling and other human services. The next chapter, Chapter 10, takes a more in-depth look at professional helping relationships, particularly counseling processes, and the implications of certain approaches and skills when used with clients from diverse backgrounds.

10

Counseling and Cultural Diversity

In the first chapter, this text introduced concepts of diversity and counseling. That introduction briefly commented about how discussion of diversity often raises two opposing views—one placing value on uniformity, conformity, and similarity of culture and another embracing and celebrating cultural differences. In addition, the chapter mentioned the inherent conflict between basic values upon which the United States was born, including ones of equality, freedom, and acceptance, and the contradictory prevalence of segregationist, egocentric, and individualistic views held by many Americans throughout history and in today's society. The apparent conflict between these perspectives was highlighted to emphasize the challenge that professional counselors and other helpers have in working with clients who are culturally different from them, or with groups of diverse clients. As noted, diversity of U.S. population is expanding at rapid pace. Future counselors and human service professionals can expect their clientele to reflect this greater diversity, and therefore, to be effective helpers, they will want to be knowledgeable of cultural differences and learn appropriate ways to become aware of the varying worldviews clients bring to various helping relationships.

This chapter explores counseling and diversity in greater depth. In it, I invite you to examine more closely some cultural aspects of counseling itself. This chapter presents models and skills that might be useful to counselors in working with diverse populations. In addition, it introduces issues about assessment, diagnosis, and intervention, describes group procedures with diverse clients, and considers ways counselors might help beyond their day-to-day counseling relationships with clients. We begin with an examination of some cultural values inherent in counseling relationships.

Cultural Aspects of Counseling

In general, multicultural counseling textbooks mention traditional counseling approaches—those that emerged largely from European schools of psychotherapeutic theory—with caution regarding their efficacy with culturally diverse clients. Over the past few decades, much study and speculation have contemplated whether traditional approaches work effectively across cultures, or if culture-specific approaches are more useful. Today, most popular approaches to counseling have come from theorists in Western Europe or the United States. According to Wohl (2000), "Any system of psychotherapy is embedded within a particular cultural-historical context, which shaped and conditioned the thought processes and values of both its practitioners and the clientele for which it was designed" (p. 75). Therefore, questions about the efficacy of such theories across diverse groups remain. At the same time, research of culture-specific approaches has yet to show promising results regarding their effectiveness. "The fundamental notion is that traditional psychotherapies can be used, but they must be adapted and flexibility applied by taking into account social, economic, cultural, ethnic, and political determinants of the patient's situation" (Wohl, 2000, p. 77).

In this section, we consider aspects of cultural difference that could have an effect on counseling relationships, specifically the processes selected by counselors to help particular clients from diverse backgrounds. If research of culture-specific approaches continues to reveal less than favorable results regarding effectiveness (much more research is needed to draw any conclusion about this matter), and if traditional approaches retain some value when used with appropriate flexibility, then professional counselors will want to know how to translate and adapt traditional approaches with the clients they serve.

Counseling Approaches and Skills

A premise of most approaches to counseling, particularly the earliest theories, is that clients come to counseling to solve problems. As such, typical models of counseling begin with a deficit perspective of the client, or a problem-oriented assessment of the client's situation. In essence, this is a remedial view of counseling as opposed to a developmental one. The trouble with a remedial perspective is that it gives the counseling relationship a narrow focus on a person's internal processes and ignores the external contributions of family, culture, and community. Approaches that are effective with clients from varied cultural backgrounds tend to take a more holistic perspective, considering the contribution of many factors and how individuals incorporate them into unique worldviews. As an example, if a client at a university counseling center discusses dissatisfaction with academic progress, a limited focus might recommend study skills intervention to help the student improve time management and other behaviors related to effective studying. Although stronger study skills might be helpful to this student, a more holistic assessment of other factors, including family expectations, physical well-being, peer relationships, and cultural perspectives about educational achievement, might help the counselor and client formulate broader, more developmental interventions with greater likelihood of encouraging the client to examine educational plans and make appropriate decisions. Given a broad range of options available to the student, plans and decisions might even include a conclusion to leave the university and pursue other career avenues and life choices.

Problem-oriented, remedial views of counseling can also limit the possibilities for broader helping relationships. In contrast, holistic and developmental approaches seek to find strengths that people possess and positive influences held by the family and commu-

Exercise 10.1

Instructions: Recall an experience from the past or current time that challenged you in some significant way. Consider the internal strength(s) you mustered in addressing this issue and write them down. Also, account for the support and values that came from external sources such as family, cultural background, and community, and list those. After compiling your two lists, assess how effective you would have been without one or the other in dealing with your identified problem.

Inner Strengths	***External Support***
____________	____________
____________	____________
____________	____________
____________	____________
____________	____________
____________	____________

nity to which they belong. Clients in counseling or other helping relationships have often faced challenges of racial, social, cultural, economic, and religious oppression. To overcome these experiences, they might benefit from an exploration of their inner strength as well as the power they receive from family, community, and culture over a lifetime, and with which they still identify. Exercise 10.1 offers you an opportunity to examine a challenge that you have experienced or are facing presently, and consider the internal strengths and external influences of family, culture, and community that empowered you in dealing with the situation.

Counselor Preparation. Another aspect of counseling that has cultural implications relates to the skills encouraged and reinforced in counselor preparation. These include listening, attending, self-disclosure, and interpretation among others. Ivey, D'Andrea, Ivey, and Simek-Morgan (2002) noted that attending behaviors are culturally specific. Consequently, no single form of attending is appropriate across cultural groups. For some clients, nonverbal cues might be more important in their assessment and acceptance of a counseling relationship than verbal content expressed by culturally different counselors. Differences in patterns of eye contact, body language, vocal tone and speech rate, physical space, and time orientation exist between European–North American and other cultures (Ivey et al., 2002). Helms and Cook (1999) added that many attending skills tend to convey a passive or nondirective approach to counseling. By contrast, when counselors use expressive skills, they offer clients more direction and interpretation. Accordingly, some clients might prefer more structured approaches and directive interventions, and these preferences might emanate from cultural influences.

Self-disclosure is another skill advocated in counselor preparation. Counselors use self-disclosure to tell something about themselves in expressing empathy and understanding about a client's situation. At the same time, self-disclosure by clients is fundamental to traditional counseling processes. To this end, Robinson (2005) questioned the appropriateness of encouraging all clients to self-disclose information about themselves. She speculated, "Isn't it possible for some clients actually to feel violated, given the unidirectional nature of the counseling exchange that could be conceived of as inconsistent with community and reciprocity" (p. 176). Using or encouraging self-disclosure without consideration of cultural differences, therefore, might prove counterproductive when counseling clients of various cultural backgrounds.

Interpretation is a skill that has different meaning depending on the author or instructor presenting it. From a conventional perspective, "Interpretation in the psychodynamic model has traditionally been made from an individualistic, ego psychology frame of reference that locates the problem and decision making in the individual" (Ivey et al., 2002, p. 135). In contrast, an expanded use of interpretation skills in counseling relationships includes dimensions of family, ethnic group, gender, or other social/cultural considerations. By helping clients interpret their behavior or situation within the context of family values, gender-orientation issues, ethnic or racial history, or other cultural aspect, counselors use interpretation to move from an individualistic to a collective perspective.

Ultimately, all these attending and related skills intend to help counselors and other professionals express empathic understanding toward their clients. Yet, from a cross-cultural or multicultural perspective, empathy is more than simply tending to or understanding the person in the process. Empathy also manifests itself in the multitude of ways that counselors demonstrate their understanding of how family and community connect, or interact, with individual clients. The ability to express accurate and authentic empathy across diverse client groups is a reflection of *cultural intentionality* by counselors and the counseling profession as a whole.

Counselor Intentionality. Intentionality is the control people have of their purpose and direction in given situations. Such control is greatly influenced by people's self-perceptions and their worldview (Schmidt, 2002). Within the counseling process, a counselor and client's intentionality interact and either moves the relationship forward or inhibits its progress. Culture is essential to this interaction and movement. As Harper (2003) emphasized, "Culture is important in counseling because it plays a significant role in influencing the worldviews of both the counselor and the client, and the worldviews of both participants in the counseling process can affect the quality and outcome of the counseling relationship" (p. 2). Consequently, cultural intentionality is the "ability to communicate thoughts, words, and behaviors with self and others in a cultural context" (Ivey et al., 2002, p. 2).

A counselor's intentionality guides awareness of how values related to language, social class, racial identity, ethnic and cultural heritage, spiritual and religious beliefs, sexual orientation, family background, residency, psychological health, and ecstatic or traumatic experiences affect clients' worldviews. Because researchers have yet to define specific skills to use with diverse populations, counselors remain challenged to use existing models and approaches in appropriate and careful ways across cultures (Schmidt, 2002).

Cultural Bias in Counseling

Some fundamental tenets of professional counseling might possess inherent biases when considered in cultural contexts. Because culture is a primary influence in guiding people to choose perceptions, draw conclusions, and establish beliefs that create their *self*-concepts and worldviews, it also is a mitigating factor in explaining people's attitudes and reactions to counseling. At the same time, as noted earlier, traditional counseling theories and processes consist of elements and beliefs that, by definition, involve biases that may be contrary to other cultural values. For example, Robinson (2005) noted that counseling, as taught and practiced in the United States, promotes many middle-class biases such as the notions of success, competition, perseverance, self-reliance, Standard English, and privilege. By nature of the required entry into the counseling profession—graduate-level preparation—many of these aspects and values are commonplace among people who express interest in becoming professional counselors. The cost of a graduate education, the need to persist toward educational goals, the implied competition among students to excel, and the reliance on proper use of English are indicative of a few middle-class biases.

Other values embraced by counseling that might be counterproductive in attempting to help a diverse clientele include the emphasis placed on confidentiality and personal space. Cultures that embrace the notions of shared community and connectedness may not value personal space and privacy, including confidences, to the same degree that American culture does. Consequently, a culturally different client might wonder how the counselor's insistence on confidentiality will be helpful if no one else in the community will be included in the process. According to Pedersen (1997), some cultures might perceive the notion of privacy as a self-serving idea that is contrary and perhaps detrimental to community goals.

Related to inherent bias in counseling concepts and counselor preparation is the fundamental notion of normalcy, which we explored briefly in Chapter 8 about family, culture, and self-concept development. Traditional approaches to counseling use normalcy as a form of measurement to define the nature and severity of clients' problems. That is, how does a client's behavior relate to expected behaviors of a comparable (normal) population? Such measurement assumes that all people, and therefore all cultures, are of the same or similar customs, beliefs, and values. Only with such assumptions can we define "normalcy." This stance may prove problematic and even erroneous when working with clients from varied cultural and ethnic backgrounds. As noted throughout this text, counselors who work with a wide range of clients find that normal behavior, beliefs, and customs are relative to cultural backgrounds. Although some universal beliefs might apply across humankind, the issues and concerns that clients often bring to counseling relationships interact with cultural traditions, which for culturally diverse clients frequently conflict with the expectations (i.e., normalcy) of mainstream society. Helping clients make appropriate decisions about these conflicts and concerns while accepting and respecting their cultural heritage is a primary goal of effective counselors.

Exercise 10.2 invites you to explore potential biases that might exist by virtue of the fact that you are preparing to enter the counseling or other helping profession. Consider the values presented in the exercise, and assess your potential biases.

Exercise 10.2

Instructions: Read the list of values below, and in the right-hand column rate your adherence to each belief on a scale of 0–3, with 3 meaning strong adherence. After the assessment, consider the values you hold most strongly and whether they might contain potential biases when counseling clients from varied cultural backgrounds. Share your thoughts in a small group or in class.

Values	*My Personal Rating*			
Perseverance	0	1	2	3
Self-Reliance	0	1	2	3
Educational Achievement	0	1	2	3
Financial Wealth	0	1	2	3
Spirituality	0	1	2	3
God, the Creator of All Things	0	1	2	3
Humanism	0	1	2	3
Standard English	0	1	2	3
Bilingual or Multilingual Proficiency	0	1	2	3
Success	0	1	2	3
Culture and Ethnicity	0	1	2	3
Family	0	1	2	3
Community	0	1	2	3
Personal Privacy	0	1	2	3
Personal Space	0	1	2	3
Normal Behavior	0	1	2	3

Results: Summarize your self-assessment of these values and what meaning they might have for you when counseling people who are different from you. What values might be most problematic for you in striving to become a culturally effective counselor?

Being a Culturally Effective Counselor

Critique of traditional approaches to counseling as well as common skills advocated in counselor preparation programs raises questions about what is appropriate when working with diverse clientele. In this and subsequent sections, we examine some models and skills presented in the counseling literature and used by culturally effective counselors. In addition, we consider assessment, diagnosis, intervention, and group procedures with diverse populations.

Multicultural Approaches

Despite criticism of Western approaches to counseling, many popular theories are useful across client groups, provided that counselors and other professional helpers use them with cultural sensitivity and relevancy. In earlier chapters of this book, we considered aspects of several theories that might have value when applied appropriately with culturally diverse clients. They included the notions of the creative self and social interest proposed by Alfred Adler (Sweeney, 1998), the use of internal dialogue in therapy as explained by Meichenbaum (1977) and others, and the significance of social modeling in the development of self-efficacy (Bandura, 1998) among many other theoretical perspectives.

Adaptation of traditional counseling approaches to meet the needs of clients is challenging. According to some authorities, it might be futile. Weinrach and Thomas (1998) remarked, "It is unreasonable to expect the existing counseling theories to address every potential client's aesthetic, behavioral, developmental, economic, emotional, cultural, psychological, psychosexual, physical, social, and spiritual need. . . . There is no perfect counseling theory, nor will there be one in the foreseeable future" (p. 117). At the same time, advocates of multicultural approaches to counseling warn, "Traditional counseling techniques need to be as dynamic as culturally different clients. The objective is not to substitute multicultural counseling for traditional theories but to hold all theories accountable in the attempt to achieve good counseling in a culturally diversified population" (Pedersen, 1996, p. 236).

Debate about whether traditional theories and approaches have value or specific multicultural models are needed to work with a broader spectrum of clients continues in the literature with no clear end in sight. Current options other than adaptation of traditional approaches are limited, and as Weinrach and Thomas (1998) observed, the identity models developed thus far (some of which were presented in earlier chapters of this text) "tend to be more descriptive than prescriptive" (pp. 116–117). Consequently, although many identity models make important contributions to understanding stages of self-development within a cultural or ethnic context, they do not provide clear alternative models to traditional theoretical approaches to counseling.

In addition to identity theories of self-development and appropriate application of traditional theories, the multicultural literature has presented some integrative models of counseling and therapy. These approaches typically apply aspects of various traditional theories to address the needs of clients while accepting and respecting cultural differences. Here we review six such approaches. The first is optimal theory and its Belief Systems Analysis (BSA) approach to counseling (Speight et al., 1991).

Optimal Theory. Introduced in Chapters 3 and 4, optimal theory offers a holistic approach to counseling (Myers et al., 1991; Speight et al., 1991). Based on traditional African culture, which according to archeological evidence and anthropological conclusions forms the beginning of all human culture, optimal theory emphasizes *process* in the counseling relationship—the movement from a "suboptimal view of the world that fosters societal '-isms' to an optimal view of the world that values diversity" (p. 33). The counseling approach that translates optimal theory into practice is Belief Systems Analysis (BSA), which combines "psychodynamic, cognitive-behavioral, and humanistic-existential aspects" (p. 33). As such, BSA is an adaptation and integration of some traditional theories into a holistic approach.

This model focuses on early life experiences that influenced socialization, thought processing, and emotional and behavioral development, all of which contribute to a person's self-awareness, self-understanding, and self-acceptance. The degree to which people achieve optimal development in these areas relates to how understanding and accepting they can be of others. "In this light, as self-knowledge increases, acceptance of others increases. Conversely, the less self-knowledge one possesses, the more unaccepting one is of others" (Speight et al., 1991, p. 33). By exploring client's perceptions of self and the experiences that have contributed to these self-views, BSA helps clients learn about sub-optimal and optimal perspectives, understand the consequences of their behavior, and "become empowered to begin changing their experience of life" (p. 34).

Multilevel Model of Counseling. Another approach to counseling with diverse clients is the multilevel model of counseling (MLM) (Bemak & Chung, 2002). Proposed as an approach to working with refugees in helping them meet their unique needs, MLM has also been suggested as a model for counseling immigrants (Bemak & Chung, 2000). As such, the model has application across cultural and ethnic groups for individuals and families that are newly immigrated to a country or region of a country. MLM is a "psychoeducational model that comprises cognitive, affective, and behavioral interventions inclusive of cultural foundations and their relation to community and social processes" (Bemak & Chung, 2000, p. 208). An integrative model that incorporates cognitive, humanistic, and behavioral philosophies, MLM consists of four levels of intervention that may be implemented separately or concurrently. "The emphasis or utilization of one level or combination of levels is based upon an assessment by the psychotherapist" (Bemak & Chung, 2000, p. 208).

Level I of MLM is mental health education. Through educative processes, the counselor informs clients of the therapeutic procedures and relationships they will encounter including types of assessments, the interpreter's role (if necessary), time considerations, dynamics of the counseling relationship, and discussion of any medications recommended. At this introductory level, the counselor also encourages clients to explore their role in the counseling process and their expectations about the helping relationship. Although an introductory level, mental health education may also be revisited throughout the counseling process (Bemak & Chung, 2002).

Level II applies traditional individual, group, or family approaches to counseling and therapy. As noted in this text, traditional approaches tend to be founded in Western beliefs and philosophies, and consequently may consist of values and behaviors unfamiliar to some clients, particularly recent immigrants and refugees. Therefore, when applying Level II, counselors remain sensitive to the cultural differences brought to the helping relationship by clients. Ultimately, success in this level of helping will depend on the credibility counselors and other professional helpers achieve with their clients. Bemak and Chung (2000, 2002) emphasized that to be successful, counselors and therapists who work with diverse clientele must be knowledgeable of research surrounding the application of traditional approaches with clients from varied cultures.

At the third level of MLM, counselors encourage clients to master their newly adopted culture and surroundings. Level III helps diffuse potential frustration and anger clients might experience regarding how governmental and other systems work, ways to access services from various organizations, and where to seek information and assistance about employment, housing, education, insurance, health care, or financial aid. Acquiring useful information to negotiate social systems empowers clients, enabling them to acculturate more smoothly and address other aspects of societal adjustment, such as hostile reaction to immigrants, discrimination, and racism, more effectively. At this level of intervention, group processes, including family counseling, are encouraged. Through various types of group intervention, clients gain support from other members who have faced or are facing similar challenges in acculturating to a new culture. In addition, group support can assist with the issue of biculturalism, the integration of a new culture with the client's culture of origin. Bemak and Chung (2000) observed, "This is crucial for the development of a healthy and positive cultural identity of self, which in turn, impacts on all other facets of one's life" (p. 210).

Level IV of the multilevel model of counseling acknowledges the importance of both traditional approaches and indigenous methods of healing. Bemak and Chung (2002) noted that the World Health Organization has described how the integration of Western approaches with indigenous healing practice results in more effective outcomes. Respect for nontraditional healing methods, valued by culturally diverse clients from many parts of the world, is essential to the establishment of credible helping relationships, and incorporation of appropriate and legitimate methods "enhance the psychotherapeutic process" (Bemak & Chung, 2002, p. 225). One challenge for counselors and other professional helpers during this level of care is to help clients assess the legitimacy, relevancy, and effectiveness of all healing methods considered in the process. At the same time, counselors must evaluate the abilities and efficacy of indigenous caregivers in determining whether to collaborate and integrate their services into the counseling relationship and/or educational programs.

Multicultural Counseling and Therapy. A third model of counseling, multicultural counseling and therapy (MCT), is described "as a metatheoretical approach that recognizes that all helping methods ultimately exist within a cultural context" (Ivey et al., 2002, p. 292). Along with the two previous models, MCT, therefore, is an integrative approach. It offers a framework for counseling that encourages clients to be free in examining their self-concepts in relation to other people and in ways that have social and cultural meaning for themselves and for those who are close to them. In this respect, "Interdependence is basic to philosophy and action in MCT [which] seeks to work with the individual and family in an egalitarian fashion" (p. 293).

MCT recognizes the risk of integrating traditional Eurocentric approaches to counseling when working with clients across cultures. Each traditional theory is founded on a particular worldview with an ethnocentric perspective, which as noted in an earlier chapter, values individualism, independence, self-reliance, and rationalism—thoughts contrary to many other world cultures. To counteract the cultural biases inherent in the traditional approaches integrated by MCT, Ivey and colleagues (2002) introduced multicultural aspects with traditional approaches and encouraged the incorporation of nontraditional methods to reflect the beliefs and practices of all clients.

As a universal approach to counseling that integrates traditional and nontraditional methods of healing, MCT is more than individual counseling. It may include a variety of interventions that call upon support networks, including family and community organizations, to help clients in the process. MCT does not oppose any of the popular Western approaches, "but rather seeks to add culture as a center while respecting older traditions" (Ivey et al., 2002, p. 297). Three major propositions underlie the practice of Multicultural counseling and therapy (MCT):

Proposition I emphasizes the metatheory philosophy of MCT. By definition, it is a theory among and about theories that provides a structure for understanding and adapting various approaches to counseling, including traditional and nontraditional methods of healing.

Proposition II holds that *self*-identities develop and interact with a multitude of multilevel personal, collective, and universal experiences, as well as with varied cultural contexts. In working with a diverse clientele, "the totality and interrelationship of experiences and context need to be considered" (Ivey et al., 2002, p. 306).

Proposition III posits that cultural identity is the primary agent within the self-development process in adopting attitudes and beliefs about oneself, one's cultural group, others from different groups, and society's dominant group. These attitudes and beliefs are not only influenced by cultural factors but also by perceptions of superior–subordinate relationships that exist among various cultures and groups. These perceptions interacting with levels of cultural identity (including racial and ethnic identity) attained by both the counselor and client influence how problems are defined and what issues receive focus in the counseling relationship.

Existential Worldview Theory. Ibrahim (2003) presented another approach, named the existential worldview theory of counseling. It proposes five "universal principles that challenge all people at some time in their lives" (p. 200). These principles, or value domains, include (1) an understanding of human nature; (2) a focus on social and familial relationships; (3) perceptions about all of nature; (4) an understanding of time; and (5) an awareness of life-cycle activities that people of all cultures experience. Examples of such life-cycle activities are birth and death and coupling or marriage (Ibrahim, 2003).

In this model of existential counseling, "Worldview is the mediating variable that can help the therapist operationalize goals, process, and outcome in counseling" that are consistent with client's perceptions and cultural values (Ibrahim, 2003, p. 200). Furthermore, Ibrahim (2003) noted that a person's worldview is reliably related to racial and cultural identity. As proposed in this text, *self*-view, composed of all aspects of identity development, is foundational to a person's ultimate worldview. Assessment tools, developed by Ibrahim to help counselors and clients evaluate and understand their self- and worldviews include the Scale to Assess Worldview (SAWV; Ibrahim & Owen, 1994) and the Cultural Identity Checklist (CICL; Ibrahim, 1999).

By merging traditional cognitive and humanistic perspectives, existential worldview theory attempts to help clients understand their private thought processes and patterns, and when cognitions seemingly interfere with healthy life choices and beneficial behaviors, clients are empowered to make adjustments in their thinking and behavioral patterns. At the same time, existential worldview counselors help clients distinguish between external and internal factors that are fundamental causes of or influences on situations and concerns they have identified in the counseling relationship. To summarize, as an integrative approach to counseling, existential worldview theory assesses and clarifies aspects of self-identity and worldview. With that self-knowledge and awareness, clients are better able to appreciate "the strength of their cultural or racial group in surviving and finding their rightful place with their social, political, and cultural world" (Ibrahim, 2003, p. 203).

Stylistic Model. Another framework for counseling with diverse clients is the Stylistic Model presented by McFadden (2003). Based on the premise that cultural identity consists of many layers, Stylistic counseling, "requires successfully uncovering those layers on behalf of both the client and the counselor" (p. 210). Three basic dimensions compose the model in a hierarchical structure. The foundational dimension is the client's historical and cultural background, which consists of experiences and perceptions surrounding the following:

1. Ethnic/racial isolation
2. Family patterns
3. Cultural traditions
4. Dynamics of oppression
5. Monocultural memberships
6. Leaders and heroes
7. Value systems
8. Historical movements
9. Language patterns

The second tier (or layer) of the model is psychosocial development, consisting of the following:

1. Ethnic/racial identity
2. Personality formation
3. Human dignity
4. Psychological security
5. Social forces
6. Perception of others
7. Self-inspection
8. Mind building
9. Self-development

Scientific-ideological is the final tier, or layer, of the model and it includes elements and perceptions of ideological and scientific relevance to the counseling relationship and the client's development. This tier also includes nine elements:

1. Ethnic/racial relations
2. Meaningful alternatives
3. Economic potency
4. Logic-behavioral chains
5. Media influences
6. Relevant programs
7. Individual goals
8. Politics
9. Institutional goals

The Stylistic Model is an integrative structure that allows counselors to "apply their particular theoretical orientation in the counseling relationship, and thereby assist clients in accomplishing their goals" (McFadden, 2003, p. 228). By addressing each of the 27 elements of the structure, beginning with cultural-historical perceptions and experiences and building knowledge and awareness based on the subsequent exploration of the other tiers, the Stylistic Model invites counselors to apply various approaches and use personal styles of counseling in helping their clients.

Invitational Counseling. In a self-concept approach to counseling, Purkey and Schmidt (1996) introduced a communication model based on the tenets and assumptions of Invitational Education (Purkey & Novak, 1996). Although this model is a general approach to counseling and not specific to multicultural counseling, many of its components are similar to those of approaches presented in this section. One important difference between invitational counseling and other integrative approaches presented here is that, as noted in Chapter 2, although culture and ethnicity greatly influence perceptions of an emerging person, they might not necessarily be the foundation blocks upon which the *self* develops. We can illustrate this difference by revisiting McFadden's (2003) Stylistic Model, presented earlier. Using the tiers (layers) of that approach, invitational counseling might view either the second tier, psychosocial development, or the third tier, scientific-ideological, as foundational with cultural-historical elements assuming relative importance depending on the perceptions of the client. As such, rather than determining which layer is foundational in every instance, invitational counseling might use the 27 elements proposed by the Stylistic Model in combination with its "Five-P's" assessment to gather information from the client's point of view, which is most significant in addressing identified issues and concerns.

As an integrated approach, invitational counseling embraces a broad perspective of the services needed to help clients meet the diverse challenges of today's world. At the same time, it encourages counselors and other professional helpers to move beyond alleviation of immediate concerns towards an exploration of relatively boundless potential for future human development (Purkey & Schmidt, 1996).

Founded on the assumptions of perceptual psychology and self-concept theory, invitational counseling acknowledges the power of human perception and its impact on self-development. Furthermore, it advocates for counseling programs and services that incorporate beneficial human relationships, improved physical environments, and respectful systems in which all people, regardless of culture or ethnicity, can thrive. Professional counselors who apply the principles of invitational counseling adhere to four fundamental beliefs:

1. Every person wants to be accepted and affirmed as valuable, capable, and responsible, and wants to be treated accordingly.
2. Every person has the power to create beneficial messages for her- or himself and others, and because each person has this power, each person has this responsibility.
3. Every person possesses relatively untapped potential in all areas of learning and human development.
4. Human potential is best realized by creating places, programs, policies, and processes intentionally designed to invite optimal development and encourage people to realize this potential in themselves and others.

The invitational approach identifies four continuous levels of functioning across a spectrum of helpful and harmful behaviors, which encompass an infinite range of purposeful and accidental actions called intentional and unintentional behaviors. The four levels of functioning are the following:

I. *Intentionally Disinviting.* People who behave in purposefully hurtful and harmful ways—towards either themselves or other people—function at the lowest desirable level. When people are intentionally disinviting, they *intend* to demean, degrade, and destroy the value and worth of themselves and/or others. Racism, sexism, and other oppressive beliefs, when intentionally acted upon, are at this level of functioning.

II. *Unintentionally Disinviting.* Sometimes hurtful and harmful messages happen even when people do not intend them. When behaviors are ill timed, careless, misguided, or exaggerated, they might be misinterpreted by others. Actions based on misconceptions and stereotypic views fall in this category. Although the harm that results from such behavior might be unintended, the damage is nonetheless hurtful, counterproductive, and sometimes irreparable.

III. *Unintentionally Inviting.* Occasionally counselors observe positive results from their actions, even though they are uncertain what they did to achieve such outcomes. For instance, counselors who begin helping relationships without establishing an understanding of the client's worldview and the client's purpose in seeking assistance, likely will be unsure of where the relationship is going, and unaware of what they are doing. However, because these counselors might have good intentions, their relationships might prove beneficial to a wide range of clients. One danger of functioning at this level is that a lack of knowing what one is doing makes it uncertain, and perhaps unlikely, that consistently effective relationships will be achieved. Such lack of consistency may prevent counselors from repeating successful relationships with other culturally different clients.

IV. *Intentionally Inviting.* Consistently successful counselors aim for the highest level of professional functioning with all their clients. They dependably demonstrate command of helping skills while remaining sensitive to cultural contexts, maintain a broad knowledge base, and demonstrate unconditional regard for themselves and others. Counselors who function at a high level of professional practice consistently create intentional messages that enable all clients to feel valued and worthwhile. These beneficial messages encourage optimal human development that helps clients construct healthy self-views and corresponding worldviews.

In addition to the four levels of functioning, invitational counseling identifies five factors that contribute to, or detract from, human development. These five factors are people, places, policies, programs, and processes, and individually and combined, they function at one or more of the levels described above. We might readily understand that people behave at different levels of functioning, but it is less obvious how the other four factors send positive or negative messages that influence human development. A few examples might help:

Policies that emphasize punitive approaches, such as school regulations that fail students according to some arbitrary cutoff score on state-mandated tests, do little to invite all students to the celebration of learning. Rather, they ignore the significance of cultural diversity and collective worldviews.

Places that demonstrate disrespect by being unsanitary, unsafe, or inaccessible dissuade and discourage people in deceptive, yet powerful ways.

Programs that neglect or ignore cultural or individual differences, or *processes* adopted for the convenience of an elite few, may disinvite people who feel slighted or set apart from the rest of the population.

Invitational counseling is compatible with other approaches. Purkey and Schmidt (1996) listed four elements of compatibility: (1) an acceptance of a perceptual orientation to understanding human behavior [self-view and worldview]; (2) an emphasis on self-concept as a dynamic force in human development; (3) an unwavering respect for human respect and dignity; and (4) the encouragement of wide applicability [advocacy and social justice]. As a belief system and guide for professional practice, the invitational model can be integrated with compatible approaches in working with an array of clients.

Invitational counseling uses understandable language to describe complex human relationships. For this reason, the concepts of inviting and disinviting, and being intentional and unintentional, can be taught to clients at all developmental levels. With clients who speak languages different from the counselor, a first step might be to ask clients to substitute suitable and meaningful terms for invitational concepts from their native language.

Clients can be taught the concepts of invitational functioning and use this knowledge to assess their own development and relationships with others. Invitational concepts also can be the framework around which counselors and clients examine concerns in individual and group sessions. As clients understand their concerns from an invitational perspective, they are able to distinguish external causes from internal perceptions, understand related responsibilities, and choose behaviors to address identified situations and concerns. By teaching invitational levels of functioning within a cultural context, counselors empower clients to make decisions and give positive direction to their lives.

The counseling approaches presented above comprise a sample of models proposed in the literature. Each claims to be an integrative or holistic approach, and some use traditional psychotherapeutic models in conjunction with nontraditional methods of healing when appropriate to do so in the helping relationship. The description of these approaches out of necessity has been brief. Readers who wish more information about these integrative approaches should consult the references cited in this section. In addition to various approaches to counseling presented in the multicultural literature, traditional helping skills have been examined by some authorities in the context of cultural diversity. The next section summarizes some skills that might increase counselor effectiveness when working with culturally diverse client populations.

Skills of a Culturally Effective Counselor

Over the decades of what has been called the multicultural movement, counseling and other helping professions have attempted to learn skills and behaviors to use or not use with particular ethnic and cultural groups. Basic to this perspective is the belief that clients from diverse cultures require different approaches to counseling and subsequently different skills and behaviors used by counselors to establish effective helping relationships. As noted in this chapter and earlier in this text, this philosophy began with the conclusion that traditional therapeutic approaches, mostly formulated by European or Euro-American theorists, were too narrow to relate appropriately to a broader, diverse population of potential clients (Schmidt, 2002).

Lack of research findings to verify specific skills for particular populations has led some authorities to posit that the helping professions need to consider therapeutic behaviors and skills with universal characteristics applicable across cultures (Ivey et al., 2002; Patterson & Hidore, 1997; Pedersen & Ivey, 1993; Schmidt, 2002). Others challenge this perspective about universal approaches, noting that to broaden the multicultural focus too much may diminish the cultural diversity that truly exists. This debate between universal and culture-specific approaches has continued for nearly 30 years among multicultural proponents in the counseling profession. It is the distinction between emic and etic perspectives. Emically oriented counselors embrace approaches that are indigenous to the culture of clients being served, while etically oriented counselors assume that differences between cultures are measurable and some universal concepts and approaches to counseling are useful across cultures (Draguns, 2002). As Ivey and colleagues (2002) have noted, this issue continues to be a hotly contested one. Nevertheless, some counselors believe that the profession is moving forward with universal characteristics being applied with cultural intentionality. Perhaps there is some value in considering both etic and emic perspectives when working with culturally diverse clients. For example, Draguns (2002) concluded, "On the most general level, it can be said that psychotherapy, wherever it is applied, constitutes a blend of universally effective and culturally specific components" (p. 43).

Many traditional aspects of counseling, as noted in this chapter, are not appropriate or effective with certain non-Western groups. However, some universality of helping characteristics may exist. Draguns (2002) stated, as one illustration, that empathy "would appear to be a more fundamental and stable feature [of helping], provided it is communicated in a culturally meaningful and acceptable fashion and not necessarily couched in words or expressed directly" (p. 43).

Some authorities have written in general terms about counseling behaviors and skills that might influence effective helping relationships. Erickson and Al-Timimi (2004) mentioned several actions counselors might want to consider when working with Arab American clients. Here, their suggestions are adapted to apply to a broader population of clients (p. 244):

- Examine feelings, thoughts, and beliefs about the client's ethnicity and culture. Attack and dispute misconceptions, and reflect upon reactions to diverse cultures.
- Become a discerning consumer of how media depicts people of the client's ethnicity and culture. Become aware of how different cultures are viewed through the media's lens by the larger population, and understand how the majority perspective affects the lives of clients.
- Examine information that disputes common stereotypic views about clients' ethnicity and culture, and use appropriate information to incorporate cultural strengths into the counseling process

In addition to these general actions, other more specific behaviors appear in the multicultural literature to assist counselors in working across cultures. The following list is compilation from other literature (Pedersen, 2004; Ponterotto & Pedersen, 1993; Smith, Richards, & MacGranley, 2004). In general, counselors and other professional helpers working with clients from different cultural backgrounds should be able to:

- Perform honest self-analysis and personal reflection when working with culturally diverse clients. As noted throughout this text, self-knowledge is a critical element in being a successful helper with any client (Schmidt, 2002).
- Demonstrate genuine regard and respect for the beliefs and values of clients who are different from them. Acceptance and respectfulness when demonstrated with genuine understanding of cultural beliefs and customs will help bridge most differences that exist.
- Share with clients the nature and expectations of the counseling relationship, types of assessments used, interventions available, and legal rights that might pertain to their specific situation. Clients from cultures where counseling is not a common healing process will need honest and clear explanations of what will happen in the relationship. They also will benefit from learning about their rights under the U.S. legal system, which may be quite different from their native governments.
- Increase trust between them and clients to establish a healthy and collaborative working relationship. Trust is fundamental to any counseling relationship regardless of cultural differences between counselor and client. With culturally diverse clients, however, the effort to gain trust may be greater than with culturally similar clients.
- Send accurate and clear verbal and nonverbal messages and interpret verbal and nonverbal responses with an equal level of accuracy, being certain to clarify messages sent and received to avoid misunderstanding. Rules for encoding messages are culturally learned. The greater the differences between counselor and client, the more likelihood for misunderstanding. "Internal dialogue, therefore, becomes very important to the competent use of multicultural counseling skills" (Pedersen, 2004, p. 22). As noted in this text, internal dialogue (self-talk) is an important construct in self-concept development. Similarly, when counseling with clients, internal dialogue by both counselors and clients influences the development of healthy, productive relationships.
- Use culturally sensitive assessment procedures and intervention techniques that are relevant for the client. We will explore assessment and intervention in more detail later in this chapter. Suffice to say that assessment and intervention must be clearly explained and chosen with adequate understanding of cultural implications.
- Use relevant multicultural theory and research. Although relatively new, multicultural literature and research continues to add to the knowledge base of professional counseling. Effective counselors and other helpers who work with diverse clientele stay abreast of research findings and professional trends.
- Advocate to diminish the effects of institutional obstacles and discriminatory policies and practices faced by clients. Sometimes, the most important intervention performed by counselors will not take place in the counseling relationship. Rather, it

will be social advocacy and professional actions taken on behalf of clients to help institutions and organizations change discriminatory or otherwise unjust practices.

- Collaborate and consult with family, community leaders, spiritual mentors, and traditional healers when appropriate. Support for clients might come from a variety of sources. Tapping these sponsors and supporters is a sign of strength for the counselor, who appreciates the communal power that family, friends, and community offer to members of their group.
- Anticipate and plan for surprises and challenging situations. Because clients have rich backgrounds consisting of varied thought and behavior patterns, effective counselors remain prepared for the unexpected.

In this section, we have examined briefly some general skills and actions that counselors working with diverse clientele might consider. In the next section, we consider how some specific procedures—assessment, diagnosis, and treatment—relate to counseling diverse clientele.

Assessment, Diagnosis, and Treatment

Assessment is an important phase of any helping relationship. Neglect of proper assessment or misuse of assessment procedures and instruments will likely lead counselors to give misguided direction and make erroneous decisions in the process of helping. In counseling, assessment consists of interviews, existing records such as medical charts or educational transcripts, projective, aptitude, achievement, and other forms of testing, observations, and self-report questionnaires among other instruments and procedures.

According to Smith (2004), assessment procedures in counseling establish direction by gathering important information, identifying relevant aspects, and helping to formulate a hypothesis or diagnosis. He also noted, "the primary objective of assessment is to inform treatment decisions" (p. 100). Unfortunately, not all procedures and instruments used by counselors and other helping professionals have cultural sensitivity, so the use of their results to inform responsible treatment plans are suspect. The deficiency of many assessment instruments is due, in large part, to the narrow population on which they were developed. As Herlihy and Watson (2003) concluded, "most norming populations employed in the development of traditional approaches to assessment and testing within counseling tend to have been of European extraction and middle class" (p. 369).

Selection of assessment procedures and instruments is a critical consideration when counseling across cultural groups. Baruth and Manning (1999) cautioned, "Two important concerns in multicultural assessment are (a) the universal validity of psychological constructs or concepts and (b) the effects of misdiagnosis because of lack of recognition of culture-based factors" (p. 385). To minimize risk of misusing assessments, they offered five questions for counselors to consider:

1. What aspects of the client's life should the counselor assess, and do those aspects have cultural implications?

2. What assessment procedures or instruments reflect cultural views, so that counselors may evaluate identified aspects accurately and responsibly?
3. What evidence exists that selected assessment procedures and instruments are culturally sensitive and appropriate?
4. What safeguards exist to help counselors interpret assessment results accurately and appropriately for all clients?
5. What ethical and legal guidelines direct the counselor's use of assessment instruments and procedures with culturally diverse clients? (Adapted from Baruth & Manning, 1999, p. 385)

Similar to Baruth and Manning's five questions, Smith (2004) warned that counselors who rely on traditional approaches to counseling, thereby narrowing their focus on apparent client problems, risk limiting the breadth of assessment possibilities, thus failing "to assess other possible sources of influence" regarding the client's concerns (p. 99). To ensure quality assessment, Smith (2004) suggested that counselors

1. Know why the assessment is being done and its potential impact on the client.
2. Understand the implications of assessment on the overall helping relationship.
3. Determine risks of performing an assessment as opposed to moving forward with a preliminary intervention.
4. Put safeguards in place to ensure relevant information is obtained from the assessment and prevent inaccurate hypotheses or diagnoses.
5. Examine and understand inherent biases in standardized measurement instruments for particular clientele.
6. Know how to communicate assessment findings clearly and accurately to clients. (Adapted from Smith, 2004, p. 100)

Smith (2004) also reported that some schemata exist to help counselors process assessments with cultural sensitivity. For example, Hays (2001) presented the acronym ADDRESSING for counselors to consider an array of factors when assessing culturally diverse clients:

A Age and generational influences
DD Developmental and acquired disabilities
R Religion and spiritual orientation
E Ethnicity and race
S Socioeconomic status
S Sexual orientation
I Indigenous heritage
N National origin
G Gender

Similarly, D'Andrea and Daniels (2001) prescribed an arrangement of factors, which they referred to as the RESPECTFUL model. They suggested counselors consider the following factors:

R Religious and spiritual identity
E Ethnic, cultural, and racial background
S Sexual identity
P Psychological maturity
E Economic class standing and background
C Chronological-development challenges
T Threats to well-being and trauma
F Family history, values, and dynamics
U Unique physical characteristics
L Location of residence and language differences

The above examples illustrate ways that multicultural authorities believe "effective counselors minimize ethnocentrism and maximize culturally appropriate information" when using assessment procedures and instruments in counseling relationships (Baruth & Manning, 1999, p. 384). By considering a multitude of factors and applying assessment procedures in contextual framework, counselors are in stronger position to make accurate diagnoses and decisions with their clients about direction for the helping relationship.

The role of diagnosis in counseling relationships has had historic debate in the profession. As the counseling profession expanded its role from vocational and educational settings of the early twentieth century to broader mental health arenas into this twenty-first century, diagnosis has become more accepted as an important step in the process of assessing and making decisions about appropriate treatment. Most significant has been the economic realities of serving clients in the mental health arena and the American Counseling Association and related divisions' drive for parity in health insurance reimbursements for clinical counselors, which has encouraged their use of prevailing diagnostic systems, particularly the *Diagnostic and Statistical Manual of Mental Disorders* (DSM-IV-TR) of the American Psychiatric Association (2000).

From a multicultural perspective, the challenge has been to create diagnostic procedures and systems with minimal cultural bias, a nearly impossible task. As Smith (2004) observed, "Just as it is virtually impossible to develop an [assessment] instrument that is free of bias, it is impossible to find a diagnostic system that is completely free of bias, particularly because such systems rely heavily on clinical judgment" (p. 103).

Diverse clients might display emotions in such varied ways that their expression might be misinterpreted and, therefore, misdiagnosed by counselors or other helping professionals. Public display of demonstrative crying and wailing over loss or other distress is common in some cultures but socially aberrant in others. Similarly, possessions by spirits, suicidal tendencies, and extraordinarily dishonorable personal behavior have various causal interpretations across diverse cultures (Smith, 2004).

Use of the DSM system presents both practical and ethical problems noted by Herlihy and Watson (2003). Later, in Chapter 11, we will explore the ethical issues related to counseling clients of varied cultural backgrounds in detail. As a practical issue, the DSM's medical model approach to diagnosis excludes contextual factors, thus "failing to consider the impact of social-political-cultural factors in clients' lives" (Herlihy & Watson, 2003, p. 371).

DSM categories reinforce mental health views of the dominant culture in U.S. society. Research has indicated that members of the dominant culture receive less severe diagnoses than minority group members do for display and assessment of similar symptoms (Herlihy & Watson, 2003). At the same time, the DSM does not take into account how oppression, poverty, and discrimination of groups and individuals contribute to feelings of worthlessness and powerlessness that often lead to depression, a factor associated with other mental disorders. Still, some authors have noted progress in revised editions of the DSM. Wohl and Aponte (2000) surmised, "The inclusion of cultural variables in psychiatric disorders and the identification of culture-bound syndromes in DSM-IV begins to provide a cultural context for the diagnosis and treatment of a number of disorders" (p. 296). They went on to caution, however, that much more work needs to be done with future versions of the manual.

Use of traditional medical models and systems of diagnosis perpetuate notions of sexism within the helping professions. They define normal developmental problems of women in terms of disease and illness. Consequently, the medical professional prescribes more "drugs and particularly psychotropic medications" for women than men (Herlihy & Watson, p. 371).

The above examples offer a small sample of issues raised by the use of limited assessment and diagnostic measures when counseling across cultures. Bemak and Chung (2000) emphasized that when counselors failed to consider a client's "conceptualization and expression of mental illness and the attainment of conceptual equivalence between clinician and client" effective assessment and diagnosis "will be difficult if not impossible, and it may lead to inappropriate treatment and perhaps to high dropout rates from mainstream mental health services" (p. 207). In contrast, when counselors apply appropriate assessment procedures and make culturally responsible diagnoses, their treatment decisions will receive more confidence from clients.

The counseling profession continues to search for treatment modalities and interventions that are appropriate with all client groups. In recent decades, the profession has made strides focusing on the essential understanding, acceptance, and sensitivity required when working with clients whose cultural and ethnic backgrounds vary significantly from the counselors serving them. Nevertheless, such knowledge and understanding will only be effective when matched with appropriate methods of treatment and intervention. As Parham and Brown (2003) explained, "It is important that practitioners of this newfound sensitivity not get stuck in a time warp by assuming that personal compassion or heightened sensitivity combined with outdated or inappropriate methods and constructs are a recipe for therapeutic success" (p. 83). Much more research will be required to identify timely and appropriate treatment methods and other interventions to apply with varied clients in counseling relationships.

Thus far, in this and other chapters, broad statements have attempted to describe general approaches to counseling with diverse clientele. These included information about relating with clients, learning about specific cultures and the constructs they embrace, understanding cultural implications of certain assessment instruments and procedures, and appreciating different worldviews, especially perceptions of mental health, healing methods, and counseling as defined and practiced in the United States. In the closing paragraphs of this section on assessment, diagnosis, and treatment, we consider specific information currently found in the multicultural literature about treatment and intervention.

One treatment suggestion found in the literature that applies across many cultural groups is attention to helping resources beyond the immediate counseling relationship. In particular, treatment modalities that include family members (including extended family members), religious or spiritual leaders, language interpreters, and community resources may have greater likelihood of success than ones that simply focus on the therapist's role with the client (Arredondo & Perez, 2003; Parham & Brown, 2003; Sandhu, Leung, & Tang, 2003). This idea resonates particularly with counselors and other professionals who represent institutions such as schools, mental health clinics, universities, and other agencies. It parallels a point made in an earlier book when I wrote, "The question for us [counselors] is, what can we do beyond our individual and small-group helping relationships to ensure that the organizations and agencies we represent consistently demonstrate helpful and beneficial behaviors toward the people we aim to serve?" (Schmidt, 2002, p. 96). A key issue for counselors in determining when and how to expand the helping relationship and include other elements is to assess the internal concerns of the person in conjunction with the external factors that might benefit from collaboration with family, community, and other constituents.

Information and education also have an important role in counseling with diverse clients. Too often, counselors and therapists neglect these vital processes in deference to more clinical and therapeutic ones. Yet, for many clients, their concerns and issues stem from lack of information or knowledge of how to access various services in the community. Counseling such clients without supplementing the relationship with pertinent and relevant information might prove frustrating for both client and counselor. As a simplistic example, providing career counseling to a hungry man so he can get a job to earn money and buy food might not be as effective, or efficient, as giving him information about how to qualify for social assistance such as food stamps.

The counseling literature has advocated interventions to use with clients of diverse backgrounds. For example, bibliocounseling (also called bibliotherapy) is a technique that has many uses with children, adolescents, and adults. McFadden and Banich (2003) advocated the use of bibliotherapy strategies across different theoretical approaches "that counselors can use transculturally [because] it has many uses such as bridging a cultural gap between counselor and client, changing affect, and building mechanisms for coping skills" (p. 293). Wehrly (2003) gave an example of using bibliotherapy with a multiracial client with a female high school student. Through reading selections from a pertinent book, keeping notes about feelings, and sharing these feelings with the counselor, the client is able to experience identification, catharsis, and insight about her Jewish and African American background.

Another determination regarding intervention and treatment for counselors is whether to use individual or group counseling methods. As DeLucia-Waack and Donigian (2004) noted, the European assumption that group work is more powerful than counseling individuals might not hold true across all cultures. Yet, many world cultures could perceive group counseling in favorable light because groups provide an optimal setting for personal exploration and growth, promote sharing and cooperation, and foster collaboration and acceptance while restraining selfish and other egocentric behaviors (DeLucia-Waack & Donigian, 2004). In the next section of this chapter, we take a closer look at what the counseling literature says about group work with diverse clientele.

Group Procedures with Diverse Clients

Beginning with Helen Driver's introduction of small groups in 1958, the counseling profession has advocated use of group procedures in a variety of settings to address a range of remedial, developmental, and preventive issues (Corey & Corey, 2002; Gazda, 1989; Gladding, 1999; Jacobs, Masson, & Harvill, 2002). More recently, the multicultural literature has mentioned group counseling, therapy, and other procedures in working with diverse clients. Han and Vasquez (2000) observed that group procedures may have relevance for members of culturally diverse and underrepresented groups who feel isolated, experience stress in interpersonal relationships, and might benefit from support that often comes from group work in counseling and other therapeutic or educational processes. Furthermore, they suggested, "Group therapy has particular value for ethnic and racial minorities who struggle with issues of confidence, self-esteem, empowerment, and identity" (Han & Vasquez, 2000, p. 110).

DeLucia-Waack and Donigian (2004) found that the principles of facilitating effective individual counseling with culturally diverse clients also apply to successful leadership of culturally sensitive counseling groups. To be successful, group leaders must gain awareness of their own culture, values, and identity. At the same time, leaders become informed and knowledgeable about cultural differences, varying worldviews, and identity processes that influence members of groups they facilitate. In this respect, group leaders understand the dynamics and differences between individualistic and collective philosophies, appreciate how thought processes and disclosure of feelings might vary across cultures, use culturally sensitive structured activities and unstructured experiences to enhance group process, and value the overall role of the leader in successful groups.

DeLucia-Waack and Donigian (2004) noted that many but not all societies "have rituals that take place in group setting, with various functions: festivities, prayer, and/or healing" (p. 43). They further suggested that many cultures might view "the healing powers of a group and may encourage members . . . to accept and participate in counseling groups" (pp. 43–44). Successful leaders are, therefore, careful to understand clients' perspectives about group participation and the ways group members' views are influenced by cultural beliefs.

Han and Vasquez (2000) recommended group work to emphasize "interpersonal learning involving feedback and experimentation" through which members "explore both maladaptive and more adaptive ways of functioning in the group and, ultimately, outside the group" (p. 111). Although theories of group process, along with other popular counseling theories, are greatly influenced by Eurocentric assumptions particularly related to universality and individualism, group work can value diversity if facilitators maintain appropriate cultural sensitivity, develop necessary competence, and incorporate a positive sense of multiple identities into an accurate and affirming *self*-view for all group members (Han & Vasquez, 2000).

Establishing groups to address concerns of clients requires careful consideration of all aspects of designing, forming, and leading groups normally expected in group work. Group composition—whether to be homogeneous or heterogeneous across ethnic identity, gender, nationality, level or acculturation, and other factors—is one of the first decisions a leader makes. Elements such as development of trust, desire for self-disclosure, need for diverse feedback, and hope of relationship building are important in this decision-making process. For example, if development of trust is a primary element in a particular group, a homogeneous membership might prove productive because members would be most comfortable with people from similar backgrounds. If, however, building relationships in mainstream society is a primary goal, a heterogeneous group might offer more opportunity to receive useful information and helpful feedback from members whose cultural backgrounds differ. Screening and selecting group members with cultural intentionality in conjunction with the primary purposes of the group are essential in establishing either heterogeneous or homogeneous groups.

Group work with diverse clients takes many forms. Therapeutic, developmental, and educational/preventive groups all have value when formed and led with a high level of cultural sensitivity. Durant and McFadden (2003) noted that groups are effective interventions to help people who have similar concerns and cultural backgrounds learn information and express themselves to "feel less isolated and more free to unlock feelings" (p. 299).

Group work is also an acceptable process to use when counselors want to help clients beyond immediate personal and social concerns. Through group work, counselors and other professionals can help clients address broader issues such as social justice and conflict resolution. In addition, counselors can use goals accomplished through groups to become more active in advocating for the larger population of people who are being discriminated, neglected, ignored, or otherwise mistreated by mainstream society.

Advocacy, Conflict Resolution, and Social Justice

Multicultural literature cites sociopolitical forces as significant elements contributing to prejudices towards race, gender, social class, and other statuses that affect self-identity and worldview. However, only recently has the counseling literature included references to an expanded role for professional counselors and therapists as social activists who advocate for clients. Such advocacy encourages counselors to move beyond existing helping relationships and to mediate problems caused by institutional policies and programs that intentionally or unintentionally discriminate against people of particular ethnicity, racial heritage, gender, sexual orientation, or other status. Advocates also use the social system to seek justice for individuals and groups that have been denied access to services or other legal rights guaranteed in a democratic society.

Focus on advocacy beyond typical individual and group interventions in a therapeutic or educational setting is an extension of multiculturalism, the "fourth force" in counseling (Pedersen, 1999). Perhaps continued emphasis on advocacy and action towards social justice beyond narrowly focused helping relationships may become a fifth force in the development of counseling theory. As D'Andrea and Daniels (2004) forecasted, "the newly emerging social justice counseling movement has the potential to provide additional fuel that will further drive the paradigmic changes that are occurring in the profession" (p. 24).

Some authorities suggest that professional counselors and therapists often ignore the effects of sociopolitical influences on situations clients present as well as on their functioning as providers of mental health services. For example, Thompson (2004) proposed, "people are exposed to an implicit conditioning that suppresses and distorts their knowledge about these forces in society" and further, "therapists who become aware of this conditioning will likely respond by holding onto their distorted views about reality" (p. 35). In a similar vein, Brooks, Haskins, and Kehe (2004) emphasized the importance of counselors and other therapists who work with African American clients to understand the continuing effects of racial discrimination and "understand the sociopolitical issues of slavery and oppression" (p. 156).

Helms and Cook (1999) also suggested a broader role for counselors and other helping professionals. "Many clients from oppressed groups could benefit from a therapist who takes on the role of an advocate," they noted (p. 189), explaining that counselors and therapists often hold positions of sociopolitical power within institutions and systems that might be problematic for certain clients. One caveat from Helms and Cook (1999) is that effective counselors must remain judicious about which situations to assert their authority on behalf of clients, and be careful not usurp the power "the client has to speak for himself or herself" (p. 189). Often, an approach that encourages clients to be assertive, teaches conflict resolution, negotiation, and bargaining skills, and fosters collaborative relationships between counselors and clients helps maintain a client's authority and autonomy while noting progress in the identified situation.

As noted earlier, the *invitational counseling* model is one that suggests active involvement by counselors beyond existing helping relationships (Purkey & Schmidt, 1996; Schmidt, 2002). In this approach, a "Five Ps" assessment paradigm encourages counselors and other helpers to examine the people, places, policies, programs, and processes affecting a client's situation and, more inclusively, an entire group's participation in the social, educational, economic, or other system. By assessing the Five Ps, counselors acknowledge that problematic situations "do not reside within individuals, but rather within individuals' ecosystems of which the person is only part" (Purkey & Schmidt, 1996, p. 97). Factors such as the Five Ps are important for the separate and combined influence of people's ecosystems. By gathering information and data about these elements, counselors and clients are better equipped to advocate changes. Exercise 10.3 asks you to remember a time in your life when a problem was more systemic than internal in nature.

Exercise 10.3

Instructions: Think of a problem you once experienced that in your assessment was largely due to external conditions, such as other people's actions toward you, a program that excluded you, an unfair policy, a place that was abhorrent or objectionable, or a process that precluded participation. Describe the situation to a classmate and answer the following questions:

1. What did you do to remedy the situation?
2. Were you satisfied with the action you chose?
3. If you were counseling a client today with a similar concern, what would you do?

Counseling Inferences

This chapter brings together many of the foundational aspects of self-concept development and cultural influence with various approaches to counseling. In becoming competent as culturally effective counselors, we ultimately must know ourselves, understand variances in the rich cultures of the clients we serve, and appreciate the sometimes subtle and sometimes obvious biases inherent in popular approaches to counseling. One of the first steps in this process of becoming competent in cross-cultural counseling is to understand the many different terms used by the profession to define and describe counseling with clients from varied cultures.

The diversity of cultures in this world is reflected in the multitude of terms created by the counseling profession to discuss the process of counseling people of various cultures. Harper (2003) is one among many authorities who has attempted to clarify "the expanding potpourri of culturally characterized concepts that are used in the counseling literature to describe a counseling relationship between counselors and clients who have different cultural backgrounds" (p. 2). Among these terms are *multicultural counseling, cross-cultural counseling, counseling across cultures, transcultural counseling, culture-centered counseling, intercultural counseling, diversity-sensitive counseling, culture-specific counseling,* and *counseling the culturally different.* Various authors use some terms, such as *cross-cultural counseling* and *intercultural counseling,* interchangeably. In addition, some authorities note distinct differences between some of these descriptors, while others see no differences in the same terms. It is ironic to some extent that in a field devoted to understanding and appreciating diversity so many terms have emerged to describe and define the process of counseling, yet there continues to be disagreement or at least varying opinions about their meaning and use. Nevertheless, competent counselors want to be aware of these terms, develop an understanding of what they all mean for their practice of counseling with all clients, and appreciate that there are different views about these terms within the counseling profession. From Harper's (2003) perspective, "multicultural counseling and cross-cultural counseling are probably the most frequently used language among the currently and recently used culture- and counseling concepts (p. 3). Of course, frequency of use may not be the ultimate measure of whether to adopt particular language in your practice of counseling. Becoming competent as counselor means choosing a language that has value and significance for you as a professional.

The language you choose must also be compatible with approaches you adapt in working with particular clients. This chapter presented several integrative approaches that have potential in working effectively with clients from various cultural and ethnic backgrounds. Most significant about the approaches briefly described in this chapter is their willingness to adapt traditional counseling beliefs and skills to culturally sensitive helping relationships. Furthermore, most of the models readily acknowledged the value of nontraditional healing methods when appropriate assessment and application of such approaches occurs. Readers and students who find one or more of these models to be of interest in their professional development are encouraged to explore primary and related sources in depth.

11

Ethical and Legal Issues

The counseling profession is guided by ethical standards established by several professional organizations including the National Board of Certified Counselors (NBCC), the American Counseling Association (ACA), and its many divisions. In addition, related professional associations such as the American Psychological Association (APA), American Association of Marriage and Family Therapists (AAMFT), and the National Association of Social Workers (NASW) also set standards of ethical practice for their members, many of which provide counseling services.

In most instances, ethical standards are guidelines that assist counselors and other professional helpers in making appropriate judgments about their services for clients and relationships with other professionals. As Helms and Cook (1999) indicated, however, sometimes preparation programs and authorities on ethical behavior present standards as absolute rules that professional helpers must follow to the letter. Such a stance creates additional dilemmas for counselors and therapists who work with diverse client populations because consideration of cultural differences is not always apparent within specific ethical standards (Pedersen, 2002). Regarding this predicament, Helms and Cook (1999) concluded, "we realized that these rules were antithetical to the cultural values of some of our clients. . . . Consequently, it has become necessary for us to become more flexible in our application of certain 'tried and true' therapy methods so that we might sustain authentic relationships with our clients" (p. 186).

This chapter presents on overview of ethical issues and laws that have significance in the practice of cross-cultural or multicultural counseling. It will present standards that specifically address helping relationships with diverse clientele as well as standards that create dilemmas for practicing counselors and other helping professionals. Cultural competencies related to ethical practice of counseling are also considered. In addition, the chapter reviews historic legislation that affected the lives of oppressed groups in the United States as well as contemporary legislation that attempts to protect civil rights. We begin with an overview of ethical standards established by NBCC and ACA that relate to counseling with diverse clients.

Ethical Standards

As noted, several different professional associations have established codes of ethical practice for the helping professions. In the following sections, we limit coverage to the ethical codes of the National Board of Certified Counselors (NBCC) and the American Counseling Association (ACA). Readers, however, are encouraged to review other codes that relate more specifically to their professional field of practice. Examples of such codes might come from one or more of the divisions of the ACA, such as the Ethical Code for the International Association of Marriage and Family Counselors (Gladding, 2002), or one of the national associations representing psychologists, social workers, or marriage and family therapists.

National Board of Certified Counselors

The preamble of the Code of Ethics for National Board of Certified Counselors (2003) states that the NBCC "certifies counselors as having met standards for the general and specialty practice of professional counseling" (p. 1). The code is divided into seven sections: (A) General, (B) Counseling Relationship, (C) Counselor Supervision, (D) Measurement and Evaluation, (E) Research and Publication, (F) Consulting, and (G) Private Practice. A review of all the standards under each section found that only a few standards address directly or indirectly counseling practice across cultural groups.

Standard A.5 indirectly relates to services provided for clients who are financially unable to afford them. It states, "In establishing fees for professional counseling services, certified counselors must consider the financial status of clients. In the event that the established fee status is inappropriate for a client, assistance must be provided in finding comparable services at acceptable costs" (NBCC, 2003, p. 2). Because clients from diverse backgrounds and cultures frequently are new immigrants or refugees to this country, they seldom have the financial resources to pay for social services or counseling sessions. Likewise, clients from historically oppressed groups might suffer similar financial burdens. General standard A.5 of the NBCC code attempts to guide professional counselors in navigating this ethical issue. Yet, the standard also raises additional issues if counselors are unable to locate "comparable services at acceptable costs." If a counselor's fees are inappropriate for particular clients, and the counselor or other helper is unsuccessful in referring those clients to sources they can afford, the standard provides no further guidance. The question remains, if all attempts at finding appropriate and acceptable services fail, what is the responsibility of the counselor to the client who sought assistance? This challenge would likely be the reality in rural communities that struggle to provide adequate services to citizens and other residents.

Standard A.12 more directly addresses ethical issues when working with diverse clients. It states, "Through an awareness of the impact of stereotyping and unwarranted discrimination (e.g., biases based on age, disability, ethnicity, gender, race, religion, or sexual orientation), certified counselors guard the individual rights and personal dignity of the client in the counseling relationship" (NBCC, 2003, p. 2). This standard is a general statement about protecting the rights and self-respect of clients. Implicit in the standard is the responsibility of counselors to monitor their biases and prejudices that might negatively affect the helping relationship. Although the standard does not specifically state so, the intent is that counselors are also obligated to refer clients when their biases or prejudices threaten productive relationships. For example, a professional counselor who has strong moral convictions against homosexuality probably could not begin to offer genuine empathic assistance to a young person struggling with the decision of whether to come out.

Under Measurement and Evaluation, Standard D.10 of the NBCC code advises that counselors must use caution when selecting assessment instruments and understand the limitations when interpreting test results or other measurements. In addition, counselors who use measurement instruments in the practice must "ensure that periodic review and/or retesting are made to prevent client stereotyping" (NBCC, 2003, p. 7). This standard is important when selecting ability tests, achievement batteries, job placement inventories, or other instruments that might unfairly categorize clients due to cultural differences or language barriers. Counselors have the responsibility of ensuring that the measurement instruments and procedures they use with clients are the most appropriate assessments available and that the interpretation of results are accurate considering a variety of cultural contexts.

American Counseling Association

The preamble to the American Counseling Association's Code of Ethics (1995) includes the statement, "Association members recognize diversity in our society and embrace a cross-cultural approach in support of the worth, dignity, potential, and uniqueness of each individual" (p. 1). The code consists of eight sections, and several sections either directly or indirectly address diversity issues. The eight sections include (A) The Counseling Relationship, (B) Confidentiality, (C) Professional Responsibility, (D) Relationships with Other Professionals, (E) Evaluation, Assessment, and Interpretation, (F) Teaching, Training, and Supervision, (G) Research and Publication, and (H) Resolving Ethical Issues.

Several general and specific standards of the ACA code address counselors' practice with diverse clients. For example, in Section A.1, Client Welfare, under the subheading Family Involvement, the code encourages counselors to recognize the important role of families in clients' welfare and to involve families in the counseling process when appropriate to do so. Another example of a general standard is in Section E, Evaluation, Assessment, and Interpretation, under the subheading Client Welfare. It cautions counselors to use assessment techniques, results, and interpretations appropriately and to take steps to prevent their misuse by others.

More direct standards in the ACA code are found in Section A.2, Respecting Diversity. In this section, a statement on nondiscrimination warns against practices that discriminate by "age, color, culture, disability, ethnic group, gender, race, religion, sexual orientation, marital status, or socioeconomic status." This standard is reiterated in Section C.5, Public Responsibility, which, in addition to the identity factors listed in Section A.2, includes direction for counselors not to discriminate in a manner that negatively influences the relationship "for any other reason." A second standard in this section, titled Respecting Differences, directs counselors to understand various cultures of clients with whom they work, and to learn how the counselors' cultural background, perceptions, values, and beliefs might influence counseling relationships.

Section C.5 mentioned above also warns against sexual harassment, "defined as sexual solicitation, physical advances, or verbal or nonverbal conduct that is sexual in nature, that occurs in connection with professional activities or roles." Sexual harassment includes intentional behaviors of a sexual nature that are not welcomed, offensive, and create a disinviting work environment, or are intense enough to be considered harassment in the context they are expressed.

According to the ACA code, cultural sensitivity is expected when diagnosing mental disorders. Section E.5 includes statements that counselors should recognize cultural influences, socioeconomic status, and cultural experiences in describing clients' problems and diagnosing mental disorders.

Section E.8, Diversity in Testing, specifically cautions counselors about using assessment procedures and interpreting clients' performance when the normative group upon which the instruments were developed and standardized do not include representation of a client's gender, culture, or ethnic or racial group. This standard again emphasizes the knowledge counselors must have about the effects that status variables related to diversity have on the administration and interpretation of test results.

National Organization for Human Service Education

Chapter 1 introduced the National Organization for Human Service Education (NOHSE, 2004a) and its ethical standards. As do the NBCC and ACA, this national organization includes ethical standards to guide human service professionals in their work with diverse clients. In the section titled, "The Human Service Professional's Responsibility to the Community and Society," statements #16 through #21 address issues of diversity. Statement #16, for example, guides professionals to advocate for all members of society, especially people from groups with a history of discrimination. Likewise, Statement #17 warns against discrimination or preference for clients based on all of the status variables covered in this text. Awareness about and respect for all clients are advocated in Statements #18 and #19, and sensitivity to sociopolitical issues is covered by Statement #20. The need for continuing education and preparation to meet the needs of diverse clientele is the focus of Statement #21.

The ethical standards mentioned in the previous paragraphs illustrate some specific and general guidelines for counselors and human service providers to follow. As noted earlier, these standards are guidelines. As the counseling and other helping professions have become more accepting, knowledgeable, and sensitive to cultural diversity among client populations, authorities in the multicultural arena have advocated for the use and interpretation of standards within situational and cultural contexts. Pedersen (2002), for example, observed, "Clients or counselors from different cultural backgrounds might follow the same ethical guidelines in identical situations by displaying different behaviors" (p. 13). Consequently, when following particular ethical codes while working with diverse clientele, professionals might find themselves in an ethical dilemma, feeling forced to choose between the stated standard and what the counselor believes is most appropriate within a cultural context. Such dilemmas highlight practical distinctions that professional counselors and human service providers might make in working across cultural groups.

Ethical Distinctions

Pedersen (2002) warned that the ACA code of ethics and similar professional standards (e.g., NOHSE) include presumptions that if adopted literally would culturally encapsulate counselors or other helping professionals. He pointed to serious discrepancies between the cultural context within which the code was developed and the cultural context within which it is applied by professional counselors. "These discrepancies have resulted in patterns of implicit cultural bias that may require counselors to choose between being ethical or following the codes" (Pedersen, 2002, p. 18) Finally, he asserted that the ACA code includes 16 suppositions that present cross-cultural challenges to counselors, and probably for other professional helpers:

1. An individualistic perspective is favored.
2. Dependency is a negative trait.
3. Freedom of choice is not destructive.
4. Differences are best overlooked.
5. Counselors act in the place of parents.
6. All counselors have cultural self-awareness.
7. All dual relationships are inappropriate.
8. Counselors should withdraw from conflict.
9. A universal money economy exists.
10. Privacy is a universally held value.
11. Universal guidelines for counselor competency exist.
12. Counseling is narrowly defined.
13. Quantitative data are superior to qualitative data.
14. Assessment measures do not always require validation.
15. Teachers do not learn from students.
16. Ethical guidelines are perfect. (Adapted from Pedersen, 2002, pp. 18–19)

Several authorities have questioned the absolute wording of some ACA standards in relation to work with culturally diverse clients (Helms & Cook, 1999; Pedersen, 2002; Sue, Arredondo, & McDavis, 1992). Beginning with the preamble mentioned earlier, the ACA code receives criticism because of its apparent or implicit focus on individualistic philosophy rather than respecting both collective and individualistic points of view. Pedersen (2002) stated that if the ACA code cannot embrace both philosophies, it "at least needs to make its dependence on individualistic values explicit for the benefit of those who do not share the assumption that the individual is more important than the group" (p. 16). Pederson (2002) continued to analyze several standards regarding their interpretation in a cultural context. For example, Section A.1.c of the code links counselors' effectiveness to their ability to respect a client's freedom in making life choices. The notion of freedom of choice may not always be compatible with collectivist views, which elevate the role of family, community, or other groups influential in a client's life. Likewise, Section A.2.a warns counselors to avoid discriminatory behavior, which at first glance seems to be an appropriate ethical standard. However, when counseling, as noted throughout this text, many different identity factors and statuses interact and counselors might want to help their clients discriminate or differentiate among "many potentially salient cultural identities" (Pedersen, 2002, p. 16). Consequently, a standard that for all appearances intends to be culturally appropriate actually may tie the hands of counselors who work with diverse clients and understand the influence of an array of cultural identities.

Confidentiality is an important part of counseling relationships, and one that the ACA code of ethics highlights in Section B, as well as Statement #3 of the Ethical

Standards of Human Service Professionals (NOHSE, 2004a). However, as some authorities have noted, the notion of personal privacy is another ideal that may have roots in individualistic values. Robinson (2005) argued that emphasis on confidentiality also promotes a middle-class value, which biases counselors. Furthermore, Pedersen (2002) explained that the ideal of personal privacy is not as highly held in many collectivistic societies as in individualistic ones because it encourages egocentric, self-interested behaviors that may be counterproductive to the goals of society. Counselors and other professional helpers who want to behave in an ethical manner interpret codes of ethical standards with the best interest of clients and communities in mind. Exercise 11.1 invites you to review several other standards of ethical practice from the ACA Code of Ethics and interpret them within a cultural context.

As noted throughout the previous section, interpretation and use of ethical standards requires thoughtful consideration of how standards might apply within a cultural context. Applying various standards with clients across cultures and within cultures is complex and challenging. This challenge is largely due to the difficulty in establishing written standards that present appropriate boundaries for counselors while allowing them to remain flexible enough in their professional judgment when working with a broad range of clients. In par-

Exercise 11.1

Practicing Ethically with All Clients

Instructions: Read each of the standards below and write a critique noting any cultural conflicts or questions raised by the standard. Share your critique in class. A sample of responses is at the end of this chapter.

1. "If it becomes apparent that counselors may be called upon to perform potentially conflicting roles, they clarify, adjust or withdraw from roles appropriately" (ACA Code, 1995, Section A.8).

   Critique: ______________________________

   ____

   ____

2. "Counselors make every effort to avoid dual relationships with clients that could impair professional judgment or increase the risk of harm to clients" (ACA Code, 1995, Section A.6).

   Critique: ______________________________

   ____

   ____

3. "Counselors recognize that culture affects the manner in which clients' problems are defined. Clients' socioeconomic and cultural experience is considered when diagnosing mental disorders." (ACA Code, 1995, Section E.5).

   Critique: ______________________________

   ____

   ____

ticular, counselors and human service professionals must ask how a standard relates to collectivistic views and values embraced by clients and/or the cultures that influence their development and daily functioning. Being competent to adapt ethical standards appropriately for all clients is imperative for counselors and other professional helpers. In the next section, we examine some multicultural competencies established and published in recent years.

Multicultural Competency

Earlier chapters of this text have alluded to competencies and skills that successful counselors acquire and apply when assisting culturally diverse clients. Chapter 9, for example, covers the skills of the multicultural counselor, discusses appropriate assessment, diagnosis, and treatment decisions, and briefly presents group procedural issues in working with diverse populations. In addition, the "Counseling Inferences" section of each chapter has addressed some competencies in general terms. This section presents more specific information about the development of multicultural competencies.

The Professional Standards Committee of the Association for Multicultural Counseling and Development (AMCD) is credited with developing basic competencies and standards of practice for multicultural counseling (Sue, Arredondo, & McDavis, 1992). This landmark document delineated essential cultural competencies across three major categories: counselor awareness, knowledge, and skills. A few years later, Arredondo, Toporek, Brown, Jones, Locke, Sanchez, and Stadler (1996) provided further explanation about how counselors apply these competencies in practice. Specifically, they illustrated how awareness, knowledge, and skills manifest themselves in attitudes, beliefs, understanding, and interventions chosen by counselors. The following sections briefly summarize the three basic categories with a few explanations and apply them across the helping professions. Readers are encouraged to review the original references for detailed explanation and understanding of these competencies.

Competency I: Counselor's Awareness of Own Cultural Values and Biases

Attitudes and Beliefs. Competent counselors and human service professionals believe that self-awareness, particularly about their own culture's influences, and sensitivity to their cultural heritage are essential. They realize the impact culture has had on their *self*-development, in both positive and negative ways, and are able to identify particular cultural groups, values, and beliefs that have had the most significant influence in developing their self-view and overall worldview. Furthermore, they are aware of how they translate these perceptions into common thoughts, personal feelings, and daily behavior. Exercise 11.2 asks you to explore some attitudes and beliefs that might affect your performance as a culturally effective counselor or human service professional.

Successful professional counselors and helpers are also aware of the multitude of ways that cultural background and experience might influence thought processes, decision making, and problem-solving behaviors. Identity factors such as race, religion, sexual

Exercise 11.2

My Cultural Awareness

Instructions: Complete the sentences about your racial, cultural, ethnic, sexual, and other identities. After completing each sentence, contemplate how these views and beliefs might affect your functioning as an effective helper. What might you do to increase or heighten your cultural awareness?

1. About my racial identity, I believe ______________________________
2. About other races, and in particular ______________, I believe ______________
3. About my sex, I believe ______________________________
4. In general, I believe members of the opposite sex ______________________________
5. The most important person in my life has been (or is) ______________________________
6. The most important group to which I belong is ______________________________
7. I believe that sexual orientation ______________________________
8. People who have a different sexual orientation than I do ______________________________
9. What I know about my own culture ______________________________
10. About religion, I believe ______________________________
11. My awareness of diverse religions ______________________________
12. People who follow no religion ______________________________
13. My ethnic awareness ______________________________
14. Awareness of my family background and roots ______________________________
15. The most influential aspects in my development have been ______________________________

orientation, and others are understood as significant contributors to *self*-development and psychological/cognitive processes for both counselors and their clients.

Additional attitudes and beliefs associated with this first competency relate to counselors' understanding of their professional limitations when working across cultures. Such limitations may be related to lack of knowledge, undeveloped skills, or unwavering beliefs and values that hinder the establishment of effective counseling relationships. In addition, these attitudes and beliefs might limit a helper's effectiveness due to discomfort regarding certain differences in identity factors that exist in the relationship between the counselor and client. As examples, counselors and other therapists sometimes have difficulty with racial issues presented by clients, struggle with differences regarding religious beliefs, or are unable to overcome prejudices about particular groups that hold different views or lifestyles, such as homosexuals.

Knowledge. Culturally competent professional helpers attain knowledge about their cultural heritage, including racial and ethnic identity, and understand how this background influences their definitions of and beliefs about normality and abnormality in counseling relationships. In addition, their knowledge includes an understanding of how racism, sexism, classism, and other forms of oppression, discrimination, and stereotypic behavior influence the effectiveness of professionals, particularly their functioning with diverse clients. Furthermore, successful counselors and therapists know how a particular racial, cultural, ethnic, or other social identity grants them certain unearned privileges. By being White, tall, male, heterosexual, physically attractive, able-bodied, or affluent, some people may receive privileges that society denies to other persons or groups that do not share these characteristics.

Self-knowledge includes an understanding by counselors and other professionals of how clients might perceive and interpret their behaviors and functions in the helping process. Knowing that certain verbal and nonverbal behaviors may be inappropriate or why selected assessment or intervention strategies might prove counterproductive with particular clients is indicative of a culturally sensitive and knowledgeable professional.

Skills. Counselors and other professionals who are culturally aware continuously seek educational opportunities and learning experiences to expand their knowledge and capability. In addition, they willingly consult with colleagues and other professionals as appropriate to verify their understanding of particular cases and counseling practices when working with challenging situations. Similarly, they know when to refer cases to ensure that all clients receive the best possible care, and they remain informed about appropriate, culturally sensitive referral sources in their community.

Another skill related to becoming a culturally aware and sensitive helper relates to a continuous search for understanding oneself as a racial/cultural being who actively works to establish a nonracist identity and, furthermore, seeks to create a nonracist society. This skill parallels the characteristics of advocacy and social justice explored in Chapter 9 of this text. Counselors and human service professionals who use their skills to establish a nonracist identity while seeking to create nonracist societies move beyond typical counseling relationships to more proactive interventions in the larger community.

Competency II: Counselor's Awareness of Clients' Worldviews

Attitudes and Beliefs. Effective helpers understand how their beliefs, including biases and prejudices, will enable or prevent them from becoming aware of how clients view themselves and the world around them. Specifically, culturally competent counselors and therapists understand how their reactions toward clients and stereotypic views might inhibit their ability to establish effective helping relationships. Genuine awareness of their biases and stereotypic thinking enables competent professionals to refer clients to more appropriate sources for assistance. As counselors and other helpers are able to move toward less judgmental positions regarding specific races, cultures, or groups, they expand the clientele they are able to serve effectively.

Knowledge. To fully appreciate the worldviews of all clients, competent counselors and human service providers learn about the various cultures of their client population. This knowledge is broad and includes information about cultural heritage, values, customs, and behavioral differences. It also includes information about how social and political events have shaped and influenced cultural beliefs. In particular, knowledge of how history of oppression, racism, poverty, and other societal forces such as media portrayal have affected

Exercise 11.3

My Daily Experience with Diversity

Instructions: Consider each of the statements below and assess your overall diversity experiences in daily living.

1. My neighborhood reflects diversity by the different races represented.
2. My next-door neighbors are of different ethnic/cultural origin than I am.
3. I work (or attend school) with a diverse group of colleagues (classmates).
4. My closest friends reflect diversity in culture, ethnicity, racial identity, religious beliefs, and/or gender.
5. The most recent social functions I attended were mixed racially and culturally.
6. When I go out socially, I prefer settings that reflect diversity.
7. I am active in community activities that encompass diversity.
8. I am often in the minority at social or community events.
9. I attend various places of worship to experience diverse practices and traditions.
10. My favorite group activity or function usually includes diverse membership.

---

certain cultural groups is important to develop awareness and sensitivity regarding clients' worldviews. Lastly, cultural knowledge helps counselors and other professionals understand how various identity factors interact with personality development and disturbances, life and career choices, and help-seeking behaviors as well as be aware of appropriate and inappropriate counseling interventions with particular clients.

Skills. To better understand the worldviews of clients, competent professionals study and learn about the latest research findings in the multicultural and counseling fields. They continue to participate in educational experiences that will help them learn about cultural diversity. In addition, competent helpers seek to broaden their personal and social experiences by actively participating in social functions, forming acquaintances and friendships, and assisting with community projects that increase their contact with diverse groups and expand their knowledge of various cultures while combating preconceived notions. Exercise 11.3 helps you examine your daily interaction with diverse cultures.

Competency III: Culturally Appropriate Intervention Strategies

Attitudes and Beliefs. An essential attitude held by culturally competent counselors and other professionals is to respect religious and spiritual beliefs of clients, and particularly how clients might express spiritual views and values through feelings of grief, pain, and sorrow. Counselors and human service providers also maintain open attitudes about indigenous healing and helping processes that rely on community and networking avenues. When appropriate, culturally effective helpers coordinate their services with indigenous healers and/or community networks that are often essential among diverse populations. Other attitudes related to this competency involve values and beliefs about bilingualism.

Effective professionals encourage bilingual practices in their work and in society. They view bilingualism as an advantage rather than a disadvantage. In contrast, obsession with the maintenance and endorsement of a single language severely limits the richness of a diverse society.

Knowledge. An understanding of how traditional philosophies and theories of counseling might conflict with diverse cultures helps culturally competent professionals appreciate the Euro-American context within which counseling approaches were first established. Counselors and therapists balance this understanding with knowledge of cultural differences that stand in opposition to commonly held and promoted perspectives about so-called appropriate counseling and therapeutic methods.

Other knowledge acquired by culturally competent helpers concerns historic institutional barriers that have prevented, and continue to prevent, diverse populations from receiving appropriate care in existing mental health systems. Knowledge about such barriers enables counselors and others to be proactive in advocating for clients and seeking alternative methods of treatment when traditional systems fail to serve clients equitably. This knowledge includes an understanding of potential biases in assessment instruments and procedures, and subsequent misuse and misguided interpretation of assessment results.

Knowledge of family structures and functions including values and beliefs of diverse cultures is also important as noted in an earlier chapter of this text. Truly competent professionals are able to put aside personal values and beliefs that might conflict with family values and beliefs of their clients. By knowing community resources that will respect diverse family structures and values, counselors are better able to assist diverse groups of clients.

Finally, knowledge of social forces and community practices that continue as vestiges of discrimination, oppression, racism, and other conditions or beliefs negatively affecting the mental health and well-being of members of society, particularly those who receive assistance from counselors and other professional helpers, is essential. As noted earlier, proactive counselors and human service providers are knowledgeable about laws, policies, programs, and other aspects of society at the local and national levels that have negative impacts on diverse populations.

Skills. Many skills relate to the selection and use of appropriate interventions. First, competent professionals are capable of sending and receiving a variety of verbal and nonverbal messages in the helping relationship. Furthermore, they are able to adapt and alter their communication styles to fit the needs of clients. By communicating effectively with all clients, counselors and therapists are better able to discern if clients' problems are a result of external forces rather than internal thought processes.

Successful helpers are also able to help their clients negotiate institutional regulations and policies that might unduly inhibit or unjustly discriminate. In addition, they have skills to reach out to other professionals, religious and spiritual leaders, and indigenous healers when appropriate. The skills used to reach out also enable counselors and other helpers to seek alternative processes when language is a barrier. By locating interpreters and seeking information and publications written in languages understood by clients, they demonstrate acceptance of and respect for diversity.

Assessment skills are another area of competency. Successful counselors and human service professionals are skilled in the use and interpretation of traditional instruments and procedures, but they consistently use those skills with cultural awareness and sensitivity. Likewise, they use skill and understanding to assess and educate others in an effort to eradicate biases and prejudices that have persisted in society and fostered oppressive and discriminatory practices. Equally important, professional helpers use their assessment and educational skills to inform clients of their rights and about what to expect within the helping relationship.

Human Service Education

Before leaving this section on preparation and education of helping professionals, we consider again the standards of the National Organization for Human Service Education (NOHSE, 2004a). Section II of those standards includes 17 statements—#38 through #54. Each statement provides guidance to human service educators about principles and processes for preparing competent human service professionals. They include language about academic freedom, explicit program goals and objectives, relevant curriculum, quality supervision in field experiences, and other aspects of strong education programs of study to ensure preparation of competent professionals. The introduction to these statements encourages educators to be informed by and accountable to the standards of their respective disciplines. The American Counseling Association, the National Board of Certified Counselors, and the National Organization for Human Service Education are included in the list of organizations that represent various professional disciplines.

The preceding sections summarize counselor competencies and explanations presented in the multicultural literature (Arredondo et al., 1996). In addition to learning about these competencies and gaining awareness, knowledge, and skills to apply them consistently and accurately with clients, counselors and human service professionals also want to know about laws and other policies that have affected diverse populations in the past and continue to do so in present-day society. The next section presents an overview of legislation and legal issues that have influenced the multicultural movement.

Laws, Legal Issues, and Diverse Clients

The United States is founded on democratic principles of freedom, equality, and justice for all people. These principles are the ideals that inspired people from various backgrounds to migrate from their homelands first to the New World, later to the American colonies, and finally to the United States. The American Revolution was fought to build upon these ideals and create a nation unlike any other the world had seen. Many historic documents, from the Declaration of Independence to the Constitution of the United States of America, were drafted and passed with this magnanimous goal in mind. Yet, the history of the United States, much like the history of many other cultures and countries, has not always lived up to its high-minded, moral ideals.

The diverse groups that comprise this great country, from the Native Americans whose ancestors first migrated across the Bering Strait to settle in unknown lands to contemporary immigrants from war-torn or otherwise oppressive parts of the world, have not always been received, accepted, or treated equitably and fairly. Worse, the African slave trade of the seventeenth and eighteenth centuries left an indelible mark of oppression, torture, incarceration, and massacre that defy all democratic principles and beliefs upon which this country was supposedly founded. Furthermore, that legacy played a significant role in a four-year Civil War that tore this country apart, and remains a sore topic of political and social concern among families in many communities 150 years later.

In this section, we explore some of the legislation and court rulings that have violated as well as fostered democratic ideals so valued by the United States. This exploration is by design a brief overview and not intended to cover all the significant events that have contributed to legal development and civil liberties in this country. The first few paragraphs cover notable immigration and citizenship laws and civil rights legislation.

Search for Freedom: A Chronology of Immigration and Citizenship Legislation

One of the first acts related to immigration and citizenship passed shortly after the United States became an independent nation. The *Naturalization Law of 1790* granted the rights of citizenship to all *free White* people who had immigrated or would immigrate to the United States, gave proof of their intentions to reside in the country, took an oath of allegiance, and resided in the country for one full year. Thus, one of the first acts of the U.S. Congress was to denote racial differences and bestow only upon free White persons the ability to become U.S. citizens. This racial difference would remain federal law until 1952, although some Asian groups were allowed citizenship during the 1940s.

In 1798, Congress passed the *Alien and Sedition Acts* giving the president power to deport any foreign person considered dangerous to the United States. It also made it a crime to speak or publish false, scandalous, or otherwise malicious material about the president or Congress. An amended Naturalization Act required a fourteen-year residency for prospective citizens, but four years later, Congress reduced that period to five years, which remains the waiting period today.

The *Chinese Exclusion Act* of 1882 halted immigration of Chinese laborers until 1892, when Congress continued the law, and then, in 1902, Congress enacted the ban permanently. This was the first time the U.S. Congress used racial identity or national origin to limit immigration into the country. The ability to speak and understand the English language first became a requirement for naturalization in 1906. A few years later, in 1917, Congress overrode President Wilson's veto and passed a literacy requirement—the capability of reading forty words in some language—for all immigrants. In addition, this bill greatly restricted the immigration of people from Asia. With the exception of Japan and the Philippines, this law prohibited all immigration from other countries in Asia.

The "Gentlemen's Agreement" of 1907 between the United States and Japan provided a curious relationship regarding immigration. The United States promised not to ban immigration from Japan, and the Japanese government agreed not to issue passports to laborers wanting to travel to the United States. However, farm workers from Japan were able to migrate to Hawaii. President Theodore Roosevelt further restricted Japanese immigration by declaring an executive order that prohibited any secondary migration from Hawaii to the continental United States.

By the 1920s, the United States had begun using a quota system that would limit the number of European immigrants to a set percentage of a nationality's representation in the 1910 census. A bill in 1921 set the limit at 3 percent, which largely favored people from northern Europe over those from Italy, Greece, and other southern and eastern European countries. At the same time, Asian people continued to be excluded from these quota systems.

The *Johnson-Reed Act* of 1924 continued the effort to use racial identity or national origin as a guiding principle of what America should look like. Congress now set immigration quotas based on the ethnic composition of the U.S. population in the 1920 census. The result was greater discrimination by race as the nation sought to keep "America for Americans," a popular slogan among the dominant culture of the time. Still, the Congress was not absolute in its goal for ethnic purity. When politically expedient to do so, exceptions were made. For example, during World War II, Congress passed a bill allowing a small number of Chinese immigrants as token appreciation to its ally, China.

U.S. resistance toward immigration continued in the 1950s with passage of the *Internal Security Act,* which prohibited the entrance of any foreign person who might participate in activities not viewed in the public interest or that otherwise posed a danger to safety and welfare. President Truman vetoed the bill, but Congress passed it over his objection. This time period included heightened fear of Communism, so the bill included sections that permitted barring and deporting foreigners who held membership in the U.S. Communist Party or who threatened national security. During this decade, Congress passed the *McCarran-Walter Act of 1952,* also known as the *Immigration and Nationality Act,* and continued the immigration quota system. Some changes made by Congress, however, opened opportunities for many people whose racial identity would have previously prohibited their immigration to the United States. Also included in this bill was the requirement that the ability to read, write, speak, and understand English was a criterion for naturalization.

From the 1960s to the present day, the United States has continued to shape its immigration policy, moving closer to the ideals upon which the country was originally founded. In 1965, for example, Congress eliminated racial identity as a criterion. Immigration from Western hemisphere countries remained favored over other countries, but the government would be remedy that prejudice by the mid-1970s. In the 1980s, Congress passed laws to grant amnesty to undocumented residents while passing other legislation to prevent employers from hiring illegal aliens. Through the 1990s and into the twenty-first century, Congress continued to fine-tune immigration legislation and raise the number of people who could come to the United States legally. However, economic conditions and employment opportunities for U.S. citizens influence public opinion and subsequently legislation regarding immigration. For example, in 1996, the *Illegal Immigration Reform and Immigrant Responsibility Act* passed, which placed new restrictions, tightened the borders, and made it more difficult for undocumented people to gain political asylum in the United States. This law greatly expanded the grounds for deporting even long-resident immigrants. These and other harsh restrictions were muted somewhat by the next Congress, which passed several pieces of legislation to reinstate some benefits to immigrants, help war refugees become permanent residents, and raise the number of skilled workers that U.S. employers may bring into the country on temporary visas.

With the beginning of the twenty-first century, the U.S. Congress continued positive movement with its pro-immigration legislation. For example, it opened opportunities for immigrants who have family or employer sponsors to obtain legal status. Also, the *Child Citizenship Act of 2000* granted automatic citizenship to certain foreign-born, biological, or adopted children when they entered the United States as lawful permanent residents. During this time, Congress also modified the naturalization law to allow severely disabled immigrants to become citizens even if they were unable to understand the Oath of Allegiance (sources for material used in this section on immigration laws include Cose, 1992; Crawford, 1992, 2000; Jones, 1992, 1995).

Equality and Justice for All: A History of Legislation and Court Rulings

The largest group of disenfranchised citizens in the United States has been women. By law, women were second-class citizens who after marriage did not have the right to own property, maintain wages, sign legal contracts, or vote in government elections. In addition, custom and traditional thought believed that women should obey their husbands to the extent of agreeing with the husband's stance on a variety of issues without expressing personal opinions. As noted in an earlier chapter, women during this period did not speak out in public forums. These customs and traditions were challenged beginning in 1848 with the first Women's Rights Convention held in Seneca Falls, New York. This convention had its roots in the antislavery movement to which many women belonged. Lucretia Mott and Elizabeth Cady Stanton were two of the leaders who decided to hold a convention to consider social, political, and religious rights of women. Some of the most important results from this convention were discussions and resolutions about women's right to vote.

The Civil War preempted any progress in the early women's movement. For the next four years, a horrific war and the antislavery movement took center stage in U.S. politics. Although women across the country periodically held meetings and conventions, nothing substantial resulted from these gatherings. Some leaders focused effort on freeing the slaves with hope that once this noble goal was accomplished, women might realize similar civil liberties. When the war ended, however, the vote of newly freed slaves won favor over women's suffrage.

Suffrage for Women. The American Equal Rights Association, founded in 1866 by Elizabeth Cady Stanton and other leaders, began the serious effort to win women's rights. Unfortunately, constitutional amendments would cause friction in the organization, splitting the women's movement into two major factions. The 14th Amendment, passed by Congress in 1868, narrowly limited citizenship and voting rights to males. The amendment prohibited states from denying and diminishing the basic rights of all citizens and equal protection and due process under the law. One result of this amendment was to encourage former Confederate states to give Black men the right to vote. Ironically, other states with freed men that remained loyal to the Union could still deny Black suffrage. Two years later, the 15th Amendment gave voting rights to all Black men. Some within the women's suffrage movement fought against the amendment because it allowed the government to continue denying the right to vote to women. As a result, the women's movement split in disagreement about how to proceed. Consequently, two organizations emerged. The National Woman Suffrage Association (NWSA) began in New York under the guidance of Elizabeth Stanton and Susan B. Anthony. About the same time, two other women, Lucy Stone and Julia Ward Howe, established the American Woman Suffrage Association (AWSA) in Boston. In the 1890s, the two associations came back together to form the National American Woman Suffrage Association (NAWSA) with Elizabeth Stanton as its head.

In 1878, the first Woman's Suffrage Amendment was introduced in Congress. Many women's groups across the country lobbied for this legislation. Groups such as the National Council of Jewish Women (NCJW), the National Association of Colored Women (NACW), and the Women's Trade Union League kept this dream alive through the end of the 1800s and into the early 1900s. Although slowed by World War I, the women's suffrage movement picked up speed again after the war and on August 26, 1920, Congress ratified the 19th Amendment to the Constitution, which President Woodrow Wilson signed. The 19th Amendment orders that the right to vote cannot be denied or abridged by the federal government or any state government because of sex.

This historic event launched the women's movement into political and social arenas heretofore untouched by female citizens. With suffrage won, the National American Woman Suffrage Association (NAWSA) ended, but other organizations such as the League of Women Voters and the National Woman's Party (NWP) followed. One of the major efforts of the NWP was to propose the Equal Rights Amendment (E.R.A.) in 1923. The measure intended to remove all vestiges of sex discrimination in society, and although it failed to pass through Congress at that time, the push for this amendment continued. In 1972, the U.S. Senate passed the amendment thanks to the efforts of many organizations, including the National Organization for Women (NOW), but to this date the amendment has yet to be ratified. There was by no means unanimous consensus among women's groups about the E.R.A. For example, after it passed the Senate, the National Committee to Stop ERA formed under the leadership of Phyllis Shafley. Over the next 30-plus years, several conventions, court rulings, and efforts to reintroduce the amendment occurred. In 1983, the U.S. Congress failed to pass the E.R.A. with the House of Representatives falling six votes short of the required two-thirds majority for it to pass (National Organization for Women, n.d.).

As noted, shortly after the women's movement began in the mid-1800s, several states seceded from the Union and into Civil War. Although historians do not agree whether slavery was the quintessential reason for the war (Dew, 2002), the issue of slavery became the fulcrum upon which the future of the nation balanced. Government action to free the slaves during the war, although criticized as being disingenuous by some contemporary authorities, was the beginning of the Civil Rights Movement in the United States.

Civil Rights and Affirmative Action. On September 22, 1862, President Abraham Lincoln issued *The Emancipation Proclamation,* which stated that all slaves held within states rebelling against the Union would be free. Embedded in this document were many exceptions, and to this day, historians debate the motives behind and authenticity of Lincoln's actions. Some even speculate that it was a public relations ploy to discourage Great Britain from supporting the confederacy (DiLorenzo, 2001). In addition, other authorities question whether the proclamation actually freed many slaves because so many border states and states under control of the Union army were exempt.

Other historians cite events and speeches of Lincoln's during his political career that seem to embrace beliefs of White supremacy and an inclination to keep Whites and Blacks separated (Bennett, 2000; Miller, 2002). Certainly, numerous statements attributed to Lincoln question his intentions. One of the most famous comes from his second debate for the Illinois senatorial nomination with Stephen Douglas on August 27, 1858, in which Lincoln argued:

> I will say, then, that I am not, nor ever have been, in favor of bringing about in any way the social and political equality of the white and black races—that I am not, nor ever have been, in favor of making voters or jurors of Negroes, nor of qualifying them to hold office, nor to intermarry with white people; and I will say in addition to this that there is a physical difference between the white and black races which I believe will forever forbid the two races from living together on terms of social and political equality.

Later, during his presidency, Lincoln seemed to affirm some of these views as he spoke and wrote about the Civil War. In an often-quoted response to Horace Greeley, then editor of the *New York Tribune,* Lincoln wrote a letter on August 22, 1862, in which he stated:

> My paramount object in this struggle is to save the Union, and is not either to save or to destroy slavery. If I could save the Union without freeing any slave I would do it, and if I could save it by freeing all the slaves I would do it; and if I could save it by freeing some and leaving others alone I would also do that.

Other historians dispute the interpretation that Lincoln was not genuine in wanting to free the slaves, noting that many other quotes demonstrate his horror toward slavery and compassion for Black people. For example, in a speech to the 140th Indiana Regiment in 1865, Lincoln said, "Whenever [I] hear any one arguing for slavery I feel a strong impulse to see it tried on him personally." Furthermore, his acceptance speech for the Republican nomination for the U.S. Senate from Illinois in June of 1858 seemed to clarify his anti-slavery position:

> A house divided against itself cannot stand. I believe this government cannot endure permanently half slave and half free. I do not expect the Union to be dissolved—I do not expect the house to fall—but I do expect it will cease to be divided. It will become all one thing, or all the other. Either the opponents of slavery will arrest the further spread of it, and place it where the public mind shall rest in the belief that is in the course of ultimate extinction; or its advocates will push it forward till it shall become alike lawful in all the States, old as well as new, North as well as South.

The foregoing discussion notwithstanding, *The Emancipation Proclamation* presented a defining moment in U.S. history because, at the very least, it conveyed for U.S. citizens and other world populations the appearance that the main thrust of the Civil War was to put an end to slavery. Although the proclamation itself did little to end slavery, the 13th Amendment to the Constitution accomplished that goal with passage in 1865. Thus began the long march toward civil rights, equal education, and affirmative action in this country.

Several legal events were precursors to the Civil Rights Movement in this country. For example, the 13th, 14th, and 15th amendments mentioned earlier gave limited rights to freed slaves. Nevertheless, legal barriers continued. One of the most notable was the 1896 U.S. Supreme Court ruling in *Plessy v. Ferguson* that upheld a "separate but equal" doctrine allowing local governments to deny Blacks access to the same facilities and institutions, such as schools, that were accessible to Whites. Without question, the facilities and institutions established for Blacks from this point on were indeed separate, but they were far from equal.

The separate-but-equal culture began changing when President Franklin D. Roosevelt signed an executive order in 1941 banning hiring policies based on race by industries that had defense contracts with the federal government. This order was the result of lobbying efforts sparked by A. Philip Randolph, a civil rights activist who first organized the March on Washington Movement (MOWM). His actions vaulted Randolph into the public and political arena as a leading civil rights figure of the period. In 1948, his efforts resulted in another significant executive order, signed by President Harry S Truman, which prohibited racial segregation in the military. In the 1950s and 1960s, Randolph joined with Dr. Martin Luther King, Jr., to continue the nonviolent group action begun by MOWM, and together they organized the history-making March on Washington where Dr. King delivered his famous "I Have a Dream" speech in 1963 (George Meany Center for Labor Studies, n.d.).

In 1953, President Truman urged the Committee on Government Contract Compliance, a temporary committee established in 1951, to insist that the U.S. Bureau of Employment Security develop and implement a policy of nondiscrimination in hiring and employment procedures. This was an initial step in establishing fair employment practices for diverse cultural and ethnic groups in the United States (Truman Presidential Museum & Library, n.d.).

In one of the most important events of the Civil Rights Movement came in 1954 when the U.S. Supreme Court overturned *Plessy v. Ferguson* (separate but equal) in *Brown v. Board of Education.* The ruling came about as a result of an appeal by the National Association for the Advancement of Colored People (NAACP) and the family of Linda Brown, a third-grade student from Topeka, Kansas, of the decision by a U.S. District Court to uphold *Plessy v. Ferguson.* In the Supreme Court decision, Chief Justice Earl Warren stated that the doctrine promoting "separate but equal" had no place in public education. Consequently, the High Court struck down *Plessy v. Ferguson* and required that public schools across the United States desegregate. The process of school desegregation, however, would take many years, inviting heated debate, violent outbursts, and "White flight" to private schools across the country.

The Civil Rights Movement received another boost in 1961 when newly inaugurated President John F. Kennedy issued an executive order to establish a Committee on Equal Employment Opportunity. For the first time, a federal mandate used the term "affirmative action" to ensure that people seeking employment and those already employed were treated equitably without regard to ethnicity, race, religious beliefs, or national origin. This led the way for passage of the Civil Rights Act of 1964, which expanded application of the principles put forth in President Kennedy's original executive order.

Following the assassination of President Kennedy in November of 1963 and shortly after President Lyndon B. Johnson took office, the Civil Rights Act of 1964 passed through Congress. It declared that "No person in the United States shall, on the ground of race, color or national origin, be excluded from participation in, be denied the benefits of, or be subjected to discrimination under any program or activity receiving federal financial assistance" (U.S. Department of Justice, n.d.).

Several executive orders and other initiatives by President Johnson and others continued to expand and clarify government policy to provide equal opportunity and ban discriminatory practices. At first these initiatives addressed racial, religious, and national origin as targets of discrimination, but soon after they included a ban on discriminatory practice based on sex.

Federal efforts to prohibit discrimination in the workplace transferred to the Department of Labor and continued during the administration of President Richard M. Nixon. During this period, the government encouraged affirmative action practices that would increase the proportion of underrepresented groups, including women, in the workforce. In implementing such policies, the government focused on the same identity variables, such as race and gender, that it insisted not be considered by employers when making hiring decisions. This contradiction has not been overlooked by groups opposing affirmative action initiatives. Today, the debate about affirmative action, often including references to moral rights and reverse discrimination, continues across the country and in the political arena. Scholars seem to agree that implementation of some affirmative action initiatives resulted in limited injustices to certain people or groups. At the same time, many believe that some injustice may be unavoidable in moving the government and country toward a higher moral goal of justice and equality for all.

Court cases and legislation continue to address many issues affecting diversity in this country. For example, in the landmark case of *Lau v. Nichols* (1974), the U.S. Supreme Court unanimously found "there was 'no equality of treatment' when more than half the students of Chinese descent in San Francisco received no instruction to overcome English-language deficiencies" (Fischer & Sorenson, 1996). The Court reversed a lower-court ruling and found that the absence of appropriate instruction in English denied Chinese students equal opportunity to participate in public educational programs. Similarly, in another California case, *Larry P. v. Riles* (1979), the African American parents of a young boy argued that the use of biased intelligence tests resulted in the identification and placement of a disproportionate number of African American students in classes for the Educable Mentally Retarded (EMR). A federal court judge placed the burden of proof on the schools to demonstrate that the tests, largely standardized on White, middle-class populations, were valid measures when used with Black students. Failure of the school system to demonstrate such validity led the court to rule against the use of such intelligence tests with African American students. The ruling was affirmed by the Ninth Circuit Court of Appeals in 1984 (Fischer & Sorenson, 1996). In 1992, the same judge who ruled in the original case rescinded his decision that led to a 1986 ban for all use of intelligence tests with African American students for special education placement. Yet, he did not reverse the original ruling that discontinued the use of intelligence tests for placing students in EMR classes.

All the cases and legislation that occurred from the mid-1840s until the late twentieth century helped move U.S. government and society closer to its ideal goals of equality and justice for all. Despite this progress another cultural group, unidentified by lawmakers and social activists, remained underserved and disenfranchised. People with disabilities were still denied access to many facilities, institutions, employment opportunities, and other services of society. This inequity changed with passage of the Americans with Disabilities Act of 1990.

Americans with Disabilities Act of 1990. The United States includes many people who have physical limitations and disabilities, such as blindness, hearing loss, and lack of mobility, and mental challenges brought on by disease, birth defects, or other conditions. With all the progress made in civil rights for U.S. citizens, before 1990 people with disabilities continued to be denied access to programs, jobs, and services simply because of their condition.

Signed into law on July 26, 1990, the Americans with Disabilities Act (ADA) purports to make society more accessible to people with these challenges. Consisting of five sections (titles), the bill requires the following:

- Businesses must provide reasonable accommodations for people with disabilities. Such accommodations might include but are not limited to changing physical environments and space planning, reorganizing jobs, and altering equipment. In addition, the government monitors application and hiring practices, salaries, benefits, medical examinations, and other employment processes that might affect opportunities for workers with disabilities (Title I).
- Accessibility to all public services for all citizens including people with disabilities. Therefore, public transportation systems, such as public buses and trains, must have lifts, ramps, or other structures to allow accessibility for people with disabilities (Title II).
- Construction and renovations must include structures and equipment to allow accessibility for people with disabilities. In addition, existing public facilities must remove barriers to services if possible. Public facilities include businesses and institutions such as restaurants, hotels, grocery stores, retail stores, and privately owned transportation systems (Title III).
- Companies that offer communications services, such as public telephone service, provide relay services to individuals who use telecommunication devices for the deaf (TTYs), or have similar equipment available (Title IV).
- Businesses, public institutions, organizations, and individuals are prohibited from coercing or threatening, or retaliating against, disabled persons or those who assist people with disabilities in asserting their rights under the law.

Since passage of ADA, buildings, programs, policies, and services have undergone significant changes to make U.S. society more accessible to all people. From alterations in city sidewalks that allow people in wheelchairs to navigate streets and intersections safely to the multiple uses of new technology to assist speech-, sight-, and hearing-impaired persons to have better employment opportunities, the effects of ADA are visible and important for creating a society based on democratic principles. All these accommodations combined with the history and accomplishments of the Civil Rights Movement in America are important for counselors and other helping professionals to know about and understand in terms of their influence on a broad range of clients.

Exercise 11.4

Legal Issues, Events, and Actions
For the next couple of weeks scan news articles and stories in newspapers, magazines, and through other media about legal actions or events that have implications for people of diverse cultures. Research a particular issue or event and form a plan of action you might take as a helper to advocate for clients that might be affected by this incident.

This section has reviewed some of the major legislation and notable court cases that have had an impact on people of diverse cultures in the United States since the nineteenth century. Successful counselors and other helping professionals that serve diverse populations stay informed about legal decisions, legislation, and administrative policies that affect the welfare of their clients. Exercise 11.4 urges you to explore recent events and government actions that have legal implications for cross-cultural counseling or advocacy for disenfranchised groups and oppressed individuals.

Counseling Inferences

Throughout this text, we explored the awareness, knowledge, and skills demanded by the social and cultural foundations of counseling and other professional helping relationships. This chapter paid particular attention to ethical standards of practice, multicultural competencies, and awareness of laws and legal issues that relate to counseling relationships. The content of this chapter infers, as do all the other chapters, that successful professionals are aware of the historical context in which diverse populations have experienced discrimination and oppression through legislation and execution of unfair and unjust laws as well as court decisions based on unwarranted bias and unprovoked prejudice. By being aware of historical transgressions by government in the passage and implementation of discriminatory laws, counselors and other helping professionals are in a stronger position to recognize contemporary efforts to use legislation or administrative policies to unjustly deny, degrade, or otherwise disenfranchise individuals or groups of people because of ethnic, racial, cultural, religious, sexual orientation, disability, or other identity status. At the same time, this knowledge might help counselors and human service providers advocate for equitable laws and policies to strengthen society's commitment to democratic principles.

This chapter also highlights important competencies developed over time by authorities in the multicultural arena. Proficiency in these cultural competencies, in addition to command of fundamental competencies advocated by the counseling profession, is requisite to being an effective professional who delivers services within appropriate boundaries of acceptable ethical standards of practice. Narrative 11.1 illustrates how one counselor remembers a case in which she used her position and understanding of legal process to help a mother obtain citizenship for an adopted daughter.

NARRATIVE 11.1 • *Measures of Success*

Professionally, I have learned to measure success in small increments. By this, I mean you must learn to appreciate the small accomplishments of clients because if you don't, you are setting yourself up for burnout or dissatisfaction with your job.

I have one case that stands out in my mind. I helped a mother obtain U.S. citizenship for her adolescent daughter, who was adopted in Africa. Due to a government coup, the mother and daughter had to leave the country hurriedly. After arriving in the U.S., the daughter suffered a prolonged seizure and high fever, causing some brain damage. Because her citizenship paperwork was not complete, the daughter lost her health benefits. I worked months with an attorney to help this mother obtain citizenship for her daughter. This case was my biggest professional success because I was able to help this family, and in turn, opened so many doors for the young lady who was my client.

Adequate understanding of and proficient use of counseling competencies depends on current awareness and knowledge of developments in the profession, including an understanding of salient research findings that guide professional practice. The final chapter of this text briefly explores research and professional issues regarding social and cultural foundations of counseling. In addition, the chapter considers future issues that might influence the practice of counseling across diverse populations.

Sample Responses to Exercise 11.1

Practicing Ethically with Diverse Clients

1. "If it becomes apparent that counselors may be called upon to perform potentially conflicting roles, they clarify, adjust or withdraw from roles appropriately" (ACA Code, 1995, Section A.8).

   Critique: When working with diverse clients, counselors might inevitably find themselves in, if not conflicting, possibly overlapping roles because the nature of collectivistic societies encourages expanded relationships. Pedersen (2002) suggested that the code might better assist counselors by offering direction "on how to reframe these multiple roles in ways that are complementary and faithful to the intention of the code" (p. 17).

2. "Counselors make every effort to avoid dual relationships with clients that could impair professional judgment or increase the risk of harm to clients" (ACA Code, 1995, Section A.6).

   Critique: Several authorities have maintained that dual relationships are often unavoidable, particularly in rural communities where few counselors or other helping professionals practice. At the same time, not all dual relationships are damaging to the helping process or harmful to clients. Counselors who work with diverse clientele must balance their desire to follow this standard with their clients' need to form trusting relationships, even if the process includes some appearance of dual relationships.

3. "Counselors recognize that culture affects the manner in which clients' problems are defined. Clients' socioeconomic and cultural experience is considered when diagnosing mental disorders." (ACA Code, 1995, Section E.5).

Critique: Although this standard seems appropriate, its interpretation is left very open and "entirely up to the individual counselor" (Pedersen, 2002, p. 17). As such, the cultural biases of the counselor still loom large over the process of diagnosis. More specific guidelines for implementing this standard may be necessary.

12

Research Issues and Future Considerations for Counseling Diverse Populations

This text has attempted to provide a broad overview of social and cultural foundations related to the practice of professional counseling, particularly as these foundations relate to self-development. In presenting these expanded concepts, each chapter has taken a specific focus. This concluding chapter highlights research issues and future considerations for the counseling profession as it strives to gain greater understanding of the social and cultural concepts that illuminate and delineate helping processes.

Counseling is both an artful and scientific profession (Nystul, 1999; Schmidt, 2004). By remaining flexible, using creative processes, and incorporating media, art, drama, and other modalities into helping relationships, professional counselors call upon their artful talents. At the same time, effective counselors rely on research evidence to lend credibility to the creative processes they select, promote competent practice, and contribute to the efficacy of the counseling profession (Nystul, 1999).

Because the multicultural arena is relatively young, much more research of the proposed models and of the usefulness of multicultural competencies mentioned in this text is needed. In this next section, we explore some research issues and future direction for counseling across diverse clientele. Counselors who serve clients from diverse backgrounds, as with professional counselors in general, want to base their practices on the most current research findings available.

Research Issues and Concerns

Successful counselors rely on the intentional selection and application of appropriate theoretical positions in conjunction with dependable assessment and communication skills. When working with diverse clients, professional counselors and other helpers demonstrate their knowledge of research findings and suppositions about the multicultural effectiveness of culturally diverse counselors. The following sections provide brief summaries of what the counseling research indicates about measurement problems, matching of clients and counselors, outcomes in counseling, and methodological issues in multicultural counseling research.

Measuring Cultural Perspectives

All aspects of counseling connect in some way to the process of measurement. For example, typical counseling relationships begin with counselors working with clients to gather information, look at previously collected data such as test results, mental health records, career inventories, or survey information, observe behaviors, and use other procedures to learn about each client and the concerns that they bring to the helping relationship. These processes combine to establish an overall assessment of the client's perceptions, behaviors, attitudes, abilities, and other characteristics that might help the counselor and client choose an appropriate direction for the counseling relationship. In cross-cultural counseling, researchers have examined several assessment tools and scales intended to help counselors measure aspects such as acculturation and cultural identity.

Roysircar (2003) highlighted a few scales developed to measure acculturation. Among these scales, some researchers have indicated that the focus of each may differ between *etic* and *emic* perspectives. An etic perspective emphasizes universal attributes across cultures and similarities among human beings. As such, a measurement scale or assessment procedure developed from an etic viewpoint will consist of beliefs the observer maintains about universal characteristics and traits that apply to all people regardless of their cultural background. Two instruments developed from this perspective are the Multigroup Ethnic Identity Measure (MEIM) (Phinney, 1992) and the Minority-Majority Relations Scale (MMRS) (Sodowsky et al., 1991). Although not widely used or intensely examined, some research of these instruments indicate validity in predicting degrees of acculturation among different ethnic groups. According to Roysircar (2003), the MEIM and MMRS "provide information that facilitates generalizations across ethnic groups and allow researchers to make comparative analysis" (p. 169).

In contrast to the etic perspective, an emic point of view relies on culture-specific variables, respecting clients' native culture and the meaning they confer on particular events, behaviors, and customs. Measures that emanate from an emic viewpoint place greater value on sociocultural variables and the influence they have on the degree to which certain individuals acculturate successfully. These variables might include the way a person immigrated (e.g., voluntary or involuntary), language, ancestral heritage, religious or spiritual beliefs, generational views, and others. Emic measures tend to illustrate the variance and heterogeneity within different ethnic groups in terms of people's degree of acculturation (Roysircar, 2003). (See Exercise 12.1.)

Racial/Ethnic Matching

Another research area concerns differences between counselors and clients. Specifically, researchers have examined clients' preferences for counselors based on racial or ethnic

Exercise 12.1

Emic and Etic Perspectives in Research
Locate news or research articles that report some social/cultural phenomenon. Based on the definitions and descriptions in this chapter, determine whether the study and findings seem to reflect an *emic* or *etic* point of view. Share your article and conclusions with the class.

characteristics and on counselors' reactions to clients that were racially or ethnically different from them (Helms & Cook, 1999). Overall, the research has failed to provide consistent findings about clients' preferences for counselors of the same racial or ethnic background. At the same time, studies of clients' preferences do not "reveal anything about how clients can be expected to behave if they do encounter a therapist" who belongs to a "disfavored group" (Helms & Cook, 1999, p. 305). Although findings are inconsistent, some research results have suggested that counselors and therapists might apply more severe diagnoses regarding clients' mental health to culturally different clients than to clients who are of the same ethnic/racial identity as the counselor. Helms and Cook (1999) noted several studies from the 1980s found that differing diagnoses that seemed to be related to racial and ethnic differences. Equally notable, they observed that "Black women relative to other racial groups were much more likely to be diagnosed as schizophrenic rather than depressed relative to their women counterparts of other races" (p. 306).

More research is required to better understand what dynamics might interact within counseling relationships when counselors and clients have dissimilar racial/ethnic backgrounds. More important than matching and mismatching counselors and clients in this effort might be to examine sociocultural variables, self-development factors, and cultural traits in studying the dynamics that lead to successful counseling relationships between apparently diverse counselors and clients. Therefore, how clients and counselors perceive racial identity, what elements they identify as contributing most to their self-development, and whether they tend to embrace individualistic or collectivistic views may be more important factors than studying Black counselors with Black or White clients, Asian clients with White or Asian counselors, and so forth. As Helms and Cook (1999) concluded, "studying racial and cultural matching actually offers very little useful information about the management or expression of such factors in the therapy process" (p. 309).

Ponterotto, Costa, and Werner-Lin (2002) also noted the limitations of earlier research and called for new direction in the study of counselor–client preferences. "It appears to us that attempting to predict counselor preferences based on race, ethnicity, gender, or acculturation level may be too limited, and these constructs, even collectively, cannot account for clinically significant variance in predictive equations" (p. 402). In particular, these authors advocated for more qualitative approaches using in-depth interviews to illustrate the important relationships among vital factors (e.g., sociocultural variables) that influence counseling processes and outcomes (see Exercise 12.2.).

Exercise 12.2

Imagining an Unmatched Helping Relationship

Imagine yourself in some type of helping relationship where you have asked for assistance with a family relationship issue. The person who appears before you is of different cultural/racial/ethnic identity than you. As the relationship proceeds, imagine the thoughts and feelings you might experience. What would be your most important concern? Write down your reactions, and share them with a small group of classmates.

Outcomes

Effectiveness of counseling services is measured, in part, by the results realized by clients. Sometimes these results are levels of satisfaction expressed by clients about their counseling experiences. Other times, outcomes might be observable changes in behaviors and/or relationships that clients set as goals for counseling. Research of outcomes in the context of counseling with diverse clients, particularly regarding the effectiveness of certain multicultural models, is lean at best. As Helms and Cook (1999) noted, some researchers have used racial matching as a variable to examine in outcome studies, but no clear findings are available. Their critique suggested that other variables besides racial matching of clients with counselors might prove more productive in studying counseling outcomes. For example, the impact of race on identity and the influence of racism, ethnocentrism, and culture on self-development might be more viable factors to measure in terms of effectiveness of counseling relationships. Furthermore, Baruth and Manning (1999) stressed that communication differences between researchers and subjects might be important cultural considerations that influence the collection and interpretation of data.

Helms and Cook (1999) listed a half dozen research studies and resources that considered "race or some aspect of culture as psychological variables" (p. 311). In summarizing these works, they indicated that issues studied included expressed collectivistic and individualistic views in counseling, gender as a nominal variable, and racial dynamics in counseling relationships. Furthermore, they advocated for more qualitative designs in research of these variables. As mentioned earlier, Ponterotto, Costa, and Werner-Lin (2002) also advocated more attention on qualitative research designs. They emphasized, "a tremendous need for and opportunity in constructivist and critical theory research paradigms as operationalized in qualitative research approaches. . . . It is clear to us that qualitative approaches will become increasingly popular in psychology generally and in multicultural counseling specifically" (p. 411). Process and outcome issues and the need to expand choices of research design lead to broader discussion of methodological considerations in multicultural counseling research.

Methodological Issues

Multicultural researchers have highlighted several methodological issues to add to the previously discussed research challenges. Among the issues related to research methodology are the tasks of finding and selecting appropriate samples, having clear conceptual/theoretical frameworks, designing sound studies, locating or developing valid instruments for measuring research variables, and controlling for confounding variables (Kurasaki, Sue, Chun, & Gee, 2000; Ponterotto et al., 2002).

Sampling has been a historic problem in multicultural research. Finding adequate and representative sample sizes and encouraging reluctant participants, who distrust government agencies such as universities that often do the research, present some of the challenges. As a result, past research has frequently relied on inadequate samples or too-broad populations. For example, past studies of Asian cultures have included participants from a wide range of populations including Chinese, Japanese, Koreans, Vietnamese, Indonesians, and others. Similarly, study of Latinos might include representatives from Mexico, Central

America, South America, Puerto Rico, United States, and other countries. As noted in earlier chapters, divergence within broad cultural groups is sometimes as great as the differences between global groups. Generalizing findings from such broad samples is therefore problematic.

Another problem with past research has been an overreliance on certain populations, such as samples of college students. Ponterotto and colleagues (2002) noted that easily accessible populations, such as college students, add to criticism of multicultural research. Samples of college students do not necessarily represent the community at large—for example in factors related to sexual orientation, ethnicity, and spirituality—so studies that attempt to generalize findings to the broader population risk confidence in their results.

Kurasaki and colleagues (2000) highlighted the difficulty of controlling for confounding variables in multicultural research. Confounding effects result when it is impossible for researchers to discern which variables contribute most to the variance in measurements taken. For example, in a study of children who are of different ages and were born in different years the variables of age and year born might become confounded. That is, the researcher might not be able to determine to what extent measured differences in dependent variables were due to a child's age or the fact that the child was born in a particular year. In multicultural research, variables studied are broad constructs, such as ethnicity. Many other variables such as social class, racial identity, and residency interrelate and interact with ethnicity. Therefore, researchers must find a way to control these variables, so they minimize confounding effects. Alternatively, as Helms and Cook (1999) proposed, "racial or ethnic classifications per se should fall outside of the domain of counseling and psychotherapy theory, research, and practice" (p. 312). They argued that research efforts to study particular classifications of counselors and clients lacked practical value in day-to-day mental health services, where "it is quite unlikely that the therapist can control or manipulate either the therapist's own racial classification or the client's" (p. 312).

Another methodological challenge, and one mentioned in a previous section, is the use of valid instruments to measure identified variables. Developing and finding valid measurement and assessment instruments, such as standardized tests, is a significant problem given the diverse meanings that cultures assign to psychological events, constructs, and characteristics. For example, Kurasaki and colleagues (2000) discussed the differences in characteristics of intelligence noted between some East African cultures and American society. In the United States, we value speed in performing ability tasks, but among some people of East Africa, "slow, deliberate thought is considered a part of intelligence" (p. 239).

Methodological challenges must be addressed for multicultural counseling research to make reliable progress. Authorities in this research arena have used critiques of past research designs and sampling techniques to speculate about future direction for the profession.

Future Direction in Multicultural Research

Researchers have highlighted several themes that should receive attention in the coming years. Among these topics, one of the most prevalent is a focus on the process of multicultural counseling (Baruth & Manning, 1999; Helms & Cook, 1999). Although research efforts have made an important contribution to the literature and understanding of cultural perspectives in counseling, more research will help the profession move beyond current explanation and speculation about diversity issues in counseling toward more definitive understanding of cultural essentials that influence counseling relationships and outcomes. Kurasaki and colleagues (2000) listed four targets for future research, and the first mentioned was to ascertain "how cultural elements influence treatment processes and outcomes among ethnic minorities" (p. 246).

In addition, research needs to investigate the relationship, if any, between essential cultural factors and group-specific treatment modalities or counseling techniques. Research has yet to show clear and consistent value and efficacy of culture-specific procedures in counseling. Another focus listed by Kurasaki and colleagues (2000) is for researchers to examine more thoroughly within-group differences and how those differences might influence counseling strategies used with new immigrants, highly acculturated immigrants, and children of immigrants. They suggested that effective strategies might vary considerably. Lastly, Kurasaki and colleagues (2000) encouraged researchers to identify the most effective counseling skills with diverse clientele and ways to prepare new counselors in attaining those skills.

Baruth and Manning (1999) also listed several directions for future research. Many of these ideas have already been discussed, but additional ideas include the following:

- Focus on developmental aspects, particularly life-span stages of the client within a cultural context.
- Evaluate the impact of multicultural preparation for counselors.
- Investigate identity development as related to minority and majority status in society.
- Study multiple oppressions and their effects on client progress in counseling.
- Investigate the impact of counselors' prejudice on diagnosis, intervention, and outcome.

Harper and McFadden (2003) also mentioned a number of directions for multicultural counseling research. In addition to those discussed above, they advocated for expanded methods of data collection beyond the typical self-report surveys and questionnaires that have notable limitations affecting validity, reliability, and ways data are expressed in the research. They suggested use of direct observational techniques such as in-person, videotaped, and one-way-mirror designs. In addition, they encouraged research to study a wider range of counseling issues including career development, addictions, nontraditional methods of helping/healing, and culture and family functioning among others.

In addition to furthering research efforts about counseling with diverse clients, the aforementioned objectives for future study might also be appropriate in examining new trends in client populations and related counseling concerns. This text has presented an overview of social and cultural foundations that influence counseling relationships. As history has shown, social and cultural development is ever-changing. Therefore, counseling professionals might expect new issues and trends to emerge in the coming years.

Future Trends and Issues

Forecasting is often a dangerous venture, so that is not the intent of this section. Nevertheless, social scientists and demographers anticipate many trends and shifts in population in the next few decades both in the United States and worldwide. When linked to professional issues for counselors and other professional helpers, these movements and developments relate to the social and cultural foundations of counseling practice. Here, we examine a few possible trends.

As noted earlier in this text, the expectation is for the U.S. population to become increasingly diverse in the coming years. In part, this expanding diversity will be due to continued immigration to this country. Bemak and Chung (2000) pointed to political upheaval and instability in many regions of the globe, combined with social change, economic stress, and civil strife as contributors to this trend. In addition, natural catastrophes often displace people who search for assistance outside their native lands. In many instances, these pressures and calamities affect people in developing nations and regions who subsequently migrate to more developed countries such as the United States. "The trends have shown that immigrants and refugees have been moving and will continue to move from developing to more developed countries including the United States" (Bemak & Chung, 2000, p. 200).

Presently, U.S. policy continues to accept a large number of immigrants each year. As noted in Chapter 11, however, support for legislation regarding immigration has had its ebb and flow depending on the political atmosphere in the United States and global conditions. Still, the United States has generally maintained lenient policies toward immigrants and refugees in comparison to other developed countries. There is no way of being certain where immigration policy might stand in the coming years, but if history is any measure, we could assume that an expanding U.S. population will continue to reflect broad diversity of nationalities, language, and culture.

For counselors who work with diverse clients, the increased range of people who will need assistance in the future translates into reliance on competencies for helping across cultures and ethnic groups. Harper and Deen (2003) surmised, "Victims of globalization, war, oppression, and terrorism will continue to seek refuge of economic sufficiency in countries other than their homeland, and the survivors of violence and natural catastrophes will continue to need grief counselors or some form of psychological support" (p. 160). Demand for such services by an increasingly diverse clientele will therefore underscore the importance of continuing research on multicultural competencies to develop best practices as well as appropriate counselor preparation for working with clients across cultures.

Another trend mentioned in the literature will be an increase in multiracial identities and perhaps a corresponding decrease in race as a social classification and status identity. Increased equity across the broader population with decreased control by the dominant White culture in the United States might encourage more socialization among diverse groups including greater numbers of interracial marriages and subsequently more multiracial members of society. According to Wehrly (2003), racially mixed marriages in the United States more than quintupled from the 1960s (150,000) through 1990 (over 1 million). This trend continued into the twenty-first century, with the 2000 U.S. census' *Profile of General Demographic Characteristics* noting that nearly 7 million people indicated they were of two or more races. This phenomenon suggests that initially counselors will require models and approaches to assist multiracial clients in adjusting to their families and communities. In particular, counselors will want to help these clients focus on their cultural strengths rather than racial differences, thereby celebrating their diversity. As this trend progresses and racial identity becomes less important as a social construct, clients of multiracial heritage might have less concern about which race(s) is (are) most significant to their development.

As mentioned in Chapter 7, indicators point to an ever-increasing older population in the United States. This trend will affect all ethnic and cultural groups. For example, older adults are the fastest-growing segment within the African American community. About one-tenth of African Americans are over 65 years old, approximately 3 million citizens (U.S. Bureau of the Census, 2001). Other groups are experiencing the same phenomenon of an increasing aging population.

An increasingly older citizenry brings forth many issues for counselors and the families they serve. As noted earlier, ageism is a form of social/cultural discrimination that targets older citizens and prevents them from fully participating in society. Frequently, age is a status that is denied access to career paths, given limited health care insurance, and questioned about the autonomy of its members. At the same time, the reality of an increasing life span across all segments of society makes the likelihood of financial stress, psychological deterioration, health-related problems, and social isolation significant issues for older clients and their families. In some instances, as Narrative 12.1 illustrates, health-related challenges can rob people of their awareness, perception, and understanding, three qualities requisite for continued self-development. In the future, counselors who work with families across cultural groups will rely on skills to help with aging members.

Robinson (2005) noted some negative effects on a society that practices forms of ageism. For example, U.S. culture's obsession with and emphasis on youthfulness translates into a denial of the aging process. The perpetuation of such beliefs—the rejection and denunciation of older members of society—while a significant portion of the population becomes increasingly older elevates the likelihood of discriminatory practices against senior citizens as well as other groups viewed in disfavor by the majority. Such discriminatory habits and procedures diminish the moral fabric of a society.

NARRATIVE 12.1 • *I Danced with My Mother*

In the middle of writing this book, I had an opportunity to visit my mother and father in New Mexico. It had been several years since we were together, and now that Mom had Alzheimer's disease, the trip took on added significance. At the age of 82, she was physically able, but her memory was limited to events of the moment and recollections of her mother and her life as a child.

Nine years previously, I had attended the wedding of a sister and remembered dancing with Mom at the reception. She always loved to dance, and particularly enjoyed dancing with one of her "boys." Now, during this latest trip I would have the opportunity to dance with her one more time.

Another sister, who lives with her family near Mom and Dad, made dinner for the family one evening during my visit. After dinner, my sister and I entertained the family, playing the guitar and singing. At one point, Mom stood up and started dancing alone. I got up and danced with her as my sister continued to play and sing. It was a wonderful moment, and one that Mom seemed to enjoy.

It occurred to me, as Mom and I twirled across the floor, that her dancing skills had not diminished since we last danced at the wedding years before. Yet, there was a difference. At the wedding, she knew with whom she was dancing. Now, she was simply enjoying the activity with a man she admired for the moment. As I reflected on this poignant scene, both the power and fragility of human perception became clearer to me. I was more aware of the contribution perception makes to self-development over a lifetime, and simultaneously, realized how quickly the power of human perception can be extinguished, whether due to physical deterioration or other condition, regardless of one's status in society.

Chapter 9 discussed the influence of socioeconomic class on self-development and discriminatory practices against diverse populations. The future does not look promising for progress toward freeing people from impoverished conditions, either in the United States or globally. In the United States, social equality and access to services continue to be threatened by seemingly ever-growing disparities in financial status across the population. Government reports indicate that overall, poverty in the United States has declined, but figures also indicate that many minority groups suffer greater degrees of poverty than the average levels. As an example, about 21 to 24 percent of Hispanic/Latino and African American families were below the poverty level in 2002 in comparison to 9.6 percent for the total population. In addition, nearly 17 percent of children under the age of 18 and over 10 percent of people 65 years and older lived in poverty (Institute for Research on Poverty, 2001). Poverty rates in 2002 also varied depending on the regions and areas where people lived. Variance is noticeable between inner city and suburban families and for families in rural areas where the poverty rate in 2001 was over 14 percent. In 2002, the poorest region in the United States was the South (13.8%) with the Midwest showing the lowest rate of poverty (10.3%) (Institute for Research on Poverty, 2001).

Counselors and other professional helpers who work with diverse individuals and groups appreciate the economic disparities that separate and distinguish their clients from the larger population. As noted in Chapter 10, these counselors might find a proactive stance of social advocacy the most effective way to help disadvantaged clients. Aponte and Johnson (2000b) noted the plight of ethnically diverse groups that were over represented among the most impoverished families and the challenges they bring to counseling relationships. "They are frequently poor, have relatively less formal education, suffer employment problems, housing problems, and little hope for improvement of these circumstances" (p. 289). The hopelessness expressed by Aponte and Johnson (2000b) about impoverished and disenfranchised clients and families puts added emphasis on proactive strategies that counselors might use beyond typical helping relationships and counseling processes.

In addition to being aware of future issues and trends specific to diverse client populations, counselors and other human service providers want to stay abreast of professional issues that might have an impact on their practice. The counseling and human service professions have expanded in the United States over the past several decades and now there are international efforts emerging. Harper and Deen (2003) commented that the spread of professional counseling to other countries and cultures requires different ideas and approaches that consider "cultural needs, ways, and values" and are "sensitive and relevant to its [the culture's] members and target clientele group" (p. 159). The same is true for related helping professions.

Similarly, technological advances mentioned in an earlier chapter present increasing opportunities for providing various human services and information to clients worldwide (Harper & Deen, 2003). Ethical standards and communication competencies across cultural groups will be important as counselors and other helpers from different parts of the world begin to offer services for a broader clientele. This reality, coupled with the prediction that the needs of a diverse population will continue to warrant services of the helping professions, creates the challenge of providing more appropriate and effective counseling and other interventions to a wider population. Such a challenge will also demand more and better prepared culturally effective counselors and human service workers. As Wohl and Aponte (2000) explained, "The twenty-first century will see no reduction in the service requirements of this population, nor in the requirement that people be trained to serve them" (p. 286).

Counseling Inferences

Among the most significant inferences for helping professionals regarding the content of this chapter is the knowledge that we have much yet to learn about theoretical frameworks and communication skills to be effective with a broad range of clients. For this reason, it seems imperative for counselors and other helpers to embrace some form of conceptual structure, such as self-concept theory, social identity theories, social-cognitive models, and cultural identity models covered in this text. As research studies are able to validate or reject various theories or parts of theories, counselors and other helpers will be in a stronger position to choose models with confidence that these models have efficacy for working with all clients. Until that time, counselors want to use existing models within a social/cultural context that demonstrates awareness, understanding, sensitivity, and skill advocated by current competencies published and promoted by the counseling and human service professions.

Another inference from research literature in this field is that professional helpers and clients from diverse backgrounds can form effective helping relationships depending on the level of awareness and skill the professional is able to demonstrate. Furthermore, sensitivity to language barriers and a proactive stance to overcome such obstacles is imperative when working across cultures. Throughout this text, you have completed exercises, many of which related to or assessed your awareness of culture, prejudice, and biases that might hamper effective helping with diverse clientele. Many of these activities were intended to help you assess your cultural encapsulation, a concept first introduced by C. Gilbert Wrenn (1962), a pioneer in the counseling profession.

A counselor's cultural encapsulation threatens the likelihood of productive counseling relationships with diverse clients on five different levels or fronts. First, a culturally encapsulated counselor tends to define the world and life according to a single set of assumptions about culture and how culture influences human development. Second, encapsulated counselors lack sensitivity to cultural differences, and furthermore, assume that their perceptions and beliefs are the only correct ones. A third aspect of assumptions made by culturally encapsulated helpers is that their beliefs are irrefutable and not dependent on rational or factual information. When shown evidence to the contrary, they dismiss it as untrue or untrustworthy. Fourth, encapsulated professionals rely on limited techniques and brief strategies regardless of the cultural implications for clients. Lastly, encapsulated helpers tend to form personal and professional opinions from a narrow, self-referenced perspective, ignoring other possible viewpoints and particularly those that include divergent cultural meaning (Pedersen, 2002). In the first chapter of this text, Exercise 1.4 encouraged you to explore your cultural encapsulation. Now that you have come to the end of this book, Exercise 12.3 invites you to explore and assess your level of cultural encapsulation more specifically.

A final thought about future directions and issues in multicultural or cross-cultural counseling is that the world is ever changing. Although we might expect conflicts between cultures, oppression of various groups, and discrimination of individuals and groups to continue across the globe, we might also imagine a time when diversity is celebrated and cultural influences recognized for the rich contribution they make to collective values as

Exercise 12.3

Counselor's Cultural Encapsulation

Instructions: Read each statement and rate yourself on a scale of 1 to 5, with 5 meaning greater likelihood that the statement is true for you. After rating each item, total your score. This is not a standardized inventory and no normative sample exists, but we might wonder if the higher your score the more encapsulated your cultural beliefs might be. More important than your score is to compare the results of this exercise with your response to Exercise 1.4, which you completed earlier in the text.

I tend to

1.	Measure people according to "normal" standards of behavior regardless of their background.	1	2	3	4	5
2.	Believe that individual rights and goals are more important than the collective group in all situations.	1	2	3	4	5
3.	Believe the collective group is more important than individual wishes in all situations.	1	2	3	4	5
4.	Define professional limitations narrowly and discourage collaborative, interdisciplinary relationships.	1	2	3	4	5
5.	Use abstract terms (e.g., normal) to describe mental health with little regard to cultural nuances.	1	2	3	4	5
6.	Always view dependency as an undesirable psychological or developmental trait.	1	2	3	4	5
7.	Ignore or devalue the relevance of people's support systems to their overall psychological health and self-development.	1	2	3	4	5
8.	Disregard scientific evidence that does not convey a cause-and-effect relationship.	1	2	3	4	5
9.	Expect people to adjust and fit in to the present social system.	1	2	3	4	5
10.	Disregard people's heritage and cultural background when helping them solve problems, because it is more important to deal with the here and now.	1	2	3	4	5
11.	Assume that I am free of racial, social, and cultural biases.	1	2	3	4	5
12.	Believe that through counseling people can make appropriate changes in their lives if they will only try.	1	2	3	4	5

Source: Adapted from Pedersen (2002) and Schmidt (2004).

well as individual development. In the United States, counselors and other human service providers will play an important, active role in helping future clients cope with past aggression, oppression, and discrimination while proactively helping them to incorporate their collectivistic beliefs with individual aspirations to forge better lives for themselves, their families, and communities. To provide assistance effectively, professional counselors and other helpers will require a working knowledge of social and cultural foundations, a keen awareness of their own cultural background, and compassionate understanding of how that background might interact with all their clients.

Appendix

Diversity Websites

This appendix includes several websites that may be helpful to counselor and human service education students and professors. Readers must use appropriate caution when ordering and purchasing materials from any Internet site, or assuming information on any site is accurate. Neither the author nor publisher endorses products, statements, or other information presented on the sites listed in this appendix. This resource list presents examples of where counselors and other helpers can access multicultural information over the Internet. There are seemingly limitless websites with helpful information, yet caution is necessary. Professional helpers who use the Internet for information have an ethical responsibility to ensure the accuracy and appropriateness of material and information obtained when offering sites as resources to clients or other professionals.

The websites in this appendix are in alphabetical order. In addition to these sites, readers will find other Internet sources listed among the references for this text.

1. Aboard the Underground Railroad (http://www.cr.nps.gov/nr/travel/underground/ugrrhome.htm). History of the underground railroad, from the National Register. Includes information about the slave trade, antislavery initiatives, and the Civil War.
2. The African-American Journey (http://www.pbs.org/aajourney/). A PBS site about the African American journey in the United States.
3. African Proverbs, Sayings, and Stories (http://www.afriprov.org/). Excellent source with explanations about proverbs, sayings, and stories used in the African American community.
4. Africans in America (http://www.pbs.org/wgbh/aia). A PBS site about slavery in America. Includes a teacher's guide.
5. African Voices (http://www.mnh.si.edu/africanvoices/). From the Smithsonian Institute, this site focuses on African culture's influence worldwide.
6. American Counseling Association (ACA) (http://www.counseling.org). Website of the American Counseling Association. Information about the divisions of the association, including the Association for Multicultural Counseling and Development.
7. ACA Code of Ethics and Standards of Practice (http://www.counseling.org/resources/ethics.htm). Information about the code of ethics for professional counselors.
8. ACA Government Relations Link (http://capwiz.com/counseling/home/). This site offers up-to-date information on the latest policies and laws related to counseling diverse clients and other professional issues.

9. American Irish Historical Society (http://www.aihs.org/). Official site of the AIHS, which educates people about Irish heritage and the contributions of Irish Americans to American society.
10. Anti-Defamation League (http://www.adl.org/). This site has many topics about terrorism, education, and religious freedom. Includes a wide variety of information about fighting prejudice and racism.
11. Arab American Institute (http://www.aaiusa.org/). An informative site that gives current events from around the world that may be of importance to Arabian cultures.
12. Arab Net (http://www.arab.net/). Consists of information about many Arab countries and their histories, and includes news articles written by leading journalists in the Arab world.
13. Asian Society (http://www.asiansociety.org/). Informative site about Asian cultures and populations.
14. Association for Gay, Lesbian & Bisexual Issues in Counseling (AGLBIC) (http://www.aglbic.org/). A Division of the American Counseling Association, the AGLBIC maintains this site with membership information and other resources for professional counselors.
15. Ayudate (http://www.ayudate.org/). A bilingual site for English-speaking and Spanish-speaking people who need information and resources. Sponsored by the North Carolina Governor's Office.
16. Black Oral History Collection (http://www.wsulibs.wsu.edu/holland/masc/xblack oralhistory.html). A site about Black oral history. Offers a collection of books, places, maps, and other related material.
17. The Booker T. Washington Papers (http://www.historycooperative.org/btw/). Offers the different writings of Booker T. Washington as well as photos of the era and information about related historical events.
18. Center for the Study of White American Culture: A Multiracial Organization (http://www.euroamerican.org). According to the site, the mission of this organization is to support cultural exploration and self-discovery among white Americans and continued dialogue among people of all races and cultures.
19. Centropa (http://www.centropa.org/). Subtitled "Jewish History in Central and Eastern Europe," this website has several links and a wealth of information.
20. Chinese-American Cultural Bridge Center (http://www.cacbc.org/). Official site of a nonprofit organization to promote cross-cultural awareness and fellowship among people of Chinese and American culture.
21. Circle of Stories (http://www.pbs.org/circleofstories/). A PBS site with information about Native American legends and storytelling.
22. Civil Rights Project: Harvard University (http://www.civilrightsproject.harvard.edu/index.html). Offers resources, research, and articles that describe modern day acts of segregation and racism.
23. Congress of Russian-Americans (http://www.russian-americans.org/). The Congress of Russian-Americans is a national organization that works to preserve Russian spiritual and cultural heritage in the United States and protect the rights of Russian Americans.

24. Counselors for Social Justice Website (http://www.counselorsforsocialjustice.org/). The official website for this organization, a division of ACA. Gives relevant news, ways to apply for membership, and activities of the organization.
25. Cultural Competence in Serving Children & Adolescents with Mental Health Problems (http://www.mentalhealth.org/publications/allpubs/CA-0015/default.asp). Discusses mental health in children. A source of information about different organizations that advocate for children.
26. Drop Me Off in Harlem (http://artsedge.kennedy-center.org/exploring/harlem/). Discusses the history of Harlem and lists people (singers, artists, performers, etc.) who had a major influence on Harlem and its rebirth.
27. Electric Magazine of Multicultural Education (http://www.eastern.edu/publications/emme/). Quarterly online magazine has articles in full text to read, review, and use.
28. Freedom Never Dies: The Legacy of Harry T. Moore (http://www.pbs.org/harrymoore/). A PBS site about the life and murder of civil rights activist Harry T. Moore and his wife, Harriette.
29. German American National Congress (Deutsch Amerikanischer National Kongress, DANK) (http://www.dank.org/). This organization works to bring together Americans of German decent to preserve their heritage and pursue interests toward this goal.
30. *GLSEN* (http://www.glsen.org/templates/index.html). Promotes safety in school systems for gays, lesbians, bisexuals, and transgender people.
31. Heritage: Civilization and the Jews (http://ww.pbs.org/wnet/heritage/). A comprehensive PBS site on Jewish history.
32. Indian Country Today (http://www.indiancountry.com/). An online newspaper about Native Americans. News reports and other timely information.
33. Institute on Domestic Violence in the African American Community (http://www.dvinstitute.org/). A rich resource about violence among African Americans. Provides different links to other sites that promote antiviolence.
34. The Internet Sacred Text Archives (http://www.sacred-texts.com/index.htm). Site includes information about different world religions.
35. Islam: Empire of Faith (http://www.pbs.org/empires/islam/). An excellent educational site about Islam.
36. IslamiCity (http://www.islamicity.com/). Provides various sections with international news and current events in Islamic culture. Includes sections on social, political, economic, religious, educational, family, youth, and interfaith issues.
37. The Jewish Museum (http://www.thejewishmuseum.org/home/). An informative site about Jewish history and culture.
38. Jews, Movies & Broadcasting (http://entertainingamerica.thejewishmuseum.org/online/). A site of the Jewish Museum, it mentions the contribution of entertainers from the Jewish community who enriched America through their music, dance, and humor.
39. Jump, Jim Crow (http://www.lib.berkeley.edu/~ljones/Jimcrow/index.html). Includes everything to know about Jim Crow.
40. Kiss, Bow, or Shake Hands? (http://www.gctcustoms.com/omnibus.html). An interesting site about unique traits and customs from diverse cultures.

41. Life Interrupted: The Japanese American Experience in WWII in Arkansas (http://www.lifeinterrupted.org/intro.html/). A site that explains the internment and education of the Japanese during World War II. Specific information about Japanese interment camps in Arkansas during World War II.
42. The Martin Luther King, Jr., Paper Project (http://www.stanford.edu/group/King/). Biographical information on Dr. Martin Luther King, Jr., with lists of speeches and other pertinent documents.
43. Mashantucket Pequot Museum & Research Center (http://www.pequotmuseum.org/Home/). Site that describes the Mashantucket Pequot Museum with a brief description of the exhibits, research, and other features about Native Americans.
44. In the Middle: A Report of Multicultural Boomers Coping with Family and Issues (http://www.aarp.org/inthemiddle/). A study that examined how the "sandwich" generation is coping with their parents and children.
45. The Middle East Institute (MEI) (http://www.mideasti.org/). Official home page of MEI. Features articles and forums for professionals to gather information about the Middle East and Islam.
46. Model Minority: A Guide to Asian American Empowerment (http://modelminority.com/). Offers commentaries, news articles, poems, and other documents about the Asian American experience.
47. A More Perfect Union: Japanese Americans and the U.S. Constitution (http://americanhistory.si.edu/perfectunion/experience/index.html). This site offers a complete history of Japanese people in America.
48. Multicultural Music & Songs to Build an Appreciation of Diversity (http://songsforteaching.homestead.com/Diversity.html). A site listing song lyrics and sound clips of songs related to diversity. Useful site for finding songs to work with children about diversity issues.
49. Multicultural Pavilion (http://curry.edschool.virginia.edu/go/multicultural/). Informative site, rich in resources.
50. National Black Child Development Institute (http://www.nbcdi.org/). An organization for African Americans, the NBCDI site has a support site and information about forthcoming conferences.
51. National Civil Rights Museum (http://www.civilrightsmuseum.org/). An overview and interactive tour of the National Civil Rights Museum.
52. National Council of La Raza (http://www.ncir.org/). Site of the National Council of La Raza, an organization that advocates for Hispanic Americans. It has hundreds of different topics for Hispanic/Latino populations.
53. National Italian American Foundation (http://www.niaf.org/). Official site of NIAF, this organization works to preserve Italian American heritage and culture.
54. National Latino Alliance for the Elimination of Domestic Violence (http://www.dvalianza.org/). A bilingual site that provides information to help eliminate violence in Latino communities.
55. Native American Internet Resources (http://falcon.jmu.edu/~ramseyil/native.htm). This site offers bibliographies, stories, histories, and links to other sites for Native Americans.

56. The Network of Alliances Bridging Race and Ethnicity (http://www.jointcenter.org/nabre/index.htm). A well-organized site that has helpful information and articles about ethnicity.
57. The New Americans (http://www.pbs.org/kcet/newamericans/). Summary of a documentary that aired in March of 2004 about immigrants trying to live the American dream.
58. North American Slave Narratives (http://docsouth.unc.edu/neh/neh.html). A link to libraries of The University of North Carolina. Includes books on slavery listed in alphabetical order.
59. Open Hearts, Closed Doors (http://www.virtualmuseum.ca/Exhibitions/orphans/english/). Tells the story of different families and individuals who suffered through the Holocaust, particularly Jewish orphans who immigrated to Canada after World War II.
60. Pew Hispanic Center (http://www.pewhispanic.org/index.jsp). Discusses the diverse Hispanic culture and population. Site is operated by the Pew Trust. Its mission is to improve the understanding of the Hispanic culture.
61. The Pluralism Project (Religious Pluralism) (http://www.pluralism.org/). This site has research projects about different cultures and religious diversity in the United States.
62. Polish American Association (http://www.polish.org/). An official site of PAA, this organization provides programs and services to support Polish Americans.
63. Race—The Power of an Illusion (http://www.pbs.org/race/000/). Information about this popular video series from PBS.
64. Ralph Bunche: An American Odessey (http://www.pbs.org/ralphbunche/). A biography of Ralph Bunche, UN mediator, scholar, and first person to be awarded the Nobel Prize for Peace, by PBS.
65. The Rise and Fall of Jim Crow (http://www.pbs.org/wnet/jimcrow/). This PBS site is a documentary of the Jim Crow era of American history.
66. Southern Poverty Law Center (http://www.splcenter.org/). This site offers an array of information including current news links to different sites, for example, the teaching of tolerance.
67. The Story of Africa (http://www.bbc.co.uk/worldservice/africa/features/storyofafrica/index.shtml). This site has much information about the past history and current history of African Americans. Tells the history of the African continent.
68. Substance Abuse & Mental Health Services Administration (http://www.samhsa.gov/). Mental health and substance abuse information.
69. Through the Lens of Time (http://www.library.vcu.edu/jbc/speccoll/cook/). Offers a variety of photographs of African Americans taken from the 1860s to the 1930s.
70. Thurgood Marshall (http://chnm.gmu.edu/courses/122/hill/marshall.htm). A biography of Supreme Court Justice Thurgood Marshall. Displays a time line of his life.
71. Tolerance (http://www.tolerance.org/index.jsp). A wealth of ideas for building tolerance from the Southern Poverty Law Center. Includes a section to explore your hidden prejudices.
72. We Shall Overcome: Historical Places of the Civil Rights Movement (http://www.cr.nps.gov/nr/travel/civilrights/). A good starting point when trying to find different websites about the history of African Americans and the Civil Rights Movement.

73. Welcome to African American History (http://www.watson.org/~lisa/blackhistory/index.html). A project about African American history, this site has links to many different sites to learn about African American heritage.
74. What is race? (http://www.pbs.org/race/000_General/000_00-Home.htm). A useful site and a good starting point to answer the question "What is race?"
75. White Privilege: Swimming in Racial Preference (http://www.tolerance.org/news/article_print.jsp?id=722) and White Supremacy: No One Is Innocent (http://www.tolerance.org/news/article_print.jsp?id=800). Both articles by Tom Wise focus on unearned privilege and inheritance.
76. Yellowbridge (http://www.yellowbridge.com/). A commercial site set up as a guide to Chinese culture and entertainment with a Chinese American focus.

References

Abraham, N. (1995). Arab Americans. In R. J. Vecoli, J. Galens, A. Sheets & R. V. Young (Eds.), *Gale encyclopedia of multicultural America* (Vol. 1, pp. 84–98). New York: Gale Research Inc.

Abudabbeh, N. (1996). Arab Families. In M. McGoldrick, J. Giordano & J. K. Pearce (Eds.), *Ethnicity and family therapy* (2nd ed., pp. 333–343). New York: Guilford.

Abudabbeh, N., & Nydell, M. K. (1993). Transcultural counseling and Arab Americans. In J. McFadden (Ed.), *Transcultural counseling: Bilateral and international perspectives* (pp. 261–284). Alexandria, VA: American Counseling Association.

Allen, B. P., & Adams, J. Q. (1992). The concept "Race": Let's go back to the beginning. *Journal of Social Behavior and Personality, 7,* 163–168.

Allen, L. S., & Gorksi, R. A. (1992). Sexual orientation and the size of the anterior commissure in the human brain. *Proceedings of the National Academy of Science, USA, 89,* 7199–7202.

Allport, G. W. (1937). *Personality: A psychological interpretation.* New York: Holt, Reinhart & Winston.

Allport, G. W. (1955). *Becoming: Basic considerations for a psychology of personality.* New Haven, CT: Yale University Press.

Alston, M. H., Rankin, S. H., & Harris, C. A. (1995). Suicide in African American elderly. *Journal of Black Studies, 26,* 31–35.

American Counseling Association. (1995). *Code of Ethics.* Retrieved February 6, 2004, from http://aca.convio.net/site/DocServer/ACA.Code_of_Ethics.pdf?docID=361.

American Psychiatric Association (2000). *Diagnostic and Statistical Manual of Mental Disorders* (4th ed.), DSM-IV-TR. Washington, DC: American Psychiatric Association.

Aponte, J. F., & Bracco, H. F. (2000). Community approaches with ethnic populations. In J. F. Aponte & J. Wohl (Eds.), *Psychological intervention and cultural diversity* (2nd ed., pp. 131–148). Boston: Allyn and Bacon.

Aponte, J. F., & Crouch, R. T. (2000). The changing ethnic profile of the United States in the twenty-first century. In J. F. Aponte & J. Wohl (Eds.), *Psychological intervention and cultural diversity* (pp. 1–17). Boston: Allyn and Bacon.

Aponte, J. F., & Johnson, L. R. (2000a). The impact of culture on the intervention and treatment of ethnic populations. In J. F. Aponte & J. Wohl (Eds.), *Psychological intervention and cultural diversity* (pp. 18–39). Boston: Allyn and Bacon.

Aponte, J. F., & Johnson, L. R. (2000b). *Ethnicity and supervision: Models, methods, processes, and issues.* In J. F. Aponte & J. Wohl (Eds.), *Psychological intervention and cultural diversity* (2nd ed., pp. 268–285). Boston: Allyn and Bacon.

Arredondo, P. (1992). *Latina/Latino counseling and psychotherapy: Tape 1. Cultural consideration for working more effectively with Latin Americans.* Amherst, MA: Microtraining and Multicultural Development.

Arredondo, P., & Perez, P. (2003). Counseling paradigms and Latina/o Americans: Contemporary considerations. In F. D. Harper & J. McFadden (Eds.), *Culture and counseling: New approaches* (pp. 115–132). Boston: Allyn and Bacon.

Arredondo, P. A., & Rice, T. M. (2004). Working from within: Contextual mental health and organizational competence. In T. Smith (Ed.), *Practicing multiculturalism: Affirming diversity in counseling and psychology* (pp. 76–96). Boston: Allyn and Bacon.

Arredondo, P., Toporek, R., Brown, S. P., Jones, J., Locke, D. C., Sanchez, J., & Stadler, H. (1996). Operationalization of the multicultural competencies. *Journal of Multicultural Counseling & Development, 24,* 42–78.

Asnes, M. (2003, December). The affluent American. *Money, 32* (13), 40–41.

Atlas, J. G., Smith, G. T., Hohlstein, L. A., McCarthy, D. M., & Kroll, L. S. (2002). Similarities and differences between Caucasian and African American college women on eating and dieting expectancies, bulimic symptoms, dietary restraint, and disinhibition. *International Journal of Eating Disorders, 32,* 326–334.

Bacigalupe, G. (2000). *El Latino:* Transgressing the Macho. In M. A. Fukuyama & G. Carey, *Family therapy with Hispanics: Toward appreciating diversity* (pp. 29–57). Boston: Allyn and Bacon.

Baldwin, J. (1993). *Nobody knows my name.* New York: Vintage.

Bandura, A. (1971). *Social learning theory.* New York: General Learning Press.

Bandura, A. (1973). *Aggression: A social learning analysis.* Englewood Cliffs, NJ: Prentice-Hall.

Bandura, A. (1986). *Social foundations of thought and action: A social cognitive theory.* Englewood Cliffs, NJ: Prentice-Hall.

Bandura, A. (1997). *Self-efficacy: The exercise of control.* New York: W. H. Freeman.

Bandura, A. (1998). Self-efficacy. In H. Friedman (Ed.), *Encyclopedia of mental health.* San Diego, CA: Academic Press.

Bandura, A., & Walters, R. (1963). *Social learning and personality development.* New York: Holt, Rinehart & Winston.

Barber, B. (1992). Neofunctionalism and the social system. In P. Colony (Ed.), *The dynamics of social systems* (pp. 36–55). London: Sage.

Bartlett, J. (1992). *Barlett's familiar quotations* (16th ed.). Boston: Little, Brown and Company.

Baruth, L. G., & Manning, M. L. (1999). *Multicultural counseling and psychotherapy: A lifespan perspective* (2nd ed.). Upper Saddle River, NJ: Prentice-Hall.

Bem, D. J. (2000). Exotic becomes erotic: Interpreting the biological correlates of sexual orientation. *Archives of Sexual Behavior, 29,* 531–548.

Bemak, F., & Chung, R. C. (2000). Psychological intervention with immigrants and refugees. In J. F. Aponte & J. Wohl, *Psychological intervention and cultural diversity* (2nd ed., pp. 200–213). Boston: Allyn and Bacon.

Bemak, F., & Chung, R. C. (2002). Counseling and psychotherapy with refugees. In P. B. Pedersen, J. G. Draguns, W. J. Lonner & J. E. Trimble (Eds.), *Counseling across cultures* (5th ed., pp. 209–232). Thousand Oaks, CA: Sage.

Bennett, L. (2000). *Forced into glory: Abraham Lincoln's white dream.* Chicago: Johnson Publishing.

Berry, J. W. (1980). Acculturation as varieties of adaptation. In A. M. Padilla (Ed.), *Acculturation: Theory, models and some new findings* (pp. 9–25). Boulder, CO: Westview Press.

Bissell, K. L. (2002). I want to be thin like you: Gender and race as predictors of cultural expectations for thinness and attractiveness in women. *New Photographer, 57,* 4–12.

Blaine, B. (2002, May). Selling stereotypes: Weight loss informercials, sexism, and weightism. In *Sex Roles: A Journal of Research.* Retrieved June 16, 2004, from http://articles.findarticles.com/p/articles/mi_m2294/is_2002_May/ai_94407545/print.

Block, C. J., & Carter, R. T. (1996). White racial identity attitude theories: A rose by any other name is still a rose. *Counseling Psychologist, 24,* 327.

Bloom, J. W., & Walz, G. R. (Eds.). (2000). *Cybercounseling and cyberlearning: Strategies and resources for the Millennium.* Alexandria, VA: American Counseling Association.

Bogucki, P. I. (1999). *The origins of human society.* Malden, MA: Blackwell.

Borisoff, D., & Merrill, L. (1992). *The power to communicate: Gender differences as barriers* (2nd ed.). Prospects Heights, IL: Waveland.

Boyd-Franklin, N. (1989). *Black families in therapy: A multisystems approach.* New York: Guilford.

Bradshaw, C. K. (1994). Asian and Asian American women: Historical and political considerations in psychotherapy. In L. Comas-Díaz & B. Greene (Eds.), *Women of color: Integrating ethnic and gender identities in psychotherapy* (pp. 72–113). New York: Guilford.

Brooks, L. J., Haskins, D. G., & Kehe, J. (2004). Counseling and psychotherapy with African American clients. In T. B. Smith (Ed.), *Practicing multiculturalism: Affirming diversity in counseling and psychotherapy* (pp. 145–166). Boston: Allyn and Bacon.

Brown, J. D. (1998). *The Self.* Boston: McGraw-Hill.

Bryant, J., & Zillman, D. (2002). *Media effects: Advances in theory and research.* Mahwah, NJ: Erlbaum.

Bureau of Justice Statistics (2002). *Homicide trends in the U.S.* Washington, DC: U.S. Department of Justice. Retrieved December 6, 2003, at http://www.ojp.usdoj.gov/bjs/homicide/teens.htm.

Butler, R. N. (1969). Ageism: Another form of bigotry. *The Gerontologist, 9,* 243–246.

Campbell, B. G. (1975). *Human evolution: An introduction to man's adaptations.* Chicago, IL: Aldine.

Carter, R. T. (1991). Cultural values: A review of empirical research and implications for counseling. *Journal of Counseling & Development, 70,* 164–173.

Casas, M., & Pytluk, S. (1995). Hispanic identity development: Implications for research and practice. In J. Ponterotto, M. Casa, L. Suzuki & C. Alexander (Eds.), *Handbook for multicultural counseling.* Thousand Oaks, CA: Sage.

Cass, V. C. (1979). Homosexuality identity formation: Testing a theoretical model. *Journal of Homosexuality, 4,* 219–235.

Cass, V. C. (1984). Homosexual identity: A concept in need of definition. *Journal of Homosexuality, 9,* 105–126.

Chang, S. C. (1988). The nature of self: A transcultural view. Part I: Theoretical aspects. *Transcultural Psychiatric Research Review, 25* (3), 169–204.

Chickering, A. (1969). *Education and Identity.* San Francisco: Jossey-Bass.

Chickering, A., & Reisser, L. (1993). *Education and identity* (2nd ed.). San Francisco: Jossey-Bass.

Child Abuse Data. (2003). Las Vegas, NV: WE CAN, Inc. Retrieved December 3, 2003, from http://www.reviewjournal.com/communitylink/wecan/page4.htm.

Child Trends Data Bank (2003). Table 1: Homicide, Suicide, and Firearm Deaths among Youth Ages 15–19. Retrieved December 6, 2003, from http://www.childtrendsdatabank.org/tables/70_Tables-1.htm.

Cohen, A. A., & Mendes-Flohr, P. (1972). *Contemporary Jewish religious thought.* New York: Charles Scribner's Sons.

Cokley, K. O. (2001). Gender differences among African American students in the impact of racial identity on academic psychosocial development. *Journal of College Student Development, 42,* 480–487.

Coleman, E. (1982). Developmental stages of the coming out process. In J. Gonsiorek (Ed.), *Homosexuality and psychotherapy: A practitioner's handbook of affirmative models* (pp. 31–44). New York: Haworth Press.

Combs, A. W. (Ed.). (1962). *Perceiving, behaving, becoming.* Washington, DC: Association for Supervision and Curriculum Development.

Combs, A. W., Avila, D. L., & Purkey, W. W. (1978). *Helping relationships: Basic concepts for the helping professions* (2nd ed.). Boston: Allyn and Bacon.

Combs, A. W., & Gonzalez, D. M. (1994). *Helping relationships: Basic concepts for the helping professions* (4th ed.). Boston: Allyn and Bacon.

Comstock, D. (Ed.). (2005). *Diversity and development: Critical contexts that shape our lives and relationships.* Belmont, CA: Brooks/Cole.

Comstock, D., & Qin, D. (2005). Relational-cultural theory. A framework for relational development across the life span. In D. Comstock (Ed.), *Diversity and development: Critical contexts that shape our lives and relationships* (pp. 25–45). Belmont, CA: Brooks/Cole.

Connell, E. S. (2001). *Deus lo volt! A chronicle of the Crusades.* Washington, DC: Counterpoint Press.

Cooley, C. H. (1902). *Human nature and social order.* New York: Charles Scribner's Sons.

Corey, M. S., & Corey, G. (2002). *Groups: Process and Practice* (6th ed.). Pacific Grove, CA: Brooks/Cole.

Cose, E. (1992). *A nation of strangers: Prejudice, politics, and the populating of America.* New York: Morrow.

Council for Accreditation of Counseling and Related Educational Programs (2001). *The 2001 Standards.* Retrieved March 20, 2004, at http://www.counseling.org/cacrep/default.htm.

Crago, M., Shisslak, C. M., & Estes, L. S. (1996). Eating disturbance among American minority groups: A review. *International Journal of Eating Disorders, 19,* 239–248.

Crandall, C. (1994). Prejudice against fat people: Ideology and self-interest. *Journal of Personality and Social Psychology, 66,* 882–894.

Crandall, C., & Martinez, R. (1996). Culture, ideology, and antifat attitudes. *Personality and Social Psychology Bulletin, 22,* 1165–1176.

Crawford, J. (1992). *Hold your tongue: Bilingualism and the politics of "English only."* Reading, MA: Addison Wesley.

Crawford, J. (2000). *At war with diversity: U.S. language policy in an age of anxiety.* Buffalo, NY: Multilingual Matters.

Crespi, T. D., & Howe, E. A. (2000, March). Families in crisis: Considerations and implications for school counselors. *Counseling Today, 42* (9), 6.

Cross, W. (1971). The Negro to Black conversion experience. *Black World, 20,* 13–25.

Cross, W. (1991). *Shades of Black.* Philadelphia: Temple University Press.

Cross, W. (1995). The psychology of Nigrescence: Revising the Cross model. In J. Ponterotto, M. Casas, L. Suzuki & C. Alexander (Eds.), *Handbook of multicultural counseling.* Thousand Oaks, CA: Sage.

Cross, W. E., Jr., Smith, L., & Payne, Y. (2002). Black identity: A repertoire of daily enactments. In P. B. Pedersen et al., *Counseling across cultures* (5th ed., pp. 93–107). Thousand Oaks, CA: Sage.

Cross, W. E., Jr., & Strauss, L. (1998). The everyday functions of African American identity. In J. K. Swim & C. Strangor (Eds.), *Prejudice: The target's perspective* (pp. 268–279). San Diego, CA: Academic Press.

Cruikshank, M. (2003). *Learning to be old: Gender, culture, and aging.* Lanham, MD: Rowman & Littlefield.

Curra, J. (2000). *The relativity of deviance.* Thousand Oaks, CA: Sage.

D'Andrea, M., & Daniels, J. (2001). Respectful counseling: An integrative multidimensional model for counselors. In D. Pope-Davis & H. Coleman (Eds.), *The intersection of race, class, and gender in multicultural counseling* (pp. 417–466). Thousand Oaks, CA: Sage.

D'Andrea, M., & Daniels, J. (2004, January). Multicultural competence and social justice: Some New Year's resolutions. *Counseling Today, 46* (7), 24–25.

Davenport, D. S., & Yurich, J. M. (1991). Multicultural gender issues. *Journal of Counseling & Development, 70,* 64–71.

Davis, C. (1997). Body image, exercise, and eating disorders. In K. R. Fox (Ed.), *The physical self: From motivation to well-being* (pp. 143–174). Champaign, IL: Human Kinetics.

Davis-Berman, J. (1990). Physical self-efficacy, perceived physical status, and depressive symptomatology in older adults. *Journal of Psychology, 124,* 207–216.

DeLucia-Waack, J. L., & Donigian, J. (2004). *The practice of multicultural group work: Visions and perspectives from the field.* Belmont, CA: Brooks/Cole–Thompson Learning.

Dew, C. B. (2002). *Apostles of disunion: Southern secession commissioners and the causes of the Civil War.* Charlottesville: University of Virginia Press.

Dewey, J. (1930). *Individualism old and new.* New York: Minton, Balch & Co.

Dill, B. T. (1994). Race, class, and gender: Prospects for an all-inclusive sisterhood. In L. Stone (Ed.), *The education feminism reader* (pp. 42–56). New York: Routledge.

DiLorenzo, T. J. (2001). Lincoln's economic legacy. Retrieved February 19, 2004, from http://www.mises.org/fullarticle.asp?record=607&month=29.

Dobbins, J. E., & Skillings, J. H. (1991). The utility of race labeling in understanding cultural identity: A conceptual tool for the social science practitioner. *Journal of Counseling & Development, 70,* 37–44.

Downes, D., & Rock, P. (2003). *Understanding deviance* (4th ed.). New York: Oxford.

Draguns, J. G. (2002). Universal and cultural aspects of counseling and psychotherapy. In P. B. Pedersen, J. G. Draguns, W. J. Lonner & J. E. Trimble (Eds.), *Counseling across cultures* (5th ed., pp. 29–50). Thousand Oaks, CA: Sage.

Driver, H. I. (1958). *Counseling and learning through small group discussion.* Madison, WI: Monona Publications.

Durant, C. E., & McFadden, J. (2003). Preventive counseling in a multicultural society. In F. D. Harper & J. McFadden (Eds.), *Culture and counseling: New approaches* (pp. 296–312). Boston: Allyn and Bacon.

Eliason, M. J. (1995). Accounts of sexual identity formation in heterosexual students. *Sex Roles, 32,* 821–834.

Ellis, A. E. (1996). *Better, deeper, and more enduring brief therapy: The rational emotive behavior therapy approach.* New York: Brunner/Mazel.

Emmons, L. (1992). Dieting and purging behavior in Black and White high school students. *Journal of the American Dietetic Association, 92,* 306–312.

Erickson, C. D., & Al-Timimi, N. R. (2004). Counseling and psychotherapy with Arab American clients. In T. B. Smith (Ed.), *Practicing multiculturalism: Affirming diversity in counseling and psychology* (pp. 234–254). Boston: Allyn and Bacon.

Erikson, E. (1968). *Identity: Youth and crisis.* New York: Norton.

Evans, N. J. (2003). Psychosocial, cognitive, and typological perspectives on student development. In S. R. Komives & D. B. Woodard, Jr. (Eds.), *Student services: A handbook for the profession* (4th ed., pp. 179–202). San Francisco: Jossey-Bass.

Evans, N. J., Forney, D. S., & Guido-DiBrito, F. (1998). *Student development in college: Theory, research, and practice.* San Francisco: Jossey-Bass.

Falco, K. (1991). *Psychotherapy with lesbian clients: Theory into practice.* New York: Brunner/Mazel.

Fassinger, R. E. (2000). Gender and sexuality in human development: Implications for prevention and advocacy in counseling psychology. In S. D. Brown & R. W. Lent (Eds.), *Handbook of counseling psychology* (pp. 346–378). New York: John Wiley.

Festinger, L. (1954). A theory of social comparison processes. *Human Relations, 7,* 117–140.

Field, L. D. (1996). Piecing together the puzzle: Self-concept and group identity in biracial black/white youth. In M. P. P. Root (Ed.), *The multiracial experience: Racial borders as the new frontier* (pp. 211–226). Thousand Oaks, CA: Sage.

Fischer, L., & Sorenson, G. P. (1996). *School law for counselors, psychologists, and social workers* (3rd ed.). White Plains, NY: Longman.

Fishman, S. B. (2000). *Jewish life and American culture.* Albany: State University of New York Press.

Flexner, S. B. (Ed.). (1993). *Random House Unabridged Dictionary* (2nd ed.). New York: Random House.

Flores, M. T. (2000a). Demographics: Hispanic populations in the United States. In M. T. Flores & G. Carey (Eds.), *Family therapy with Hispanics: Toward appreciating diversity* (pp. 297–311). Boston: Allyn and Bacon.

Flores, M. T. (2000b). La familia Latina. In M. T. Flores & G. Carey (Eds.), *Family therapy with Hispanics: Toward appreciating diversity* (pp. 3–28). Boston: Allyn and Bacon.

Freeman, H. P. (2004). Poverty, culture, and social injustice determinants of cancer disparities. *CA—A Cancer Journal for Clinicians, 54* (2), 72–78.

Freud, S. (1946). *The ego and mechanisms of defense.* New York: International Universities Press.

Fukuyama, M. A., & Sevig, T. D. (2002). Spirituality in counseling across cultures. In P. B. Pedersen, J. G. Draguns, W. J. Lonner & J. E. Trimble (Eds.), *Counseling across cultures* (5th ed., pp. 273–295). Thousand Oaks, CA: Sage.

Garrett, M. T. (1995). Between two worlds: Cultural discontinuity in the dropout of Native American youth. *School Counselor, 42,* 186–195.

Garrett, J. T., & Garrett, M. T. (1994). The path of good medicine: Understanding and counseling Native American Indians. *Journal of Multicultural Counseling and Development, 22,* 134–144.

Gazda, G. M. (1989). *Group counseling: A developmental approach* (4th ed.). Boston: Allyn and Bacon.

Geertz, C. (1973). The integrative revolution: Primordial sentiments and civil politics in the new states. In C. Geertz (Ed.), *The interpretation of cultures* (pp. 255–310). New York: Basic Books.

George Meany Center for Labor Studies (n.d.). A. Philip Randoph, 1889–1979: Civil Rights Activist. Retrieved February 18, 2005 from http://www.georgemeany.org/archives/activist.html.

Gibbs, J. P. (2003). Conceptions of deviant behavior: The old and the new. In D. H. Kelly & E. J. Clarke (Eds.), *Deviant behavior* (6th ed., pp. 14–19). New York: Worth.

Gillett, J., & White, P. G. (1992). Male bodybuilding and the reassertion of hegemonic masculinity: A critical feminist perspective. *Play and culture, 5,* 358–369.

Gilligan, C. (1982). *In a different voice: Psychological theory and women's development.* Cambridge, MA: Harvard University Press.

Gladding, S. T. (1999). *Group work: A counseling specialty* (3rd ed.). Upper Saddle River, NJ: Merrill/Prentice-Hall.

Gladding, S. T. (2000). *Counseling: A comprehensive profession* (4th ed.). Upper Saddle River, NJ: Prentice-Hall.

Gladding, S. T. (2002). *Family therapy: History, theory, and practice* (3rd ed.). Upper Saddle River, NJ: Prentice-Hall.

Gloria, A. M., Ruiz, E. L., & Castillo, E. M. (2004). Counseling and psychotherapy with Latino and Latina clients. In T. B. Smith (Ed.), *Practicing multiculturalism: Affirming diversity in counseling and psychology* (pp. 167–189). Boston: Allyn and Bacon.

Goldstein, K. (1939). *The organism.* New York: American Book Company.

Gonzalez, G. M. (1997). The emergence of Chicanos in the twenty-first century: Implications for counseling, research, and policy. *Journal of Multicultural Counseling & Development, 25,* 94–106.

Goode, E. (2002). *Deviance in everyday life: Personal accounts of unconventional lives.* Prospects Heights, IL: Waveland.

Gould, M. C., & Gould, H. (2003). A clear vision for equity and opportunity. *Phi Delta Kappan, 85,* 324–328.

Groesz, L. M., Levine, M. P., & Murnen, S. K. (2002). The effect of experimental presentation of thin media images on body satisfaction: A meta-analytic review. *International Journal of Eating Disorders, 31* (1), 1–16.

Gysbers, N. C. (1996). Beyond career development—Life career development revisited. In R. Feller & G. Walz (Eds.), *Career transitions in turbulent times* (pp. 11–20). Greensboro: ERIC Counseling and Student Services Clearinghouse, University of North Carolina at Greensboro.

Hall, E. T. (1983). *The dance of life: The other dimension of time.* New York: Anchor Books.

Hamachek, D. (1992). *Encounters with the self* (4th ed.). New York: Harcourt Brace Jovanovich.

Han, A. L., & Vasquez, M. J. T. (2000). Group intervention and treatment with ethnic minorities. In J. F. Aponte & J. Wohl (Eds.), *Psychological intervention and cultural diversity* (2nd ed., pp. 110–130). Boston: Allyn and Bacon.

Hanna, F. J., & Green, A. (2004). Asian shades of spirituality: Implications for multicultural school counseling. *Professional School Counseling, 7,* 326–333.

Harper, F. D. (2003). Background: Concepts and history. In F. D. Harper & J. McFadden (Eds.), *Culture and counseling: New approaches* (pp. 1–19). Boston: Allyn and Bacon.

Harper, F. D., & Deen, N. (2003). The international counseling movement. In F. D. Harper & J. McFadden (Eds.), *Culture and counseling: New approaches* (pp. 147–163). Boston: Allyn and Bacon.

Harper, F. D., & McFadden, J. (2003). Conclusions, trends, issues, and recommendations. In F. D. Harper & J. McFadden (Eds.), *Culture and counseling: New approaches* (pp. 379–393). Boston: Allyn and Bacon.

Harrison, A. O. (1989). Mental health issues of African-American women and adults. In R. L. Jones (Eds.), *Black adult development and aging* (pp. 91–115). Berkeley, CA: Cobb & Henry.

Hartman, H., & Hartman, M. (1999). Jewish identity, denomination and denominational mobility. *Social Identities, 5,* 279–312.

Hays, P. (2001). *Addressing cultural complexities in practice: A framework for clinicians and counselors.* Washington, DC: American Psychological Association.

Heckert, D. M. (2003). Positive deviance: A classificatory model. In D. H. Kelly & E. J. Clarke (Eds.), *Deviant behavior* (6th ed., pp. 20–32). New York: Worth.

Hehir, T. (2002). Eliminating ableism in education. *Harvard Educational Review, 72* (1). Retrieved June 21, 2004, from http://gseweb.harvard.edu/~hepg/hehir.htm.

Hejleh, M. (2003). *The countries and people of Arabia.* Retrieved November 6, 2003, from http://www.hejleh.com/countries/.

Helms, J. E. (1984). Toward a theoretical explanation of the effects of race on counseling: A Black and White model. *The Counseling Psychologist, 12,* 153–165.

Helms, J. E. (1995). An update of white and people of color racial identity model. In J. G. Ponterotto, J. M. Casa, L. A. Suzuki & C. M. Alexander (Eds.), *Handbook of multicultural counseling* (pp. 181–198). Thousand Oaks, CA: Sage.

Helms, J. E. (2003). Racial identity in the school environment. In P. Pedersen & J. C. Carey (Eds.), *Multicultural counseling in schools* (2nd ed., pp. 44–58). Boston: Allyn and Bacon.

Helms, J. E., & Cook, D. A. (1999). *Using race and culture in counseling and psychotherapy.* Boston: Allyn and Bacon.

Helms, J. E., & Parham, T. A. (1984). *Racial identity attitude scale.* Unpublished manuscript.

Helms, J. E., & Talleyrand, R. M. (1997). Race is not ethnicity. *American Psychologist, 52,* 1246–1247.

Henderson, Z. P. (1993). Racial poverty gap exists among elderly. *Human Ecology, 21* (3), 31.

Henriques, G. R., Calhoun, L. G., & Cann. A. (1996). Ethnic differences in women's body satisfaction: An experimental investigation. *Journal of Social Psychology, 136,* 689–697.

Herlihy, B., & Watson, A. E. (2003). Ethical issues and multicultural competence in counseling. In F. D. Harper & J. McFadden (Eds.), *Culture and counseling: New approaches* (pp. 363–378). Boston: Allyn and Bacon.

Herring, R. D. (1991). Counseling Native American youth. In C. C. Lee & B. L. Richardson (Eds.), *Multicultural issues in counseling: New approaches to diversity* (pp. 37–47). Alexandria, VA: American Counseling Association.

Herring, R. D. (1999). Experiencing a lack of money and appropriate skin color: A personal narrative. *Journal of Counseling and Development, 77,* 25–27.

Hetherington, E. M., & Kelly, J. (2002). *For better of for worse: Divorce reconsidered.* New York: Norton.

Ho, M. K. (1987). *Family therapy with ethnic minorities.* Newbury Park, CA: Sage.

Hoffman, A. M., & Summers, R. W. (Eds.). (2001). *Teen violence: A global view.* Westport, CT: Greenwood.

Hofstede, G. (1991). *Cultures and organizations: Software of the mind.* London: McGraw-Hill.

Hogg, M. A. (2003). Social identity. In M. R. Leary & J. P. Tangney (Eds.), *Handbook of self and identity* (pp. 462–479). New York: Guilford.

Hooker, E. (1957). The adjustment of the male overt homosexual. *Journal of Projective Techniques, 21,* 18–31.

hooks, b. (2000). *where we stand: CLASS MATTERS.* New York: Routledge.

Howard-Hamilton, M. F., & Frazier, K. (2005). Identity development and the convergence of race, ethnicity, and gender. In D. Comstock (Ed.), *Diversity and development: Critical contexts that shape our lives and relationships* (pp. 67–90). Belmont, CA: Brooks/Cole.

Howe, H., II (1991). American 2000: A bumpy ride on four trains. *Phi Delta Kappan, 73,* 192–203.

Ibrahim, F. A. (1999). Transcultural counseling: Existential worldview theory and cultural identity. In J. McFadden (Ed.), *Transcultural counseling* (2nd ed., pp. 23–58). Alexandria, VA: American Counseling Association.

Ibrahim, F. A. (2003). Existential worldview counseling theory: Inception to Applications. In F. D. Harper & J. McFadden (Eds.), *Culture and counseling: New approaches* (pp. 196–208). Boston: Allyn and Bacon.

Ibrahim. F. A., & Owen, S. V. (1994). Factor analytic structure of the Scale to Assess Worldview. *Current Psychology, 13,* 201–209.

Institute for Research on Poverty. (2001). *Who is poor?* Madison: University of Wisconsin. Retrieved January 3, 2001, from http://www.ssc.wisc.edu/irp.faqs/faq3.htm.

Institute for Research on Poverty (2003). *Who was poor in 2002?* Madison: University of Wisconsin. Retrieved November 6, 2003, from http://www.ssc.wisc.edu/irp/faqs/faq3.htm.

Ivey, A. E. (1993). *Developmental strategies for helpers: Individual, family and network interventions.* North Amherst, MA: Microtraining Associates.

Ivey, A. E. (2000). *Developmental therapy: Theory into practice.* North Amherst, MA: Microtraining Associates.

Ivey, A. E., D'Andrea, M., Ivey, M. B., & Simek-Morgan, L. (Eds.). (2002). *Theories of counseling and psychotherapy: A multicultural perspective* (5th ed.). Boston: Allyn and Bacon.

Jackson, M. (1997). Counseling Arab Americans. In C. Lee (Ed.), *Multicultural issues in counseling: New Approaches to diversity* (2nd ed., pp. 333–349). Alexandria, VA: American Counseling Association.

Jackson, M. L., & Vontress, C. E. (2003, July). Where has culture in counseling gone? *Counseling Today, 46* (1), 7, 10.

Jacobs, E. E., Masson, R. L., & Harvill, R. L. (2002). *Group counseling: Strategies and skills* (4th ed.). Pacific Grove, CA: Brooks/Cole.

Jacobson, L. (2002). Kindergarten study links learning deficits to poverty. *Education Week, 22* (5), 10.

James, W. (1890). *Principles of psychology.* New York: Henry Holt & Co.

Johnson, A. G. (1995). *The Blackwell dictionary of sociology: A user's guide to sociological language.* Cambridge, MA: Blackwell.

Johnson, C., & Petrie, T. (1995). The relationship of gender discrepancy of eating attitudes and behaviours. *Sex Roles, 33,* 405–416.

Johnson, R. M. (2000). *Rural health response to domestic violence: Policy and practice issues.* Washington, DC: U.S. Department of Health and Human Services. Retrieved December 12, 2003, from http://www.ruralhealth.hrsa.gov/pub/domviol.htm.

Joint Center for Poverty Research. (2001). Rural dimensions of welfare reform. Chicago: Northwestern University/University of Chicago. Retrieved January 3, 2001, from http://www.jcpr.org/conference/ruralbriefing.html#selectfindings.

Jones, M. A. (1992) *American immigration* (2nd ed.). Chicago: University of Chicago Press.

Jones, M. A. (1995). *The limits of liberty: American history, 1607–1992.* Oxford, UK: Oxford University Press.

Jones, S. (1993). *The language of genes. Biology, history and the evolutionary future.* London: HarperCollins.

Jones, S. R., & McEwen, M. K. (2000). A conceptual model of multiple dimensions of identity. *Journal of College Student Development, 41,* 405–414.

Jordan, J. V., & Hartling, L. M. (2002). New developments in relational-cultural theory. In M. Ballou & L. S. Brown (Eds.), *Rethinking mental health and disorders: Feminist perspectives* (pp. 48–70). New York: Guilford.

Jourard, S. M. (1964). *The transparent self: Self-disclosure and well-being.* Princeton, NJ: Van Nostrand Reinhold.

Jourard, S. M. (1968). *Disclosing man to himself* (2nd ed.). New York: Van Nostrand Reinhold.

Jung, C. G. (1953). Two essays on analytical psychology. *Collected works* (Vol. 7, Bollinger Series XX). New York: Pantheon.

Kaplan, H. B., & Johnson, R. J. (2001). *Social deviance: Testing a general theory.* New York: Kluwer Academic/Plenum.

Kazdin, A. E. (2001). *Behavior modification in applied settings* (6th ed.). Belmont, CA: Wadsworth.

Kegan, R. (1994). *In over our heads: The mental demands of modern life.* Cambridge, MA: Harvard University Press.

Kelly, D. H., & Clarke, E. J. (2003). *Deviant behavior* (6th ed.). New York: Worth.

Kelly, G. A. (1955). *The psychology of personal constructs.* New York: W. W. Norton.

Kimura, D. (2002, May). Sex differences in the brain. *Scientific American.com.* Retrieved September 12, 2003, from http://www.sciam.com/print_version.cfm?articleID=00018E9D-879D-1D06-8E49809EC588EEDF.

Kluckhohn, F. R., & Strodtbeck, F. L. (1961). *Variations in value orientations.* Evanston, IL: Row, Peterson.

Kohlberg, L. (1976). Moral stages and moralization: The cognitive-developmental approach. In T. Lickona (Ed.), *Moral development and behavior: Theory, research, and social issues* (pp. 31–53). New York: Holt, Rinehart & Winston.

Kosmin, B. A., & Mayer, E. (2001). Profile of the U.S. Muslim population. *American Religious Identification Survey 2001* (ARIS Report No. 2). New York: CUNY. Retrieved December 30, 2003, from http://www.gc.cuny.edu/studies/aris_part_two.htm.

Kreeger, K. Y. (2002, February). Sex-based differences continue to mount. *The Scientist, 16* (4). Retrieved September 12, 2003, from http://www.thescientist.com/yr2002/feb/research_020218.html.

Kretschmer, E. (1925). *Physique and character* (2nd ed.). W. J. H. Spratt, Trans. New York: Harcourt, Brace and World.

Kurasaki, K. S., Sue, S., Chun, C., & Gee, K. (2000). Ethnic minority intervention and treatment research. In J. F. Aponte & J. Wohl (Eds.), *Psychological intervention and cultural diversity* (2nd ed., pp. 234–249). Boston: Allyn and Bacon.

LaFromboise, T. D. (1988). American Indian mental health policy. *American Psychologist, 43,* 388–397.

LaFromboise, T. D., Trimble, J. E., & Mohatt, G. V. (1990). Counseling intervention and American Indian tradition: An integrative approach. *The Counseling Psychologist, 18,* 628–654.

Landrine, H. (1992). Clinical implications of cultural differences: The referential versus the indexical self. *Clinical Psychology Review, 12,* 401–415.

Langston, D. (2001). Tired of playing Monopoly? In M. L. Anderson & P. Hill Collins (Eds.), *Race, class, and gender: An anthology* (4th ed., pp. 125–134). Belmont, CA: Wadsworth/Thomson Learning.

Larry P. v. Riles, 495 F. Supp. 926 (N.D. Cal. 1979), *aff'd in part,* 793, f.2d 969 (9th Cir. 1986).

Lau v. Nichols, 414 U.S. 563 (1974).

Le, C. N. (2003). Religion, spirituality, and faith. *Asian-Nation: The landscape of Asian America.* Retrieved December 16, 2003, from http://www.asian-nation.shtml.

Lee, C. C. (2000). Cybercounseling and empowerment: Bridging the digital divide. In J. W. Bloom & G. R. Walz (Eds.), *Cybercounseling and cyberlearning: Strategies and resources for the Millennium* (pp. 85–91). Alexandria, VA: American Counseling Association.

LeVay, S. (1993). *The sexual brain.* Cambridge, MA: MIT Press.

LeVay, S., & Hamer, D. (1994). Evidence for a biological influence in male homosexuality. *Scientific American, 270,* 44–49.

Lewis, L., & Benet, S. (2003, December). Measuring progress. *Black Enterprise, 34* (5), 30.

Liu, W. M., & Pope-Davis, D. B. (2004). Understanding classism to effect personal change. In T. B. Smith (Ed.), *Practicing multiculturalism: Affirming diversity in counseling and psychology* (pp. 295–310). Boston: Allyn and Bacon.

MacDonald, D. (2004). Collaborating with students' spirituality. *Professional School Counseling, 7,* 293–300.

Maddux, J. E., & Gosselin, J. T. (2003). Self-efficacy. In M. R. Leary & J. P. Tangney (Eds.), *Handbook of self and identity* (pp. 218–238). New York: Guilford.

Maki, M. T., & Kitano, H. H. L. (2002). Counseling Asian Americans. In P. Pedersen et al. (Eds.), *Counseling across cultures* (5th ed., pp. 109–131). Thousand Oaks, CA: Sage.

Maslow, A. H. (1968). *Toward a psychology of being* (2nd ed.). New York: Van Nostrand Reinhold.

McBee, S. M., & Rogers, J. R. (1997). Identifying risk factors for gay and lesbian suicidal behavior: Implications for mental health counselors. *Journal of Mental Health Counseling, 19,* 143–155.

McCarn, S. R., & Fassinger, R. E. (1996). Revisioning sexual minority identity formation: A new model of lesbian identity and its implications for counseling and research. *Counseling Psychologist, 24,* 508–534.

McEwen, M. K. (2003). New perspectives on identity development. In S. R. Komives, D. B. Woodard, Jr., & Associates (Eds.), *Student services: A handbook for the profession* (4th ed., pp. 203–233). San Francisco, CA: Jossey-Bass.

McFadden, J. (2003). Stylistic Model for counseling across cultures. In F. D. Harper & J. McFadden (Eds.), *Culture and counseling: New approaches* (pp. 209–232). Boston: Allyn and Bacon.

McFadden, J., & Banich, M. (2003). Using bibliotherapy in transcultural counseling. In F. D. Harper & J. McFadden (Eds.), *Culture and counseling: New approaches* (pp. 285–295). Boston: Allyn and Bacon.

McGoldrick, M. (2003). Culture: A challenge to concepts of normality. In F. Walsh (Ed.), *Normal family processes: Growing diversity and complexity* (pp. 235–259). New York: Guilford.

McIntosh, P. (1989, July/August). White privilege: Unpacking the invisible White knapsack. *Peace and Freedom,* 10–12.

Mead, G. H. (1934). *Mind, self, and society.* Chicago: University of Chicago Press. (Revised 1967.)

Megarry, T. (1995). *Society in prehistory: The origins of human culture.* New York: New York University Press.

Meichenbaum, D. (1977). *Cognitive behavior modification: An integrative approach.* New York: Plenum Press.

Mercado, M. M. (2000). The invisible family: Counseling Asian American substance abusers and their families. *The Family Journal, 8,* 267–272.

Midgley, M., & Hughes, J. (1997). Are families out of date? In H. L. Nelson (Ed.), *Feminism and families* (pp. 55–68). New York: Routledge.

Miller, W. L. (2002). *Lincoln's virtues: An ethical biography.* New York: Knopf.

Morales, E. S. (1989). Ethnic minority families and minority gays and lesbians. *Journal of Homosexuality, 17,* 217–239.

Murray, B. (2003). Latino religion in the United States: Demographic shifts and trends. Retrieved December 16, 2003, from http://www.facsnet.org/issues/faith/espinosa.php.

Myers, D. G. (2004). *Psychology* (7th ed.). New York: Worth.

Myers, L. J., Speight, S. L., Highlen, P. S., Cox, C. I., Reynolds, A. L., Adams, E. M., & Hanley, P. (1991). Identity development and worldview: Toward an optimal conceptualization. *Journal of Counseling & Development, 70,* 54–63.

National Board of Certified Counselors. (2003). *Code of Ethics.* Greensboro, NC: Author.

National Board of Certified Counselors. (2004). *National Certified Counselor 2004 Application Packet.* Retrieved on March 20, 2004, from http://www.nbcc.org.

National Center for Children in Poverty. (1999). *Poverty and brain development in early childhood.* Retrieved May 27, 2004, from Columbia University website: http://www.nccp.org/pub_pdb99.html.

National Center for Health Statistics. (2003). Table 27. Life expectancy at birth, at 65 years of age, and at 75 years of age, according to race and sex: United States, selected years 1900–2001. Retrieved December 10, 2003, from http://www.cdc.gov/nchs/about/major/dvs/mortdata.htm.

National Institute on Aging. (2003). *What's your aging IQ?.* Washington, DC: U.S. Department of health and Human Services. Retrieved July 1, 2004, from http://www.niapublications.org/pubs/agingiq/indiex.asp.

National Institute of Mental Health. (2003). U.S. suicide rates by age, gender, and racial group. Retrieved December 6, 2003, from http://www.nimh.nih.gov/research/suichart.cfm.

National Organization for Human Service Education (2004a). Ethical Standards of Human Service Professionals. Retrieved May 31, 2004, from http:www.nohse.com/ethstand.html.

National Organization for Human Service Education (2004b). The Human Service Worker. Retrieved May 31, 2004, from http:www.nohse.com/hsworker.html.

National Organization for Women (n.d.) Chronology of the Equal Rights Amendment, 1923–1996. Retrieved February 18, 2004, from http://www.now.org/issues/economic/cea/history/html.

National Projections Program. (2000). *Projected life expectancy at birth by race and Hispanic origin, 1999 to 2100.* Washington, DC: U.S. Bureau of the Census.

Native American Spirituality. (2003). Charlottesville: University of Virginia. Retrieved December 16, 2003, from http://religiousmovements.lib.viginia.edu/nrms/naspirit.html.

Nystul, M. S. (1999). *Introduction to counseling: An art and science perspective.* Boston: Allyn and Bacon.

O'Boyle, E. J. (1998). *Personalist economics: Moral convictions, economic realities, and social action.* Boston: Kluwer Academic.

Olson, D. H. (2000). *Marriage and the family: Diversity and strengths* (3rd ed.). Mountain View, CA: Mayfield.

Ontario Consultants on Religious Tolerance. (2003). *Religious identification in the U.S.* Retrieved December 16, 2003, from http://www.religioustolerance.org/chr_prac2.htm.

Ossana, S. M., Helms, J. E., & Leonard, M. M. (1992). Do "womanist" attitudes influence college women's self-esteem and perceptions of environmental bias? *Journal of Counseling & Development, 70,* 402–408.

Overboe, J. (1999). Difference in self: Validating disabled people's lived experience. *Body and Society, 5* (4), 17–29.

Oyserman, D., Coon, H. M., & Kemmelmeier, M. (2002). Rethinking individualism and collectivism: Evaluation of theoretical assumptions and meta-analyses. *Psychological Bulletin, 128,* 3–72.

Padilla, A. M. (1980). The role of cultural awareness and ethnic loyalty in acculturation. In A. M. Padilla (Ed.), *Acculturation: Theory, models, and some new findings* (pp. 47–84). Boulder, CO: Westview Press.

Palmore, E. (1990). *Ageism: Negative and positive.* New York: Springer.

Papalia, D. E., & Olds, S. W. (1992). *Human development* (5th ed.). New York: McGraw-Hill

Parham, T. A., & Brown, S. (2003). Therapeutic approaches with African American populations. In F. D. Harper & J. McFadden (Eds.), *Culture and counseling: New approaches* (pp. 81–98). Boston: Allyn and Bacon.

Parker, K. D., Ortega, S. T., & Hill, M. N. (1999). Gender differences in self-esteem: The impact of religious, sociodemographic and familial factors among Black Americans. *Challenge: A Journal of Research on African American Men, 10* (2), 37–53.

Parks, E. E., Carter, R. T., & Gushue, G. V. (1996). At the crossroads: Racial and womanist identity development in Black and White women. *Journal of Counseling & Development, 74,* 624–631.

Parks, S. D. (2000). *Big questions, worthy dreams: Mentoring young adults in their search for meaning, purpose, and faith.* San Francisco: Jossey-Bass.

Patterson, C. H., & Hidore, S. (1997). *Successful psychotherapy: A caring, loving relationship.* Northvale, NJ: Aronson.

Pedersen, P. B. (1996). The importance of both similarities and differences in multicultural counseling: Reaction to C. H. Patterson. *Journal of Counseling & Development, 74,* 236–237.

Pedersen, P. B. (1997). The cultural context of the American Counseling Association Code of Ethics. *Journal of Counseling and Development, 76,* 23–28.

Pedersen, P. B. (1999). *Multiculturalism as a Fourth Force.* Philadelphia, PA: Brunner/Mazel.

Pedersen, P. B. (2000). *Handbook for developing multicultural awareness* (3rd ed.). Alexandria, VA: American Counseling Association.

Pedersen, P. B. (2002). Ethics, competence, and other professional issues in culture-centered counseling. In P. B. Pedersen et al. (Eds.), *Counseling across cultures* (5th ed., pp. 3–27). Thousand Oaks, CA: Sage.

Pedersen, P. (2004). The multicultural context of mental health. In T. B. Smith (Eds.), *Practicing multiculturalism: Affirming diversity in counseling and psychology* (pp. 17–32). Boston: Allyn and Bacon.

Pedersen, P. B., & Carey, J. C. (2003). *Multicultural counseling in schools* (2nd ed.). Boston: Allyn and Bacon.

Pedersen, P. B., Draguns, J. G., Lonner, W. J., & Trimble, J. E. (Eds.). (2002). *Counseling across cultures* (5th ed.). Thousand Oaks, CA: Sage.

Pedersen, P., & Ivey, A. E. (1993). *Cultured-center counseling.* New York: Greenwood.

Phinney, J. S. (1992). The Multigroup Ethnic Identity Measure: A new scale for use with diverse groups. *Journal of Adolescent Research, 7* (2), 156–176.

Piaget, J. (1952). *The origins of intelligence in children.* New York: International University Press.

Poindexter-Cameron, J., & Robinson, T. L. (1997). Relationships among racial identity attitudes, womanist identity attitudes, and self-esteem in African American college women. *Journal of College Student Development, 38,* 288–296.

Polk, W. A. C. (2000). *Memoirs of an Oreo: A social history.* New York: Writers Club Press.

Polsky, H. W. (2002). *How I am a Jew: Adventures into my Jewish-American identity.* Lantham, MD: University Press of America.

Ponterotto, J. G. (1988). Racial consciousness development among White counselor trainees: A stage model. *Journal of Multicultural Counseling & Development, 16,* 146–156.

Ponterotto, J. G., Costa, C. I., & Werner-Lin, A. (2002). Research perspectives in cross-cultural counseling. In P. Pedersen, J. G. Draguns, W. J. Lonner & J. E. Trimble (Eds.), *Counseling across cultures* (5th ed., pp. 395–420). Thousand Oaks, CA: Sage.

Ponterotto, J. G., & Pedersen, P. B. (1993). *Preventing prejudice: A guide for counselors and educators.* Newbury Park, CA: Sage.

Popenoe, R. (2004). *Feeding desire: Fatness, beauty, and sexuality among a Saharan people.* New York: Routledge.

Porter, R. Y. (2000a). Clinical issues and intervention with ethnic minority women. In J. F. Aponte & J. Wohl (Eds.), *Psychological intervention and cultural diversity* (2nd ed., pp. 183–199). Boston: Allyn and Bacon.

Porter, R. Y. (2000b). Understanding and treating ethnic minority youth. In J. F. Aponte & J. Wohl (Eds.), *Psychological intervention and cultural diversity* (2nd ed., pp. 167–182). Boston: Allyn and Bacon.

Poston, W. S. C. (1990). The Biracial Identity Development model: A needed addition. *Journal of Counseling and Development, 69,* 152–155.

Purkey, W. W. (1970). *Self-concept and school achievement.* Englewood Cliffs, NJ: Prentice-Hall.

Purkey, W. W. (2000). *What students say to themselves: Internal dialogue and school success.* Thousand Oaks, CA: Corwin Press.

Purkey, W. W., & Novak, J. M. (1996). *Inviting school success: A self-concept approach to teaching, learning, and democratic practice* (3rd ed.). Belmont, CA: Wadsworth.

Purkey, W. W., & Schmidt, J. J. (1996). *Invitational counseling: A self-concept approach to professional practice.* Pacific Grove, CA: Brooks/Cole.

Raeff, C. (1997). Maintaining cultural coherence in the midst of cultural diversity. *Developmental Review, 17,* 250–261.

Ramirez, D. A. (1996). Multiracial identity in a color-conscious world. In M. P. P. Root (Ed.), *The multiracial experience: Racial borders as the new frontier* (pp. 49–62). Thousand Oaks, CA: Sage.

Rauscher, L., & McClintock, J. (1996). Ableism curriculum design. In M. Adams, L. A. Bell & P. Griffen (Eds.), *Teaching for diversity and social justice* (pp. 198–231). New York: Routledge.

Reynolds, A. L., & Pope, R. L. (1991). The complexities of diversity: Exploring multiple oppressions. *Journal of Counseling and Development, 70,* 174–180.

Reynolds, J. (2005). Familial and relational transitions across the life span. In D. Comstock (Ed.), *Diversity and development: Critical contexts that shape our lives and relationships* (pp. 269–298). Belmont, CA: Brooks/Cole.

Richmond, L. J. (2003). Counseling European Americans. In F. D. Harper & J. McFadden (Eds.), *Culture and counseling: New approaches.* Boston: Allyn and Bacon.

Ridley, M. (1999). *Genome: The autobiography of a species in 23 chapters.* New York: HarperCollins.

Roald, A. S. (2001). *Women in Islam: The Western experience.* New York: Routledge.

Robinson, B. (1994). *Ageism.* Retrieved June 29, 2004, from University of California, Berkeley, website: http://ist-socrates.berkeley.edu/~aging/ModuleAgeism.html.

Robinson, T. L. (2005). *The convergence of race, ethnicity, and gender: Multiple identities in counseling* (2nd ed.). Upper Saddle River, NJ: Prentice-Hall.

Rodeheaver, D. (1990). *Aging curriculum content for education in the social-behavioral sciences: Module VII: Ageism.* New York: Springer.

Rogers, C. R. (1951). *Client-centered therapy: Its current practice, implications, and theory.* Boston: Houghton Mifflin.

Rogers, C. R. (1986). Client centered therapy. In I. L. Kuthash & A. Wolf (Eds.), *Psychotherapist's casebook* (pp. 197–208). San Francisco: Jossey-Bass.

Root, M. P. P. (1990). Resolving "other" status: Identity development of biracial individuals. In L. S. Brown & M. P. P. Root (Eds.), *Diversity and complexity in feminist therapy* (pp. 185–205). New York: Haworth Press.

Root, M. P. P. (Ed.). (1992). *Racially mixed people of America.* Newbury Park, CA: Sage.

Root, M. P. P. (Ed.). (1996). *The multicultural experience: Racial borders as the new frontier.* Thousand Oaks, CA: Sage.

Root, M. P. P. (1998). Multiracial Americans: Changing the face of Asian America. In L. C. Lee & N. W. Zane (Eds.), *Handbook of Asian American psychology* (pp. 261–287). Thousand Oaks, CA: Sage.

Root, M. P. P. (1999). The biracial baby boom: Understanding ecological constructions of racial identity in the 21st century. In R. Hernandez-Sheets & E. R. Hollins (Eds.), *Racial and ethnic identity in school practices: Aspect of human development* (pp. 67–90). Mahwah, NJ: Erlbaum.

Root, M. P. P. (2002). Methodological issues in multiracial research. In G. C. N. Hall & S. Okazaki (Eds.), *Asian American psychology: The science of lives in context* (pp. 171–193). Washington, DC: American Psychological Association.

Roseberry-McKibbin, C. (2001). Serving children from the culture of poverty. *ASHA Leader, 6* (20), 4–7.

Rosenthal, S. T. (2001). *Irreconcilable differences? The waning of the American Jewish love affair with Israel.* Hanover, NH: Brandeis University Press.

Rowe, W., Bennett, S. K., & Atkinson, D. R. (1994). White racial identity models: A critique and alternative proposal. *Counseling Psychologist, 22,* 129–146.

Roysircar, G. (2003). Understanding immigrants: Acculturation theory and research. In F. D. Harper & J. McFadden (Eds.), *Culture and counseling: New approaches* (pp. 164–195). Boston: Allyn and Bacon.

Sadker, M., & Sadker, D. (1987). *Sex and equality handbook for schools.* New York: Longman.

SAMHSA. (2003). Highlights of latest national data on drug abuse. Retrieved December 5, 2003, from http://www.samhsa.gov/oas/oasftp.htm.

Sandhu, D. S. (1997). Psychocultural profiles of Asian and Pacific Islander Americans: Implications for counseling and psychotherapy. *Journal of Multicultural Counseling and Development, 25,* 7–22.

Sandhu, D. S., Leung, S. A., & Tang, M. (2003). Counseling approaches with Asian Americans and Pacific Islander Americans. In F. D. Harper & J. McFadden (Eds.), *Culture and counseling: New approaches* (pp. 99–114). Boston: Allyn and Bacon.

Schlossberg, N. K., Waters, E. B., & Goodman, J. (1995). *Counseling adults in transition* (2nd ed.). New York: Springer.

Schmidt, J. J. (1994). *Living intentionally & making life happen* (Rev. Ed.). Greenville, NC: Brookcliff.

Schmidt, J. J. (2002). *Intentional helping: A philosophy for proficient caring relationships.* Upper Saddle River, NJ: Prentice-Hall.

Schmidt, J. J. (2004). *A survival guide for the elementary/middle school counselor* (2nd ed.). San Francisco: Jossey-Bass.

Scupin, R. (Ed.). (2003a). *Race and ethnicity: An anthropological focus on the United States and the World.* Upper Saddle River, NJ: Prentice-Hall.

Scupin, R. (2003b). Ethnicity. In R. Scupin (Ed.), *Race and ethnicity: An anthropological focus on the United States and the world* (pp. 67–89). Upper Saddle river, NJ: Prentice-Hall.

Seabrook, J. (2003). *A world growing old.* London: Pluto Press.

Shapiro, J. P. (1994). *No pity: People with disabilities forging a new civil rights movement.* New York: Random House.

Sheldon, W. H. (1954). *Atlas of men: A guide for somatotyping the adult male at all ages.* New York: Harper & Row.

Shore, R. (1997). *Rethinking the brain: New insights into early development.* New York: Families and Work Institute.

Smith, D. (2003). The older population in the United States: March 2002. *U.S. Census Bureau Current Population Reports* (P20-546). Washington, DC: U.S. Bureau of the Census.

Smith, G. (2001, July 20). Backtalk: The brother in the wheelchair. *Essence,* p. 162.

Smith, T. B. (2004). A contextual approach to assessment. In T. B. Smith (Eds.), *Practicing multiculturalism: Affirming diversity in counseling and psychology* (pp. 97–119). Boston: Allyn and Bacon.

Smith, T. B., Richards, P. S., & MacGranley, H. (2004). Practicing multiculturalism: An introduction. In T. B. Smith (Eds.), *Practicing multiculturalism: Affirming diversity in counseling and psychology* (pp. 3–16). Boston: Allyn and Bacon.

Sodowsky, G. R., Lai, E. W. M., & Plake, B. S. (1991). Moderating effects of sociocultural variables on acculturation attitudes of Hispanics and Asian Americans. *Journal of Counseling & Development, 70,* 194–204.

Sokolovsky, J., & Vesperi, M. D. (1991). The cultural context of well-being in old age. *Generations, 15* (1), 21–25.

Sophie, J. (1985). A critical examination of stage theories of lesbian identity development. *Journal of Homosexuality, 12,* 39–51.

Sparkes, A. C. (1997). Reflections on the socially constructed physical self. In K. R. Fox (Ed.), *The physical self: From motivation to well-being* (pp. 83–110). Champaign, IL: Human Kinetics.

Speight, S. L., Myers, L. J., Cox, C. I., & Highlen, P. S. (1991). A redefinition of multicultural counseling. *Journal of Counseling & Development, 70,* 29–36.

Spickard, P. R. (1992). The illogic of American racial categories. In M. P. P. Root (Ed.), *Racially mixed people in America* (pp. 12–23). Newbury Park, CA: Sage.

Spickard, P. R. (2000). What must I be? Asian Americans and the question of multiethnic identity. In J. Y. S. Wu & M. Song (Eds.), *Asian American Studies.* New Brunswick, NJ: Rutgers University Press.

Steigerwald, F. (2003). Diversity issues in family work. In D. M. Kaplan & Associates (Ed.), *Family counseling for all counselors* (pp. 203–246). Greensboro, NC: CAPS Publications.

Stein, E. (1999). *The mismeasure of desire: The science, theory, and ethics of sexual orientation.* New York: Oxford University Press.

Stewart, P. J., & Strathern, A. (2002). *Violence: Theory and ethnography.* New York: Continuum.

Stone, A. (2003, August 19). The digital divide that wasn't. *BusinessWeek Online.* Retrieved December 10, 2003, from http://www.businessweek.com/technology/content/aug2003/tc200308194285tc126.htm.

Striegel-Moore, R. H., Schreiber, G. B., Lo, A., Crawford, P., Obarzanek, E., & Rodin, J. (2000). Eating disorder symptoms in a cohort of 11- to 16-year-old black and white girls: The NHLBI growth and health study. *International Journal of Eating Disorders, 27,* 49–66.

Sue, D. W., Arredondo, P., & McDavis, R. J. (1992). Multicultural counseling competencies and standards: A call to the profession. *Journal of Counseling and Development, 70,* 644–688.

Sue, D. W., & Sue, D. (1999). *Counseling the culturally different: Theory and practice* (3rd ed.). New York: John Wiley.

Sue, S. (1998). In search of cultural competencies in psychology and counseling. *American Psychologist, 53,* 440–448.

Sullivan, P. (1998). Sexual identity development: The importance of target or dominant group membership. In R. L. Sanlo (Ed.), *Working with lesbian, gay, bisexual, and transgender college students: A handbook for faculty and administrators* (pp. 3–12). Westport, CT: Greenwood.

Super, D. E. (1990). A life-span, life-space approach to career development. In D. Brown & L. Brooks (Eds.), *Career choice and development: Applying contemporary theories to development* (2nd ed., pp. 197–261). San Francisco: Jossey-Bass.

Sweeney, T. J. (1998). *Adlerian counseling: A practitioner's approach* (4th ed.). Philadelphia, PA: Accelerated Development.

Tafoya, T. (1989). Circles and cedar: Americans and family therapy. *Journal of Psychotherapy and the Family, 6,* 71–98.

Tajfel, H., & Turner, J. C. (1979). An integrative theory of intergroup conflict. In W. G. Austin & S. Worchel (Eds.), *The social psychology of intergroup relations (*pp. 33–47). Monterey, CA: Brooks/Cole.

Tajfel, H., & Turner, J. C. (1986). The social identity theory of ingroup behavior. In S. Worchel & W. G. Austin (Eds.), *Psychology of intergroup relations* (pp. 7–24). Chicago, Nelson-Hall.

Therman, E., & Susman, M. (1993). *Human chromosomes: Structure, behavior, and effects* (3rd ed.). New York: Springer-Verlag.

Thompson, C. E. (2004). *Awareness and identity: Foundational principles of multicultural practice.* In T. B. Smith (Ed.), *Practicing multiculturalism: Affirming diversity in counseling and psychology* (pp. 35–56). Boston: Allyn and Bacon.

Thompson, M., Ellis, R., & Wildavsky, A. (1990). *Cultural theory.* Boulder, CO: Westview Press.

Thornton, M. C. (1996). Hidden agendas identity theories, and multiracial people. In M. P. P. Root (Ed.), *The multiracial experience: Racial borders as the new frontier* (pp. 101–120). Thousand Oaks, CA: Sage.

Thurman, P. J., Plested, B., Edwards, R. W., Chen, J., & Swaim, R. (2000). Intervention and treatment with ethnic minority substance abusers. In J. F. Aponte & J. Wohl (Eds.), *Psychological intervention and cultural diversity* (2nd ed., pp. 214–233). Boston: Allyn and Bacon.

Toppo, G. (2003, June 11). Children gaining in well-being. *USA Today.* Retrieved December 7, 2003, from http://search.epnet.com/direct.asp?an=JOE397403679503&db=f5h.

Triandis, H. C. (1994). *Culture and social behavior.* New York: McGraw-Hill.

Triandis, H. C. (1995). *Individualism and collectivism.* Boulder, CO: Westview Press.

Trimble, J. E., & Thurman, P. J. (2002). Ethnocultural considerations and strategies for providing counseling services to Native American Indians. In P. B. Pedersen et al. (Eds.), *Counseling across cultures* (5th ed., pp. 53–91). Thousand Oaks, CA: Sage.

Troiden, R. R. (1989). The formation of homosexual identities. *Journal of Homosexuality, 17,* 43–73.

Truman Presidential Museum & Library. (n.d.). Harry S Truman Papers Staff Member and Office Files: Philleo Nash Files (1939–1953). Retrieved February 20, 2004, from http://www.trumanlibrary.org/hstpaper/nashhst.htm.

Urrabazo, R. (2000). Therapeutic sensitivity to the Latino spiritual soul. In M. T. Flores & G. Cary (Eds.), *Family therapy with Hispanics: Toward appreciating diversity* (pp. 205–227). Boston: Allyn and Bacon.

U.S. Bureau of the Census. (2000a). *Statistical Abstract of the United States: 2000.* Washington, DC: Department of Commerce.

U.S. Bureau of the Census. (2000b). *Profile of general demographic characteristics.* Washington, DC: U.S. Department of Commerce.

U.S. Bureau of the Census. (2001). *Age: 2000.* Washington, DC: U.S. Department of Commerce.

U.S. Bureau of the Census. (2003). *Historical poverty tables* (Table 4). Washington, DC: Department of Commerce. Retrieved November 6, 2003, from http://www.census.gov/hhes/poverty/hstpov4.html.

U.S. Department of Education. (2000). To assure the free and appropriate public education of all children with disabilities. *Twenty-second annual report to Congress on implementation of the Individuals with Disabilities Education Act.* Washington, DC: Author.

U.S. Department of Justice. (n.d.). Title VI of the Civil Rights Act of 1964. Retrieved February 20, 2004, from http://www.usdoj.gov/crt/cor/coord/titlevi.htm.

Vacc, N., & Loesch, L. (2000). *Professional orientation to counseling* (3rd ed.). Philadelphia: Brunner-Routledge.

Violence Policy Center. (2003). *Hispanics and firearms violence.* Washington, DC: Author. Retrieved December 6, 2003, from http://www.vpc.org/studies/hispone.htm.

Volpe, J. S. (1996). *Effects of domestic violence on children and adolescents: An overview.* Commack, NY: The American Academy of Experts in Traumatic Stress. Retrieved December 6, 2003, from http://www.aaets.org/arts/art8.htm.

Vygotsky, L. S. (1935/1978). *Mind in society: The development of higher psychological processes.* Cambridge, MA: Harvard University Press.

Vygotsky, L. S. (1962). *Thought and language.* Cambridge, MA: MIT Press.

Wachtel, S. S. (Ed.). (1994). *Molecular genetics of sex determination.* San Diego, CA: Academic Press.

Walsh, F. (2003). Changing families in a changing world. In F. Walsh (Ed.), *Normal family processes: Growing diversity and complexity* (pp. 3–26). New York: Guilford.

Wang, L. (1994). Marriage and family therapy with people from China. *Contemporary Family Therapy: An International Journal, 16,* 25–37.

Weber, L. (1998). A conceptual framework for understanding race, class, gender, and sexuality. *Psychology of Women Quarterly, 22,* 13–32.

Weeber, J. E. (1999). What could I know of racism? *Journal of Counseling and Development, 77* (1), 20–23.

Wehrly, B. (2003). Breaking barriers for multiracial individuals and families. In J. F. Aponte & J. Wohl (Eds.), *Psychological intervention and cultural diversity* (2nd ed., pp. 313–323). Boston: Allyn and Bacon.

Weinrach, S. G. (2002). The counseling profession's relationship to Jews and the issues that concern them: More than a case of selective awareness. *Journal of Counseling & Development, 80,* 300–314.

Weinrach, S. G. (2003). I am my brother's (and sister's) keeper: Jewish values and the counseling process. *Journal of Counseling & Development, 81,* 441–444.

Weinrach, S. G., & Thomas, K. R. (1998). Diversity-sensitive counseling today: A postmodern clash of values. *Journal of Counseling & Development, 76,* 115–122.

Wentz, L. (2003, July). Cultural crossover. *Advertising Age, 74* (27), S1–2.

Whitfield, S. J. (1999). *In search of American Jewish culture.* Hanover, NH: Brandeis University Press.

Williams, B. (2003). The worldview dimensions of individualism and collectivism: Implications for counseling. *Journal of Counseling & Development, 81,* 370–374.

Wilson, M. N., Kohn, L. P., & Lee, T. S. (2000). Cultural relativistic approach toward ethnic minorities in family therapy. In J. F. Aponte & J. Wohl (Eds.), *Psychological intervention and cultural diversity* (2nd ed., pp. 92–109). Boston: Allyn and Bacon.

Wohl, J. (2000). Psychotherapy and cultural diversity. In J. F. Aponte & J. Wohl (Eds.), *Psychological intervention and cultural diversity* (2nd ed., pp. 75–91). Boston: Allyn and Bacon.

Wohl, J., & Aponte, J. F. (2000). Common themes and future prospects for the twenty-first century. In J. F. Aponte & J. Wohl (Eds.), *Psychological intervention and cultural diversity* (2nd ed., pp. 286–300). Boston: Allyn and Bacon.

Wood, J. V. (1989). Theory and research concerning social comparisons of personal attributes. *Psychological Bulletin, 106,* 231–248.

Woodard, D. B., Jr., & Komives, S. R. (2003). Shaping the future. In S. R. Komives, D. B. Woodard, Jr., & Associates (Eds.), *Student services: A handbook for the profession* (4th ed., pp. 637–655). San Francisco: Jossey-Bass.

Woolf, L. M. (1998). *Ageism.* Retrieved June 29, 2004, from Webster University website: http://www.webster.edu/~woolflm/agesim.html.

Worster, D. (1994). *Nature's economy: A history of ecological ideas.* Cambridge, UK: Cambridge University Press.

Worthington, R. L., Savoy, H. B., Dillon, F. R., & Vernaglia, E. R. (2002). Heterosexual identity development: A multidimensional model of individual and social identity. *The Counseling Psychologist, 30,* 496–531.

Wrenn, C. G. (1962). The culturally encapsulated counselor. *Harvard Educational Review, 32,* 444–449.

Yin, S. (2003, November). The art of staying at home. *American Demographics, 25* (9), 17.

Zane, N., Morton, T., Chu, J., & Lin, N. (2004). Counseling and psychotherapy with Asian American clients. In T. B. Smith (Ed.), *Practicing multiculturalism: Affirming diversity in counseling and psychology* (pp. 190–214). Boston: Allyn and Bacon.

Zuckerman, M. (1990). Some dubious premises in research and theory on racial differences: Scientific, social, and ethical issues. *American Psychologist, 45,* 1297–1303.

Author Index

Subject Index